W9-DCW-976

Rick Steves'

IRELAND
2008

Rick Steves & Pat O'Connor

LEGEND

- —M4— Freeway/Motorway
- —A4— Other Roads
- —— Major Rail Line
- ✈ Airport
- 🌲 National Park or Natural Wonder

Gaeltacht (Gaelic-speaking) Regions

Dingle Recommended location*

Sligo Just passing through**

- ■ Ruin, Museum, other Point of Interest
- 🏰 Castle/Monument/Palace

* Black locations are places of interest to tourists, sized by importance.

** Gray locations are places of little or no interest to tourists and are sized by population.

0 km — 50 kilometers

0 miles — 50 miles

Atlantic

Ocean

Bloody Foreland

Bunbeg •

Dungloe •

Glencoumbkille

Donegal

D O

Ballyshannon •

N15

Drumcliff (Yeats' Grave) ■ • Sligo

N16

Lough Gill

MAYO

Belmullet

N59 • Ballina

Achill Island

Lough Conn

Clare Island

S L I G O

N17

N5

Carrick-on-Shannon •

Westport

Croagh Patrick

• **Knock**

Leenane

N59

Kylemore Abbey 🏰

CONNEMARA 🌲

Cong

N17

Strokestown •

Clifden

Ashford Castle

Lough Corrib

Roscommon

Longford

N59

N84

Loug Ree

Rossaveel

Salthill • **Galway**

N6 Athlone

Dún Aenghus ■ **Kilronan**

Dunguaire •

Clonmacnoise ■

Aran Islands

Ballyvaughan •

Kinvarra

Doolin •

THE BURREN

I R E L

CLIFFS OF MOHER

• **Lisdoonvarna**

Lahinch **N18**

Lough Derg

Birr

CLARE

• **Ennis**

Roscrea

N7

N67

N68

Bunratty Castle & Folk Park ■

T I P P E R A R Y

Kilkee •

Shannon ✈

Killimer •

Tarbert •

Limerick

Shannon

N8

DINGLE PENINSULA

Gallarus Oratory

Tralee

Limerick Junction •

N24

Rock of Cashel ■

• **Cashel**

Slea Head

N86

N69

N21

Tipperary •

N8

Caher •

Clonmel

Blasket Islands

Dingle • (An Daingean)

Minard Castle ■

Inch Strand

Kerry Airport ✈

KERRY

Killarney

Mallow •

N20

Valentia Island

N72

N72

N25

RING OF KERRY

Muckross House ■

Port-magee •

Dungarvan •

Sneem •

Kenmare

Blarney 🏰

N72

Skellig Michael

Derrynane House ■

Macroom

N22

Midleton Youghal

BEARA

N71

Glengarriff •

Cork

✈

N25

Ardmore

Bantry Bay

• **Bantry**

• **Cobh**

N71

R600

Kinsale

Skibbereen •

Drombeg Stone Circle ■

To Roscoff, France

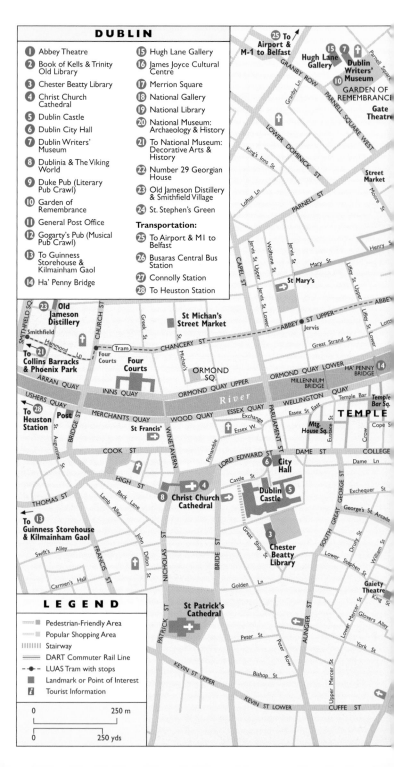

DUBLIN

1. Abbey Theatre
2. Book of Kells & Trinity Old Library
3. Chester Beatty Library
4. Christ Church Cathedral
5. Dublin Castle
6. Dublin City Hall
7. Dublin Writers' Museum
8. Dublinia & The Viking World
9. Duke Pub (Literary Pub Crawl)
10. Garden of Remembrance
11. General Post Office
12. Gogarty's Pub (Musical Pub Crawl)
13. To Guinness Storehouse & Kilmainham Gaol
14. Ha' Penny Bridge
15. Hugh Lane Gallery
16. James Joyce Cultural Centre
17. Merrion Square
18. National Gallery
19. National Library
20. National Museum: Archaeology & History
21. To National Museum: Decorative Arts & History
22. Number 29 Georgian House
23. Old Jameson Distillery & Smithfield Village
24. St. Stephen's Green

Transportation:
25. To Airport & M1 to Belfast
26. Busaras Central Bus Station
27. Connolly Station
28. To Heuston Station

LEGEND

- Pedestrian-Friendly Area
- Popular Shopping Area
- Stairway
- DART Commuter Rail Line
- LUAS Tram with stops
- Landmark or Point of Interest
- Tourist Information

0   250 m

0   250 yds

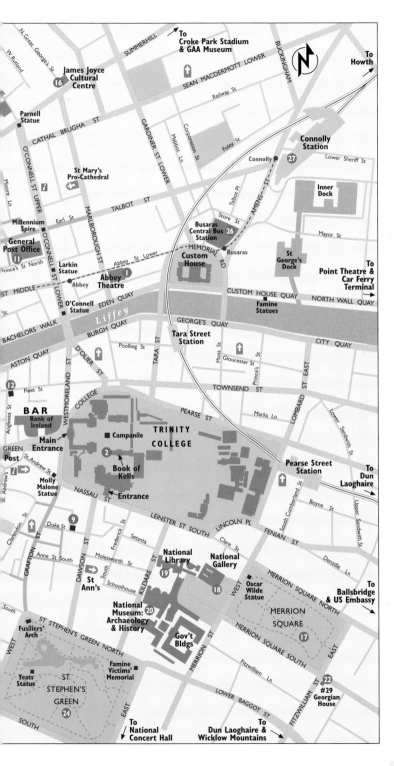

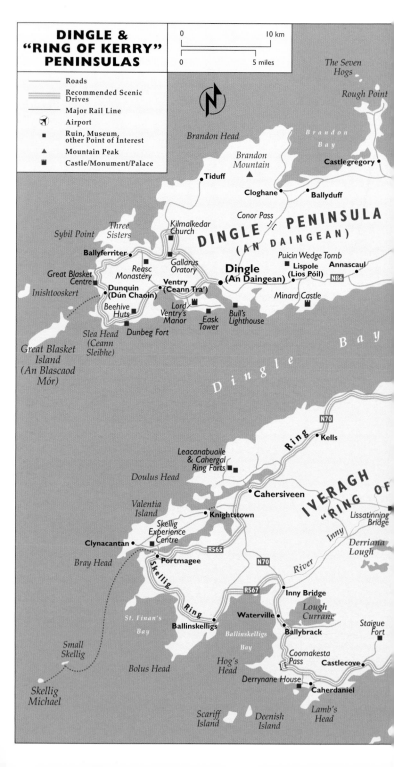

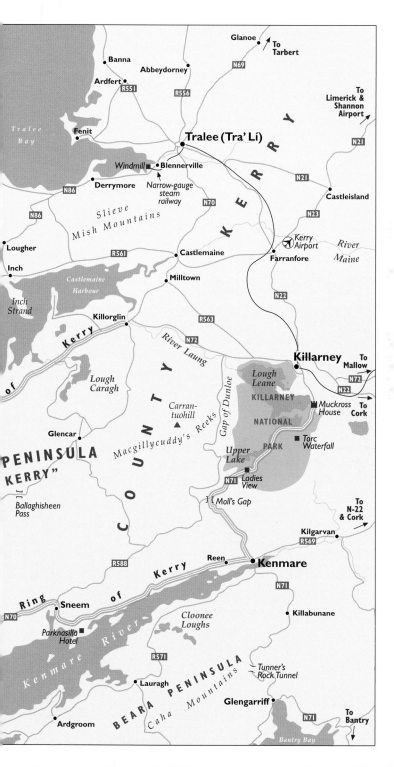

Rick Steves'

IRELAND

2008

AVALON
TRAVEL

CONTENTS

Top Destinations in Ireland

Portrush & Antrim Coast

Derry & County Donegal

Belfast

Connemara & County Mayo

Aran Islands

Galway

Near Dublin

Dublin

Burren & County Clare

Dingle Peninsula (An Daingean)

Kilkenny & The Rock of Cashel

Kenmare & The Ring of Kerry

Kinsale & Cobh

Waterford & County Wexford

DCH

INTRODUCTION

Flung onto the foggy fringe of the Atlantic pond like a mossy millstone, Ireland drips with mystery, drawing you in for a closer look and then surprising you. An old farmer cuts turf from the bog, while his son staffs the tech hotline for an international software firm. Buy them both a pint in a pub that's whirling with playful conversation and exhilarating traditional music. Pious, earthy, witty, brooding, proud, and unpretentious, Irish culture is an intoxicating potion to sip or slurp—as the mood strikes you.

This book breaks Ireland into its top big-city, small-town, and rural destinations. It gives you all the information and opinions necessary to wring the maximum value out of your limited time and money in each of these locations. If you plan three weeks or less for Ireland and have a normal appetite for information, this lean and mean book is all you'll need. If you're a travel-info fiend, this book sorts through all the superlatives and provides a handy rack upon which to hang your supplemental information.

Experiencing Irish culture, people, and natural wonders economically and hassle-free has been my goal for three decades of traveling, tour guiding, and travel writing. With this new edition, I pass on to you the lessons I've learned, updated for your trip in 2008.

The places I cover are balanced to include a comfortable mix of exciting big cities and great-to-be-alive-in small towns. Note that this book covers the highlights of the entire island, including Northern Ireland. While you'll find the predictable biggies (such as the Book of Kells, Brú na Bóinne, and the Cliffs of Moher), I've also mixed in a healthy dose of Back Door intimacy (rope-bridge hikes, holy wells, and pubs with traditional Irish music). I've been selective. On a short trip, visiting both the monastic ruins of Glendalough and Clonmacnoise is redundant; I cover only the best—Glendalough. There are plenty of great manor-house gardens; again, I recommend just the top one—the Gardens of Powerscourt.

The best is, of course, only my opinion. But after spending a third of my adult life exploring and researching Europe, I've developed a sixth sense for what travelers enjoy. The places featured in this book will give anyone the "gift of gab."

About This Book

Rick Steves' Ireland 2008 is a personal tour guide in your pocket. Better yet, it's actually two tour guides in your pocket: The co-author of this guidebook is Pat O'Connor. Pat is the Ireland specialist and senior Ireland tour guide at my company, Rick Steves' Europe Through the Back Door. I have enjoyed traveling in Ireland for many years, but nobody has a more Irish name than Pat—whose travel passion has long been the Emerald Isle. Together, Pat and I keep this book up-to-date and accurate (though for simplicity we've shed our respective egos to become "I" in this book).

This book is organized by destinations, each one a mini-vacation on its own, filled with exciting sights and homey, affordable places to stay. In the following chapters, you'll find:

Planning Your Time, a suggested schedule with thoughts on how best to use your limited time.

Orientation includes tourist information, tips on public transportation, local tour options, helpful hints, and an easy-to-read map designed to make the text clear and your arrival smooth.

Self-Guided Walks take you through interesting neighborhoods, with a personal tour guide in hand.

Sights provides a succinct overview of the most important sights, arranged by neighborhood, with ratings:

▲▲▲—Don't miss.

▲▲—Try hard to see.

▲—Worthwhile if you can make it.

No rating—Worth knowing about.

Sleeping describes my favorite hotels, from budget deals to splurges.

Eating serves up good-value restaurants, ranging from inexpensive pubs to fancier options.

Transportation Connections to nearby destinations by train, bus, and plane, and route tips for drivers.

Ireland: Past and Present gives you an overview of Irish history, a look at contemporary Ireland, a taste of the Irish language, and an Irish–Yankee vocabulary list.

The **appendix** is a traveler's tool kit, with a handy packing checklist, recommended books and films, instructions on how to use the telephone, useful phone numbers, and the procedure for dealing with lost credit cards. You'll also find detailed information on driving and public transportation, as well as a climate chart, festival list, and a hotel reservation form.

Study this book and put together the plan of your travel dreams. Then have a great trip! Traveling like a temporary local, and taking advantage of the information here, you'll enjoy the absolute most out of every mile, minute, and dollar. As you visit places I know and love, I'm happy you'll be meeting my favorite Irish people.

PLANNING

Trip Costs

Five components make up your trip cost: airfare, surface transportation, room and board, sightseeing and entertainment, and shopping and miscellany.

Airfare: A basic round-trip flight from the US to Dublin costs $600–1,200 (even cheaper in winter), depending on what city you fly from and when. If your travels take you beyond Ireland, consider saving time and money in Europe by flying "open jaw" (into one city and out of another; for instance, into Dublin and out of Paris).

Surface Transportation: For a three-week whirlwind trip of all my recommended Irish destinations, allow $275 per person for public transportation (train tickets and key buses), or $500–800 per person for car rental (based on two people sharing a three-week rental), including gas and insurance. A car rental is cheapest when reserved from the US. Since Ireland's train system has gaps, you'll usually save money by simply buying train and bus tickets as you go, rather than buying a railpass (see "Transportation," page 398).

Room and Board: You can manage well in Ireland on an average of $120 a day per person for room and board (allow less for villages and more for Dublin). A $120-per-day budget allows $15 for lunch, $30 for dinner, $5 for snacks or a Guinness, and $70 for lodging (based on two people splitting a $140 double room that includes breakfast). That's doable, particularly outside Dublin. Students and tightwads eat and sleep for $50 a day ($25 for a bed in a hostel, $25 a day for meals—mostly picnics—and snacks).

Sightseeing and Entertainment: In big cities, figure about $8–10 per major sight (e.g., the Book of Kells at Dublin's Trinity College-$10), $4 for minor ones (climbing church towers), $12–15 for guided walks, $35–45 for day-trip bus tours, and up to $70 for splurge experiences (such as the Dunguaire Castle medieval banquet or a flight to the Aran Islands). For information on the various passes that are available for Ireland's sights, see page 14.

An overall average of $35 a day works for most. Don't skimp here. After all, this category is the driving force behind your trip—you came to sightsee, enjoy, and experience Ireland.

Shopping and Miscellany: Figure roughly $2 per postcard, tea, or ice-cream cone, and $5 per pint of beer. Shopping can vary

Ireland's Best Three-Week Trip by Car

Day	Plan	Sleep in
1	Fly into Dublin, rent car, Glendalough	Kilkenny
2	Kilkenny with side-trip to Cashel	Kilkenny
3	Waterford	Waterford
4	Explore Wexford	Waterford
5	Cobh	Kinsale
6	Kinsale	Kinsale
7	Muckross House and Farms	Kenmare
8	Ring of Kerry	Dingle
9	Dingle Peninsula loop	Dingle
10	Blaskets, Dingle town (laundry and rest)	Dingle
11	Cliffs of Moher, Burren, Dunguaire Castle banquet	Galway
12	Galway	Galway
13	Aran Islands	Aran Islands
14	Tour Connemara and County Mayo	Westport
15	Drive to Northern Ireland	Derry
16	Side-trip to Donegal	Derry
17	Explore Derry, then drive to Portrush	Portrush
18	Explore Antrim Coast	Portrush
19	Belfast	Belfast
20	Drive to Valley of the Boyne sights, return car	Dublin
21	Dublin	Dublin
22	Dublin	Dublin
23	Fly home	

While this three-week itinerary (stretched to 23 days by using weekends at each end) is designed to be done by car, most of it can be done by train and bus. For three weeks without a car, spend your first three nights in Dublin, using buses and taxis. Cut back on the recommended sights with the most frustrating public transportation (Ring of Kerry, Valley of the Boyne, Connemara, and Counties Mayo, Wexford, and Donegal). You can book day

in cost from nearly nothing to a small fortune. Good budget travelers find that this category has little to do with assembling a trip full of lifelong and wonderful memories.

When to Go

July and August are peak season—my favorite time—with long days, the best weather, and the busiest schedule of tourist fun.

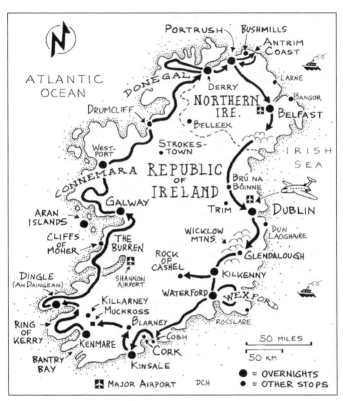

ATLANTIC
OCEAN

PORTRUSH · BUSHMILLS
ANTRIM
COAST

DONEGAL
DERRY
NORTHERN
IRE.
BELLEEK
BELFAST

DRUMCLIFF

STROKES-
TOWN

WEST-
PORT

LARNE
BANGOR

IRISH
SEA

CONNEMARA
REPUBLIC
OF
IRELAND

GALWAY

BRÚ NA
BÓINNE

TRIM
DUBLIN

ARAN
ISLANDS

CLIFFS
OF
MOHER

THE
BURREN

WICKLOW
MTNS.

DUN
LAOGHAIRE

GLENDALOUGH

SHANNON
AIRPORT

ROCK
OF
CASHEL

KILKENNY

WEXFORD

DINGLE
(AN DAINGEAN)

WATERFORD

KILLARNEY
MUCKROSS
BLARNEY

ROSSLARE

RING
OF
KERRY

KENMARE

COBH

CORK

50 MILES

BANTRY
BAY

KINSALE

50 KM

MAJOR AIRPORT   DCH

● = OVERNIGHTS
• = OTHER STOPS

tours by bus for some of these areas at local tourist offices. For at
least two people traveling together, taxis—though expensive—
can work in a pinch if bus schedules don't fit your plans (i.e., Cork
to Kinsale, Waterford to New Ross, Dublin to Trim). If you have
time for only one idyllic peninsula on your trip, I'd suggest the
Dingle Peninsula over the Ring of Kerry (for specifics, see sidebar
on page 171).

Prices and crowds don't go up as dramatically in Ireland as
they do in much of Europe. Still, travel during "shoulder season" (May, early June, Sept, and early Oct) is easier and a bit
less expensive. Shoulder-season travelers get minimal crowds,
decent weather, the full range of sights and tourist fun spots, and
the ability to grab a room almost whenever and wherever they
like—often at a flexible price. Winter travelers find absolutely no

Major Holidays and Weekends

Popular places are even busier on weekends...and inundated on three-day weekends, when hotels, trains, and buses can get booked up before, during, and after the actual holiday. Holidays can bring many businesses to a grinding halt. Plan ahead and reserve your accommodations and transportation well in advance. Mark these dates in red on your travel calendar: New Year's Day; St. Patrick's Day (March 17, celebrated March 15–19 in Dublin in 2008); Good Friday through Easter Monday (March 21–24 in 2008); Christmas; December 26; and New Year's Day. In addition, Ireland recognizes these UK and Ireland-only Bank Holiday Mondays in 2008, which close banks and bring crowds for the long weekend: May 5 and 26, June 2, August 4 and 25, and October 27. In Belfast in Northern Ireland, some businesses close for the week leading up to the controversial July 12th Orangemen marches (see page 291).

Reserve in advance for Dublin for any weekend, for Galway during its many peak-season events (listed on page 229), and for Dingle throughout July and August. Also check the list of festivals and holidays on page 409 of the appendix.

crowds and soft room prices, but shorter sightseeing hours. Some attractions are open only on weekends or are closed entirely in the winter (Nov–Feb). The weather can be cold and dreary, and nightfall draws the shades on sightseeing well before dinnertime. While Ireland's rural charm falls with the leaves, city sightseeing is fine in the winter.

Plan for rain no matter when you go. Just keep traveling and take full advantage of "bright spells." The weather can change several times in a day, but rarely is it extreme. As the locals say, "There is no bad weather, only inappropriate clothing." Bring a jacket and dress in layers. Daily averages throughout the year range between 42°F and 70°F. Temperatures below 32°F cause headlines, and days that break 80°F—while increasing in recent years—are still rare. For more information, see the climate chart in the appendix.

While sunshine may be rare, summer days are very long. Dublin is as far north as Edmonton, Canada, and Portrush is as far north as Ketchikan on the Alaskan panhandle. The summer sun is up from 5:00 until 22:00. It's not uncommon to have a gray day, eat dinner, and enjoy hours of sunshine afterward.

Sightseeing Priorities

Depending on the length of your trip, here are my recommended priorities:

Know Before You Go

Your trip is more likely to go smoothly if you plan ahead.

Since **airline carry-on restrictions** are always changing, visit the Transportation Security Administration's website (www.tsa.gov/travelers) for an up-to-date list of what you can bring on the plane with you...and what you have to check. Remember to arrive with plenty of time to get through security. If you're flying into Dublin from London, note that you are allowed only one carry-on (no extras like a purse or backpack); check Britain's website for the latest (www.dft.gov.uk).

Call your **debit and credit card companies** to let them know the countries you'll be visiting, so that they'll accept (and not deny) your international charges. Confirm what your daily withdrawal limit is; consider asking to have it raised so you can take out more cash at each ATM stop.

Be sure that your **passport** is valid at least six months after your ticketed date of return to the US. If you need to get or renew a passport, it can take up to three months (for more on passports, see www.travel.state.gov).

Book your rooms well in advance if you'll be traveling during any major **holidays** (see "Major Holidays and Weekends," on previous page). It's smart to reserve rooms in peak season if you'd like to stay in my lead listings (particularly for B&Bs in June, July, and August) and definitely for your first night.

3 days:	Dublin
5 days, add:	Dublin, Dingle Peninsula
7 days, add:	Galway, a day in Belfast
9 days, add:	County Clare/Burren
11 days, add:	Northern Ireland's Antrim Coast
15 days, add:	Aran Islands, Wicklow Mountains
19 days, add:	Kinsale, Waterford, Valley of the Boyne
23 days, add:	Ring of Kerry, Connemara, Derry, Donegal

(This includes virtually everything on the "Ireland's Best Three-Week Trip by Car" map and itinerary on pages 4 and 5.)

Travel Smart

Your trip to Ireland is like a complex play—easier to follow and to really appreciate on a second viewing. While no one does the same trip twice to gain that advantage, reading this book in its entirety before your trip accomplishes much the same thing.

Most people fly into Dublin and remain there for a few days. If you're picking up a car at Dublin Airport, consider a gentler small-town start in Trim or Kilkenny, and let Dublin be the finale at the end of your trip. You'll be more rested and ready to tackle Dublin.

Just the FAQs, Please

Whom do I call in case of emergency?
Dial 999 for police or medical emergencies.

What if my credit card is stolen?
Act immediately. See "Damage Control for Lost Cards," page 388, for instructions.

How do I make a phone call to, within, and from Ireland?
For detailed dialing instructions, refer to page 393.

How can I get tourist information about my destination?
Ireland has a national tourist information office in the US (see page 383) and offices in virtually every destination covered in this book. Note that Tourist Information is abbreviated **TI** in this book.

What's the best way to pack?
Light. For a recommended packing list, see page 413.

Does Rick have other resources that could help me?
For more on my guidebooks, public television series, free audio-tours, public radio show, website, guided tours, travel bags, accessories, and railpasses, see page 384.

Are there any updates to this guidebook?
Check www.ricksteves.com/update for changes to the most recent edition of this book.

Can you recommend any good books or movies for my trip?
For suggestions, see pages 386–388.

Design an itinerary that enables you to visit the various sights at the best possible times. As you read this book, make note of festivals, colorful market days, and when sights are closed. Saturdays are virtually weekdays with earlier closing hours and no rush hour (though transportation connections can be less frequent than on weekdays). Sundays have the same pros and cons as they do for travelers in the US (special events, limited hours, closed shops and banks, limited public transportation, no rush hours). Popular destinations are even more popular on weekends, especially sunny weekends, which are sufficient cause for an impromptu holiday in this soggy corner of Europe.

To give yourself a little rootedness, minimize one-night stands. It's worth a long drive after dinner to be settled into a town for two nights. B&Bs are also more likely to give a good price to someone staying more than one night.

Be sure to mix intense and relaxed periods in your itinerary. Every trip (and every traveler) needs at least a few slack days. Pace

Do you have information on driving, train travel, and flights?
See pages 398–409 in the appendix.

How much do I tip?
Relatively little. For tips on tipping, see page 389.

Will I get a student or senior discount?
While discounts (called "concessions" in Ireland) are not listed in this book, many Irish sights are discounted for seniors (loosely defined as those who are retired or willing to call themselves a senior), youths (ages 8–18), students, groups of 10 or more, and families.

How can I get a VAT refund on major purchases?
See the details on page 389.

Does Ireland use the metric system?
Both the Republic of Ireland and Northern Ireland use the metric system for everything but driving measurements. Weight and volume are typically calculated in metric: A kilogram is 2.2 pounds and a liter is about a quart. The weight of a person is measured by "stone" (one stone equals 14 pounds). Temperatures are generally given in both Celsius and Fahrenheit.

On the road, the Republic of Ireland is still converting from miles to kilometers, and you'll likely see signs in both (especially in rural destinations). Northern Ireland uses miles and posts speed limits in miles per hour.

For more metric conversions, see page 411.

yourself. Assume you will return.

Reread this book as you travel, and visit local tourist information offices. Upon arrival in a new town, lay the groundwork for a smooth departure; write down the schedule for the train or bus you'll take when you depart.

Plan ahead for laundry, picnics, and Internet stops. Get online at Internet cafés or your hotel to research transportation connections, confirm events, check the weather, and get directions to your next hotel. Buy a phone card and use it for reservations, reconfirmations, and double-checking hours.

Connect with the culture. You speak the language—use it! Slow down and ask questions—most locals are eager to point you in their idea of the right direction. Keep a notepad in your pocket for organizing your thoughts. Wear your money belt, and learn the local currency and how to estimate prices in dollars. Those who expect to travel smart, do.

PRACTICALITIES

Red Tape: You need a passport—but no visa or shots—to travel in Ireland. Your passport must be valid for at least six months beyond the time you leave Ireland. Pack a photocopy of your passport in your luggage in case the original is lost or stolen.

Time: In Ireland—and in this book—you'll use the 24-hour clock. It's the same through 12:00 noon, then keep going: 13:00, 14:00, and so on. For anything over 12, subtract 12 and add p.m. (14:00 is 2:00 p.m.).

Like Great Britain, Ireland is one hour earlier than most of continental Europe. Ireland is also five/eight hours ahead of the East/West Coasts of the US; the exceptions are the beginning and end of Daylight Saving Time. Ireland and Europe "spring forward" the last Sunday in March (two weeks after most of North America), and "fall back" the last Sunday in October (one week before North America). For a handy online time converter, try www.timeanddate.com/worldclock.

Business Hours: Most stores throughout Ireland are open Monday through Saturday from roughly 10:00–17:30, with a late night on Wednesday or Thursday (until 19:00 or 20:00), depending on the neighborhood. On Sunday, when some stores are closed, street markets are lively with shoppers.

Watt's Up? Ireland's electrical system is different from North America's in two different ways: the shape of the plug (three square prongs—not the two round prongs used in continental Europe) and the voltage of the current (220 volts instead of 110 volts). For your North American plug to work in Ireland, you'll need an adapter plug, sold inexpensively at travel stores in the US. As for the voltage, most newer electronics or travel appliances (such as hair dryers, laptops, and battery chargers) automatically convert the voltage—if you see a range of voltages printed on the item or its plug (such as "110–220"), it'll work in Ireland and Europe. Otherwise, you can buy a converter separately in the US (about $20).

News: Americans keep in touch via the *International Herald Tribune* (published almost daily via satellite throughout Europe). Every Tuesday, the European editions of *Time* and *Newsweek* hit the stands with articles of particular interest to travelers. Sports addicts can get their daily fix online or from *USA Today*. Good websites include http://news.bbc.co.uk and www.europeantimes.com. Many hotels have CNN or BBC television channels.

MONEY

Banking

Throughout Europe, cash machines (ATMs) are the standard way for travelers to get local currency. Bring plastic—credit and/or debit cards—along with several hundred dollars in hard cash as an emergency backup (but bring smaller bills—banks in Ireland have had problems with phony $100 bills, and will not accept them). It's smart to bring two cards, in case one gets demagnetized or eaten by a temperamental machine. Travelers checks are a waste of time (long waits at slow banks) and a waste of money (in fees).

Cash from ATMs

To use a cash machine to withdraw money from your account, you'll need a debit card (ideally with a Visa or MasterCard logo for maximum usability), plus a PIN code. Know your PIN code in numbers; there are only numbers—no letters—on European keypads.

Before you go, verify with your bank that your card will work overseas, and alert them that you'll be making withdrawals in Europe; otherwise, the bank may not approve transactions if it perceives unusual spending patterns.

Try to take out large sums of money to reduce your per-transaction bank fees. If the machine refuses your request, don't take it personally. Just try again and select a smaller amount.

Even in mist-kissed Ireland, you'll need to keep your cash safe. Thieves target tourists. Use a money belt—a pouch with a strap that you buckle around your waist like a belt, and wear under your clothes. A money belt provides peace of mind, allowing you to carry lots of cash safely. Don't waste time every few days tracking down a cash machine—withdraw a week's worth of money, stuff it in your money belt, and travel!

Credit and Debit Cards

For purchases, Visa and MasterCard are more commonly accepted than American Express. Just like at home, credit or debit cards work easily at larger hotels, restaurants, and shops, but smaller businesses prefer payment in local currency (in small bills—break large bills at a bank or larger store).

Credit and debit cards—whether used for purchases or ATM withdrawals—often come with additional, tacked-on "international

Exchange Rates

I've priced things throughout this book in local currencies. The Republic of Ireland uses the euro currency. Northern Ireland, which is part of the United Kingdom, has retained its traditional currency, the British pound sterling. Border towns in the North might take euros, but at a lousy exchange rate.

1 euro (€1) = about $1.30
1 British pound (£1) = about $2

Republic of Ireland: Like dollars, one euro (€) is broken down into 100 cents. You'll find coins ranging from 1 cent to 2 euros and bills ranging from 5 euros to 500 euros. To roughly convert prices in euros to dollars, add 30 percent to Irish prices: €20 is about $26, €50 is about $65, and so on.

Northern Ireland: The British pound sterling (£), also called a "quid," is broken into 100 pence (p). Pence means "cents." You'll find coins ranging from 1p to £2 and bills from £5 to £50. Some travelers try to kid themselves that pounds are dollars. But when they get home, that £1,000-pound Visa bill isn't asking for $1,000...it wants $2,000. To avoid this shock, double prices in Northern Ireland to estimate dollars.

Northern Ireland issues its own currency worth the same as an English pound. If you'll be traveling on to Great Britain, note that English and Northern Ireland's Ulster pounds are technically interchangeable in both regions, although Ulster pounds are "undesirable" in Britain. Banks in either region will convert your Ulster pounds into English pounds at no charge. Don't worry about the coins, which are accepted throughout Great Britain and Northern Ireland.

transaction" fees of up to 3 percent plus $5 per transaction. To avoid unpleasant surprises, call your bank or credit-card company before your trip to ask about these fees.

Using a new scheme called "dynamic currency conversion," some merchants might charge you in dollars for credit-card transactions—but they set their own exchange rate, which is almost always a much worse deal than if you simply pay in the local currency (euros in the Republic of Ireland, pounds in Northern Ireland). According to Visa, you have the right to decline this "service" and be charged in the local currency.

If your cards are lost or stolen, see page 388 for advice on what to do.

SIGHTSEEING

Sightseeing can be hard work. Use these tips to make your visits to Ireland's finest sights meaningful, fun, fast, and painless.

Plan Ahead

Set up an itinerary that allows you to fit in all your must-see sights. Most sights keep stable hours, but you can easily confirm the latest by checking with the local TI.

Don't put off visiting a must-see sight—you never know when a place will close unexpectedly for a holiday, strike, or restoration. If you'll be visiting during a holiday, find out if a particular sight will be open by phoning ahead or visiting its website.

When possible, visit key museums first thing (when your energy is best) and save other activities for the afternoon. Hit the highlights first, then go back to other things if you have the stamina and time.

Depending on the sight, there are ways to avoid crowds. This book offers tips on specific sights. Try visiting very early, at lunch, or very late. Evening visits are usually peaceful, with fewer crowds.

At the Sight

All sights have rules, and if you know about these in advance, they're no big deal.

Some important sights have metal detectors or conduct bag searches that will slow your entry.

Most museums require you to check daypacks and coats. They'll be kept safely. If you have something you can't bear to part with, stash it in a pocket or purse. If you don't want to check a small backpack, carry it under your arm like a purse as you enter. From a guard's point of view, a backpack is generally a problem while a purse is not.

Cameras are normally allowed, but not flashes or tripods

(without special permission). Flashes damage oil paintings and distract others in the room. Even without a flash, a handheld camera will take a decent picture (or buy postcards or posters at the museum bookstore). Video cameras are usually allowed.

Some museums have special exhibits in addition to their permanent collection. Some exhibits are included in the entry price, while others come at an extra cost (which you may have to pay even if you don't want to see the exhibit).

Many sights rent audioguides, which generally offer excellent recorded descriptions of the art (about €3). If you bring along your own pair of headphones and a Y-jack, two people can share one audioguide and save. Guided tours (usually €4 and widely ranging in quality) are most likely to occur during peak season.

Expect changes—paintings can be on tour, on loan, out sick, or shifted at the whim of the curator. To adapt, pick up any available free floor plans as you enter, and ask museum staff if you can't find a particular painting.

Most important sights have an on-site café or cafeteria (usually a good place to rest and have a snack or light meal). The WCs are free and generally clean.

Museums have bookstores selling postcards and souvenirs. Before you leave, scan the postcards and thumb through the biggest guidebook (or skim its index) to be sure you haven't overlooked something that you'd like to see.

Most sights stop admitting people 30–60 minutes before closing time, and some rooms close early (generally about 45 minutes before the actual closing time). Guards usher people out, so don't save the best for last.

Every sight or museum offers more than what is covered in this book. Use the information in this book as an introduction—not the final word.

Sightseeing Passes

Ireland offers two different passes (each covering a different set of sights) that can save you money. The first is smart for anyone, and the second works best for two people traveling together. Twosomes who love to sightsee should get both passes.

The **Heritage Card** gets you into 85 historical monuments, gardens, and parks maintained by the OPW (Office of Public Works) in the Republic of Ireland. It will pay off if you plan on visiting half a dozen or more included sights over the course of your trip (€21, seniors

age 60 and older-€16, students-€8, families-€55, covers entry to all Heritage sights for one year, comes with handy map and list of sights' hours and prices, purchase at any Heritage sight or Dublin's tourist information office on Suffolk Street, tel. 01/605-7700 or 01/647-6587, fax 01/661-6764, www.heritageireland.ie, heritagecard@opw.ie). People traveling by car are most likely to get their money's worth out of the card.

If, instead of getting the Heritage Card, you pay for the sights individually, your costs will add up fast. Adult entry prices range from €1.60 to €10.30. An energetic sightseer with three weeks in Ireland will probably pay to see nearly all 20 of the following sights (covered in this book): Dublin Castle-€4.50, Kilmainham Gaol-€5.30 (Dublin), Brú na Bóinne (Knowth and Newgrange tombs and Visitors Centre)-€10.30, Hill of Tara-€2.10, Old Mellifont Abbey-€2.10, Trim Castle-€3.70 (Valley of the Boyne), Glendalough Visitors Centre-€2.90 (Wicklow Mountains), Kilkenny Castle-€5.30 (Kilkenny), Rock of Cashel-€5.30 (Cashel), Reginald's Tower-€2.10 (Waterford), Charles Fort-€3.70 (Kinsale), Desmond Castle-€3 (Kinsale), Muckross House and Farm-€8.65 (near Killarney), Derrynane House-€2.90 (Ring of Kerry), Great Blasket Centre-€3.70 (near Dingle), Ennis Friary-€1.60 (Ennis), Dún Aenghus-€2.10 (Inishmore, Aran Islands), Connemara National Park-€2.90 (near Galway), Newmills Corn and Flax Mill-€2.90, and Glenveagh Castle and National Park-€2.90 (Donegal). This totals €77.95; a pass saves you €56.95 (about $74) per person over paying individual entrance fees. It also moves you through ticket lines quicker. Note that scheduled tours given by OPW guides at any of these sites are included in the price of admission—regardless of whether you have the Heritage Card—and that the card covers no sights in Northern Ireland.

Ambitious travelers covering more ground should seriously consider the **Heritage Island Explorer Touring Guide** (€6), which does not overlap with the above Heritage sights and gives a

THE ESSENTIAL TOURING GUIDE TO IRELAND'S MAJOR VISITOR ATTRACTIONS & HERITAGE TOWNS

variety of discounts (usually 2-for-1 discounts, but occasionally 20 percent off) at sights in both the Republic and Northern Ireland. This is a great no-brainer deal for two people traveling together—you just need to buy one Touring Guide, so you'll save the cost of the guide after only a couple stops. (Solo travelers might have to go to half a dozen sights before the discounts recoup the initial €6.) You can buy the guide at TIs and participating sights, but study the full list of sights first (tel. 01/236-6890, fax 01/236-6895, www.heritageisland.com). Discounted sights mentioned in this guidebook include: Trinity College Library (Book of Kells), Christ Church Cathedral, Dublin City Hall, Dublinia, Hugh Lane Gallery, Old Jameson Distillery, Jameson Distillery Chimney Viewing Tower, Guinness Storehouse, Gaelic Athletic Association Museum (all aforementioned sights in Dublin), Power & Glory (in Trim), Gardens of Powerscourt (Enniskerry), Bru Boru Cultural Centre (Rock of Cashel), Waterford Crystal Factory, *Dunbrody* Famine Ship (New Ross), Irish National Heritage Park (Wexford), Kinsale Regional Museum (Kinsale), Queenstown Story (Cobh), Old Midleton Distillery (Midleton), Blarney Castle (County Cork), Skellig Experience Centre (Valentia Island on Ring of Kerry), Kerry the Kingdom Museum, Siamsa Tíre Theatre (Tralee), Burren Centre (Kilfenora), Galway Atlantaquaria Aquarium (Galway), Clare Museum, Glór Irish Music Centre (Ennis), Kylemore Abbey (Letterfrack), Strokestown Park National Famine Museum (Strokestown), Ulster Museum, W5 Science Centre (Belfast), Ulster Folk and Transport Museum (Cultra), Tower Museum (Derry), Belleek Pottery Visitors Centre (Belleek), and Ulster American Folk Park (Omagh).

SLEEPING

I favor accommodations (and restaurants) handy to your sight-seeing activities. Rather than list hotels scattered throughout a city, I choose two or three favorite neighborhoods and recommend the best accommodations values in each, from $25 bunk beds to fancy-for-my-book $240 doubles. Outside of Dublin you can expect to find good doubles for $80–140, including tax and a cooked breakfast.

I look for places that are friendly; clean; a good value; located in a central, safe, quiet neighborhood; and not mentioned in other guidebooks. I'm more impressed by a handy location and a fun-loving philosophy than hair dryers and shoeshine machines.

I've described my recommended accommodations using a Sleep Code (see page 17). Prices listed are for one-night stays in peak season, include a hearty breakfast (unless otherwise noted), and assume you're booking direct and not through a TI.

You should find prices listed in this book to be good through 2008 (except for major holidays and festivals—see page 409). Prices can soften off-season, for stays of two nights or longer, or for payment in cash (rather than by credit card). Always mention that you found the place through this book—many of the hotels listed offer special deals to my readers.

When establishing prices with a hotelier or B&B owner, confirm if the charge is per person or per room (if a price is too good to be true, it's probably per person). Because many places in Ireland

Sleep Code

To help you easily sort through the accommodations listed, I've divided the rooms into three categories based on the price for a standard double room with bath.

$$$ Higher Priced
$$ Moderately Priced
$ Lower Priced

To give maximum information in a minimum of space, I use this code to describe accommodations listed in this book. Prices are listed per room, not per person. Unless otherwise noted, credit cards are accepted and breakfast is included.

S = Single room, or price for one person in a double.
D = Double or twin room. (I specify double- and twin-bed rooms only if they are priced differently, or if a place has only one or the other. When reserving, you should specify.)
T = Three-person room (often a double bed with a single).
Q = Four-person room (adding an extra child's bed to a T is usually cheaper).
b = Private bathroom with toilet and shower or tub.
s = Private shower or tub only. (The toilet is down the hall.)
   According to this code, a couple staying at a "Db-€100" hotel would pay a total of €100 (about $130) per night for a room with a private toilet and shower (or tub). The hotel accepts credit cards or cash. You can assume credit cards are accepted unless otherwise noted.

charge per person, small groups often pay the same for a single and a double as they would for a triple. Note: In this book, room prices are listed per room, not per person.

The Republic of Ireland and Northern Ireland have banned smoking in the workplace (pubs, offices, taxicabs, etc.), but some hotels still have a floor or two of rooms where guests are allowed to smoke. If you don't want a room that a smoker might have occupied before you, make sure you let the hotelier know when you make your reservation. About 80 percent of my recommended B&Bs prohibit smoking. While some places allow smoking in the sleeping rooms, breakfast rooms are nearly always smoke-free.

"Twin" means two single beds, and "double" means one double bed. If you'll take either one, let them know, or you might be needlessly turned away. Most hotels offer family deals, which means that parents with young children can easily get a room with an extra child's bed or a discount for larger rooms. Call to negotiate the price. Teenage kids are generally charged as adults. Kids under

Laundry

If you're not washing your clothes in the sink in your room, it's a good idea to plan ahead for when you'll need to do laundry. Figure on an average of about €9–12 per load (up to €15 for smaller towns with only one launderette).

Most launderettes in Ireland are drop-off rather than self-serve. Drop-off operations are a smarter use of your valuable travel time. The €5 you might save plugging coins into a self-serve washer/dryer is not worth the two or three hours you'll waste when you could be out enjoying a local sight.

Drop your load off first thing in the morning, and pick it up late that afternoon (washed, dried, and kind of folded). If you wait until too late in the morning to drop it off, they might not be able to get it done for you by closing time that day (be sure to confirm closing time when you drop it off). Note that most places are closed on Sunday; waiting to pick up your load until Monday morning may cramp your plans. When I know I might be distracted by sightseeing, I set my alarm watch to go off late in the afternoon to remind me to pick up my laundry.

If you've packed only basic, practical wash-and-wear clothes, you have nothing to fear from an Irish launderette. If you're traveling with your favorite silk kimono, don't tempt fate—it might come back leprechaun-size.

five sleep almost free.

Many places listed have three floors of rooms and steep stairs; expect good exercise and be happy you packed light. Elevators are rare except in the larger hotels. If you're concerned about stairs, call and ask about ground-floor rooms or pay for a hotel with a lift (elevator).

Be careful of the terminology: An "en suite" room has a bathroom (toilet and shower/tub) actually inside the room; a room with a "private bathroom" can mean that the bathroom is all yours, but it's across the hall; and a "standard" room has access to a bathroom down the hall that's shared with other rooms. Figuring there's little difference between "en suite" and "private" rooms, some places charge the same for both. If you want your own bathroom inside the room, request "en suite."

If money's tight, ask for a standard room. You'll almost always have a sink in your room. And, as more rooms go "en suite," the hallway bathroom is shared with fewer standard rooms.

Note that to be called a "hotel," a place technically must have certain amenities, including a 24-hour reception (though this rule is loosely applied). A place called "townhouse" or "house" is like a big B&B or a small family-run hotel—with fewer amenities but more character than a "hotel." TVs are standard in rooms.

Ireland has a rating system for hotels and B&Bs. These stars and shamrocks are supposed to imply quality, but I find that they mean only that the place sporting symbols is paying dues to the tourist board. Rating systems often have little to do with value.

If you're traveling beyond my recommended destinations, you'll find accommodations where you need them. Any town with tourists has a TI that books rooms or can give you a list and point you in the right direction. In the absence of a TI, ask people on the street or in pubs and restaurants for help. The Republic of Ireland also has a nationwide room-booking phone number; within Ireland, dial 1-800-363-626 (Mon–Sat 9:00–20:00, closed Sun).

B&Bs

Compared to hotels, bed-and-breakfast places give you double the cultural intimacy for half the price. In 2008, you'll generally pay €40–60 (about $52–78) per person for a double room in a B&B in Ireland. Prices include a big cooked breakfast. The amount of coziness, teddies, tea, and biscuits tossed in varies tremendously.

B&Bs range from large guest houses with 15–20 rooms to small homes renting out a spare bedroom, but they typically have six rooms or fewer. The philosophy of the management determines the character of a place more than its size and facilities offered. Avoid places run as a business by absentee owners. My top listings are run by people who enjoy welcoming the world to their breakfast table.

If you have a reasonable but limited budget, skip hotels and go the B&B way. If you can use a telephone and speak English,

you'll enjoy homey, friendly, clean rooms at a great price by sticking to my listings. Book direct—if you have a TI book a room for you, it'll take a 10 percent commission from the B&B and may charge you up to €5. If you book direct, the B&B gets it all (and you'll have a better chance of getting a discount). I have negotiated special prices with this book (often for cash).

B&Bs come with their own etiquette and quirks. Keep in mind that B&B owners are at the whim of their guests—if you're getting up early, so are they; and if you check in late, they'll wait up for you. It's polite to call ahead to confirm your reservation the day before, and give them a rough estimate of your arrival time. This allows them to plan their day and run errands before or after you arrive...and also allows them to give you specific directions for driving or walking to their place.

A few tips: B&B proprietors are selective as to whom they invite in for the night. At some B&Bs, children are not welcome. Risky-looking people (two or more single men are often assumed to be troublemakers) find many places suddenly full. If you'll be staying for more than one night you are a "desirable." In popular weekend-getaway spots, you're unlikely to find a place to take you for Saturday night only.

If my listings are full, ask for guidance. (Mentioning this book can help.) Owners usually work together and can call up an ally to land you a bed.

B&Bs serve a hearty "Irish fry" breakfast (for more about B&B breakfasts, see page 24). You'll figure out quickly which parts of the "fry" you like and don't like. B&B owners prefer to know this up front, rather than serve you the whole shebang and have to throw out uneaten food. Because your B&B owner is also the cook, there's usually a quite limited time span when breakfast is served (typically about an hour, starting usually around 8:00). It's an unwritten rule that guests shouldn't show up at the very end of the breakfast period and expect a full cooked breakfast—instead, if you're running late, aim to arrive at least 10 minutes before breakfast ends. If you do arrive at the last minute (or if you need to leave before breakfast is served), most B&B hosts are happy to let you help yourself to cereal, fruit, and coffee; ask politely if it's possible.

B&Bs are not hotels: If you want to ruin your relationship with your hostess, treat her like a hotel clerk. Americans often assume they'll get new towels each day. The Irish don't, and neither will you. Hang them up to dry and reuse.

In almost every B&B, you'll encounter unusual bathroom fixtures. The "pump toilet" has a flushing handle that doesn't kick in unless you push it just right: too hard or too soft, and it won't go. Be decisive but not ruthless. There's also the "dial-a-shower," an electronic box under the shower head where you'll turn a dial to select the heat of the water, and (sometimes with a separate dial or button) turn on or shut off the flow of water. Virtually all rooms have sinks.

Some B&Bs stock rooms with a hot-water pot, cups, tea bags, and coffee packets (if you prefer decaf, buy a jar at a grocery, and dump into a baggie for easy packing). Electrical outlets sometimes come with switches on the outlet to turn the current on or off; if your electrical appliance isn't working, flip the switch.

Most B&Bs come with thin walls and doors. This, combined with people walking down the hall to use the bathroom, can make for a noisy night. If you're a light sleeper, bring earplugs. And please be quiet in the halls and in your rooms (talk softly, and keep the TV volume low)...those of us getting up early will thank you for it.

Your B&B bedroom might not include a phone. In the mobile-phone age, street phone booths can be few and far between. Some B&B owners will allow you to use their phone, but understandably don't want to pay for long-distance charges. If you must use their phone, show them your international calling card (see page 391) and keep the call short (5–10 minutes max). If you plan to be staying in B&Bs and making frequent calls, consider buying an Irish mobile phone (see page 391).

A few B&B owners are also pet owners. And, while pets are rarely allowed into guest rooms, and B&B proprietors are typically very tidy, those with pet allergies might be bothered. I've tried to list which B&Bs have pets, but if you're allergic, ask about pets when you reserve.

Making Reservations

Given the quality of the gems I've found for this book, I'd recommend that you reserve your rooms in advance, particularly if you'll be traveling during peak season. Book several weeks ahead, or as soon as you've pinned down your travel dates. Note that some national holidays merit your making reservations far in advance (see "Major Holidays and Weekends" page 6). Just like at home, Monday holidays are preceded by busy weekends, so book the entire weekend in advance.

Some travelers make reservations as they travel, calling hotels or B&Bs a few days to a week before their visit. If you prefer the flexibility of traveling without any reservations at all, you'll have greater success snaring rooms if you arrive at your destination early in the day. When you anticipate crowds, call hotels around 9:00 on the day you plan to arrive, when the hotel clerk knows who'll be checking out and just which rooms will be available.

To make a reservation in advance, contact hotels directly by email, phone, or fax. Email is the clearest and most economical way to make a reservation. In addition, many hotel websites now have online reservation forms. If phoning from the US, be mindful of time zones (see page 10). To ensure you have all the information you need for your reservation, use the form in this book's appendix (also at www.ricksteves.com/reservation). If you don't get a reply to your email or fax, it usually means the hotel is already fully booked.

When you request a room for a certain time period, use the European style for writing dates: day/month/year. Hoteliers need to know your arrival and departure dates. For example, for a two-night stay

Vouchers

Many US travel agents sell vouchers for lodging in Ireland. In essence, you're paying ahead of time for your lodging, with the assurance that you'll be staying in B&Bs and guesthouses that live up to certain standards. I don't recommend buying into these, since your choices will be limited to only the places in Ireland that accept vouchers. Sure, there are hundreds in the program to choose from. But in this guidebook, I list any place that offers a good value—a useful location, nice hosts, and a comfortable and clean room—regardless of what club they do or do not belong to. Lots of great B&Bs choose not to participate in the voucher program because they have to pay to be part of it, which would slice their already thin profit even further. And many Irish B&B owners lament the long wait they endure between the date a traveler stays with them and the date the voucher company reimburses them. In short, skip it. The voucher program is just another middleman between you and the innkeeper.

in July I would request "2 nights, arrive 16/07/08, depart 18/07/08." Consider in advance how long you'll stay; don't just assume you can extend your reservation for extra days once you arrive.

If the response from the hotel gives its room availability and rates, it's not a confirmation. You must tell them that you want that room at the given rate.

The hotelier will sometimes request your credit-card number for a one-night deposit. While you can email your credit-card information (I do), some people prefer to share that personal info via phone call, fax, or secure online reservation form (if the hotel has one on its website).

If you must cancel your reservation, it's courteous to do so with as much advance notice as possible (simply make a quick phone call or send an email). Family-run hotels and B&Bs lose money if they turn away customers while holding a room for someone who doesn't show up. Understandably, some hoteliers bill no-shows for one night. Hotels in larger cities such as Dublin sometimes have strict cancellation policies (for example, you might lose a deposit if you cancel within two weeks of your reserved stay, or you might be billed for the entire visit if you leave early); ask about cancellation policies before you book.

Always reconfirm your room reservation a few days in advance from the road. Most places will hold a room until 16:00, but if you'll be arriving later, let them know.

On the small chance that a hotel loses track of your reservation, bring along a hard copy of their emailed or faxed confirmation.

Big, Cheap, Modern Hotels

Hotel chains—popular with budget tour groups—offer predict-
ably comfortable, no-frills accommodations at reasonable prices.
These hotels are popping up in big cities in Ireland. They can be
located near the train station, in the city center, on major arterials,
and outside the city center. What you lose in charm, you gain in
savings.

These hotels are ideal for families, offering simple, clean, and
modern rooms for up to four people (two adults/two children) for
€100–140, depending on the location. Note that couples or families (up to four) pay the same price for a room. Most rooms have a
double bed, single bed, five-foot trundle bed, private shower, WC,
and TV. Hotels usually have an attached restaurant, good security, an elevator, and a 24-hour staffed reception desk. Of course,
they're as cozy as a Motel 6, but many travelers love them. You can
book online (be sure to check their websites for deals) or over the
phone with a credit card, then pay when you check in. When you
check out, just drop off the key, Lee.

The biggies are Jurys Inn (call their hotels directly or book
online at www.jurysdoyle.com), Comfort/Quality Inns (Republic
of Ireland tel. 1-800-500-600, Northern Ireland tel. 0800-
444-444, US tel. 800-228-5150, www.choicehotels.com), and
Travelodge (also has freeway locations for tired drivers, reservation
center in Britain tel. 08700-850-950, www.travelodge.co.uk).

Hostels

If you're traveling alone, hosteling is the best way to conquer hotel
loneliness. Hostels are also a tremendous source of local and budget travel information. You'll pay an average of €25 for a bed, €2
for sheets, and €3 for breakfast. Anyone of any age can hostel in
Ireland. While there are no membership concerns for private hostels, International Youth Hostel Federation (IYHF) hostels require
membership. Those without cards simply buy one-night guest
memberships for €2.50. You can book online for many hostels.

Ireland has hundreds of hostels of all shapes and sizes. Choose
your hostel selectively. Hostels can be historic castles or depressing
tenements, serene and comfy or overrun by noisy school groups.
Unfortunately, many of the IYHF hostels have become overpriced
and, in general, I no longer recommend them. The only time I do
is if you're on a very tight budget, want to cook your own meals,
or are traveling with a group that likes to sleep on bunk beds in
big rooms. But many of the informal private hostels are more fun,
easygoing, and cheaper. These alternatives to the IYHF hostels
are more common than ever, and allow you to enjoy the benefits
of hosteling. Hostels of Europe (www.hostelseurope.com) and
Hostels.com have good listings. Ireland's Independent Holiday

Hostels (www.hostels-ireland.com) is a network of 145 independent hostels, requiring no membership and welcoming all ages. All IHH hostels are approved by the Irish Tourist Board.

Self-Catering Cottages and Apartments

Travelers wanting to slow down and base themselves in one place for extended periods can rent a cottage or an apartment (called flats in Ireland). This type of lodging varies greatly, but almost always includes a kitchen and living room. The owners discourage short stays, and usually require a minimum one-week rental plus a deposit.

I focus on short-term-stay sleeping recommendations in this book (B&Bs, guesthouses, and hotels), rather than self-catering options. But there are a variety of organizations that specialize in this longer-term alternative. Your most reliable source for places that live up to certain standards is the Irish Tourist Board (for online info, try www.tourismireland.com).

EATING

Ireland has long been labeled the "land of potatoes," but you'll find modern-day Irish cuisine delicious and varied, from vegetables, meat, and dairy products to fresh- and saltwater fish. Try the local specialties wherever you happen to be eating.

The traditional breakfast, the "Irish Fry" (known in the North as the "Ulster Fry"), is a hearty way to start the day—with juice, tea or coffee, cereal, eggs, bacon, sausage, a grilled tomato, sautéed mushrooms, and optional black pudding (made from pigs' blood). Toast is served with butter and marmalade. This meal tides many travelers over until dinner. But there's nothing un-Irish about skipping the "fry"—few locals  actually start their day with this heavy traditional breakfast. You can simply skip the heavier fare and enjoy the cereal, juice, toast, and tea.

Picnicking saves time and money. Try boxes of orange juice (pure, by the liter), fresh bread (especially Irish soda bread), tasty Cashel blue cheese, meat, a tube of mustard, local-eatin' apples, bananas, small tomatoes, a small tub of yogurt (it's drinkable), rice crackers, gorp or nuts, plain digestive biscuits (the chocolate-covered ones melt), and any local specialties. At open-air markets and supermarkets, you can get produce in small quantities. Supermarkets often have good deli sections, packaged sandwiches, and sometimes salad bars. I often munch a relaxed "meal on wheels" in a car, train, or bus to save 30 precious minutes for sightseeing.

At classier restaurants, look for "early-bird specials," allowing you to eat well and affordably, but early (around 17:30–19:00, last order by 19:00). At a sit-down place with table service, tip around 10 percent—unless the service charge is already listed on the bill (for details, see page 389).

Pub Grub and Beer

Pubs are a basic part of the Irish social scene, and, whether you're a teetotaler or a beer-guzzler, they should be a part of your travel here. "Pub" is short for "public house." It's an extended living room where, if you don't mind the stickiness, you can feel the pulse of Ireland.

Smart travelers use the pubs to eat, drink, get out of the rain, watch the latest sporting event, and make new friends. Unfortunately, many city pubs have been afflicted with an excess of brass, ferns, and video games. Most traditional atmospheric pubs are in the countryside and smaller towns.

Pub grub gets better every year—it's Ireland's best eating value. For around $12–15, you'll get a basic hot lunch or dinner in friendly surroundings. Pubs that are attached to restaurants, advertise their food, and are crowded with locals are more likely to have fresh food and a chef than to be the kind of pub that sells only lousy microwaved snacks.

Pub menus consist of a hearty assortment of traditional dishes such as Irish stew (mutton with mashed potatoes, onions, carrots, and herbs), soups and chowders, coddle (bacon, pork sausages, potatoes, and onions stewed in layers), fish-and-chips, collar and cabbage (boiled bacon coated in bread crumbs and brown sugar, then baked and served with cabbage), boxty (potato pancake filled with fish, meat, or vegetables), and champ (potato mashed with milk and onions). Irish bread nicely rounds out a meal. In coastal areas, a lot of seafood is available, such as mackerel, mussels, and Atlantic salmon. There's seldom table service in Irish pubs. Order drinks and meals at the bar. Pay as you order, and don't tip.

I recommend certain pubs, and your B&B host is usually up-to-date on the best neighborhood pub grub. Ask for advice (but adjust for nepotism and cronyism, which run rampant).

When you say "a beer, please" in an Irish pub, you'll get a pint of Guinness (the black beauty with the blonde head). If you want a small beer, ask for a glass or a half-pint. Never rush your bartender when he's pouring a Guinness. It takes time—almost sacred time.

The Irish take great pride in their beer. At pubs, long hand pulls are used to draw the traditional, rich-flavored "real ales" up from the cellar. These are the connoisseur's favorites: They're

fermented naturally, vary from sweet to bitter, and often include a hoppy or nutty flavor. Experiment with obscure local microbrews. Short hand pulls at the bar mean colder, fizzier, mass-produced, and less interesting keg beers. Stout is dark and more bitter, like Guinness. If you don't like Guinness, try it in Ireland. It doesn't travel well and is better in its homeland. Murphy's is a very good Guinness-like stout, but a bit smoother and milder. For a cold, refreshing, basic, American-style beer, ask for a lager such as Harp. Ale drinkers swear by Smithwick's. Caffrey's is a satisfying cross between stout and ale. Try the draft cider (sweet or dry)...carefully. Teetotalers can order a soft drink.

Pubs are generally open daily from 11:00 to 23:30 and Sunday from noon to 22:30. Children are served food and soft drinks in pubs (sometimes in a courtyard or the restaurant section). You'll often see signs behind the bar asking that children vacate the premises by 20:00. You must be 18 to order a beer, and the Gardí (police) are cracking down hard on pubs that don't enforce this. A cup of darts is free for the asking.

You're a guest on your first night; after that, you're a regular. A wise Irishman once said, "It never rains in a pub." The relaxed, informal atmosphere feels like a refuge from daily cares. Women traveling alone need not worry—you'll become part of the pub family in no time.

Craic (crack), Irish for "fun" or "a good laugh," is the sport that accompanies drinking in a pub. People are there to talk. To encourage conversation, stand or sit at the bar, not at a table.

The Irish government passed a law making all pubs in the Republic smoke-free. Smokers now take their pints outside, turning alleys into covered smoking patios. An incredulous Irishman responded

to the law by saying, "What will they do next? Ban drinking in pubs? We'll never get to heaven if we don't die."

It's a tradition to buy your table a round, and then for each person to reciprocate. If an Irishman buys you a drink, thank him by saying, "Go raibh maith agat" (guh rov mah UG-ut). Offer him a toast in Irish—"Slainte" (SLAWN-chuh), the equivalent of "cheers." A good excuse for a conversation is to ask to be taught a few words of Gaelic.

Here's a goofy excuse for some *craic:* Ireland—small as it is—has many dialects. People from Cork are famous for talking very fast (and in a squeaky voice)—so fast that some even talk in letters alone. ABCD fish? (Anybody see the fish?) DR no fish. (There are no fish.) DR fish. (There are fish.) CDBDIs? (See the beady eyes?) OIBJ DR fish. (Oh aye, be Jeeze, there are fish.) For a possibly more appropriate spin, replace the fish with "bird" (girl). This is obscure, but your pub neighbor may understand and enjoy hearing it. If nothing else, you won't seem so intimidating to him anymore.

Traditional Irish Music

Traditional music is alive and popular in pubs throughout Ireland. "Sessions" (musical evenings) may be planned and advertised or impromptu. Traditionally, musicians just congregate and play for the love of it. There will generally be a fiddle, a flute or tin whistle, a guitar, a *bodhrán* (goatskin drum), and maybe an accordion or mandolin. Things usually get going around 21:30 (but note that Irish punctuality is unpredictable). Last call for drinks is around 23:30.

The music often comes in sets of three songs. The wind and string instruments embellish melody lines with lots of tight orna-

mentation. Whoever happens to be leading determines the next song only as the song the group is playing is about to be finished. If he wants to pass on the decision, it's done with eye contact and a nod. A *ceilidh* (KAY-lee) is an evening of music and dance... an Irish hoedown.

Percussion generally stays in the background. The *bodhrán* (BO-run) is played with a small, two-headed club. The performer's hand stretches the skin to change the tone and pitch. You'll sometimes be lucky enough to hear a set of bones crisply played. These are two cow ribs (boiled and dried) that are rattled in one hand like spoons or castanets, substituting for the sound of dancing shoes in olden days.

Watch closely if a piper is playing. The Irish version of bagpipes, the *uilleann* (ILL-in) pipes are played by inflating the airbag (under the left elbow) with a bellows (under the right elbow) rather than with a mouthpiece like the Scottish Highland bagpipes. *Uilleann* is Gaelic for "elbow," and the sound is more melodic,

How Was Your Trip?

Were your travels fun, smooth, and meaningful? If you'd like to share your tips, concerns, and discoveries, please fill out the survey at www.ricksteves.com/feedback. I value your feedback. Thanks in advance—it helps a lot.

with a wider range than the Highland pipes. The piper fingers his chanter like a flute to create individual notes, and uses the heel of his right hand to play chords on one of three regulator pipes. It takes amazing coordination to play this instrument well, and the sound can be haunting.

Occasionally, the fast-paced music will stop and one person will sing a lament. Called *sean nos* (Gaelic for "old style"), this slightly nasal vocal style may be a remnant of the ancient storytelling tradition of the bards whose influence died out when Gaelic culture waned 400 years ago. This is the one time when the entire pub will stop to listen as sad lyrics fill the room. Stories—often of love lost, emigration to a faraway land, or a heroic rebel death struggling against English rule—are always heartfelt. Spend a lament studying the faces in the crowd.

A session can be magical or lifeless. If the chemistry is right, it's one of the great Irish experiences. The music churns intensely while members of the group casually enjoy exploring each other's musical style. The drummer dodges the fiddler's playful bow. Sipping their pints, they skillfully maintain a faint but steady buzz. The floor on the musicians' platform is stomped paint-free, and barmaids scurry artfully through the commotion, gathering towers of empty, cream-crusted glasses. Make yourself right at home, "playing the boot" (tapping your foot) under the table in time with the music. Talk to your neighbor. Locals often have an almost evangelical interest in explaining the music.

TRAVELING AS A TEMPORARY LOCAL

We travel all the way to Europe to enjoy differences—to become temporary locals. You'll experience frustrations. Certain truths that we find "God-given" or "self-evident," such as cold beer, ice in drinks, bottomless cups of coffee, hot showers, and bigger being better, are suddenly not so true. One of the benefits of travel is the eye-opening realization that there are logical, civil, and even better alternatives.

If there is a negative aspect to the image the Irish have of Americans, it's that we are big, loud, aggressive, impolite, rich, superficially friendly, and a bit naive.

Given our reluctance to work with the world on climate change issues, the Irish don't respond well to Americans complaining about being too hot or too cold. Bring a sweater in winter, and in summer, be prepared to sweat a little like everyone else.

While the Irish look bemusedly at some of our Yankee excesses—and worriedly at others—they nearly always afford us individual travelers all the warmth we deserve. Judging from all the happy feedback I receive from travelers who have used this book, it's safe to assume you'll enjoy a great, affordable vacation—with the finesse of an independent, experienced traveler.

Thanks, and have a grand holiday!

BACK DOOR TRAVEL PHILOSOPHY
From *Rick Steves' Europe Through the Back Door*

Travel is intensified living—maximum thrills per minute and one of the last great sources of legal adventure. Travel is freedom. It's recess, and we need it.

Experiencing the real Europe requires catching it by surprise, going casual..."Through the Back Door."

Affording travel is a matter of priorities. (Make do with the old car.) You can travel—simply, safely, and comfortably—nearly anywhere in Europe for $100 a day plus transportation costs. In many ways, spending more money only builds a thicker wall between you and what you came to see. Europe is a cultural carnival, and, time after time, you'll find that its best acts are free and the best seats are the cheap ones.

A tight budget forces you to travel close to the ground, meeting and communicating with the people, not relying on service with a purchased smile. Never sacrifice sleep, nutrition, safety, or cleanliness in the name of budget. Simply enjoy the local-style alternatives to expensive hotels and restaurants.

Extroverts have more fun. If your trip is low on magic moments, kick yourself and make things happen. If you don't enjoy a place, maybe you don't know enough about it. Seek the truth. Recognize tourist traps. Give a culture the benefit of your open mind. See things as different but not better or worse. Any culture has much to share.

Of course, travel, like the world, is a series of hills and valleys. Be fanatically positive and militantly optimistic. If something's not to your liking, change your liking. Travel is addictive. It can make you a happier American as well as a citizen of the world. Our Earth is home to six and a half billion equally important people. It's humbling to travel and find that people don't envy Americans. Europeans like us, but, with all due respect, they wouldn't trade passports.

Globe-trotting destroys ethnocentricity. It helps you understand and appreciate different cultures. Regrettably, there are forces in our society that want you dumbed down for their convenience. Don't let it happen. Thoughtful travel engages you with the world—more important than ever these days. Travel changes people. It broadens perspectives and teaches new ways to measure quality of life. Rather than fear the diversity on this planet, travelers celebrate it. Many travelers toss aside their hometown blinders. Their prized souvenirs are the strands of different cultures they decide to knit into their own character. The world is a cultural yarn shop, and Back Door travelers are weaving the ultimate tapestry. Join in!

REPUBLIC
OF
IRELAND

REPUBLIC OF IRELAND

Though a relatively small island, Ireland has had a disproportionately large impact on the rest of the world. For hundreds of years, Ireland's greatest export has been its friendly yet feisty people. Geographically isolated in the damp attic of Dark Age Europe, Christian Irish monks tended the flickering flame of literacy, then bravely reintroduced it to the barbaric Continent. Later, pressure from wars and famines at home (combined with opportunities abroad) compelled many Irish to leave their island and scramble for a better life in far-flung America, Canada, and Australia.

The Republic of Ireland has existed since 1922, but its inhabitants proudly claim their nation to be the only modern independent state to sprout from purely Celtic roots (sprinkled with a few Vikings and shipwrecked Spanish Armada sailors for seasoning). The Romans never bothered to come over and organize the wild Irish. Through the persuasive and culturally enlightened approach of early missionaries such as St. Patrick, Ireland may also be the only country to have initially converted to Christianity without bloodshed. Irish culture absorbed the influences of Viking raiders and Norman soldiers of fortune, eventually enduring the 750-year shadow of English occupation.

Just a few decades ago, Ireland was an isolated agricultural economic backwater that had largely missed out on the Industrial Revolution. Joining the European Community (precursor to the EU) in 1973 began to turn things around, and the Irish government instituted farsighted tax laws (including a corporate tax rate of only 12.5 percent) to entice foreign corporations to set up shop here.

Today, the Republic enjoys a renaissance as its Celtic Tiger economy—the strongest in the EU—attracts expatriate Irish and new foreign investment. And as the only English-speaking country to have adopted the euro currency, Ireland is an appealing place for US corporations to set up shop as a beachhead on European turf. More than 40 percent of the Irish population is under 25 years old, leading many high-tech and pharmaceutical firms to take

Republic of Ireland

advantage of this young, well-educated labor force. Google and Yahoo have both chosen Dublin as their European headquarters. Microsoft, Intel, Dell, Apple, Oracle, and IBM all have major outposts here (welcome to the "Silicon Bog"). Pfizer makes Viagra in Ringaskiddy, County Cork. And for the first time, Ireland has also become a destination for emigrants from the Third World and the newer EU countries in Eastern Europe, who come in search of higher pay...a switch from the days when Irish fled to start new lives abroad.

Other aspects of modern life are making inroads in traditional Ireland. In 2003, shops began charging customers for plastic sacks for carrying goods (in 2007, there was a €0.22 surcharge), which has cut down on litter. In 2004, smoking was banned in all Irish pubs. Some pubkeepers grumble about lost business, but the air has cleared.

The vast majority of Irish people speak English, but you'll encounter Irish Gaelic if you venture to the western Irish fringe.

Republic of Ireland Almanac

Official Name: The Republic of Ireland (locals say Ireland or Éire).

Population: Ireland's four million people (same as Kentucky) are of Celtic stock. They speak English, though Irish (Gaelic) is spoken in pockets along the country's west coast. Nearly 9 in 10 are nominally Catholic, though only one in three attends church.

Latitude and Longitude: 53°N and 8°W. The latitude is equivalent to Alberta, Canada.

Area: With 27,000 square miles—half the size of New York State—it occupies the southwestern 80 percent of the island of Ireland. The country is small enough that radio broadcasts manage to cover traffic snarls nationwide, rather than city-wide.

Geography: The isle is mostly flat, ringed by a hilly coastline. The climate is moderate, with cloudy skies about every other day.

Biggest Cities: The capital of Dublin (1.5 million) is the only big city; one in four Irish live in the greater Dublin area, and 4 in 10 live within 50 miles. Cork has 180,000, while Limerick and Galway have about 60,000.

Economy: The Gross Domestic Product is $165 billion (similar to Louisiana's) and the GDP per capita is $41,000—one of Europe's highest, and 25 percent more than Britain's. Major money-makers include tourism and exports (especially to the US and UK) of machines, medicine, Guinness, glassware, crystalware, and software. Traditional agriculture (potatoes and other root vegetables) is fading fast, but dairy is booming.

Government: The elected president, Mary McAleese, appoints the prime minister (Bertie Ahern), who is nominated by Parliament. The Parliament consists of the 60-seat Senate, chosen by an electoral college, and the House of Representatives, with 166 seats apportioned after the people vote for a party. Major parties include Fianna Fail, Fine Gael, and Sinn Fein, the political arm of the (fading) IRA. Ireland is divided into 26 administrative counties—including Kerry, Clare, Cork, Limerick, and so on.

Flag: The Republic of Ireland's flag is made of three vertical bands of green, white, and orange.

The Average Irish: A typical Irish person is 5'6", 34 years old, has 1.86 kids, and will live to be 78. Every day, he or she drinks four cups of tea and spends $3 on alcohol.

The Irish love of conversation shines through wherever you go. The warm welcome you'll receive has its roots in ancient Celtic laws of hospitality toward stranded strangers.

At first glance, Ireland's landscape seems unspectacular, with few mountains over 3,000 feet and an interior consisting of grazing pastures and peat bogs. But its seductive beauty slowly grows on you. The gentle rainfall, called "soft weather" by the locals, really does create 40 shades of green—and quite a few rainbows as well. Ancient, moss-covered ring forts crouch in lush valleys, while stone-strewn monastic ruins and lone castle turrets brave the wind on nearby hilltops. Charming fishing villages dot the coast near rugged, wave-battered cliffs. Slow down to contemplate the checkerboard patterns created by the rock walls outlining the many fields. Examine the colorful small-town shop fronts that proudly state the name of the proprietor.

The resilient Irish character was born of dark humor, historical reverence, and an optimistic, "we'll get 'em next time" rebel spirit. Though the influence of the Catholic Church is less apparent these days, it still plays a major part in Irish life. The national radio and TV station, RTE, pauses for 30 seconds at noon and 18:00 to broadcast the chimes of the Angelus bells. A favorite Irish punch line proclaims that if you're phoning heaven, it's a long-distance call from the rest of the world, but a local call from Ireland.

DUBLIN

With reminders of its stirring history and rich culture on every corner, Ireland's capital and largest city is a sightseer's delight. Dublin's fair city will have you humming, "Cockles and mussels, alive, alive-O."

Founded as a Viking trading settlement in the ninth century, Dublin grew to be a center of wealth and commerce, second only to London in the British Empire. Dublin, the seat of English rule in Ireland for 700 years, was the heart of a "civilized" Anglo-Irish area (eastern Ireland) known as "the Pale." Anything "beyond the Pale" was considered uncultured and almost barbaric...purely Irish.

The Golden Age of English Dublin was the 18th century. The British Empire was on a roll, and the city was right there with it. Largely rebuilt during this Georgian era, Dublin—even with its tattered edges—became an elegant and cultured capital.

But nationalism, plus a realization of the importance of human rights, forever changed Dublin. The American and French Revolutions inspired Irish intellectuals to buck British rule and, after the Rebellion of 1798, life in Dublin was never quite the same. But the 18th century left a lasting imprint on the city. Squares and boulevards in the Georgian style (that's British for "Neoclassical") gave the city an air of grandeur. The National Museum, the National Gallery, and many government buildings are in the Georgian section of town. Few buildings (notably Christ Church and St. Patrick's cathedrals) survive from before this Georgian period.

In the 19th century, with the closing of the Irish Parliament, the Great Potato Famine, and the beginnings of the modern struggle for independence, Dublin was treated—and felt—more like a colony than a partner. The tension culminated in the Easter Rising of 1916, followed a few years later by independence from Britain and Ireland's tragic civil war. With many of its grand streets left in ruins, Dublin emerged as the capital of the British Empire's only former colony in Europe.

While bullet-pocked buildings and dramatic statues keep memories of Ireland's recent struggle for independence alive, it's boom time now, and the city is looking to a bright future. Locals are enjoying the strong Celtic Tiger economy while visitors enjoy a big-town cultural scene wrapped in a small-town smile.

Planning Your Time

On a three-week trip through Ireland, Dublin deserves three nights and two days. Consider this aggressive sightseeing plan:

Day 1: 10:15–Follow the Trinity College guided walk; 11:00–Visit the Book of Kells and Old Library ahead of the mid-day crowds; 12:00–Browse Grafton Street and have lunch there or picnic on Merrion Square; 13:30–See Number Twenty-Nine Georgian House (closed Mon); 15:00–Head to the National Museum: Archaeology and History branch (also closed Mon); 17:00–Return to hotel, rest, have dinner—eat well for less during early-bird specials; 19:30–Go for an evening guided pub tour (musical or literary); 22:00–Drop in on Irish music in the Temple Bar area.

Day 2: 10:00–Take the Dublin Castle tour; 11:30–Hop on one of the hop-on, hop-off buses, jumping off to see the Guinness Storehouse and Kilmainham Gaol (while in transit, you could munch a slow sandwich picnic in traffic on the open-top bus); 15:00–Leave the bus at Parnell Square, visit the Garden of Remembrance and stroll down to O'Connell Bridge, sightseeing and shopping as you like along the way; Evening–Catch a play, concert, or Comhaltas traditional music in Dun Laoghaire (DUN-leary).

With More Time: Dublin—while relatively small—can keep you busily sightseeing for a week without even leaving the center of town. And with all its music, theater, and after-hour tours—not to mention the lively pub scene—evenings are just as fun.

ORIENTATION

(area code: 01)

Greater Dublin sprawls with a million people—a fourth of the country's population. But the center of tourist interest is a tight triangle between O'Connell Bridge, St. Stephen's Green, and Christ Church Cathedral. Within this triangle you'll find Trinity College (Book of Kells), Grafton Street (top pedestrian shopping zone),

Temple Bar (trendy and touristy nightlife center), Dublin Castle, and the hub of most city tours and buses. The only major sights outside your easy-to-walk triangle are the Kilmainham Gaol, the Guinness Storehouse, and the National Museum: Decorative Arts and History branch (all west of the center).

The River Liffey cuts the town in two. Focus on the southern half, where nearly all of your sightseeing will take place. Dublin's wide main drag, O'Connell Street, starts north of the river at the Parnell monument and runs south, down to the central O'Connell Bridge. After crossing the bridge, it continues south as the major city axis (mostly as the pedestrian-only Grafton Street) to St. Stephen's Green.

The suburban port of Dun Laoghaire (described on page 83) lies south of Dublin, 20 minutes away by DART commuter train. Travelers connecting by ferry to Holyhead in Wales—or those just looking for a mellow town to sleep in outside of urban Dublin—can easily home-base here. Another option is the northern suburb of Howth (see page 87), 25 minutes away on the DART and closer to the airport.

Tourist Information

Dublin's main tourist information office (TI) is a thriving hub of ticket and info desks filling an old church (June–Sept Mon–Sat 9:00–19:00, Sun 10:30–15:00; Oct–May Mon–Sat 9:00–17:30, Sun 10:30–15:00; a block off Grafton Street on Suffolk Street, tel. 01/850-230-330 or 01/605-7700, www.visitdublin.com). It has a car-rental agency, bus-info desk, sandwich bar, more maps and books than you'll ever need, racks advertising the busy entertainment scene, and traditional knickknacks for sale. It's also a good place to pick up brochures for destinations throughout Ireland. There's another TI at the airport (daily 8:00–22:00) and one at the Dun Laoghaire ferry terminal (Mon–Sat 10:00–12:45 & 14:00–18:00, closed Sun). Smaller satellite TIs are at the north end of the Baggot Street Bridge (Mon–Fri 9:30–12:00 & 12:30–17:00, closed Sat–Sun) and halfway down the east side of O'Connell Street (Mon–Sat 9:00–17:00, closed Sun, roughly opposite General Post Office).

Pick up the TI's *The Guide* or its free newspaper, *Dubl!n,* both of which have decent city maps. The handy *Dublin's Must-Do* booklet has a small map and the latest on all of the town's sights—many more than I list here (€2.50, sold at TI bookshop without any wait).

Greater Dublin

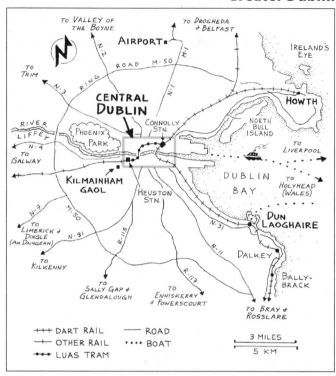

For a schedule of happenings in town, check the minimal calendar of events inside *The Guide to Dublin* newspaper (free at TI).

The excellent *Collins Illustrated Discovering Dublin Map* (€7 at TIs and newsstands) is the ultimate city map, listing just about everything of interest, along with helpful opinions and a cheat sheet of Dublin history.

Dublin Pass: This sightseeing pass is a good deal only if you like to visit lots of sights quickly (€31/1 day, €49/2 days, €59/3 days, €89/6 days, sold at TIs, www.dublinpass.com). The pass occasionally saves a few minutes when you'd otherwise need to wait in line to buy a ticket. It covers museums, churches, literature-related sights, and expensive stops like the Guinness Storehouse and the Old Jameson Distillery, plus the Aircoach airport bus (but not Airlink buses). However, the pass doesn't include the famous Book of Kells at Trinity College or any bus tours or walking tours, and many of the sights it claims to "cover" (such as the National Gallery and the Chester Beatty Library) are actually free. The booklet that comes with the pass, however, is a handy planning tool.

Arrival in Dublin

By Train: Dublin has two train stations. **Heuston Station,** on the west end of town, serves west and southwest Ireland (30-min walk from O'Connell Bridge; take taxi or bus #90, see below). **Connolly Station,** which serves the north, northwest, and Rosslare, is closer to the center (10-min walk from O'Connell Bridge). Each station has ATMs and lockers (small lockers-€4/day, large-€6/day, 7-day maximum).

The two train stations are connected by the red line of the LUAS commuter train (see "Getting Around Dublin," below) and by bus. Bus #90 runs along the river, linking both train stations, the bus station, and the city center (€1, 6/hr).

To reach Heuston Station from the city center, catch bus #90 on the south side of the river; to get to Connolly Station and Busaras Central Bus Station from the city center, catch #90 on the north side of the river. Some bus stops are "request only" stops: Be alert to the bus numbers (above the windshield) of approaching buses. When you see your bus coming, extend your arm straight out, palm outward, to flag it down.

By Bus: Bus Éireann, Ireland's national bus company, uses the **Busaras Central Bus Station** next to Connolly Station (10-min walk or short bus ride to the city center; see bus #90 info in "By Train," above).

By Plane: The airport has ATMs, change bureaus, car-rental agencies, baggage check, a café, and a supermarket at the airport parking lot (tel. 01/814-1111, www.dublinairport.ie).

Getting Between the Airport and Downtown by Bus: You have two main choices: Airlink (yellow and dark-blue bus) or Aircoach (light blue bus). Both pick up on the street directly in front of airport arrivals at ground level. Consider buying a €11 **Rambler** city-bus pass at the airport TI (see "Getting Around Dublin," page 42), which covers the Airlink bus into town—but read this first to see if Airlink is the best choice for your trip.

Airlink: Airlink buses #747 and #748 connect the airport to Busaras Central Bus Station, which is only a block from Connolly Station (€6, pay driver, 3/hr, 35 min, tel. 01/873-4222, www .dublinbus.ie). Bus #747 is best for reaching my recommended hotels near Parnell Square north of the city center. Bus #748 is better for hotels in the city center—ask the driver which stop is closest to your hotel (this bus also connects the airport with Heuston Station).

Aircoach: To reach recommended hotels near St. Stephen's Green south of the city center, the Aircoach is best (€7, covered by Dublin Pass, 3/hr, runs 5:00–23:30; pay driver and confirm best stop for your hotel, tel. 01/844-7118, www.aircoach.ie).

The cheapest (and slowest) way from the airport to downtown

Dublin is by **city bus;** buses marked #16A, #41, #41A, and #41B go to O'Connell Street (€1.90, exact change required, no change given, 4/hr, 55 min).

Getting Between the Airport and Suburbs: The best way to get to Dun Laoghaire is to take the Patton Flyer bus (€7, 1/hr, 45 min, tel. 01/284-9619, www.thepattonflyer.ie). Otherwise, take either Airlink bus #747 or #748 to Busaras Central Bus Station and transfer onto the DART light rail system (€7 for Airlink/DART combo-ticket). For Dun Laoghaire, take DART direction: Bray; for Howth, take DART direction: Howth.

Taxis from the airport into Dublin cost about €25–30; to Dun Laoghaire, about €50; to Howth, about €25.

By Ferry: Irish Ferries docks at the mouth of the River Liffey (at Dublin Docklands, near the town center), while the Stena Line docks at Dun Laoghaire (easy DART train connections into Dublin, 4/hr, 20 min). For more information, see "Transportation Connections," page 80.

By Car: Trust me, you don't want to drive in downtown Dublin. Cars are unnecessary for sightseeing in town, parking is expensive (more than €30 per day), and traffic will get your fighting Irish up. Save your car-rental days for cross-country travel between smaller towns and see this energetic city by taxi, bus, or on foot. If you're staying out in the suburbs (Dun Laoghaire or Howth), ask your innkeeper for the best place to park.

Drivers renting their car at Dublin Airport, but not staying in Dublin, can bypass the worst of the big-city traffic by making use of the recently completed M-50 ring road to whisk themselves south or west. Before you leave the airport, crack a bill (buy a newspaper or candy bar) to get €5 worth of euro coins for the tolls on the M-1 and M-50 freeway system.

Helpful Hints

High Costs: Thanks to its recent "Celtic Tiger" economic boom, Ireland now rivals Finland as the EU's most expensive country. Restaurants and lodging—other than hostels—are more expensive the closer you get to the touristy Temple Bar district (see cheaper options listed in "Sleeping," page 71). A pint of beer in a Temple Bar pub now costs €5 (a sobering thought).

Tourist Victim Support Service: This service can be helpful if you run into any problems (Mon–Sat 10:00–18:00, Sun 12:00–18:00, tel. 01/478-5295).

US Embassy: It's on 42 Elgin Road in the Ballsbridge neighborhood (Mon–Tue and Thu–Fri 8:30–11:30 for passport concerns, closed Wed and Sat–Sun, tel. 01/668-7122 or 01/668-8777, http://dublin.usembassy.gov).

Festivals: St. Patrick's Day is a five-day extravaganza in Dublin

(March 13–17 in 2008, www.stpatricksday.ie). June 16 is Bloomsday, dedicated to the Irish author James Joyce and featuring the Messenger Bike Rally. On rugby weekends (about four per year), during the all-Ireland Gaelic football and hurling finals (Sundays in September), and during summer rock concerts, hotels raise their prices and are packed. Book ahead during festivals and for any weekend.

Internet Access: Internet cafés have sprung up on nearly every street. **Central Cybercafé** is indeed central (Mon–Fri 10:00–21:00, Sat–Sun 10:00–20:00, 6 Grafton Street, tel. 01/677-8298). **Global Internet Café** is north of the River Liffey (Mon–Fri 8:00–23:00, Sat 9:00–23:00, Sun 10:00–23:00, 8 Lower O'Connell Street, tel. 01/878-0295).

Laundry: Patrick Street Launderette, a block southwest of Jurys Inn Christ Church on Patrick Street, is full-service only. Allow four hours and about €9 for a load (Mon–Fri 9:00–20:00, Sat 9:00–18:00, closed Sun, tel. 01/473-1779). The **All-American Launderette** offers self- and full-service options (Mon–Sat 8:30–19:00, Sun 10:00–18:00, 40 South Great George's Street, tel. 01/677-2779).

Car Rental: For Dublin car-rental information, see page 397.

Getting Around Dublin

You'll do most of Dublin on foot, though when you need public transportation, you'll find it readily available and easy to use.

By Bus: Buses are cheap and cover the city thoroughly. Most lines start at the four quays (pronounced "keys"), or piers, that are nearest to O'Connell Bridge. If you're away from the center, nearly any bus takes you back downtown. Tell the driver where you're going, and he'll ask for €1–2 depending on the number of stops. Bring change or lose any excess. Bus #90 connects the bus and train stations (see "Arrival in Dublin—By Train," page 40).

The bus office at 59 Upper O'Connell Street has free bus-route maps and sells two different city-bus passes (Mon 8:30–17:30, Tue–Fri 9:00–17:30, Sat 9:00–14:00, closed Sun, tel. 01/873-4222, www.dublinbus.ie). The three-day **Rambler pass** costs €11 and covers the Airlink airport bus (but not Aircoach buses or DART trains). The one-day **Short Hop pass,** which costs €8.80, includes DART trains (but not Airlink or Aircoach buses). Passes are also sold at each TI and at newsstands and markets citywide (mostly Centra, Mace, Spar, and Londis).

By DART (Train): Speedy commuter trains run along the coast, connecting Dublin with Dun Laoghaire's ferry terminal, Howth's harbor, and recommended B&Bs. Think of the DART line as a giant "C" that serves coastal suburbs from Bray in the south to Howth in the north (€2, €3.60 round-trips are valid the same day only, Eurailpass valid but you'll use up a valuable flexi-day, tel. 01/703-3504, www.iarnrodeireann.ie/dart/home). For more information, see "Getting to Dun Laoghaire" on page 83 and "Getting to Howth" on page 88.

By LUAS (Light Rail): The city's light-rail system has two main lines (red and green) that serve inland suburbs. The more useful line for travelers is the red line, connecting the Connolly and Heuston train stations at either edge of the Central 1 Zone. In between, the Busaras Central Bus Station, Smithfield, and Museum stops can be handy (€1.40, 6/hr, runs 5:30–24:30, tel. 1-800-300-604, www.luas.ie).

By Taxi: Taxis are everywhere and easy to hail (cheap for three or four people). Cabbies are honest, plentiful, friendly, and good sources of information (€3.80 minimum, €0.50 per bag, figure around €8 for most crosstown rides, €35 per hour for guided joyride).

TOURS

While Dublin's physical treasures are lackluster by European standards, the city has a fine story to tell and people with a natural knack for telling it. It's a good town for walking tours, and the competition is fierce. Pamphlets touting creative walks are posted all over town. There are medieval walks, literary walks, Georgian Dublin walks, traditional music pub crawls, and even a rock-and-stroll walk tracing the careers of contemporary Irish bands. Taking an evening walk is a great way to meet other travelers. The Dublin TI also offers series of free, good-quality "iWalks" for travelers with iPods or MP3 players (download with maps at www.visitdublin.com).

By Foot

▲▲**Historical Walking Tour**—This is your best introductory walk. A group of hardworking history graduates—many of whom claim to have done more than just kiss the Blarney Stone—enliven Dublin's basic historic strip (Trinity College, Old Parliament House, Dublin Castle, and Christ Church Cathedral). You'll get the story of their city, from its Viking origin to the present. Guides speak at length about the roots of Ireland's struggle with Britain. As you listen to your guide's story, you stand in front of buildings that aren't much to see, but are lots to talk about (May–Sept daily at 11:00 and 15:00; April and Oct daily at 11:00; Nov–March Fri, Sat, and Sun only at 11:00). All walks last two hours and cost €12 (but get the €10 "student" discount rate with this book in 2008, free for kids under 14, depart from front gate of Trinity College, private tours available, mobile 087-688-9412, 087-830-3523, or

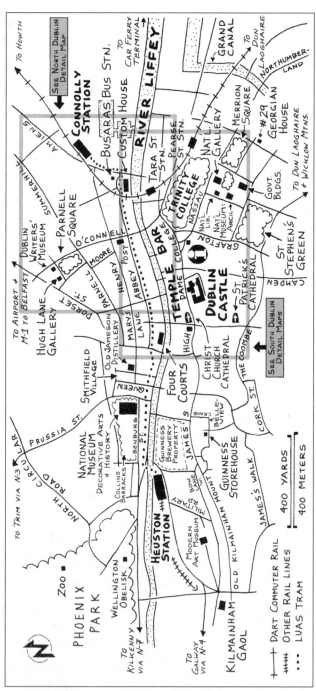

Dublin

087-305-9159, www.historicalinsights.ie).

▲▲▲**Traditional Irish Musical Pub Crawl**—This impressive and entertaining tour visits the upstairs rooms of three pubs; there, you'll listen to two musicians talk about, play, and sing traditional Irish music. While having only two musicians makes the music a bit thin (Irish music aficionados will say you're better off just finding a good jam session), the evening—though touristy—is not gimmicky. It's an education in traditional Irish music. The musicians, who also demonstrate a few instruments, clearly enjoy introducing rookies to their art and are very good at it (€13, €1 discount with this book in 2008, beer extra, allow 2.5 hours, April–Oct daily at 19:30, Nov–March Thu–Sat only, expect up to 50 tourists, meet upstairs at Gogarty's Pub at the corner of Fleet and Anglesea in the Temple Bar area, tel. 01/475-3313, www.musicalpubcrawl.com).

▲**Dublin Literary Pub Crawl**—Two actors take 40 or so tourists on a walk, stopping at four pubs. Their clever banter introduces the novice to the high *craic* of Joyce, O'Casey, and Yeats. The two-hour tour is punctuated with 20-minute pub breaks (free time). While the beer lubricates the social fun, it dilutes the content of the evening. This is an easygoing excuse to drink beer in busy pubs, hook up with other travelers, and get a dose of Irish witty lit. But if  you want straight lit and drama, find a real performance—there are many throughout the summer, such as the lunchtime hour at the Dublin Writers' Museum, described later in this chapter (€13, €1 discount with this book in 2008, April–Nov daily at 19:30, plus Sun at noon; Dec–March Thu–Sun only; you can normally just show up, but call ahead July–Aug when it can fill up; meet upstairs in the Duke Pub, off Grafton on Duke Street, tel. 01/670-5602, mobile 087-263-0270, www.dublinpubcrawl.com).

1916 Rebellion Walks—This two-hour walking tour breathes gritty life into the most turbulent year in modern Irish history, when idealistic Irish rebels launched the Easter Uprising—eventually leading to independence from Britain (€12, €2 discount with this book in 2008, daily mid-March–Oct Mon–Sat at 11:30, Sun at 13:00, no tours Nov–mid-March, depart from International Bar at 23 Wicklow Street, mobile 086-858-3847, www.1916rising.com).

By Bus (on Land and Water)

▲**Hop-on, Hop-off Bus Tours**—Two companies (Dublin City Tour and City Sightseeing/Guide Friday) offer hop-on, hop-off bus tours of Dublin, doing virtually identical 90-minute circuits. You can get on or off at your choice of about 20 stops (4/hr, daily 9:30–18:30, ticket valid for 24 hours). Buses are mostly topless, with live running commentaries. This type of tour, which runs in many European cities but isn't always well executed, is made-to-order for Dublin, and buses run so frequently that they make your sight-

seeing super-efficient. Both companies go to Guinness Storehouse and Kilmainham Gaol (although the Dublin City tour bus stops a few blocks from the Gaol). Buy your ticket on board. Each company's map, free with your ticket, details various discounts you'll get at Dublin's sights (such as the Guinness Storehouse, Viking Splash tour, Old Jameson Distillery, Dublin Writers' Museum, Dublinia, Christ Church Cathedral, and others). **Dublin City Tour** (green-and-cream buses) drivers provide a fun and quirky narration (€14, tel. 01/873-4222, www.dublinsightseeing.ie). **City Sightseeing** (red buses) and **Guide Friday** (yellow buses) cost more but come with a guide and a driver, rather than a driver who guides (€15, tel. 01/872-9010, www.irishcitytours.com).

▲**Viking Splash Tours**—If you'd like to ride in a WWII amphibious vehicle—driven by a Viking-costumed guide who's as liable to spout history as he is to growl—this is for you. The tour starts with a group roar from the Viking within us all. At first, the guide talks as if he were a Viking ("When we came here in 841..."), but soon the patriot emerges as he tags Irish history onto the sights you pass. Near the end of the 75-minute tour (punctuated by occasional group roars at passersby), you don a life jacket for a slow spin up and down a boring canal. Kids who expect a Viking splash may feel they've been trapped in a classroom, but historians will enjoy the talk more than the gimmick (€20, daily Feb–Nov 9:30–17:00, none Dec–Jan, depart about hourly from Bull Alley beside St. Patrick's Cathedral and from the north side of St. Stephen's Green opposite Dawson Street, ticket office at 64–65 Patrick Street, tel. 01/707-6000, www.vikingsplash.ie). Although it's covered, the boat is breezy—dress appropriately.

SIGHTS

Trinity College

Founded in 1592 by Queen Elizabeth I to establish a Protestant way of thinking about God, Trinity has long been Ireland's most prestigious college. Originally the student body was limited to rich Protestant males. Women were admitted in 1903, and Catholics—

though allowed entrance by the school much earlier—were given formal permission to study at Trinity in the 1970s. Today, half of Trinity's 12,500 students are women, and 70 percent are culturally Catholic (although only about 20 percent of Irish youth are churchgoing).

▲▲**Trinity College Tour**—Trinity students organize and lead 30-minute tours of their campus (look just inside the gate for posted

departure times and a ticket-seller on a stool). You'll get a rundown of the mostly Georgian architecture; a peek at student life past and present; and the enjoyable company of your guide, a witty Irish college kid (€10; includes €8 fee to see Book of Kells, where the tour leaves you; May–Sept daily 10:15–

15:40, Feb–April and Oct–Nov Sat–Sun only, no tours Dec–Jan, departs roughly every 30 min, weather permitting).

▲▲**Book of Kells in the Trinity Old Library**—The only Trinity campus interior welcoming tourists is the Old Library (just follow the signs), with its precious Book of Kells. The first-class "Turning Darkness into Light" exhibit puts the 680-page illuminated manuscript in its historical and cultural context, preparing you to see the original book and other precious manuscripts in the treasury. The exhibit is a one-way affair leading to the actual treasury, which shows only four books under glass in one display case. Make a point to spend at least half an hour in the exhibit (before reaching the actual Book of Kells). Especially interesting are the five-minute video clips showing the exacting care that went into transcribing the monk-uscripts and the ancient art of bookbinding.

Written on vellum (calfskin) in the late eighth century—by Irish monks on the island of Iona, Scotland—this enthusiastically decorated copy of the four Gospels was taken safely inland to the

Irish monastery at Kells in A.D. 806 after a series of Viking raids. Arguably the finest piece of art from what is generally called the Dark Ages, the Book of Kells shows that monastic life in this far fringe of Europe was far from dark. It has been bound into four separate volumes, and at any given time, two of the four gospels are on display. The crowd around the one glass case with the treasures can be off-putting, but hold your own and get up close. You'll see four richly decorated, 1,200-year-old

Dublin

Dublin at a Glance

▲▲▲Traditional Irish Musical Pub Crawl A fascinating, practical, and enjoyable primer on traditional Irish music. **Hours:** April–Oct daily at 19:30, Nov–March Thu–Sat only.

▲▲▲Kilmainham Gaol Historic jail used by the British as a political prison—today a moving museum of the suffering of the Irish people. **Hours:** Daily 9:30–18:00.

▲▲Historical Walking Tour Your best introduction to Dublin. **Hours:** May–Sept daily at 11:00 and 15:00; April and Oct daily at 11:00; Nov–March Fri, Sat, and Sun only at 11:00.

▲▲Trinity College Ireland's most famous school, best visited with a 30-minute tour led by one of its students. **Hours:** May–Sept daily 10:15–15:40, Feb–April and Oct–Nov Sat–Sun only, no tours Dec–Jan; weather permitting.

▲▲Book of Kells in the Trinity Old Library An exquisite illuminated manuscript, the most important piece of art from the Dark Ages. **Hours:** May–Sept daily 9:30–16:30; Oct–April Mon–Sat 9:30–16:30, Sun 12:00–16:30.

▲▲Dublin Castle The city's historic 700-year-old castle, featuring ornate English state apartments, tourable only with a guide. **Hours:** Mon–Fri 10:00–17:00, Sat–Sun 14:00–17:00.

▲▲Chester Beatty Library American expatriate's eclectic yet sumptuous collection of literary and religious treasures from Islam, the Orient, and medieval Europe. **Hours:** Mon–Fri 10:00–17:00, Sat 11:00–17:00, Sun 13:00–17:00; Oct–April closed Mon.

▲▲National Museum: Archaeology and History Interesting collection of Irish treasures from the Stone Age to today. **Hours:** Tue–Sat 10:00–17:00, Sun 14:00–17:00, closed Mon.

▲▲Grafton Street The city's liveliest pedestrian shopping mall. **Hours:** Always open.

▲▲Number Twenty-Nine Georgian House Restored 18th-century house; tours provide an intimate glimpse of middle-class

Georgian life. **Hours:** Tue–Sat 10:00–17:00, Sun 13:00–17:00, closed Mon.

▲▲**Temple Bar** Dublin's trendiest neighborhood, with shops, cafés, theaters, galleries, pubs, and restaurants—a great spot for live traditional music. **Hours:** Always open.

▲▲**O'Connell Bridge** Landmark bridge spanning the River Liffey at the center of Dublin. **Hours:** Always open.

▲▲**O'Connell Street** Dublin's grandest promenade and main drag, packed with history and ideal for a stroll. **Hours:** Always open.

▲**National Museum: Decorative Arts and History** Shows off Irish dress, furniture, silver, and weaponry with a special focus on the 1916 rebellion, fight for independence, and civil war. **Hours:** Tue–Sat 10:00–17:00, Sun 14:00–17:00, closed Mon.

▲**National Gallery** Fine collection of top Irish painters and European masters. **Hours:** Mon–Sat 9:30–17:30, Thu until 20:30, Sun 12:00–17:30.

▲**St. Stephen's Green** Relaxing park surrounded by fine Georgian buildings. **Hours:** Always open.

▲**Merrion Square** Enjoyable and inviting park with a fun statue of Oscar Wilde. **Hours:** Always open.

▲**Guinness Storehouse** The home of Ireland's national beer, with a museum of beer-making, a gallery of clever ads, and the spectacular Gravity Bar with panoramic city views. **Hours:** Daily 9:30–17:00.

▲**Gaelic Athletic Association Museum** High-tech museum of traditional Gaelic sports such as hurling and Irish football. **Hours:** July–Aug Mon–Sat 9:30–18:00, Sun 12:00–18:00; Sept–June Mon–Sat 9:30–17:00, Sun 12:00–17:00. On game Sundays, it's open only to ticket-holders.

pages—two text and two decorated cover pages. The library treasury also displays two other books—likely the Book of Armagh (A.D. 807) and the Book of Durrow (A.D. 680)—neither of which can be checked out.

Next, a stairway leads upstairs to the 200-foot-long main chamber of the Old Library (from 1732), stacked to its towering ceiling with 200,000 of the library's oldest books. Here, you'll find one of a dozen surviving original copies of the **Proclamation of the Irish Republic.** Patrick Pearse read these words outside the General Post Office on April 24, 1916, starting the Easter Rising that led to Irish independence. Read the entire thing...imagining it was yours. Notice the inclusive opening phrase and the seven signatories (each of whom was executed). Another national icon is nearby: the oldest surviving Irish harp, from the 15th century.

Cost and Hours: €8; included in €10 Trinity College tour—see above; May–Sept daily 9:30–16:30; Oct–April Mon–Sat 9:30–16:30, Sun 12:00–16:30; tel. 01/896-2308). A long line often snakes out of the building. Minimize your wait by avoiding the midday crunch (roughly 11:30–14:30). For more on the Book of Kells, see page 372 in the Ireland: Past and Present chapter.

More Sights South of the River Liffey

▲▲**Dublin Castle**—Built on the spot of the first Viking fortress, this castle was the seat of English rule in Ireland for 700 years. Located where the Poddle and Liffey Rivers came together, making a black pool (*dubh linn* in Irish), Dublin Castle was the official residence of the viceroy who implemented the will of the British royalty. In this stirring setting, the Brits handed power over to Michael Collins and the Irish in 1922. Today, it's used for fancy state and charity functions.

Standing in the courtyard, you can imagine the ugliness of the British-Irish situation. Notice the statue of justice above the gate—pointedly without her blindfold and admiring her sword. As locals say, "There she stands, above her station, with her face to the palace and her arse to the nation." The fancy interior is viewable only with a 45-minute tour, which offers a fairly boring room-by-room walk through the lavish state apartments of this most English of Irish palaces. The tour finishes with a look at the foundations of the Norman tower and the best remaining chunk of the 13th-century town wall (€4.50, covered by Heritage Card—see page 14, buy tickets in courtyard under portico opposite clock tower, 2/hr, Mon–Fri 10:00–17:00,

South Dublin

Dublin

1 Historical Walking Tour
2 Trinity College Tours
3 1916 Rebellion Walks
4 Literary Pub Crawls
  (Meet at The Duke Pub)
5 Musical Pub Crawls
  (Meet at Gogarty's Pub)
6 Viking Splash Tours
7 Dublin City Hall
8 Meeting House Square &
  Temple Bar Info Centre
9 Great George's Arcade
10 Powerscourt Townhouse
   Shopping Centre

200 YARDS
200 METERS

N

+—+ DART COMMUTER RAIL
•—•• LUAS TRAM + STOP

To BUSARAS BUS STATION
FAMINE STATUES
CUSTOM HOUSE
To CONNOLLY STATION
EDEN QUAY
CITY QUAY
TARA ST. STATION
TOWNSEND ST.
PEARSE ST.
PEARSE ST. STN.
OSCAR WILDE STATUE
MERRION SQUARE
FITZ

O'CONNELL STREET
BURGH QUAY
POOLBEG
BURGH QUAY
LIFFEY
HA' PENNY BRIDGE
PEDESTRIAN
LOTTS
ABBEY ST.
CAPEL ST.
MARY'S LANE
CHURCH ST.

HA' PENNY BRIDGE
BACHELOR'S WALK
ASTON QUAY
BANK OF IRE.
WESTMORELAND ST.
COLLEGE ST.
COLLEGE GREEN
TRINITY COLLEGE
BOOK OF KELLS
NAT'L. GALLERY
NASSAU ST.
LEINSTER ST.
KILDARE ST.
NAT'L. LIBRARY
MOLESWORTH ST.
DAWSON ST.
LINCOLN PL.
CLARE ST.
MERRION SQ.
#29 GEORGIAN HOUSE
GOVT. BLDGS.
NAT'L. MUSEUM: ARCHAEOLOGY + HISTORY
ST. STEPHEN'S GREEN N.
ST. STEPHEN'S GREEN
GATE
KING ST.
CHATHAM ST.
ANNE ST.
DUKE ST.
SUFFOLK ST.
WICKLOW ST.
EXCHEQUER ST.
DRURY ST.
GREAT GEORGES ST.
STEPHEN ST.
BOW LANE
YORK ST.
AUNGIER ST.
WHITEFRIAR ST.

FLEET ST.
TEMPLE BAR
WELLINGTON QUAY
MILLENNIUM PEDESTRIAN BRIDGE
TEMPLE BAR
SYCAMORE
DAME ST.
DAME LANE
TRINITY

O'CONNELL
LOWER
ORMOND QUAY
STRAND ST.
WOOD QUAY
FISH.
ESSEX ST.
LORD EDWARD ST.
DUBLIN CASTLE
CHESTER BEATTY LIBRARY
WERBURGH ST.

RIVER LIFFEY
INNS QUAY
FOUR COURTS
MERCHANTS QUAY
COOK ST.
HIGH ST.
CHRIST CHURCH CATHEDRAL
WINETAVERN ST.
ST. DUBLIN ST.
BRIDGE ST.
NICHOLAS ST.
ST. PATRICK'S CATHEDRAL
BULL
GOLD
BRIDE ST.
KEVIN ST.
DCH
PATRICK ST.
FRANCIS ST.
THE COOMBE

OLD JAMESON DISTILLERY
TO SMITHFIELD
TO HEUSTON STN.
SMITHFIELD
CHANCERY
STRAND
MOB

Sat–Sun 14:00–17:00, tel. 01/677-7129, www.dublincastle.ie).

▲▲Chester Beatty Library—Chester Beatty was a rich American mining engineer who retired to Ireland in 1950, later becoming its first honorary citizen. He left his priceless and eclectic collection to his adopted homeland as a public charitable trust. Today Ireland has put a modern glass roof over the parade ground separating two old army barracks and filled it with Beatty's treasures. It's a small collection, delightfully displayed and described. The top floor focuses on the world's great religions (strong on Islam and Christianity) with displays on dervish whirls, calligraphy in Islam, and early Asian Christian manuscripts. The bottom floor is all about the written word, with topics including etching, medieval book binding, and fine old manuscripts. As you wander, you'll see books carved out of jade, ornate snuff bottles, rhino-horn cups, and even the oldest surviving copy of St. Paul's letter to the Romans (A.D. 180). Other highlights include a graceful Burmese book written on palm leaves—bound together to unfold like an accordion—and a densely ornamental sunburst motif from a 500-year-old Iranian Quran (free, Mon–Fri 10:00–17:00, Sat 11:00–17:00, Sun 13:00–17:00; Oct–April closed Mon; coffee shop, tel. 01/407-0750, www.cbl.ie). You'll find the library behind Dublin Castle (follow the signs).

Dublin City Hall—The first Georgian building in this very Georgian city stands proudly overlooking Dame Street, in front of the gate to Dublin Castle. Built in 1779 as the Royal Exchange, it introduced the Georgian style (then very popular in Britain and on the Continent) to Ireland. Step inside (it's free) to feel the prosperity and confidence of Dublin in her 18th-century glory days. In 1852, it became the City Hall. Under the grand rotunda, a cycle of heroic paintings tells the city's history. (The mosaics on the floor convey such homilies as "Obedience makes the happiest citizenry.") Pay your respects to the 18-foot-tall statue of Daniel O'Connell, the great orator and liberator who, in 1829, won emancipation for Catholics in Ireland from the much-despised Protestants over in London. The greeter sits like the Maytag repairman at the information desk, eager to give you more information. Downstairs is an excellent *Story of the Capital* exhibition—storyboards and video clips of Dublin's history (€4, free audioguide, coffee shop, Mon–Sat 10:00–17:00, Sun 14:00–17:00, tel. 01/222-2204, www.dublincity.ie).

Dublinia and The Viking World—This exhibit tries valiantly to be a "bridge to Dublin's medieval past." The amateurish look at the medieval town starts with a walk through dim rooms of tableaus, followed by several halls of medieval exhibits, a scale model of old Dublin, and an interesting room devoted to medieval fairs. Then, at the top of the stairs, you get to enter the old synod (church council) hall, now devoted to exhibitions on Viking life in Dublin (€6.25, €10.20 combo-ticket includes Christ Church Cathedral—saves you €1.25, daily April–Sept 10:00–17:00, Oct–March 11:00–16:00, last entry 45 min before closing, brass rubbing, coffee shop open in summer, across from Christ Church Cathedral, tel. 01/679-4611, www.dublinia.ie).

Christ Church Cathedral—The first church on this spot was built of wood by King Sitric in Viking times (c. 1040). The present structure dates from a mix of periods: Norman and Gothic, but mostly Victorian Neo-Gothic (1870s restoration work). The unusually large crypt under the cathedral—actually the oldest building in Dublin—contains stocks, statues, and the cathedral's silver (€5 donation to church, includes downstairs crypt silver exhibition, €10.20 combo-ticket includes Dublinia, daily 9:45–18:00, free brochure with self-guided tour). Because of Dublin's British past, neither of its top two churches is Catholic. Christ Church Cathedral and the nearby St. Patrick's Cathedral are both Church of Ireland. In Catholic Ireland, these sights feel hollow. They're more famous than visit-worthy.

Evensong: At Christ Church Cathedral, a 45-minute evensong service is sung regularly several times a week (Wed–Thu at 18:00, Sat at 17:00, and Sun at 15:30; less regularly during the summer). The 13th-century St. Patrick's Cathedral, where Jonathan Swift (author of *Gulliver's Travels*) was dean in the 18th century, also offers evensong (Sun at 15:15, Mon–Fri at 17:30, but not on Wed in July–Aug).

▲▲**National Museum: Archaeology and History**—Showing off the treasures of Ireland from the Stone Age to modern times,

this branch of the National Museum is itself a national treasure. Under one dome, it's wonderfully digestible. Ireland's Bronze Age gold fills the center. Up four steps, a prehistoric Ireland exhibit rings the gold. In a corner (behind a 2,000-year-old body), you'll find the treasury, with the museum's most famous pieces (brooches, chalices, and other examples of Celtic metalwork) and an 18-minute video (played on request) that gives an overview of Irish art through the 13th century. The collection's superstar is the gold, enamel, and amber eighth-century Tara Brooch. The best Viking artifacts in town are upstairs (with the medieval collection). If you'll be visiting Cong (in Connemara, near Galway), seek out the original Cross of Cong (free, Tue–Sat 10:00–17:00, Sun 14:00–17:00, closed Mon, good café, between Trinity College and St. Stephen's Green on Kildare Street). Greatest-hits tours are given several times a day (€2, 40 min, tel. 01/677-7444—call in morning for tour schedule, www.museum.ie/archaeology). For background information, read "Irish Art" on page 371.

▲**National Museum: Decorative Arts and History**—This branch of the National Museum, which occupies the huge 18th-century stone Collins Barracks in west Dublin, displays Irish dress, furniture, weaponry, silver, and other domestic baubles from the past 700 years. History buffs will linger longest in "The Road to Independence" exhibition, offering Ireland's best coverage of its painful "Terrible Beauty" national birth. Guns, personal letters, and death masks help illustrate the 1916 Easter Rising, War of Independence against Britain, and Ireland's Civil War in 1922–1923. Croppies Acre, the large park between the museum and the river, was the site of Dublin's largest soup kitchen during the Great Potato Famine in 1845–1849 (free, Tue–Sat 10:00–17:00, Sun 14:00–17:00, closed Mon, good café; on north side of Liffey River in Collins Barracks on Benburb Street, roughly across the river from Guinness Storehouse, easy to reach by LUAS—get off at Museum stop; tel. 01/648-6453, www.museum.ie/decorative). Daily 45-minute **tours** run at 15:30 and cost €2.

▲**National Gallery**—Along with a hall that features the work of top Irish painters including Jack Yeats (the brother of the famous poet), this museum has Ireland's best collection of European masters: Vermeer, Caravaggio, Monet, and Picasso. It's impressive—although not nearly as extensive as national galleries in London or Paris. Study the floor-plan flier and take advantage of the free audioguide. Be sure to walk the series of rooms on the ground floor devoted to Irish painting and get to know artists you may never have heard of before. Visit the National Portrait Gallery on the mezzanine level for an insight into the great personalities of Ireland. You'll find Caravaggio and Vermeer on the top floor. In his *Taking of Christ,* Caravaggio, master of the chiaroscuro style, makes dramatic use of light and shadow for emphasis. Vermeer's *Lady Writing a Letter with her Maid,* one of only 35 known works by the Dutch artist, shows his trademark focus on life's quiet moments (free, Mon–Sat 9:30–17:30, Thu until 20:30, Sun 12:00–17:30, Merrion Square West, tel. 01/661-5133, www.nationalgallery.ie). The museum offers free audioguide tours (donations accepted) and free 45-minute **guided tours** (daily July–Aug at 15:00, Sun also at 14:00 and 16:00, Sept–June only on Sat at 15:00 and Sun at 14:00, 15:00, and 16:00).

National Library—Literature holds a lofty place in the Irish psyche. To feel the fire-and-ice pulse of Ireland's most famous poet and playwright, visit the well-designed W. B. Yeats exhibit in the basement of the library. It fleshes out the very human passions of this enigmatic writer, with samples of his handwritten manuscripts, a dreamy poetry alcove, and surprisingly interesting mini-documentaries of the turbulent times he lived in. Upstairs you can get some help making use of the library records to trace your genealogy (free, Mon–Wed 9:30–21:00, Thu–Fri 9:30–17:00, Sat 9:30–13:00, closed Sun, tel. 01/603-0200, Kildare Street, www.nli.ie).

▲▲**Grafton Street**—Once filled with noisy traffic, today's Grafton Street is Dublin's liveliest pedestrian shopping mall. A 10-minute stroll past street musicians takes you from Trinity College to St. Stephen's Green (and makes you wonder why American merchants are so terrified of a car-free street). Walking by a buxom statue of "sweet" Molly Malone (known by locals as "the tart with the cart"), you'll soon pass two venerable department stores: the Irish Brown Thomas and the English Marks & Spencer. Johnson's Court alley leads to the Powerscourt Townhouse Shopping Centre, which tastefully fills a converted Georgian mansion. The huge, glass-covered St. Stephen's Green Shopping Centre and the peaceful green itself mark the top of Grafton Street. For fun, gather a pile of coins and walk the street, putting each human statue into action with a donation. Consider stopping somewhere along the street for coffee with a second-floor view of the action.

▲**St. Stephen's Green**—This city park, originally a medieval commons, was enclosed in 1664 and gradually surrounded with fine Georgian buildings. Today, it provides 22 acres of grassy refuge for Dubliners. On a sunny afternoon, it's a wonderful world apart from the big city. When marveling at the elegance of Georgian Dublin, remember that during the Georgian period (when the American colonies were fighting King George), Dublin was the second most important city in the British Empire. Local big shots knew that any money wrung from the local populace not spent in Dublin would end up in London. Since it was "use it or lose it," they used it—with gusto—to beautify their city.

▲▲**Number Twenty-Nine Georgian House**—The carefully restored house at Number 29 Lower Fitzwilliam Street gives an intimate glimpse of middle-class Georgian life (which seems pretty high-class). From the sidewalk, descend the stairs to the basement-level entrance (corner of Lower Fitzwilliam and Lower Mount Streets, opposite southern corner of Merrion Square). Start with an interesting 15-minute video (you're welcome to bring in a cup of coffee from the café) before joining your guide, who takes you on a fascinating 35-minute walk through this 1790 Dublin home (€5, tours leave regularly, Tue–Sat 10:00–17:00, Sun 13:00–17:00, closed Mon, tel. 01/702-6165).

▲**Merrion Square**—Laid out in 1762, this square is ringed by elegant Georgian houses decorated with fine doors—a Dublin trademark. (If you're inspired by the ornate knobs and knockers,

there's a shop by that name on nearby Nassau Street.) The park, once the exclusive domain of the residents, is now a delightful public escape. More inviting than St. Stephen's Green, it's ideal for a picnic. To learn what "snogging" is, walk through the park on a sunny day, when it's full of smooching lovers. Oscar Wilde, lounging wittily on a boulder on the corner nearest the town center and surrounded by his clever quotes, provides a fun photo op (see photo on page 63).

▲▲**Temple Bar**—Originally a Georgian center of craftsmen and merchants, this neighborhood fell on hard times in the 19th century. The ensuing low rents attracted students and artists, giving the area a bohemian flair. With government tax incentives and lots of development money, the Temple Bar district has now become a thriving cultural (and beer-drinking) hot spot. This much-promoted center—with trendy

shops, cafés, theaters, galleries, pubs with live music, and restaurants—feels like the heart of the city. It's Dublin's "Left Bank," and like in Paris, it's on the south shore of the river. It fills the cobbled streets between Dame Street and the River Liffey. ("Bar" means a walkway along the river.)

Temple Bar is an absolute spectacle in the evening, when it bursts with revelers. The noise, rude crowds of foreigners, and inflated prices have driven most locals away. But even if you're just gawking, don't miss the opportunity to wander through this human circus. Summer weekend nights can be a real zoo. Women in funky hats, part of loud "hen" (bachelorette) parties, promenade down the main drag as drunken dudes shout from pub doorways to get their attention. Be aware that a pint of beer here is €5—about €1 more than at less-glitzy pubs just a couple blocks away (north of the River Liffey or south of Dame Street).

The central **Meeting House Square,** just off Essex Street, hosts free street theater, as well as a lively organic-produce market and a book market (Sat 10:00–18:00). The square is surrounded by interesting cultural centers. For a listing of events and galleries, visit the **Temple Bar Information Centre** (12 East Essex Street,

www.visit-templebar.com). Rather than follow particular pub or restaurant recommendations (mine are under "Eating" on page 76), venture down a few side lanes off the main drag to see what looks good. The pedestrian-only **Ha' Penny Bridge,** named for the halfpence toll people used to pay to cross it, leads from Temple Bar over the River Liffey to the opposite bank and more sights.

North of the River Liffey

▲▲ O'Connell Bridge

This bridge spans the River Liffey, which has historically divided the wealthy, cultivated south side from the poorer, cruder, north side. While there's plenty of culture north of the river, even today "the north" is considered rougher and less safe.

From the bridge, look upriver (west) as far upstream as you can see. On the left in the distance, the **big concrete building**—considered an eyesore by locals—houses the city planning commission, which ironically is in charge of making sure new buildings are built in good taste. It squats on the still-buried precious artifacts of the first Viking settlement, established in Dublin in the ninth century.

Across the river stands the **Four Courts**—the Supreme Court building. It was shelled and burned in 1922, during the tragic civil war that followed Irish independence. The national archives office burned, and irreplaceable birth records were lost, making it difficult for those with Irish roots to trace their ancestry today. The closest bridge upstream—the elegant iron **Ha' Penny Bridge** (see photo, at the top of this page)—leads left, into the Temple Bar nightlife district. Just beyond that old-fashioned, 19th-century bridge is Dublin's pedestrian **Millennium Bridge,** inaugurated in 2000. (Note that buses leave from O'Connell Bridge—specifically Aston Quay—for the Guinness Storehouse and Kilmainham Gaol.)

Turn 180 degrees and look downstream to see the tall **Liberty Hall** union headquarters—for now, the tallest building in the Republic (16 stories tall, some say in honor of the 1916 Easter Uprising)—and lots of cranes. Booming Dublin is developing downstream. The Irish (forever clever tax fiddlers) have subsidized and revitalized this formerly dreary quarter with great success. A short walk downstream along the north bank leads to a powerful series of modern statues memorializing the Great Potato Famine of 1845–1849.

North Dublin

1. Daniel O'Connell Statue
2. James Larkin Statue
3. Millennium Spire
4. Father Matthew Statue
5. Charles Stewart Parnell Monument
6. James Joyce Cultural Centre
7. Millennium Pedestrian Bridge
8. The Townhouse
9. Jurys Inn Custom House
10. Jurys Inn Parnell Street
11. Comfort Inn
12. Charles Stewart Hotel

▲▲ O'Connell Street Stroll

Dublin's grandest street leads from O'Connell Bridge through the heart of north Dublin. From the 1740s, it has been a 45-yard-wide promenade. Ever since the first O'Connell Bridge connected it to the Trinity side of town in 1794, it's been Dublin's main drag. (But it was only named O'Connell after independence was won in 1922.) These days, construction reigns as the city makes the street more pedestrian-friendly. Though lined with fast-food and souvenir shops, O'Connell Street echoes with history. Take the following stroll. The tree-lined median strip is wide, less crowded, and closer to the statues I mention here.

Statues and monuments line O'Connell Street, celebrating great figures in Ireland's fight for independence. At the base of the street stands **Daniel O'Connell** (1775–1847), known as "the

Liberator" for founding the Catholic Association and demanding Irish Catholic rights in the British Parliament.

Looking a block east down Abbey Street, you can see the

famous **Abbey Theatre**—rebuilt after a fire into a nondescript, modern building. It's still the much-loved home of the Irish National Theatre.

The statue of **James Larkin** honors the founder of the Irish Transport Workers' Union. The one monument that didn't wave an Irish flag—a tall column crowned by a statue of the British hero of Trafalgar, Admiral Horatio Nelson—was blown up in 1966...the IRA's contribution to the local celebration of the Easter Rising's 50th anniversary.

This spot is now occupied by the 390-foot-tall, stainless steel **Millennium Spire** that was finally completed in 2003. While it trumpets rejuvenation on that side of the river, it's a memorial to nothing and has no real meaning. Dubious Dubliners call it the tallest waste of €5 million in all of Europe. Its nickname? Take your pick: the Stiletto in the Ghetto, the Stiffy on the Liffey, the Pole in the Hole, the Poker near the Croker (after the nearby Croke Park), or the Spike in the Dike.

The **General Post Office** is not just any P.O. It was from here that Patrick Pearse read the Proclamation of Irish Independence in 1916, and kicked off the Easter Rising. The G.P.O. building itself—a kind of Irish Alamo—was the rebel headquarters and scene of a five-day bloody siege that followed the proclamation. Its pillars remain pockmarked with bullet holes (open for business and sightseers Mon–Sat 8:00–20:00, closed Sun).

The busy **Moore Street Market** is nearby (Mon–Sat 8:00–18:00, closed Sun). To get there, detour left (west) two blocks past the post office, down people-filled Henry Street (the locals' favorite shopping lane), then wander to the right into the market. Many of its merchants have staffed the same stalls for more than 30 years. Start a conversation. It's a great workaday scene. You'll see lots of mums with strollers—a reminder that Ireland is Europe's youngest country, with more than 40 percent of the population under the age of 25.

Back on O'Connell Street, cross back onto the median strip and continue your walk.

Modern Ireland's Turbulent Birth: A Timeline

Imagine if our American patriot ancestors had fought both our Revolutionary War and our Civil War over a span of seven chaotic years...and then appreciate the remarkable resiliency of the Irish people. Here's a summary of what happened when.

1916: A nationalist militia called the Volunteers (led by **Patrick Pearse**) and the socialist Irish Citizen Army (led by **James Connolly**) join forces in the **Easter Uprising,** but they fail to end 750 years of British rule. The uprising is unpopular with most Irish, who are unhappy with the destruction in Dublin and preoccupied with the "Great War" on the Continent. But when 16 rebel leaders (including Pearse and Connolly) are executed, Irish public opinion reverses as sympathy grows for the martyrs and the cause of Irish Independence.

Two important rebel leaders escape execution. New-York born **Eamon de Valera** is spared because of his American passport (the British don't want to anger their potential ally in World War I). **Michael Collins,** a low-ranking rebel officer who fought in the uprising at the General Post Office, perfects urban warfare strategies in prison and then blossoms after his release as the rebel's military and intelligence leader in the power vacuum that followed the executions.

1918: World War I ends and a general election is held in Ireland. Outside of Ulster, the nationalist **Sinn Fein** party wins 73 out of 79 seats in Parliament. Only four out of 32 counties vote to maintain the Union with Britain (all four are in Ulster, part of which would become Northern Ireland). Rather than take their seats in London, **Sinn Fein** representatives abstain from participating in a government they see as foreign occupiers.

1919: On January 19 the abstaining Sinn Fein members set up a rebel government in Dublin called Dail Eireann. On the same day, the first shots of the **Irish War of Independence** are fired as rebels begin ambushing police barracks which are seen as an extension of British rule. De Valera is elected by the Dail to lead the rebels, with Collins as his deputy. In one of the first moves of modern urban guerilla warfare, Collins infiltrates British

St. Mary's Pro-Cathedral, a block east of O'Connell down Cathedral Street, is Dublin's leading Catholic church. But, curiously, it's not a cathedral, even though the pope declared Christ Church one in the 12th century—and later, St. Patrick's. (The Vatican has chosen to stubbornly ignore the fact that Christ Church and St. Patrick's haven't been Catholic for centuries.) Completed in 1821, it's done in the style of a Greek temple.

Continuing up O'Connell Street, you'll find a statue of **Father Matthew,** a leader of the temperance movement of the 1830s who,

intelligence at Dublin Castle. The Volunteers rename themselves the Irish Republican Army; meanwhile the British beef up their military presence in Ireland by sending in tough WWI vets, the Black & Tans. A bloody guerilla war ensues.

1921: Having lived through the slaughter of World War I, the British tire of the extended bloodshed in Ireland and begin negotiations with the rebels. De Valera leads rebel negotiations, but then entrusts them to Collins (a clever politician, De Valera sees that whomever signs a treaty will be blamed for its compromises). Understanding the tricky position he's been placed in, Collins signs the **Anglo-Irish Treaty** in December, lamenting that in doing so he has signed his "own death warrant."

The Dail narrowly ratifies the treaty, but the Collins camp is unable to convince De Valera's supporters that the compromises are a stepping stone to later full independence. De Valera and his followers resign in protest. **Arthur Griffith,** founder of Sinn Fein, assumes the Presidential post.

In June, the anti-treaty forces, holed up in the Four Courts building, are fired upon by Collins and his pro-treaty forces—thus igniting the **Irish Civil War.** The British want the treaty to stand and even supply Collins with cannons, meanwhile threatening to re-enter Ireland if the anti-treaty forces aren't put down.

1922: In August, Griffith dies of stress-induced illness, and Collins is assassinated 10 days later. Nevertheless, the pro-treaty forces prevail, as they are backed by popular opinion and better (British-supplied) military equipment.

1923: In April, the remaining IRA forces dump (or stash) their arms, ending the Civil War...but many of their bitter vets vow to carry on the fight. De Valera distances himself from the IRA and becomes the dominant Irish political leader for the next 40 years.

some historians claim, was responsible for enough Irish peasants staying sober to enable Daniel O'Connell to organize them into a political force. (Perhaps understanding this dynamic, the USSR was careful to keep the price of vodka affordable.) The fancy Gresham Hotel is a good place for an elegant tea or beer.

A monument to **Charles Stewart Parnell** stands boldly at the top of O'Connell Street. The names of the four ancient provinces of Ireland and all 32 Irish counties (North *and* South, since this was erected before Irish independence) ring the monument, honoring

the member of Parliament who nearly won Home Rule for Ireland in the late 1800s. (A sex scandal cost Parnell the support of the Church, which let the air out of the movement for a free Ireland.)

Continue straight up Parnell Square East. At the **Gate Theatre** (on the left), Orson Welles and James Mason had their professional acting debuts.

One block up on the left, past the Gate Theater, is the **Garden of Remembrance** (free, daily 8:30–18:00). Honoring the victims of the 1916 Rising, the park was dedicated in 1966 on the 50th anniversary of the revolt that ultimately led to Irish independence. The bottom of the cross-shaped pool is a mosaic of Celtic weapons, symbolic of how the early Irish would proclaim peace by throwing their weapons into a lake or river. The Irish flag flies above the park: green for Catholics, orange for Protestants, and white for the hope that they can live together in peace. On the uphill side, across the street...

The **Dublin Writers' Museum** fills a splendidly restored Georgian mansion. No other country so small has produced such a wealth of literature (see page 374). As interesting to fans of Irish literature as it is boring to those who aren't, this three-room museum features the lives and works of Dublin's great writers (€7, includes helpful audioguide, ask about €12 combo-ticket with James Joyce Museum in Dun Laoghaire; Mon–Sat 10:00–17:00, Sun 11:00–17:00, June–Aug Mon–Fri until 18:00; coffee shop, 18 Parnell Square North, tel. 01/872-2077). For an easy, affordable, and enjoyable literary performance in summer, consider "The Writers Entertain," a one-man show (€13, July–Aug daily at 13:10, 50 min, upstairs in a fine reading room).

With hometown wits such as Swift, Yeats, Joyce, Wilde, and Shaw, Dublin has a checklist of residences and memorials to see. Aficionados of James Joyce's work may want to hike two blocks east to visit the **James Joyce Cultural Centre** (€5, June–Aug Tue–Sat 10:00–17:00, Sun 12:00–17:00, closed Mon; Sept–May closed Sun–Mon, 35 North Great George's Street, tel. 01/878-8547). There's more Joyce memorabilia in Dun Laoghaire at the **James Joyce Museum** (see page 84). Next door to the Dublin Writers' Museum is...

Dublin's Literary Life

Dublin in the 1700s, grown rich from a lucrative cloth trade, was one of Europe's most cultured and sophisticated cities. The buildings were decorated in the Georgian style still visible today. The city's Protestant elite shuttled between here and London, bridging the Anglo-Irish cultural gap.

Jonathan Swift (1667–1745), the great satirical writer, was also dean of St. Patrick's Cathedral (1713–1745) and one of the city's eminent citizens. His most famous book, *Gulliver's Travels,* poked fun at religious hardliners and the pompous bureaucrats in London who shaped England's misguided Irish policies.

Around the turn of the 20th century, Dublin produced some of the world's great modern writers.

Oscar Wilde (1854–1900), born in Dublin and a graduate of Trinity College, wowed London with his quick wit, outrageous clothes, and flamboyant personality, and scandalized them when he was outed as being gay. He satirized upper-class Victorian society in comedic plays (like *The Importance of Being Earnest,* 1895) with characters who speak very elegantly about the trivial concerns of the idle rich.

William Butler Yeats (1865–1939), also born and raised in Dublin, captured the passion of the Irish independence movement. His poem "Easter, 1916" contains the refrain that summed up how those events affected Ireland: "All are changed, changed utterly: A terrible beauty is born."

James Joyce (1882–1941) wandered the back streets of Dublin, observing its seedier side, which he captured in a modern, stream-of-consciousness style. His famous novel *Ulysses,* set on a single day (June 16, 1904), follows Dubliners on an odyssey through the city's pubs, hospitals, libraries, churches, and brothels.

And today, Ireland still produces some of the English language's greatest writers. **Seamus Heaney,** a poet who has won the Nobel and Pulitzer Prizes, published a new translation in 1999 of the Old English epic *Beowulf*—wedding the old with the new.

For more on Irish literature, see page 374.

The Hugh Lane Gallery: In a grand Neoclassical building, this has a fine, bite-size selection of Pre-Raphaelite, French Impressionist, and 19th- and 20th-century Irish paintings (free, Tue–Thu 10:00–18:00, Fri–Sat 10:00–17:00, Sun 11:00–17:00, closed Mon, tel. 01/222-5550, www.hughlane.ie). Sir Hugh went down on the *Lusitania* in 1915; due to an unclear will, his collection is shared by this gallery and the National Gallery in London.

Tucked in the back of the gallery is the **Francis Bacon Studio,** reconstructed here in its original (messy) state from its London location at the time of the artist's death in 1992. Born in Dublin and inspired by Picasso, Bacon's shocking paintings reflected his belief that "chaos breeds energy." This compact space contains touch-screen terminals, display cases of personal items, and a few unfinished works. The 10-minute film interview of Bacon may fascinate like-minded viewers...and disquiet others (free, same hours as rest of gallery).

Your walk is over. Here on the north end of town, it's convenient to visit the Gaelic Athletic Association Museum at Croke Park Stadium (described on page 67, a 20-min walk or short taxi ride away). Otherwise, hop on your skateboard and zip back to the river.

Dublin's Smithfield Village

This neighborhood is worth a look for the Old Jameson Distillery whiskey tour, a Chimney Viewing Tower offering city views, and Dublin's most authentic traditional-music pub. The sights are clustered close together, two blocks northwest of the Four Courts—the Supreme Court building. For a decent bite to eat, try the **Park Inn** restaurant, on the same square near the base of the chimney tower.

Old Jameson Distillery—Whiskey fans enjoy visiting the old distillery. You get a 10-minute video, a 20-minute tour, and a free shot in the pub. Unfortunately, the "distillery" feels fake and put together for tourists. The Bushmills tour in Northern Ireland (in a working factory, see page 318) and the Midleton tour near Cork (in the huge, original factory, page 155) are better experiences. If you do take this tour, volunteer energetically when offered the chance: This will get you a coveted seat at the whiskey taste test table at the tour's end (€9.75, daily 9:00–18:00, last tour at 17:15, Bow Street, tel. 01/807-2355).

Jameson Distillery Chimney Viewing Tower—Built in 1895 for the distillery, the chimney is now an observatory. Ride the elevator 175 feet up for a Dublin panorama not quite as exciting as the view from the Guinness Storehouse's Gravity Bar (overpriced at €6, Mon–Sat 10:00–17:00, Sun 11:00–17:00, tel. 01/817-3838).

Cobblestones Pub—Hiding in a derelict-looking building, this pub offers Dublin's least glitzy and most rewarding traditional-

Charles Stewart Parnell
(1846–1891)

Parnell, who led the Irish movement for Home Rule, served time in Kilmainham Gaol. A Cambridge-educated Protestant and Member of Parliament, he had a vision of a modern and free Irish Republic filled mostly with Catholics but not set up as a religious state. Momentum seemed to be on his side. With the British prime minister of the time, William Gladstone, in favor of a similar form of Home Rule, it looked as if all of Ireland was ripe for independence. Then a sex scandal broke around Parnell and his mistress. The press, egged on by the powerful Catholic bishops (who didn't want a free but secular Irish state), battered away at the scandal until finally Parnell was driven from office. Sadly, after that, Ireland became mired in the Troubles of the 20th century: an awkward independence (1921) featuring a divided island, a bloody civil war, and sectarian violence ever since. It's said Parnell died of a broken heart. Before he did, this great Irish statesman requested to be buried outside of Ireland.

music venue. The candlelit walls, covered with photos of honored trad musicians, set the tone with this understated sign: "Listening area, please respect musicians" (daily 17:00–23:45, trad-music sessions Mon–Wed at 21:30, Thu–Sat at 17:00, at north end of square, 100 yards from chimney tower, tel. 01/872-1799).

Outer Dublin

The Kilmainham Gaol and the Guinness Storehouse are the main sights outside of the old center. Combine them in one visit.

▲▲▲**Kilmainham Gaol (Jail)**—Opened in 1796 as both the Dublin County Jail and a debtors' prison, it was considered a model

in its day. In reality, this jail was frequently used by the British as a political prison. Many of those who fought for Irish independence were held or executed here, including leaders of the rebellions of 1798, 1803, 1848, 1867, and 1916. National heroes Robert Emmett and Charles Stewart Parnell each did time here. The last prisoner to be held here was Eamon de Valera, who later became president of Ireland. He was released on July 16, 1924, the day Kilmainham was finally shut down. The buildings, virtually in ruins, were restored in the 1960s. Today, it's a shrine to the Nathan Hales of Ireland.

Start your visit with a guided **tour** (60 min, 2/hr, includes 15-min prison history slide show in the prison chapel—spend waiting time in museum). It's touching to tour the cells and places of execution—hearing tales of terrible colonialism and heroic patriotism—alongside Irish schoolkids who know these names well. The museum is an excellent exhibit on Victorian prison life and Ireland's fight for independence. Don't miss the museum's dimly lit Last Words 1916 hall upstairs, which displays the stirring final letters that patriots sent to loved ones hours before facing the firing squad (€5.30, covered by Heritage Card—see page 14, daily 9:30–18:00, last entry 90 min before closing, tel. 01/453-5984). The humble cafeteria serves little more than sandwiches.

To get from Aston Quay or the Guinness Storehouse to Kilmainham Gaol, you can take a taxi, or catch bus #51B, #78A, or #79. Another option is to take one of the hop-on, hop-off buses (see page 45): City Sightseeing/Guide Friday stops right at Kilmainham Gaol, whereas Dublin City Tour stops 200 yards away, in front of the modern art museum in Kilmainham hospital. Both tours stop at the Guinness Storehouse.

To catch the city bus from the jail to the Guinness Storehouse: Leave the prison and take three rights—crossing no streets—to the bus stop and hop bus #51B or #78A.

▲**Guinness Storehouse**—A visit to the Guinness Storehouse is, for many, a pilgrimage. Arthur Guinness began brewing the famous stout here in 1759. By 1868, it was the biggest brewery in the world. Today, the sprawling brewery fills several city blocks. Around the world, Guinness brews more than 10 million pints a day. The home of Ireland's national beer welcomes visitors, for a price, with a sprawling modern museum, but there are no tours of the actual work-

ing brewery. The museum fills the old fermentation plant that was used from 1902 through 1988, vacated, and then opened in 2000 as a huge, shrine-like place. Step into the middle of the ground floor and look up. A tall, beer glass–shaped glass atrium—14 million pints big—leads past four floors of exhibitions and cafés to the skylight. Then look down at Arthur's original 9,000-year lease, enshrined under glass in the floor...at £45 per year it's been quite a bargain. Atop the building, the **Gravity Bar** provides visitors with a commanding 360-degree view of Dublin—with vistas all the way to the sea—and a free beer.

The actual exhibit makes brewing seem more grandiose than

it is and treats Arthur like the god of human happiness. Highlights are the cooperage (with 1954 film clips showing the master wood-keg makers plying their now virtually extinct trade), a display of the brewery's clever ads, and the Gravity Bar, which really is spectacular (€14, includes a €4 pint, discount with your hop-on hop-off bus ticket or when booked online, daily 9:30–17:00; enter on Bellevue Street, bus #78A from Aston Quay near O'Connell Bridge, or bus #123 from Dame Street and O'Connell Street; tel. 01/408-4800, www.guinness-storehouse.com). Both hop-on, hop-off bus tours stop here.

▲**Gaelic Athletic Association Museum**—The GAA was founded in 1884 as an expression of an Irish cultural awakening (see next page). It was created to foster the development of Gaelic sports, specifically Gaelic football and hurling, and to ban English sports such as cricket and rugby. The GAA played an important part in the fight for independence. This museum, at 82,000-seat Croke Park Stadium in east Dublin (a 20-min walk east of Parnell Square), offers a high-tech, interactive introduction to Ireland's favorite games. Relive the greatest moments in hurling and Irish-football history. Then get involved: Pick up a stick and try hurling, kick a football, and test your speed and balance. A 15-minute film (played on request) gives you a "Sunday at the stadium" experience (€5.50; July–Aug Mon–Sat 9:30–18:00, Sun 12:00–18:00; Sept–June Mon–Sat 9:30–17:00, Sun 12:00–17:00; on game Sundays the museum is closed to the general public; located under the stands at Croke Park Stadium—enter from St. Joseph's Avenue off Clonliffe Road; tel. 01/819-2323, http://museum.gaa.ie). The €9.50, one-hour museum-plus-stadium-tour option is worth it only for rabid fans who yearn to know which locker room is considered the unlucky one.

Hurling or Gaelic Football at Croke Park Stadium—Actually seeing a match here, surrounded by incredibly spirited Irish fans,

is a fun experience. Hurling is like airborne hockey with no injury time-outs. Gaelic football is a rugged form of soccer; you can carry the ball, but must bounce or kick it every three steps. Matches are held most Saturday or Sunday afternoons in summer (May–Aug), culminating in the hugely popular all-Ireland finals on Sunday afternoons in September. Tickets are available at the stadium except during the finals (€15–55, tel. 01/836-3222, www.gaa.ie). Choose a county to support, buy something colorful to wear or wave, and you're a temporary local screaming yourself hoarse.

Ireland's Gaelic Athletic Association

The GAA has long been a powerhouse in Ireland. Ireland's national pastimes of Gaelic football and hurling pack stadiums all over the country. When 80,000 people—paying at least €20 to €30 each—stuff Dublin's Croke Park Stadium and you consider that all the athletes are strictly amateur, you might wonder, "Where does all the money go?"

Ireland has a long tradition of using the revenue generated by these huge events to promote Gaelic athletics and Gaelic cultural events throughout the country in a grassroots and neighborhood way. So, while the players (many of whom are schoolteachers whose jobs allow for evenings and summers free) participate only for the glory of their various counties, the money generated is funding children's leagues, school coaches, small-town athletic facilities, and traditional arts, music, and dance—as well as the building and maintenance of giant stadiums such as Croke Park (which claims to be the third-largest stadium in Europe).

Gaelic sports are a heartfelt expression of Irish identity. There was a time when the Irish were not allowed to be members of the GAA if they also belonged to a cricket club (a British game). In 1921, during the War of Independence, Michael Collins (leader of the early IRA who invented urban guerrilla warfare) orchestrated the simultaneous assassination of a dozen British intelligence agents around Dublin. The Black & Tans retaliated immediately. As grizzled British WWI veterans, clad in black police coats and tan surplus army pants, they had been sent to Ireland to stamp out the rebels. Knowing Croke Park would be full of Irish Nationalists, they drove a tank onto the field during a Gaelic football match and machine-gunned the stands, killing 13 spectators as well as a Tipperary player. It was Ireland's first Bloody Sunday, a tragedy repeated over 50 years later in Derry.

Greyhound Racing—For an interesting, lowbrow look at local life, consider going to the dog races and doing a little gambling (€8; generally Wed, Thu, and Sat at 20:00; Shelbourne Park, tel. 01/668-3502). Greyhounds race most other days at Harold's Cross Racetrack (€10; Mon, Tue, and Fri at 20:00; tel. 01/497-1081).

SHOPPING

Shops are open roughly Monday–Saturday 9:00–18:00 and until 20:00 on Thursday. They have shorter hours on Sunday (if they're open at all). Good shopping areas include:

Grafton Street with its neighboring streets and arcades (such as the fun Great George's Arcade between Great George's and Drury Streets), and nearby shopping centers (Powerscourt Townhouse and St. Stephen's Green). Francis Street creaks with antiques.

Henry Street, home to Dublin's top department stores (pedestrian-only, off O'Connell Street).

Nassau Street, lining Trinity College, with the popular Kilkenny Department Store, the Irish Music store, and lots of touristy shops.

Dundrum Town Mall, a vast new suburban shopping mall (no tourists). The new LUAS light rail goes directly there from St. Stephen's Green.

Temple Bar, worth a browse any day for its art, jewelry, new-age paraphernalia, books, music, and gift shops. On Saturdays at Temple Bar's Meeting House Square, it's food in the morning (from 9:00) and books in the afternoon (until 18:00).

Street markets such as: Moore Street (produce, noise, and lots of color, Mon–Sat 8:00–18:00, closed Sun, near General Post Office), and St. Michan Street (fish, Tue–Sat 7:00–15:00, closed Sun–Mon, behind Four Courts building).

ENTERTAINMENT AND THEATER

Ireland has produced some of the finest writers in both English and Irish, and Dublin houses some of Europe's finest theaters. While Handel's *Messiah* was first performed in Dublin (1742), these days Dublin is famous for its rock bands (U2, Thin Lizzy, Sinead O'Connor, and Live Aid founder Bob Geldof's band the Boomtown Rats all got started here).

Abbey Theatre is Ireland's national theater, founded by W. B. Yeats in 1904 to preserve Irish culture during British rule (€14–20, generally nightly at 20:00, Sat matinees, 26 Lower Abbey Street, tel. 01/878-7222, www.abbeytheatre.ie). **Gate Theatre** does foreign plays as well as Irish classics (Cavendish Row, tel. 01/874-4045, www.gate-theatre.ie). The **Gaiety Theatre** offers a wide range of quality productions (King Street South, tel. 01/677-1717, www.gaietytheatre.com). Street theater takes the stage in Temple Bar on summer evenings. Browse the listings and fliers at the TI.

Point Theatre, once a railway terminus, is now the country's top live-music venue (East Link Bridge, tel. 081-871-9391, www.thepoint.ie).

At the **National Concert Hall,** the National Symphony Orchestra performs most Friday evenings (€9–30, off St. Stephen's Green at Earlsfort Terrace, tel. 01/417-0000, www.nch.ie).

Pub Action: Folk music fills the pubs and street entertainers are everywhere. The Temple Bar area thrives with music—traditional, jazz, and pop. Although it's pricier than the rest of Dublin, it really is *the* comfortable and fun place for tourists and locals (who come here to watch the tourists). **Gogarty's Pub** has top-notch sessions downstairs daily at 14:00 and upstairs nightly from 21:00 (at corner of Fleet and Anglesea, tel.

01/671-1822). Use this pub as a kickoff for your Temple Bar evening. It's also where the Traditional Irish Musical Pub Crawl starts (see page 45).

A 10-minute hike up the river west of Temple Bar takes you to a twosome with a local and less-touristy ambience. The **Brazen Head,** which lays claim to being the oldest pub in Dublin, is a hit for an early dinner and late live music (nightly from 21:30), with atmospheric rooms and a courtyard perfect for balmy evenings. They also host "Food, Folk, and Fairies" evenings. For €40, you get a hearty four-course meal punctuated by solid Irish history interwoven with more nebulous fairy tales (May–Oct Wed–Sat 19:00–22:00, 20 Bridge Street near Christchurch, pub tel. 01/677-9549, show tel. 01/492-2543, www.irishfolktours.com). **O'Shea's Merchant Pub,** just across the street, is encrusted in memories and filled with locals taking a break from the grind. They have live traditional music nightly at 21:30 (the front half is a restaurant, the magic is in the back half—enter on Bridge Street, tel. 01/679-3797).

At **Palace Pub,** climb upstairs to a cozy room that is a local favorite for traditional music sessions (at east end of Temple Bar, where Fleet Street hits Westmoreland Street, 21 Fleet Street).

Porterhouse has an inviting and varied menu, Dublin's best selection of microbrews, and live music. You can check their schedule online (€10 entrées, corner of Essex Street East and Parliament

Street, tel. 01/671-5715, www.porterhousebrewco.com/livetemplebar
.html).

The **Arlington Hotel Pub** hosts free Irish music shows, with
an Irish Rovers–type band singing ballads and a dance troupe
scuffing up the floorboards, to the delight of tour groups (shows
nightly 21:00–23:00, 23 Bachelors Walk, just off north end of
O'Connell Bridge, tel. 01/804-9100).

To sample truly traditional Irish song and dance, consider
heading to Comhaltas Ceoltoiri Éireann in nearby Dun Laoghaire
(see page 85).

Pub Crawls: For guided pub crawls (focusing on either Irish
literature or music), see page 45.

SLEEPING

Dublin is popular, and rooms can be tight. Book ahead for weekends any time of year, particularly in summer and during rugby
weekends. On Sundays in September, fans converge on Dublin
from all over the country for the all-Ireland finals in Gaelic
football and hurling. Prices are often discounted on weeknights
(Mon–Thu) and from November through February.

Big and practical places (both cheap and moderate) are most
central near Christ Church Cathedral, on the edge of Temple Bar.
For classy, older Dublin accommodations, you'll stay a bit farther
out (east of St. Stephen's Green). For a small-town escape with the
best budget values, consider staying in nearby Dun Laoghaire (see
page 83) or Howth (see page 87).

Near Christ Church Cathedral

These hotels face Christ Church Cathedral, a five-minute walk
from the best evening scene (at Temple Bar), and 10 minutes from

---

Sleep Code

(€1 = about $1.30, country code: 353, area code: 01)
S = Single, **D** = Double/Twin, **T** = Triple, **Q** = Quad, **b** = bathroom,
s = shower only. Breakfast is included and credit cards are
accepted unless otherwise noted.

To help you easily sort through these listings, I've divided
the rooms into three categories, based on the price for a standard double room with bath:

$$$ **Higher Priced**—Most rooms €130 or more.
$$ **Moderately Priced**—Most rooms between €70–130.
$ **Lower Priced**—Most rooms €70 or less.

Dublin

Dublin Accommodations

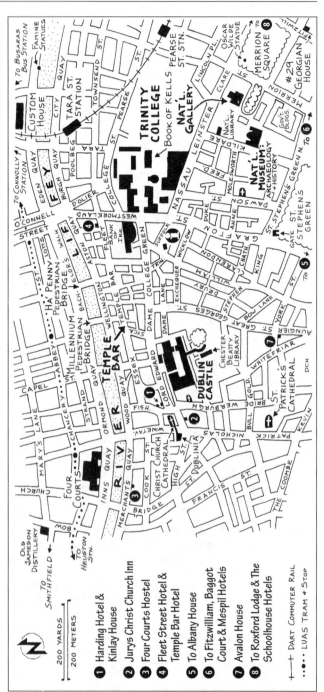

1 Harding Hotel & Kinlay House

2 Jurys Christ Church Inn

3 Four Courts Hostel

4 Fleet Street Hotel & Temple Bar Hotel

5 To Albany House

6 To Fitzwilliam, Baggot Court & Mespil Hotels

7 Avalon House

8 To Roxford Lodge & The Schoolhouse Hotels

＋ — DART COMMUTER RAIL

•••• LUAS TRAM + STOP

200 YARDS
200 METERS

the sightseeing center (Trinity College and Grafton Street). The cheap hostels in this neighborhood have some double rooms. Full Irish breakfasts, which cost €10–15 at the hotels, are half the price at the many small cafés nearby; try Bagel Haven or Chorus Café (see listings under "Eating").

$$$ Jurys Christ Church Inn, one of three Jurys Inns in downtown Dublin, is central and offers business-class comfort in all of its 182 identical rooms. This no-nonsense, American-style hotel chain has a winning keep-it-simple-and-affordable formula. If ye olde is getting old (and you don't mind big tour groups), these are a good option (€130 Sun–Thu; €150 Fri–Sat for one, two, or three adults or two adults and two kids; breakfast-€13). Its three floors are strictly non-smoking. Request a room far from the noisy elevator (book long in advance for weekends, check website for discounts, parking-€13/day, Christ Church Place, tel. 01/454-0000, fax 01/454-0012, US tel. 800-423-6953, www.jurysinn.com, info@jurysdoyle.com). The other Jurys Inns, described below, are near Connolly Station and Parnell Square.

$$ Harding Hotel is a hardworking, hardwood place with 52 newly refurbished, earth-tone rooms (Sb-€65, Db-€97 Sun–Wed, Db-€106–120 Thu–Sat, extra bed-€25, breakfast-€8.50; Rick Steves readers get 10 percent discount in 2008 if booking by email, phone, or fax, but not through websites; on weekends, request quiet upper-floor room away from fun but noisy ground-floor pub; in Copper Alley across street from Christ Church Cathedral, tel. 01/679-6500, fax 01/679-6504, www.hardinghotel.ie, info@hardinghotel.ie).

$ Kinlay House, around the corner from Harding Hotel, is the backpackers' choice—definitely the place to go for cheap beds, a central location, and an all-ages-welcome atmosphere. This huge, red-brick, 19th-century Victorian building has 200 metal, prison-style beds in spartan, non-smoking rooms. There are singles, doubles, and four- to six-bed coed dorms (good for families), as well as a few giant dorms. It fills up most days. Call well in advance, especially for singles, doubles, and summer weekends (S-€56–70, D-€62–68, Db-€66–72, dorm beds-€18–28, includes continental breakfast, free Internet access and Wi-Fi, kitchen access, launderette-€8, left luggage, travel desk, TV lounge, small lockers, lots of stairs, Christ Church, 2–12 Lord Edward Street, tel. 01/679-6644, fax 01/679-7437, www.kinlaydublin.ie, info@kinlaydublin.ie).

$ Four Courts Hostel is a 236-bed hostel beautifully located immediately across the river from the Four Courts. It's within a five-minute walk of Christ Church Cathedral and Temple Bar. Bare and institutional (as hostels typically are), it's also spacious and well run, with a focus on security and efficiency (dorm beds-€15–27, S-€47, Sb-€52, bunk D-€64, bunk Db-€70, includes small breakfast, non-smoking, elevator, Internet access, game room, laundry service, some parking-€8/day, left luggage room, 15–17 Merchant's Quay, bus #748 from airport, bus #90 from Connolly Station or Busaras Central Bus Station, tel. 01/672-5839, fax 01/672-5862, www.fourcourtshostel.com, info@fourcourtshostel.com).

Between Trinity College and Temple Bar

$$$ **Fleet Street Hotel** rents 70 decent rooms. For its size, it has a cozy ambience with character (Sb-€79–129, Db-€100–169, often midweek deals, breakfast-€6.50, non-smoking rooms, request a quiet room off the street, 19–20 Fleet Street, tel. 01/670-8122, fax 01/670-8103, www.fleethoteltemplebar.com, reservations @cbgroup.ie).

$$$ **Temple Bar Hotel** is a 130-room business-class place, very centrally located midway between Trinity College and the Temple Bar action (Sb-€80–150, Db-€120–195, Tb-€180–255, midweek discounts, non-smoking rooms, Wi-Fi, Fleet Street, Temple Bar, tel. 01/677-3333, fax 01/677-3088, www.templebarhotel .com, reservations@tbh.ie).

$$$ **Trinity College** turns its 800 student-housing rooms on campus into no-frills, affordable accommodations in the city center each summer. Look for the easy to miss Accommodations Office inside the huge courtyard, 50 yards down the wall on the left from the main entry arch (mid-June–Sept, S-€58, Sb-€70, D-€116, Db-€140, T-€174, Tb-€210, Qb-€280, all rooms have up to 3 twin beds, includes continental breakfast, cooked breakfast-€3.40 extra, tel. 01/896-1177, fax 01/671-1267, www.tcd.ie/accommodation, reservations@tcd.ie).

Near St. Stephen's Green

$$$ **Albany House**'s 43 comfortable rooms come with high ceilings, Georgian elegance, and some street noise—request a quieter room at the back (Sb-€100, Db-€140, Tb-€180, Una promises 10 percent off when booking direct with this book in 2008, nonsmoking, just 1 block south of St. Stephen's Green at 84 Harcourt Street, tel. 01/475-1092, fax 01/475-1093, www.albanyhousedublin .com, albany@indigo.ie).

$$$ **Fitzwilliam Townhouse** rents 14 good-value rooms in a Georgian townhouse near St. Stephen's Green (Sb-€89–100, Db-€120–175, Tb-€160–220, Qb-€180–240, 41 Upper Fitzwilliam Street, tel. 01/662-5155, fax 01/676-7488, www.fitzwilliamguesthouse .ie, info@fitzwilliamguesthouse.ie).

$$$ **Baggot Court Town House,** with the same owners as the Fitzwilliam (above), has 11 decent rooms a block farther from St. Stephen's Green (Sb-€89–100, Db-€120–175, Tb-€160–220, non-smoking, free parking, 92 Lower Baggot Street, tel. 01/661-2819, fax 01/661-0253, www.baggotcourt.com, baggot@indigo.ie).

$$ Avalon House, near Grafton Street, rents 281 simple, clean backpacker beds in newly refurbished rooms (dorm beds–€14–31, S–€32–36, Sb–€37–41, twin D–€60–68, twin Db–€70–78, includes continental breakfast, elevator, Internet access, launderette, helpful staff, sells Bus Éireann tickets, a few minutes off Grafton Street at 55 Aungier Street, tel. 01/475-0001, fax 01/475-0303, www.avalon-house.ie, info@avalon-house.ie).

Away from the Center, East of St. Stephen's Green

$$$ Roxford Lodge Hotel is a memorable splurge. In a quiet residential neighborhood a 20-minute walk from Trinity College, it has 20 tastefully decorated rooms awash with Jacuzzis and saunas. The €275 executive suite is honeymoon-worthy (Sb–€100–125, Db–€140–180, Tb–€150–180, Qb–€180–260, secure parking, 46 Northumberland Road, tel. 01/668-8572, fax 01/668-8158, www.roxfordlodge.ie, reservations@roxfordlodge.ie).

$$$ The Schoolhouse Hotel taught as many as 300 students in its heyday (1861–1969) and was in the middle of the bloodiest street fight of the 1916 Easter Uprising. Now it's a serene hideout with 31 pristine rooms and a fine restaurant (Sb–€149–169, Db–€149–199, discounted to €109 on Sun, book early, 2–8 Northumberland Road, tel. 01/667-5014, fax 01/667-5015, www.schoolhousehotel.com, info@schoolhousehotel.com).

$$$ Mespil Hotel is a huge, modern, business-class hotel renting 256 identical three-star rooms (most with a double and single bed, phone, TV, voice mail, and modem hookup) at a good price with all the comforts. This is a cut above Jurys Inn (Sb, Db, or Tb–€99–175, breakfast–€12, elevator, non-smoking floors, Wi-Fi, apartments for weeklong stays, 10-min walk southeast of St. Stephen's Green or bus #10, Mespil Road, tel. 01/488-4600, fax 01/667-1244, www.leehotels.com, mespil@leehotels.com).

Near Connolly Station

To locate these hotels, see the "North Dublin" map, page 58.

$$$ The Townhouse, with 80 small, stylish rooms (some with pleasant views into a central garden courtyard), hides behind a brick Georgian facade one block north of the Customs House (Sb–€70–80, Db–€115–130, Tb–€132–144, Internet access; small first-come, first-served parking lot; 47–48 Lower Gardiner Street, tel. 01/878-8808, fax 01/878-8787, www.townhouseofdublin.com, info@townhouseofdublin.com).

$$$ Jurys Inn Custom House, on Custom House Quay, offers the same value as the other Jurys Inns in Dublin, but it's less central. Its 239 rooms border the boring financial district, a 10-minute riverside hike from O'Connell Bridge. Of the three

Jurys Inns in town, this one is most likely to have rooms available (Db-€135 Sun–Thu, or €150 Fri–Sat, breakfast-€13, tel. 01/607-5000, fax 01/829-0400, US tel. 800-423-6953, www .jurysinn.com, info@jurysdoyle.com).

Near Parnell Square

To locate these hotels, see the "North Dublin" map, page 58.

$$$ Jurys Inn Parnell Street, built in 2006 as part of the steady rejuvenation of Dublin's north side, has 253 predictably soulless but good-value rooms. It's a block from the north end of O'Connell Street and the cluster of museums on Parnell Square (Db-€135 Sun–Thu, or €150 Fri–Sat, breakfast-€13, tel. 01/878-4900, fax 01/878-4999, www.jurysinn.com, jurysinnparnellst @jurysdoyle.com).

$$ Comfort Inn has 92 plain-vanilla rooms that are short on character but long on dependable, modern comforts (Db-€79–99 Sun–Thu, or €99–189 Fri–Sat, cheaper if booked online, Great Denmark Street, tel. 01/873-7700, fax 01/873-7777, www .comfortinndublin.com, info@comfortinndublin.com).

$$ Charles Stewart Hotel, big and basic, offers lots of forgettable rooms, many of them long and narrow, with head-to-toe twins. But it's in a great location for a good price (Sb-€50–64, D-€60–85, Db-€69–99, Tb-€120–140, Qb-€130–155, frequent midweek discounts, ask for a quieter room in the back, includes cooked breakfast, just beyond top end of O'Connell Street at 5–6 Parnell Square East, tel. 01/878-0350, fax 01/878-1387, www.charlesstewart .ie, info@charlesstewart.ie).

EATING

As Dublin does its boom-time jig, fine, creative eateries are popping up all over town. While you can get decent pub grub for €12 on just about any corner, consider saving that for the countryside. There's just no pressing reason to eat Irish in cosmopolitan Dublin. In fact, going local these days is the same as going ethnic. The city's good restaurants are packed from 20:00 on, especially on weekends. Eating early (18:00–19:00) saves time and money, as many better places offer an early-bird special. Many restaurants serve free jugs of ice water with a smile.

Eating Quick and Easy Around Grafton Street

Cornucopia is a small, earth-mama-with-class, proudly vegetarian, self-serve place two blocks off Grafton. It's friendly and youthful, with hearty €9 lunches and €12 dinner specials (Mon–Sat 8:30–20:00, Sun 12:00–19:00, 19 Wicklow Street, tel. 01/677-7583).

Dublin Restaurants

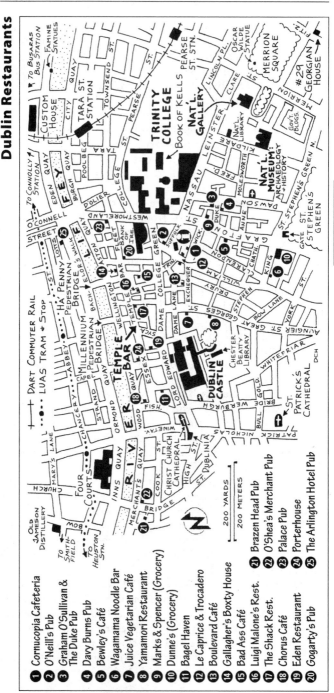

Dublin

1. Cornucopia Cafeteria
2. O'Neill's Pub
3. Graham O'Sullivan & The Duke Pub
4. Davy Burns Pub
5. Bewley's Café
6. Wagamama Noodle Bar
7. Juice Vegetarian Café
8. Yamamori Restaurant
9. Marks & Spencer (Grocery)
10. Dunne's (Grocery)
11. Bagel Haven
12. Le Caprice & Trocadero
13. Boulevard Café
14. Gallagher's Boxty House
15. Bad Ass Café
16. Luigi Malone's Rest.
17. The Shack Rest.
18. Chorus Café
19. Eden Restaurant
20. Gogarty's Pub
21. Brazen Head Pub
22. O'Shea's Merchant Pub
23. Palace Pub
24. Porterhouse
25. The Arlington Hotel Pub

O'Neill's Pub is a venerable, dark, and tangled retreat offering good grub, including dependable €10–12 carvery lunches. It's very central, located across from the main TI (daily 12:00–22:00, Suffolk Street, tel. 01/679-3656).

Graham O'Sullivan Restaurant and Coffee Shop, a cheap, cheery cafeteria, has soup, sandwiches, a salad bar, and an unpretentious ambience (Mon–Fri 8:00–18:30, Sat 8:30–17:00, Sun 11:00–16:30, 12 Duke Street). Two pubs on the same street—**The Duke** and **Davy Burns**—serve pub lunches. (The nearby Cathach Rare Books shop, at 10 Duke Street, displays a rare edition of *Ulysses* inscribed by Joyce, among other treasures, in its window.)

Bewley's Café is an old-time local favorite, offering light meals from €9 and full meals from €10–14. Sit on the ground floor among Art Deco lamps and windows by stained-glass artist Harry Clarke, or head upstairs to the bright atrium decorated by local art students (self-service Mon–Sat 8:00–22:00, Sun 9:00–22:00, 78 Grafton Street, tel. 01/672-7720). Their Mackerel seafood restaurant at the same location is also highly regarded. For a taste of witty Irish lunch theater, check out **Bewley's Café Theatre** upstairs; you can catch a fun hour-long performance while having a lunch of soup and brown bread for €14 (Mon–Sat at 13:00 during a play's run—doors open at 12:45, closed Sun, booking info tel. 086-878-4001, best to call ahead to see what's on, can sell out).

Wagamama Noodle Bar, like its popular sisters in London, is a pan-Asian slurpathon with great and healthy noodle and rice dishes (€11–15) served by walkie-talkie-toting waiters at long communal tables (daily 12:00–23:00, no reservations, often a line but it moves quickly, South King Street, underneath St. Stephen's Green Shopping Centre, tel. 01/478-2152).

South Great George's Street is lined with hardworking little eateries. **Juice** keeps vegetarians happy (daily 12:00–22:00, 73 South Great George's Street, tel. 01/475-7856).

Yamamori is a plain, mellow, and modern Japanese place serving seas of sushi and noodles (€10 lunches daily 12:30–17:30, €15–20 dinners nightly 17:30–23:00, 71 South Great George's Street, tel. 01/475-5001).

Supermarkets: **Dunne's,** on South Great George's Street, is your one-stop-shop for assembling a picnic meal (daily 7:00–24:00, across from Yamamori). They have another outlet in the basement of the St. Stephen's Green Shopping Centre. **Marks & Spencer** department store has a fancy grocery store in the basement, with fine take-away sandwiches and salads (Mon–Fri 9:00–20:00, Thu until 21:00, Sat 8:30–19:00, Sun 12:00–18:30, Grafton Street).

Eating Ethnic and Cheap in North Dublin

The **Epicurean Food Hall** offers a fun selection of food stalls with big and splittable portions. It's a hit with locals—and visitors—needing to eat cheaply (100 yards north of the Ha' Penny Bridge on Lower Liffey Street).

Eating Fast and Cheap near Christ Church Cathedral

Many of Dublin's **late-night grocery stores** sell cheap salads, microwaved meat pies, and made-to-order sandwiches (such as the Spar, open 24 hours a day, off the top of Dame Street on Parliament Street). An €8 picnic dinner back at the hotel might be a good option after a busy day of sightseeing.

Bagel Haven does fresh bagel sandwiches with quiet street-side seating. Get yours to go, and enjoy a picnic with a Georgian view in one of Dublin's grassy squares (€4 breakfasts, €5–8 lunches, Mon–Fri 7:30–16:00, Sat–Sun 10:00–16:00, hidden beside Kinlay House on Cow's Lane, tel. 01/675-9900).

Chorus Café is a friendly little hole-in-the-wall diner, perfect for breakfast or lunch with a newspaper (€4–7 breakfasts, €5–9 lunches, Mon–Fri 7:30–16:30, Sat 10:00–16:30, closed Sun, Fishamble Street, next door to the site of the first performance of Handel's *Messiah*, tel. 01/616-7088).

Dining at Classy Restaurants and Cafés

These three stylish restaurants serve well-presented food at fair prices. They're located within a block of each other, just south of Temple Bar and Dame Street, near the main TI.

Le Caprice is a fine, relaxing Italian place, with a good wine selection and a friendly staff (€15 pastas, €22–29 meals, Tue–Sun 17:30–23:15, closed Mon, 12 St. Andrew Street, tel. 01/679-4050). Consider their €21 early-bird special if your plans allow for an early dinner (finish by 20:15 if necessary).

Trocadero, across the street, serves beefy European cuisine to locals interested in a slow, romantic meal. The dressy, red-velvet interior is draped with photos of local actors. Come early or make a reservation—it's a favorite with Dublin's theatergoers (€19–30 meals, Mon–Sat 17:00–24:00, closed Sun, 3 St. Andrew Street, tel. 01/677-5545). The three-course pre-theater special is a fine value at €25 (17:00–19:00, leave by 19:45).

Boulevard Café is mod, local, trendy, and likeable, dishing up Mediterranean cuisine that's heavy on the Italian. Their salads, pasta, and sandwiches run about €8–11, and three-course lunch specials are €15 (Mon–Sat 10:00–18:00). Dinners cost around €15–23 (Mon–Sat 12:00–24:00, closed Sun, 27 Exchequer Street, smart to reserve for dinner, tel. 01/679-2131).

Eating in Temple Bar

Eden is a classy refuge serving a variety of contemporary Irish dishes in an airy space with a pleasant outdoor terrace (€20–29 dishes, daily 12:30–15:00 & 18:00–22:00, on Meeting House Square, a half-block off the busy tourist thoroughfare, tel. 01/670-5372). They offer a three-course pre-theater menu for €26 (Sun–Thu only before 19:00).

Gallagher's Boxty House is touristy and traditional—a good, basic value with creaky floorboards and old Dublin ambience. Its specialty is boxties, the generally bland-tasting Irish potato pancake filled and rolled with various meats, veggies, and sauces. The "Gaelic Boxty" is liveliest (€14–25, daily 9:00–23:00, also serves stews and corned beef, 20 Temple Bar, reservations wise, tel. 01/677-2762).

Bad Ass Café is a grunge diner—where Sinead O'Connor was once a waitress—serving cowboy/Mex/veggie/pizzas to old and new hippies. No need to dress up (€9 lunch specials with wine or beer, €13–18 dinners, daily 11:30–23:00, kids' specials, Crown Alley, just off Meeting House Square, tel. 01/671-2596).

Luigi Malone's, with its fun atmosphere and varied menu of pizza, ribs, pasta, sandwiches, and fajitas, is just the place to take your high-school date (€15–25 dishes, daily 12:00–23:00, €11 lunch menu with wine until 17:00, corner of Cecila and Fownes Streets, tel. 01/679-2723).

The Shack, while a bit pricey and touristy, has a reputation for good quality. It serves traditional Irish, chicken, seafood, and steak dishes (€17–26 entrées, daily 12:00–23:00, in the center of Temple Bar, 24 East Essex Street, tel. 01/679-0043).

TRANSPORTATION CONNECTIONS

Note that trains and buses generally run less frequently on Sundays.

From Dublin by Train from Heuston Station to: Tralee (7/day, 5/day on Sun, always via Killarney, 4 hrs), **Ennis** (2/day, 4 hrs), **Galway** (7/day, 3 hrs, recorded timetable tel. 01/805-4222).

By Train from Connolly Station to: Rosslare (5/day, 3 hrs), **Portrush** (7/day, 2/day Sun, 5 hrs, transfer in Belfast or Coleraine), **Belfast** (8/day, 2 hrs, tel. 01/836-3333). The **Dublin–Belfast train** connects the two Irish capitals in two hours at 90 mph on one continuous, welded rail (€35 one way, €50 round-trip; can cost more Fri–Sun). Train info: tel. 01/836-6222. Northern Ireland train info: tel. 048/9089-9400.

To Dun Laoghaire: See "Getting to Dun Laoghaire," page 83.

By Bus to: Belfast (16/day, most via Dublin Airport, 3.5 hrs),

Trim (10/day, 1 hr), **Ennis** (11/day, 5 hrs), **Galway** (14/day, 3.5 hrs), **Limerick** (13/day, 3.5 hrs), **Tralee** (7/day, 6 hrs), **Dingle** (4/day, 8–9 hrs, transfer at Limerick and Tralee). Bus info: tel. 01/836-6111, www.buseireann.ie.

Dublin Airport: The airport is well connected to the city center seven miles away; for transportation options into the city, see "Arrival in Dublin," page 40. Airport info: tel. 01/814-1111, www .dublinairport.ie. For a list of airlines, see below and the appendix. To sleep at Dublin Airport, a good bet is the **$$ Radisson SAS Hotel** (Db-€88–121, best prices if booked online, tel. 01/844-6000, www.hotels.radissonsas.com).

Connecting Ireland and Britain

Spend a few minutes online researching your transportation options across the Irish Sea. Most airline and ferry companies routinely offer discounts (often as much as €10) for tickets purchased from their websites. Before sorting out rail/ferry prices with individual companies, try www.sailrail.com, which deals with several companies and has fares low enough to compete with cheap airlines (some of the lowest: London–Dublin-£25, Glasgow–Belfast-£18, book in advance).

If you're going directly to London, flying is your best bet. Check **Ryanair** first (90 min, Irish tel. 081-830-3030, www .ryanair.com). Other options include **British Airways** (Irish tel. 1-890-626-747, US tel. 800-247-9297, www.britishairways.com), **Aer Lingus** (tel. 081-836-5000, www.aerlingus.com), and **bmi british midland** (Irish tel. 01/407-3036, US tel. 800-788-0555, www.flybmi.com). To get the lowest fares, ask about round-trip ticket prices and book months in advance (though Ryanair offers deals nearly all the time).

Dublin and Liverpool: SeaCat has ferries for car and foot passengers (weekly via the Isle of Man, 4 hrs, €30–35 one-way for foot passengers, tel. 800-805-055, www.steam-packet.com). Car-only

ferries are operated by both P&O Irish Sea Ferries (daily, 7.5 hrs, tel. 01/407-3434, www.poirishsea .com) and Norfolk Line (2/day, 7.5 hrs, €38–60, Tue–Sun, closed Mon, tel. 01/819-2999, www.norfolkline -ferries.co.uk). Check in one to two hours before the sailing time—call to confirm details.

Dublin and Holyhead: Irish Ferries sails between Dublin and Holyhead in North Wales. The dock is a mile east of O'Connell Bridge (5/day: 2 slow, 3 fast; slow boats—3.25 hrs, €29 one-way walk-on fare; fast boats—1.75 hrs, €32; Dublin tel. 01/638-3333, Holyhead tel. 08705-329-129, www.irishferries.com).

Dun Laoghaire and Holyhead: Stena Line sails a huge catamaran between Dun Laoghaire (near Dublin) and Holyhead in North Wales (Fri–Sun 3/day, Mon–Thu 2/day, 2 hrs, €30 one-way walk-on fare, €4 extra if paying with credit card, reserve by phone—they book up long in advance on summer weekends, Dun Laoghaire tel. 01/204-7777, recorded info tel. 01/204-7799, can book online at www.stenaline.com).

Ferries to France

Irish Ferries connects Ireland (Rosslare) with France (Cherbourg and Roscoff) every other day (less often Jan–March). While Cherbourg has the quickest connection to Paris, your overall time between Ireland and Paris is about the same (20–25 hrs) regardless of which port is used on the day you sail. One-way fares range from €40 to €100. Eurailpass holders go half-price. In both directions, departures are generally between 16:00 and 17:00 and arrive late the next morning. While passengers can nearly always get on, reservations are wise in summer and easy by phone. If you anticipate a crowded departure, you can reserve a seat for €11. Doubles (or singles) start at €44–54 per person. The easiest way to get a bed (except during summer) is from the information desk upon boarding. The cafeteria serves bad food at reasonable prices. Upon arrival in France, buses and taxis connect you to your Paris-bound train (Irish Ferries: Dublin tel. 01/855-2222, www.irishferries .com, info@irishferries.com).

Dun Laoghaire and Howth

Dun Laoghaire (dun leery) and Howth (rhymes with growth) are two peas in a pod, dangling from opposite ends of Dublin Bay's crescent-shaped shoreline. They offer quieter, cheaper lodging alternatives to Dublin. Both offer easy DART light rail access to the city center, less than a 30-minute ride away. Each houses their only worthwhile sightseeing options in pillbox martello (masonry) towers. And they were each once home to famous Irish writers: James Joyce in Dun Laoghaire and W. B. Yeats in Howth. The fundamental difference between the two is that Dun Laoghaire (south of Dublin) has the ferry port to Wales, while Howth (north of Dublin) is closer to the airport.

Dun Laoghaire

Dun Laoghaire is seven miles south of Dublin. This snoozy suburb, with the ferry terminal for Wales and easy connections to

downtown Dublin, is a great small-town base for exploring the big city.

The Dun Laoghaire harbor was strategic enough to merit a line of martello towers, built to defend against an expected Napoleonic invasion (one tower now houses the James Joyce Museum, described later in this section). By the mid-19th century, its massive breakwaters were completed, protecting a huge harbor. Ships sailed regularly from here to Wales (60 miles away), and the first train line in Ireland connected the terminal with Dublin.

Getting to Dun Laoghaire

While buses run between Dublin and Dun Laoghaire, the **DART** commuter train is much faster (4/hr, 20 min, runs Mon–Sat about 6:00–23:30, Sun from 9:00, €2 one-way, €3.60 round-trips are good same day only, Eurailpass valid but uses a flexi-day, tel. 01/703-3504, www.iarnrodeireann.ie/dart/home). If you're coming from Dublin, catch a DART train marked "Bray" and get off at the Sandycove/Glasthule or Dun Laoghaire stop, depending on which B&B you choose. If you're leaving Dun Laoghaire, catch a train marked "Howth" to get to Dublin. Get off at the central Tara Street Station if you want to sightsee in Dublin; or ride it one stop farther to Connolly Station (for train connections north, or Airlink bus connections to airport).

The **Patton Flyer** is a new bus service to and from the **airport** via the recently completed Port Tunnel. You can catch it at either the Royal Marine Hotel in Dun Laoghaire or at St. Joseph's Church in nearby Glasthule (€7, departs Dun Laoghaire starting at 4:00 and from the airport starting at 5:00 until 23:00, hourly, 45 min, tel. 01/284-9619, www.thepattonflyer.ie).

The **taxi** fare from Dun Laoghaire to central Dublin is about €35, to the airport about €50. Try ABC Taxi service (tel. 01/285-5444). With DART access into Dublin and cheap or sometimes free parking, this area is ideal for those with **cars** (which can cost more than €30/day to park in Dublin).

ORIENTATION

A busy transportation hub, Dun Laoghaire has a coastline defined by its nearly mile-long breakwaters—reaching like two muscular arms into the Irish Sea. The breakwaters are popular for strollers, bikers, bird-watchers, and fishermen.

Tourist Information: The TI is in the ferry terminal (Mon–Sat 10:00–12:45 & 14:00–18:00, closed Sun).

Helpful Hints

Internet Access: U-surf.ie provides a fast connection (€4/hr, daily 10:00–24:00, 88B Lower George's Street, tel. 01/231-1186).

Post Office: It's on Lower George's Street (Mon–Fri 9:00–18:00, Sat 9:00–13:00, closed Sun).

Laundry: Try **Jeeves,** located in the village of Glasthule, a five-minute downhill walk from Sandycove/Glasthule DART station (Mon–Sat 8:30–18:00, closed Sun, full-service only, 34 Glasthule Road, next to Daniel's Restaurant and Wine Bar, tel. 01/230-1120).

Parking: If you don't have free parking at your B&B, try the pay-and-display street-parking system; buy a ticket at machines spaced along the street, and display it on your dashboard (Mon–Fri 8:00–19:00, €1.50/hr, 3-hr max, free Sat–Sun).

Best Views: Hike out to the lighthouse, at the end of the interesting East Pier, or climb the tight, stuffy James Joyce Museum/tower (see below).

SIGHTS

James Joyce Museum—This squat martello tower at Sandycove was originally built to repel a Napoleonic invasion, but it became famous chiefly because of its association with James Joyce. The great author lived here briefly and made it the setting for the opening of his novel *Ulysses.* Today, the museum's round exhibition space is filled with literary memorabilia, including photographs and rare first editions. For a fine view, climb the claustrophobic, two-story spiral stairwell sealed inside the thick wall to reach the rooftop gun mount (€7, €12 combo-ticket with Dublin Writers' Museum, March–Oct Mon–Sat 10:00–13:00 & 14:00–17:00, Sun 14:00–18:00; when it's closed, in Nov–Feb, Joyce fans can call and make arrangements to see the museum; tel. 01/280-9265).

The sandy little cove and rounded rocks beside the tower are a safe and clean swimming spot, a local favorite for kids of all ages.

ENTERTAINMENT

For an evening of pure Irish music, song, and dance, check out the **Comhaltas Ceoltoiri Éireann,** an association working to preserve this slice of Irish culture. It got started in the 1950s when Elvis and company threatened to steal the musical heart of the new generation. Judging by the pop status of traditional Irish music these days, Comhaltas accomplished its mission. Their Seisiun evening is a stage show mixing traditional music, song, and dance (€10, July–Aug Mon–Thu at 21:00, followed by informal music session at 22:30). On Fridays all year long, they have a *ceilidh* (KAY-lee), where everyone does set dances. This style, the forerunner of square dancing, evolved from the French Quadrille dances of 200 years ago, with two couples making up a set (€8 includes friendly pointers, 21:30–24:30). At 21:00 on Tuesdays and Wednesdays (free) and Saturdays (€3), there are informal sessions by the fireside. All musicians are welcome. Performances are held at the Cuturlann na Éireann center at 32 Belgrave Square in Monkstown (near the Seapoint DART stop, or take bus #7 from Dun Laoghaire, tel. 01/280-0295, www.comhaltas.ie). Their bar is free to enter (no cover charge) and often filled with music.

SLEEPING

(€1 = about $1.30, country code: 353, area code: 01)

In Dun Laoghaire, near Sandycove DART Station

These listings are within a couple of blocks of the Sandycove/ Glasthule DART station and a 10-minute walk to the Dun Laoghaire DART station/ferry landing.

$$ Windsor Lodge rents four fresh, inviting rooms on a quiet street a block off the harbor and a block from the DART station (Db-€60–85, Tb-€90–100, family room-€90–105, 10 percent discount with this book in 2008, cash only, non-smoking, 3 Islington Avenue, tel. 01/284-6952, www.windsorlodge.ie, winlodge @eircom.net, Mary O'Farrell).

$$ Ferry House is a family-friendly place with four high-ceilinged rooms on a dead-end street (Sb-€55–65, Db-€75–80, Tb-€100–120, Qb-€120, €5 discount with this book in 2008, non-smoking, 15 Clarinda Park North just off Clarinda Park West, tel. 01/280-8301, www.ferryhousedublin.com, ferry_house@hotmail .com, Eamon and Pauline).

$ Seaview B&B, a modern house run by Mrs. Kane, has three big, cheery rooms and a welcoming guests' lounge with a bright and friendly feeling (S-€35, Db-€70 with this book in 2008, cash only, non-smoking, just above Rosmeen Gardens at 2 Granite

Dun Laoghaire

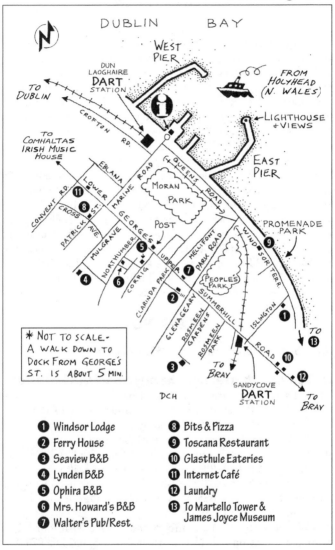

DUBLIN   BAY

WEST
PIER

DUN
LAOGHAIRE
DART
STATION

FROM
HOLYHEAD
(N. WALES)

TO
DUBLIN

LIGHTHOUSE
& VIEWS

CROFTON RD.

TO
COMHALTAS
IRISH MUSIC
HOUSE

EAST
PIER

ERLANA

MARINE ROAD

QUEEN'S ROAD

MORAN
PARK

PROMENADE
PARK

CONVENT RD.

LOWER GEORGE'S ST.

CROSS

PATRICK AVE.

POST

MELLIFONT PARK ROAD

WIND SORTER TERR.

MULGRAVE

NORTHUMBER.

UPPER

PEOPLE'S
PARK

CORRIG

CLARINDA PARK

SUMMERHILL

GLENAGEARY

ROSMEEN GARDENS

ROSMEEN PARK

ISLINGTON

TO

TO
BRAY

* NOT TO SCALE -
A WALK DOWN TO
DOCK FROM GEORGE'S
ST. IS ABOUT 5 MIN.

DCH

SANDYCOVE
DART
STATION

TO
BRAY

1 Windsor Lodge
2 Ferry House
3 Seaview B&B
4 Lynden B&B
5 Ophira B&B
6 Mrs. Howard's B&B
7 Walter's Pub/Rest.

8 Bits & Pizza
9 Toscana Restaurant
10 Glasthule Eateries
11 Internet Café
12 Laundry
13 To Martello Tower &
James Joyce Museum

Hall, tel. & fax 01/280-9105, www.seaviewbedandbreakfast.com,
seaviewbedandbreakfast@hotmail.com).

Near the Dun Laoghaire DART Station

$$ **Lynden B&B,** with a classy 150-year-old interior hiding behind
a somber front, rents four big rooms (S-€42, Sb-€45–60, D-€65,
Db-€75, 10 percent discount with this book in 2008, cash only,

past Mulgrave Street to 2 Mulgrave Terrace, tel. 01/280-6404, fax 01/230-2258, lynden@iol.ie, Maria Gavin).

$$ Ophira B&B is a historic house with four comfortably creaky rooms run by active diver, hiker, and biker John O'Connor (Db-€70–90, Tb-€90–100, Qb-€120–140, non-smoking, parking available, 10 Corrig Avenue, tel. 01/280-0997, www.ophira.ie, info@ophira.ie).

$ Mrs. Howard's B&B has four big, airy rooms (S-€40, Sb-€45, D-€64, Db-€70, cash only, TV lounge, 36 Northumberland Avenue, tel. 01/280-3262, mobile 086-102-9287, paul.northumberland @hotmail.com).

EATING

If staying in Dun Laoghaire, I'd definitely eat here and not in Dublin.

George's Street, Dun Laoghaire's main drag three blocks inland, has plenty of eateries and pubs, many with live music. **Walters Public House and Restaurant** is a bright, modern place above a pub, offering good food to a dressy crowd. The multi-terraced back patio of the pub is great for a drink on a warm evening (€16–26 meals, €8–14 pub meals, daily 17:30–22:30, 68 Upper George's Street, tel. 01/280-7442). A good bet for families is the kid-friendly **Bits and Pizza** (daily 12:00–22:30, off George's Street at 15 Patrick Street, tel. 01/284-2411).

Toscana, on the waterfront, is a popular little cubbyhole, serving hearty Italian dishes and pizza. Its prime location makes it easy to incorporate into your evening stroll. Reserve for dinner (€11–24 meals, daily 12:00–23:00, 5 Windsor Terrace, tel. 01/230-0890).

Glasthule (called simply "the village" locally, just down the street from the Sandycove/Glasthule DART station) has an array of fun, hardworking little restaurants. The big **Eagle House pub** dishes up hearty €10–19 pub meals in a wonderful atmosphere; it's a super, local joint for a late drink (Mon–Sat 12:30–21:30, Sun 12:30–19:30, tel. 01/280-4740). The nearby **Daniel's Restaurant and Wine Bar** is less atmospheric, but it's also good (€18–24 meals, Tue–Sun 18:00–23:00, closed Mon, 34 Glasthule Road, tel. 01/284-1027). **Centra** market is right next door and has your picnic makings (daily 7:00–23:00, Glasthule Road).

Howth

Eight miles north of Dublin, Howth rests on a teardrop-shaped peninsula that pokes the Irish Sea. Its active harbor teems with fishing boats bringing in the daily catch. Weary Dubliners come here for refreshing coastal cliff walks near the city. Located at the north terminus of the DART light rail line, Howth makes a good place for travelers to settle in, with easy connections to Dublin for sightseeing.

Howth was once an important gateway to Dublin. Near the neck of the peninsula is the suburb of Clontarf, where Irish High King Brian Boru defeated the last concerted Viking attack in 1014. Eight hundred years later, a squat martello tower was built on a bluff above Howth's harbor to defend it from a Napoleonic invasion that never came. The harbor then grew as a port for shipping from Liverpool and Wales. It was eventually eclipsed by Dun Laoghaire, which was first to gain rail access. Irish rebels smuggled German-supplied guns into Ireland via Howth in 1914, making the 1916 Easter Uprising possible. Today this hamlet is so sleepy, it doesn't even have a TI.

Getting to Howth

The **DART** light rail system zaps travelers between Howth and the city twice as fast as bus service (4/hr, 25 min, runs Mon–Sat about 6:00–23:30, Sun from 9:00, €2 one-way, round trips are €3.60 same day only, Eurailpass valid but uses a flexi-day, tel. 01/703-3504, www.iarnrodeireann.ie/dart/home). If you're coming from Dublin, catch a DART train marked "Howth" (not Howth Junction, Malahide, or Drogheda) and ride it to the end of the line. All trains departing Howth head straight to Dublin's Connolly Station, then continue on to Tara and Pierce Stations.

If you choose to go by **bus**, #31 or #31B links Dublin's Eden Quay and the well-marked bus stop on Howth's harborfront (60 min, €1.80). A **taxi** from the airport takes about 20 minutes and costs about €25. Try Executive Cabs (tel. 01/839-6020). With easy DART access into Dublin and plentiful parking, Howth is a good option for those with **cars** (which can cost more than €30/day to park in Dublin).

Orientation

Howth perches on the north shore of the peninsula, clustered along a quarter-mile harborfront promenade that stretches from the DART station (in the west) to the martello tower on the bluff (in the east). Its two stony piers clutch like crab claws at the Irish Sea. The West Pier has the fishing action, while the East Pier extends to a stubby 200-year-old lighthouse and views of a rugged nearby island, Ireland's Eye. Abbey Street extends south, uphill

Howth

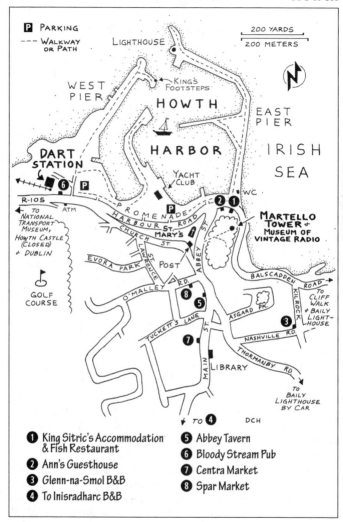

- **1** King Sitric's Accommodation & Fish Restaurant
- **2** Ann's Guesthouse
- **3** Glenn-na-Smol B&B
- **4** To Inisradharc B&B
- **5** Abbey Tavern
- **6** Bloody Stream Pub
- **7** Centra Market
- **8** Spar Market

from the harbor near the base of the martello tower bluff, becoming Main Street with most of the shops and pubs, along with the post office (Mon–Fri 9:00–13:00 & 14:15–18:00, Sat 9:00–13:00, closed Sun) and library (free Internet access, only one terminal, Mon and Wed 14:00–20:30, Tue and Thu–Sat 10:00–13:00 & 14:00–17:00, closed Sun).

With no TI, your best source of local info is your innkeeper. The only ATM in town is adjacent to the Gem Newsstand, across the street from the DART station.

SIGHTS AND ACTIVITIES

Other than coastal walks, sightseeing here pales in comparison to Dublin.

Museum of Vintage Radio—The three-story martello tower on the bluff overlooking the East Pier is the only site in Howth worth a glance. Curator Pat Herbert has spent 45 years acquiring his collection of lovingly preserved radios, phonographs, and even a Hurdy Gurdy crank-action musical oddity—all of which still work (€5, May–Oct daily 11:00–16:00, Nov–April Sat–Sun only 11:00–16:00, entry up driveway off Abbey Street).

Before leaving the compact bluff, check out the views of the harbor and the nearby island of Ireland's Eye. Spot the distant martello tower on the island's west end and the white guano coating its eastern side, courtesy of a colony of gannets.

National Transport Museum—Housed in a large shed on the castle grounds, this is a dusty waste of time unless you find rapture in old trams and buses (€3, June–Aug Mon–Fri 10:00–17:00, Sat–Sun 14:00–17:00, otherwise by appointment, tel. 01/848-0831). Howth Castle, nearby, is still in private hands and cannot be toured.

St. Mary's Abbey—Looming above Abbey Street, the current ruins date from the early 1400s. Prior to that, a church built by Norse King Sitric in 1042 stood at this site. The entrance to the ruins is above the abbey grounds, across from Café Blue's patio on Church Street.

East and West Piers—The piers make for mellow strolls after a meal. Poke your head into the various fishmonger shops along the East Pier to see the day's catch. At the end of the pier (on the leeward, downwind side), you'll find the footsteps of King George IV carved into the stone after his 1821 visit. The West Pier is a quiet jetty barbed with a squat lighthouse and the closest views of Ireland's Eye.

Hiking Trails—Trails above the eastern cliffs of the peninsula offer enjoyable, breezy exercise. For a scenic three-hour round-trip, walk past the East Pier and martello tower, following Balscadden Road uphill. You'll soon pass Balscadden House, where writer W. B. Yeats spent part of his youth (watch for plaque on left). Where the road dead-ends, you'll find the well-marked trailhead. The trail is easy to follow and soon you'll be walking south around the craggy coastline to grand views of the Bailey Lighthouse on the southeast rim of the peninsula. The gate to the lighthouse grounds is always locked, so enjoy the view from afar before retracing your steps back to Howth.

SLEEPING

$$$ King Sitric's Accommodation is Howth's best lodging option and has a fine harborfront seafood restaurant (described in "Eating"). It fills the old harbormaster's house with eight well-kept rooms and a friendly staff (Sb-€105–140, Db-€152–205, non-smoking, East Pier below martello tower, tel. 01/832-5235, fax 01/839-2442, www.kingsitric.ie, info@kingsitric.ie, Aidan and Joan MacManus).

$$ Ann's Guesthouse, next door to King Sitric's, sports four bright, airy rooms on its top floor—two with skylight views of the harbor (Sb-€70, Db-€100–120, 5 East Pier, tel. 01/832-3197, www.annsofhowth.com, annsofhowth@eircom.net, Jon and Una Cooke).

$$ Glenn-na-Smol B&B is a homey house with six unpretentious rooms in a quiet setting, a five-minute walk uphill along the coast behind the martello tower (S-€50, Db-€74, Tb-€111, Qb-€148, cash only, parking, corner of Nashville Road & Kilrock Lane, tel. 01/832-2936, rickards@indigo.ie, Sean and Kitty Rickard).

$$ Inisradharc B&B rests in the lofty suburbs above town with three tidy rooms and views of Ireland's Eye below. The steep 20-minute uphill hike from the harbor makes this a lodging option only drivers can appreciate (Db-€80–90, Tb-€125–135, non-smoking, parking, Balkill Road, tel. 01/832-2306, harbour_view @msn.com).

EATING

King Sitric's Fish Restaurant, one of Dublin's most famous seafood experiences, serves Irish versions of French classics in a dining room (upstairs) with harbor views. Chef Aidan MacManus rises early every morning to select the best of the day's catch on the pier, to be enjoyed that evening by happy customers (€22–30 meals, Mon–Sat 12:30–14:15 & 18:30–22:00, closed Sun, reservations smart, tel. 01/832-5235, www.kingsitric.ie).

For pub grub, try the **Abbey Tavern** on Abbey Street (occasional trad music and dance, call for schedule, tel. 01/839-0307 or 01/832-2006) or the **Bloody Stream Pub** in front of the DART station (tel. 01/839-5076). For picnic supplies, head to **Centra Market** (daily 7:00–22:00, Main Street) or **Spar Market** (daily 8:00–22:00, St. Lawrence Road).

NEAR DUBLIN

Not far from urban Dublin, you'll find the stony skeletons of evocative ruins sprouting from the lush Irish countryside. The story of Irish history is told by ancient burial mounds, early Christian monastic settlements, huge Norman castles, and pampered estate gardens. These sights are separated into regions: north of Dublin (the Valley of the Boyne, including Brú na Bóinne and the town of Trim) and south of Dublin (Glendalough and the Wicklow Mountains).

North of Dublin: The Valley of the Boyne

The peaceful, green Valley of the Boyne, just 30 miles north of Dublin, has an impressive concentration of historical and spiritual sights: The enigmatic burial mounds at Brú na Bóinne are older than the Egyptian pyramids. At the Hill of Tara (seat of the high kings of Celtic Ireland), St. Patrick preached his most persuasive sermon. The valley also contains the first Vatican-endorsed monastery in Ireland and several of the country's finest high crosses. You'll see Trim's 13th-century castle—Ireland's biggest—built by Norman invaders, and you can wander the site of the historic Battle of the Boyne (1690), in which the Protestants turned the tide against the Catholics, and imposed British rule until the 20th century.

Valley of the Boyne

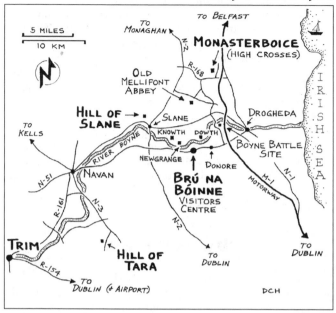

Planning Your Time

Of these sights, only Brú na Bóinne is worth ▲▲▲ (and deserves a good three hours). The others, while relatively meager physically, are powerfully evocative to anyone interested in Irish history and culture. Without a car, I'd visit only Brú na Bóinne, taking the shuttle bus from Dublin (see "Getting There" on page 95).

The region is a joy by car, because all of the described sights are within a 30-minute drive of each other. If you eat your Weetabix, you could do the entire region in a day. While sights are on tiny roads, they're well marked with brown, tourist-friendly road signs, and you'll navigate best using an Ordnance Survey atlas.

As you plan your Ireland itinerary, keep in mind that if you're flying into or out of Dublin, and want to avoid the intensity and expense of that big city, you can use Trim as an overnight base (45-min drive from airport, see accommodations listings on page 100), and tour these sights from there.

Tours of the Valley of the Boyne

If you lack a car and like tours, consider one of these round-trip tours from Dublin.

Mary Gibbon's Tours visits both Brú na Bóinne (including inside the Newgrange tomb) and the Hill of Tara in a six-hour trip (€39, €35 for students and readers with this book in 2008,

Mon–Fri only, 10:15 pickup at Dublin TI on Suffolk Street, 10:25 pickup at Royal Dublin Hotel on O'Connell Street, home by 16:30, book direct rather than through TI, tel. 086/355-1355, www .newgrangetours.com, info@newgrangetours.com).

Over the Top Tours covers everything but Brú na Bóinne and Trim. Leaving Dublin at 9:00 and returning by 17:30, they stop at the Hill of Tara, the Hill of Slane (free time for lunch), Fourknocks (prehistoric tombs, less famous than Brú na Bóinne), the Battle of the Boyne site, and the monasteries of Monasterboice and Old Mellifont Abbey (€28, departing daily at 9:00 from Dublin TI on Suffolk Street, pickup at 9:20 from Royal Dublin Hotel on O'Connell Street, 14-seat minibus, reservations required, hold seat by leaving credit-card number, Ireland toll-free tel. 1-800-424-252, Dublin tel. 01/838-6128, www.overthetoptours .com, info@overthetoptours.com).

Brú na Bóinne

Near Dublin

The famous archaeological site properly known as Brú na Bóinne—"dwelling place of the Boyne"—is also commonly referred to as "Newgrange" (actually one of the tombs). The well-organized site, worth ▲▲▲, centers on a state-of-the-art museum. Visitors are given appointments for shuttle buses that ferry small groups five minutes away, to one of two 5,000-year-old passage tombs where a guide gives a 30-minute tour. **Newgrange** is more famous, and allows you inside. **Knowth** (rhymes with south) opened more recently and is more extensive, but you can't go inside the tomb. At the turnstile, you'll buy a ticket to one or both sights, and be given bus departure times (if you plan to see both sights, note that buses depart 90 min apart). Newgrange sells out first, and comes with a longer wait. If you opt for Knowth, be sure to see the museum's replica of the Newgrange passage entrance (where a short tour and winter solstice light-show demo often occur upon request); the replica is connected to the video room. Each site is different enough and worthwhile, but for many, seeing just one is adequate. For information on the prehistoric art, see page 371.

Newgrange is one single mound, the more restored of the Brú na Bóinne sites. Dating from 3200 B.C., it's 500 years older than the pyramids at Giza. While we know nothing of the builders, it most certainly was a sacred spot dealing with some kind of Sun

God ritual. During the tour, you'll squeeze down a narrow passageway to a cross-shaped central chamber, located under a 20-foot-high igloo-type stone dome. Bones and ashes were placed here under 200,000 tons of stone and dirt to wait for a special moment. As the sun rose on the shortest day of the year (winter solstice, Dec 21), a ray of light would creep slowly down the 60-foot-long passageway. For 17 minutes it would light the center of the sacred chamber. Perhaps this was the moment when the souls of the dead would be transported to the afterlife via that mysterious ray of life-giving and life-taking light.

Knowth (the second Brú na Bóinne site) is a necropolis of several grassy mounds around one 85-yard-wide grand tomb. The big mound, covering 1.5 acres, has two passages aligned so that on the spring and fall equinoxes, rays from the rising and setting sun shine down the passageways to the center chamber. Neither of the passages is open to the public; but when you visit a room cut into the mound—designed to expose the interior construction layers—you get a glimpse down one of the passages. The Knowth site thrived from 3000 to 2000 b.c., with mysterious burial rituals and sun-tracking ceremonies to please the gods and ensure the regular progression of seasons for crops. The site then evolved into the domain of fairies and myths for the next 2,000 years, and became an Iron Age fortress in the early centuries after Christ. Around a.d. 1000, it was an all-Ireland political center, and, later, a Norman fortress was built atop the mound. You'll see plenty of mysteriously carved stones and new-feeling grassy mounds that you can look down on from atop the grand tomb.

Cost and Hours: Allow an hour for the excellent museum and an hour for each of the tombs you visit. The museum in the Brú na Bóinne Visitors Centre is included in the following prices: Newgrange-€5.80, Knowth-€4.50, covered by Heritage Card (May–Sept daily 9:00–18:30 or 19:00, slightly shorter hours off-season, Newgrange open year-round, Knowth open April–Oct only, tel. 041/988-0300).

Crowd-Beating Tips: Visits are limited, and on busy summer days those arriving in the afternoon may not get a spot (no reservations possible). In peak season, try to arrive by 9:30 to avoid a wait caused by big tour-bus crowds. Generally upon arrival you'll get a bus departure time for one or both of the passage-tomb sites (the last shuttle bus leaves 1.75 hours before closing). Spend your wait visiting the museum, watching the great seven-minute video, and munching lunch in the cheery cafeteria. You can't drive directly to the actual passage tombs.

Getting There: To reach the Brú na Bóinne Visitors Centre from Dublin by **car,** drive north on N-1 to Drogheda, where signs direct you to the center.

If you don't have a car and you're not taking a tour, hop on the Brú na Bóinne (Newgrange) **shuttle bus** that runs from Dublin directly to the Visitors Centre (€15 round-trip, departs at 8:45 and 11:00 from TI on Suffolk Street and at 9:00 and 11:15 from Royal Dublin Hotel on O'Connell Street, return trips depart at 13:00 and 16:00 from the Visitors Centre, run by Over the Top Tours, book by phone, tel. 01/860-0405).

More Sights in the Valley of the Boyne

▲Hill of Tara

This was the most important center of political and religious power in pre-Christian Ireland. While aerial views show plenty of mysterious circles and lines, wandering with the sheep among the well-worn ditches and hills leaves you with more to feel than to see. Visits are made meaningful by an excellent 20-minute video presentation and the caring 20-minute guided walk that follows (always available upon request and entirely worthwhile).

You'll see the Mound of Hostages (a Bronze Age passage grave, c. 2500 B.C.), a couple of ancient sacred stones, a war memorial, and vast views over the Emerald Isle. While ancient Ireland was a pig-pile of minor chieftain-kings scrambling for power, the high king of Tara was king of the mountain. It was at this ancient stockade that St. Patrick directly challenged the authority of the high king. When confronted by the pagan high king, Patrick convincingly explained the Holy Trinity using a shamrock: three petals with one stem. He won the right to preach Christianity throughout Ireland, and the country had a new national symbol.

This now-desolate hill was also the scene of great modern events. In 1798, passionate young Irish rebels chose Tara for its defensible position, but were routed by better organized (and more sober) British troops. (The cunning British commander had sent three cartloads of whiskey along the nearby road earlier in the day, knowing the rebels would intercept it.) In 1843, the great orator and champion of Irish liberty Daniel O'Connell gathered 500,000 Irish peasants on this hill for his greatest "monster meeting"—a peaceful show of force demanding the repeal of the Act of Union with Britain. In a bizarre final twist, a small group of British Israelites—who believed they were one of the lost tribes of Israel, ending up in Britain—spent 1899 to 1901 recklessly digging up parts of the hill in a misguided search for the Ark of the Covenant.

Stand on the Hill of Tara. Think of the history it's seen, and survey Ireland. It's understandable why this "meeting place of heroes" continues to hold a powerful place in the Irish psyche (€2.10, covered by Heritage Card, includes video and 20-min guided walk, mid-May–mid-Sept daily 10:00–18:00, last tour 17:15; otherwise, access to site is free but visitors center is closed; tel. 046/902-5903). Local guide Jean Thornton, who works on-site, brings the lumpy mounds to life; if she's on duty, request her. Wear good walking shoes because the ground is uneven and often wet.

Old Mellifont Abbey

This Cistercian abbey (the first in Ireland) was established by French monks who came to the country in 1142 to bring the Irish monks more in line with Rome. (Even the abbey's architecture was unusual, marking the first time in Ireland that a formal, European-style monastic layout was used.) Cistercians lived isolated rural lives; lay monks worked the land, allowing the more educated monks to devote all their energy to prayer. After Henry VIII dissolved the abbey in 1539, centuries of locals used it as a handy quarry. Consequently, little survives beyond the octagonal lavabo, where the monks would ceremonially wash their hands before entering the refectory to eat. The lavabo gives a sense of the grandeur that the abbey once had. The excellent 45-minute tours, available upon request and included in your admission, give meaning to the site (€2.10, covered by Heritage Card, May–Sept daily 10:00–18:00, last entry 17:15, no tours Oct–April when site is free and you can explore on your own, tel. 041/982-6459).

Monasterboice

This ruined monastery is visit-worthy for its round tower and its ornately carved high crosses—two of the best such crosses in Ireland. In the Dark Ages, these crosses, illustrated from top to bottom with Bible stories, gave monks a teaching tool as they preached to the illiterate masses. Today Monasterboice, basically an old graveyard, is always open and free.

The 18-foot-tall Cross of Murdock (Muiredach's Cross, A.D. 923, named after an abbot) is considered the best high cross in Ireland. The circle—which characterizes the Irish high cross—could represent the perfection of God. Or, to help ease pagans into Christianity, it may represent the sun, which was worshipped in pre-Christian Celtic society. Whatever its symbolic purpose, its practical function was to support the weight of the crossbeam.

Face the cross (with the round tower in the background) and study the carved sandstone. The center panel shows the Last Judgment, with Christ under a dove, symbolizing the Holy Spirit. Those going to heaven are on Christ's right, and the damned are being ushered away by a pitchfork-wielding devil on his left.

Working down, you'll see the Archangel Michael weighing souls, as the Devil tugs demonically at the scales; the adoration of the three—or four—Magi; Moses strik-ing the rock to bring forth water; scenes from the life of David; and, finally, Adam, Eve, and the apple next to Cain slaying Abel. Imagine these carvings with their original, colorful paint jobs.

Find the even-taller cross nearest the tower. It seems the top section was broken off and buried for a period, protecting it from weathering. The bottom part remained standing, enduring the erosive effect of Irish weather and smearing the once-crisp features.

The door to the round tower was originally 15–20 feet above the ground (accessible by ladder). After centuries of burials, the ground level has risen.

Battle of the Boyne Site

One of Europe's great non-sights, this is simply the pastoral riv-erside site of the pivotal battle in which the Protestant British broke Catholic resistance, establishing Protestant rule over all Ireland and Britain. Drop into the information center next to the small parking lot and ask for a guided tour (free, May–Sept daily 10:00–17:45, last tour 16:45, closed Oct–April, tel. 041/980-9950, www.battleoftheboyne.ie). The attendant will generally take you on a 45-minute historic stroll around the Oldbridge Estate, on the south bank of the river.

It was here in 1690 that Protestant King William III, with his English and Dutch army, defeated his father-in-law—who was also his uncle—Catholic King James II, and his Irish and French army. King William's forces, on the north side of the Boyne, man-aged to cross the river, and by the end of the day, James was flee-ing south in full retreat. He soon departed Ireland, but his forces fought on until their final defeat two years later. James the Second (called "James da Turd" by those who scorn his lack of courage and leadership) never returned, and died a bitter ex-monarch in France. King William of Orange's victory, on the other hand, is still celebrated in Northern Ireland every July 12, with controver-sial marches by Unionist "Orangemen."

This site was bought in 1997 by the Office of Public Works as part of the Republic's governmental efforts to honor a site sacred to Unionists in Northern Ireland—despite the fact that the battle's outcome ensured Catholic subordination to the Protestant minor-ity for the next 230 years.

Trim

The sleepy, workaday town of Trim, straddling the Boyne River, is marked by the towering ruins of Trim Castle. Trim feels littered with mighty ruins that seem to say, "This little town was big-time...700 years ago." The tall Yellow Steeple (over the river from the castle) is all that remains of the 14th-century Augustinian Abbey of St. Mary. A pleasant half-mile walk back toward Dublin takes you to the sprawling ruins of Saints Peter and Paul Cathedral (from 1206), once the largest Gothic church in Ireland. Across the 15th-century Norman bridge from the cathedral are the 13th-century ruins of the Hospital of St. John the Baptist.

If you're flying into or out of Dublin Airport and don't want to deal with big-city Dublin, Trim is perfect—an easy 45-minute, 30-mile drive away. You can rent a car at the airport and make Trim your first overnight base (getting used to driving on the other side of the road in easier country traffic), or spend your last night here before returning your car at the airport. Either way, you don't need or want a car in Dublin (where parking is expensive and sightseeing is best on foot, or by bus or taxi).

ORIENTATION

Trim's main square is a traffic roundabout, and everything's within a block or two. Most of the shops and eateries are on or near Market Street, along with banks, a supermarket, and the launderette (Mon–Sat 9:00–18:00, closed Sun, Watergate Street, tel. 046/943-7176). The post office is tucked in the back of the Spar Market (Mon–Fri 9:00–13:00 & 14:00–17:30, Sat 9:00–13:00, closed Sun, Emmet Street). The library offers 30 minutes of free Internet access (Tue and Thu 10:00–20:30; Wed, Fri, and Sat 10:00–13:00 & 14:00–17:00; closed Sun–Mon, High Street).

Tourist Information

The TI is right next to the castle entrance and includes a handy coffee shop. Drop in for a free map and take a moment to ask them about Mel Gibson's visit to film *Braveheart* (Mon–Sat 9:30–17:30, Sun 12:00–17:30, shorter hours off-season, Castle Street, tel. 046/943-7227).

SIGHTS

▲▲**Trim Castle**—This is the biggest Norman castle in Ireland. Its mighty keep towers above a very ruined outer wall in a grassy riverside park at the edge of the sleepy town. The current castle was completed in the 1220s and served as a powerful Norman statement to the restless Irish natives. It remains an impressive sight—so impressive it was used in the 1994 filming of *Braveheart* (which was actually about Scotland's—not Ireland's—fight for freedom from the English).

The best-preserved walls ring the castle's southern perimeter and sport a barbican gate that contained two drawbridges. At the base of the castle walls, notice the cleverly angled "batter" wall—used by defenders who hurled down stones that banked off at great velocity into the attacking army.

The massive 70-foot-high central keep has 20 sides. Offering no place for invaders to hide, it was tough to attack. You can go inside only with the included 45-minute tour (2/hr). In a mostly hollow shell, you'll climb a series of tightly winding original staircases and modern, high catwalks, learn about life in the castle, and end at the top with great views of the walls and the countryside (€1.60 for castle grounds, €3.70 for entrance to keep and required tour, covered by Heritage Card; roughly April–Oct daily 10:00–18:00, last entry 17:00; Nov–March Sat–Sun only 10:00–17:00, last entry 16:00; tour spots are limited, so call in peak season to save frustration of arriving to find nothing available, tel. 046/943-8619). Make time to take a 15-minute walk outside, circling the castle walls and stopping at the informative plaques that show the castle from each viewpoint during its gory glory days. Night strollers are treated to views of the castle hauntingly lit in blue-green hues.

The Power & Glory—This is a grade-schoolish 30-minute slideshow overview of the personalities and history of the castle, followed by an exhibit on life here in Norman times (€3.20, Mon–Sat 10:00–12:30 & 14:30–17:00, Sun 12:00–17:00, shorter hours offseason, in visitors center with TI next to castle, Castle Street, tel. 046/943-7227). The show and a free cup of coffee help to pass the time as you wait for your castle tour.

SLEEPING

In and Near Trim

$$ Highfield House B&B, across the street from the castle and a five-minute walk from town, is a stately 175-year-old former maternity hospital, with hardwood floors and seven spacious, high-ceilinged rooms (Sb-€50–55, Db-€80–84, Tb-€99–110, family-friendly, free Internet access and Wi-Fi; overlooks roundabout where Dublin Road hits Trim, just before castle at Maudlins Road;

Trim

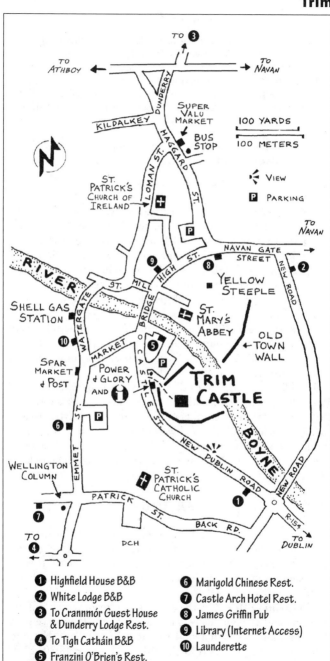

1 Highfield House B&B
2 White Lodge B&B
3 To Crannmór Guest House
   & Dunderry Lodge Rest.
4 To Tigh Catháin B&B
5 Franzini O'Brien's Rest.
6 Marigold Chinese Rest.
7 Castle Arch Hotel Rest.
8 James Griffin Pub
9 Library (Internet Access)
10 Launderette

Sleep Code

(€1 = about $1.30, country code: 353, area code: 046)
S = Single, **D** = Double/Twin, **T** = Triple, **Q** = Quad, **b** = bathroom,
s = shower only. Credit cards are accepted and breakfast is
included unless otherwise noted.

To help you easily sort through these listings, I've divided
the rooms into two categories, based on the price for a standard double room with bath:

$$ **Moderately Priced**—Most rooms more than €70.
 $ **Lower Priced**—Most rooms €70 or less.

---

tel. 046/943-6386, fax 046/943-8182, www.highfieldguesthouse
.com, highfieldhouseaccom@eircom.net, Geraldine Duignan).

$ White Lodge B&B, a 10-minute walk northwest of the
castle, has six comfortably unpretentious rooms with an oak-
and-granite lounge (Sb-€37–45, Db-€56–66, Tb-€75, Qb-€80,
free Internet access, parking, New Road, tel. 046/943-6549,
www.whitelodgetrim.com, whitelodgetrim@eircom.net, Todd
O'Loughlin).

Countryside B&Bs: These two B&Bs are in the quiet coun-
tryside about a mile outside of Trim (phone ahead for driving
directions). At **$$ Crannmór Guest House,** north of town, Anne
O'Regan decorates five rooms with cheery color schemes, and her
husband knows all the best fishing holes (Sb-€50–55, Db-€76–80,
Tb-€120, Dunderry Road, tel. 046/943-1635, fax 046/943-
8087, www.crannmor.com, cranmor@eircom.net). Mrs. Keane's
$$ Tigh Catháin B&B, southwest of town, has four bright, lacy
rooms with a comfy, rural feel (Db-€80–84, cash only, Longwood
Road, tel. 046/943-1996, www.tighcathaintrim.com, mariekeane
@esatclear.ie).

EATING

A country-market town, Trim offers basic meat-and-potatoes
lunch and dinner options. Don't waste time searching for gourmet
food. The restaurants and cafés along Market Street are friendly,
wholesome, and unpretentious (soup-and-sandwich delis close at
18:00).

Franzini O'Brien's is the only place in town with a fun din-
ner menu and enough business to make it work. They serve pasta,
steak, fish, and fajitas in a modern, candlelit ambience. Nothing's
Irish except the waiters (€15–26 dishes, Mon–Sat 18:30–22:00,

Sun 13:00–21:00, €20 two-course or €25 three-course early-bird dinners before 19:30, French's Lane, tel. 046/943-1002).

If you feel like Chinese food, **Marigold** fits the bill (Mon–Sat 17:00–24:00, Sun 16:00–24:00, Emmet Street, tel. 046/943-8788).

For a tasty splurge of gourmet cooking out in the country, get driving directions to **Dunderry Lodge,** four miles north of Trim off the Dunderry Road (Mon–Sat 19:30–21:30, Sun 12:30–14:30 & 18:30–20:30, €20 early-bird dinner Mon–Fri 17:30–19:00, tel. 046/943-1671).

The **Castle Arch Hotel,** popular with locals, serves hearty meals at reasonable prices in its bistro (€10–13 meals, daily 12:30–21:30, tel. 046/943-1516).

For an unvarnished pub experience, check out Trim's best watering hole, **James Griffin** (on High Street). It's full of local characters and old-fashioned atmosphere, with live Irish music on Monday and Thursday nights.

Groceries: **Super Valu** has everything you need to create a picnic (Mon–Sat 8:00–21:00, Sun 7:00–19:30, Haggard Street). The smaller **Spar Market** has fewer choices (Mon–Sat 8:00–21:00, Sun 9:00–21:00, Emmet Street).

TRANSPORTATION CONNECTIONS

Trim has no train station; the nearest is in Drogheda on the coast, but there are no bus connections to Trim from there.

Buses from Trim to **Dublin** (10/day, 1 hr) pick you up at the bus shelter next to the TI and castle entry on Castle Street.

South of Dublin: Glendalough and the Wicklow Mountains

The Wicklow Mountains, while only 10 miles south of Dublin, feel remote—enough so to have provided a handy refuge for opponents to English rule. Rebels who took part in the 1798 Irish uprising hid out here for years. When the frustrated British built a military road in 1800 to help flush out the rebels, the area became more accessible. Today, this same road—now R-115—takes you through the Wicklow area to Glendalough at its south end. While the valley is the darling of the Dublin day-trip tour organizers, it doesn't live up to the hype. But two blockbuster sights—Glendalough and the Gardens of Powerscourt—make a visit worth considering.

Getting Around

By car or tour, it's easy. If you lack wheels, take a tour. It's not worth the trouble on public transport.

By Car: It's a delight. Take N-11 south from Dublin Bray, then R-117 to Enniskerry (accommodation listed below), the gateway to the Wicklow Mountains. Signs direct you to the gardens and on to Glendalough. From Glendalough, if you're heading west, you can leave the valley (and pick up the highway to the west) over the famous but dull mountain pass called the Wicklow Gap.

By Tour from Dublin: Wild Wicklow Tours cover the region with an entertaining guide packing every minute with information and *craic* (good fun conversation). With a gang of 34 packed into tight but comfortable mountain-gripping buses, the guide kicks into gear from the first pickup in Dublin. Tours cover Dublin's embassy row, Dun Laoghaire, the Bay of Dublin (with the mansions of Ireland's rich and famous), the windy military road over scenic Sally Gap, and the Glendalough monasteries (€28, €25 for students and readers with this book in 2008, daily year-round, 9:10 pickup at Dublin TI on Suffolk Street, 10:00 pickup at Dun Laoghaire TI, stop for lunch at a pub—cost not included, return through Dun Laoghaire and on to Dublin by 17:30, Dun Laoghaire-ites could stay on the bus to continue into Dublin for the evening, advance booking required, tel. 01/280-1899, www.wildwicklow.ie).

Mary Gibbon's Tours visits both Glendalough and the Gardens of Powerscourt in a six-hour trip (€39, €35 students and readers with this book in 2008, 10:15 pickup at Dublin TI on Suffolk Street, 10:25 pickup at Royal Dublin Hotel on O'Connell Street, home by 17:00, call ahead to reserve—especially in high season, book direct rather than through TI, tel. 086/355-1355, www.newgrangetours.com, info@newgrangetours.com).

Over the Top Tours bypasses mansions and gardens to focus on Wicklow scenery. Stops include Glendalough, the Glenmacnass waterfall, and Blessington lakes (€28, 9:20 pickup at Gresham Hotel on O'Connell Street, 9:45 pickup at TI on Suffolk Street, return by 17:30, 14-seat minibus, reservations required, hold seat by leaving credit-card number, tel. 1-800-424-252, Dublin tel. 01/838-6128, www.overthetoptours.com).

SIGHTS

▲▲Gardens of Powerscourt

While the mansion's interior, only partially restored after a 1974 fire, isn't much, its meticulously kept aristocratic gardens are Ireland's best. The house was commissioned in the 1730s by Richard Wingfield, first viscount of Powerscourt. The gardens,

South of Dublin

created during the Victorian era (1858–1875), are called "the grand finale of Europe's formal gardening tradition...probably the last garden of its size and quality ever to be created." I'll buy that.

Upon entry, you'll get a flier laying out 40-minute and 60-minute walks. The "60-minute" walk takes 30 minutes at a slow amble. With the impressive summit of the Great Sugar Loaf Mountain as a backdrop, and a fine Japanese garden, Italian garden, and goofy pet cemetery along the way, this attraction provides the scenic greenery

I hoped to find in the rest of the Wicklow area. The lush movies *Barry Lyndon* and *The Count of Monte Cristo* were filmed in this well-watered aristocratic fantasy.

The Gardens of Powerscourt, a mile above the village of Enniskerry, cover several thousand acres within the 16,000-acre estate. The dreamy driveway alone is a mile long (€8 March–Oct, €6 Nov–Feb, daily 9:30–17:30 year-round, great cafeteria, tel. 01/204-6000, www.powerscourt.ie). Skip the associated waterfall (€5, 4 miles away).

Enniskerry: Drivers coming straight from Dublin Airport can stay overnight in Enniskerry at nearby Brook Cottage B&B, a quiet guesthouse offering comfortable beds and traditional break-fasts in a country setting (Sb-€60, Db-€90, studio with kitchen-€90; from Enniskerry clocktower go 1.7 miles up Kilgarron Hill toward Glencree, look for B&B sign on the right, turn left on Shop River Road—watch for *Children at Play* sign—and pass through green gates; tel. 01/276-6039, www.enniskerry.org, brookcottagebb@eircom.net, Mary and Jeff Drexler).

▲▲Military Road over Sally Gap

This is only for those with a car. From the Gardens of Powerscourt and Enniskerry, go to Glencree, where you drive the tiny military road over Sally Gap and through the best scenery of the Wicklow Mountains. Look for the German military cemetery, built for U-boat sailors who washed ashore in World War II. Near Sally Gap, notice the peat bogs and the freshly cut peat bricks drying in the wind. Many locals are nostalgic for the "good old days," when homes were peat-fire heated. At the Sally Gap junction, turn left, where a road winds through the vast Guinness estate. Look down on the glacial lake (Lough Tay) and the Guinness mansion (famous for jet-set parties). Nicknamed "Guinness Lake," the water looks like Ireland's favorite dark-brown stout, and the sand of the beach actually looks like the head of a Guinness beer. From here, the road meanders scenically down into the village of Roundwood and on to Glendalough.

▲▲Glendalough

The steep wooded slopes of Glendalough (GLEN-da-lock, "valley of the two lakes"), at the south end of Wicklow's military road, hides Ireland's most impressive monastic settlement. Founded by St. Kevin in the sixth century, the monastery flourished (despite repeated Viking raids) throughout the Age of Saints and Scholars until the English destroyed it in 1398. While it was finally aban-doned during the Dissolution of the Monasteries in 1539, pilgrims kept coming, especially on St. Kevin's Day, June 3. (This might have something to do with the fact that a pope said seven visits to

Glendalough had the same indulgence value as one visit to Rome.) While much restoration was done in the 1870s, most of the buildings date from the 8th–12th centuries.

The valley sights are split between the two lakes. The lower lake has the visitors center and the best buildings. The upper lake has scant ruins and feels like a state park, with a grassy lakeside picnic area and school groups. Walkers and hikers will enjoy a choice of nine different trails of varying lengths through the lush Wicklow countryside (longest loop takes four hours, hiking-trail maps available at visitors center).

Planning Your Time: Park free at the Glendalough Visitors Centre. Visit the center, wander the ruins (free) around the round tower, walk the traffic-free Green Road one mile to the upper lake, and then walk back to your car. Or you can drive to the upper lake (more free parking, except July–Aug, when it's €5). If you're rushed, skip the upper lake. Summer tour-bus crowds are terrible all day on weekends and 11:00–14:00 on weekdays.

Glendalough Visitors Centre: Start your visit here (€2.90, covered by Heritage Card, mid-March–mid-Oct daily 9:30–18:00, mid-Oct–mid-March closes at 17:00, last entry 45 min before closing, tel. 0404/45325). The 20-minute video provides a good thumbnail background on monastic society in medieval Ireland. While the video is more general than specific to Glendalough, the adjacent museum room features this particular monastic settlement. The model in the center of the room re-creates the fortified village of the year 1050 (although there were no black-and-white Frisian cows in Ireland back then—they would have been red). A browse through the interactive exhibits here shows the contribution these monks made to intellectual life in Dark Age Europe (such as illuminated manuscripts and Irish minuscule, a more compact alphabet developed in the seventh century).

From the center, a short and scenic walk along the Green Road takes you to the round tower.

The Monastic Village: Easily the best ruins of Glendalough gather around the famous 110-foot-tall round tower. Towers like this (usually 60–110 feet tall) were standard features in such settlements, functioning as bell towers, storage lofts, beacons for pilgrims, and last-resort refuges during Viking raids (though given enough warning, monks were safer hiding in the surrounding forest). The towers had a high door with a pull-up ladder. Several ruined churches (8th–12th centuries) and a sea of grave markers complete this evocative scene. Markers give short descriptions of the ruined buildings.

In an Ireland without cities, these monastic communities were mainstays of civilization. They were remote outposts where ascetics (with a taste for scenic settings) gathered to commune with God. In the 12th century, with the arrival of grander monastic orders such as the Franciscans and the Dominicans and with the growth of cities, these monastic communities were eclipsed. Today, Ireland is dotted with the reminders of this age: illuminated manuscripts, simple churches, carved crosses, and about 100 round towers.

Upper Lake: The Green Road continues one mile farther up the valley to the upper lake. The oldest ruins—scant and hard to find—lie near this lake. If you want a scenic Wicklow walk, begin here.

KILKENNY and the
ROCK OF CASHEL

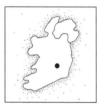

If you're driving from Dublin (on Ireland's east coast) to Dingle (on Ireland's west coast), the best two stops to break the long journey are Kilkenny, often called Ireland's finest medieval town, and the Rock of Cashel, a thought-provoking early Christian site crowning the Plain of Tipperary. With a few extra days, there are additional worthwhile destinations along the southeast coast, such as Waterford and County Wexford (described in the next chapter). Folks with even more time can continue on the scenic southern coastal route west via Cobh, Kinsale, Kenmare, and the Ring of Kerry (covered in the Kinsale/Cobh and Kenmare/Ring of Kerry chapters).

Kilkenny

Famous as "Ireland's loveliest inland city," Kilkenny gives you a feel for salt-of-the-earth Ireland. Its castle and cathedral stand like historic bookends on either end of a higgledy-piggledy High Street of colorful shops and medieval facades. It's nicknamed the "Marble City" for its nearby quarry (actually black limestone, not marble), and you can still see the white seashells fossilized within the black stone steps around town. While a small town today (fewer than 10,000 residents), Kilkenny has a big history. It used to be an important center—occasionally even the capital of Ireland in the Middle Ages.

Kilkenny is a good overnight for drivers wanting to break the journey from Dublin to Dingle (necessary if you want to spend more time in the Wicklow area and at the Rock of Cashel).

Kilkenny and Cashel

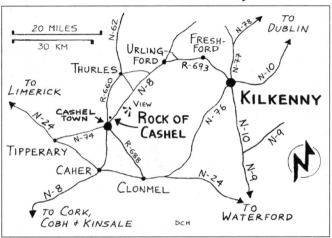

A night in Kilkenny comes with plenty of traditional folk music in the pubs (hike over the river and up John Street).

ORIENTATION

(area code: 056)

Tourist Information
The TI is a block off the bridge in the 16th-century Shee Alms poorhouse (June–Aug Mon–Fri 9:00–18:00, Sat 10:00–18:00, Sun 11:00–17:00; Sept–May closed Sun, Rose Inn Street, tel. 056/775-1500).

Arrival in Kilkenny
The train/bus station is four blocks from John's Bridge, which marks the center of town.

If arriving by car, the two handiest places to park are in the lot next to the castle (buy €1.20 parking disks at local shops, closest is Kilkenny Crystal or the TI, both on Rose Inn Street across from west end of castle parking lot, buy one for each hour you want to stay, 3 hours maximum in one parking space, scratch off your arrival time and leave it on your dash) or in the multistory parking garage on Ormonde Street (€1.60/hr, or just get the 5-day pass for €14 if staying overnight).

Helpful Hints
Internet Access and Bus Tickets: Café Net at 4 Patrick Street sells bus tickets and surf time (€4/hour, June–Aug Mon–Fri

8:00–18:00, Sat 9:00–17:00, Sun 12:00–18:00; Sept–May closed Sun; tel. 056/777-0051).

Post Office: It's on High Street (Mon–Fri 9:00–17:30, Sat 9:00–13:00, closed Sun).

Laundry: Hennessy's is at 18 Parliament Street (Mon–Sat 8:30–18:00, closed Sun).

TOURS

Bus Tours—City Sightseeing's hop-on, hop-off bus tours cover the town in one hour, making 13 stops along the way (€10, June–Sept only, pay driver; departs Kilkenny Castle at 10:30, 11:30, 12:30, 14:00, 15:00, 16:00, and 17:00; ticket valid 24 hours, www.city -sightseeing.com).

Local Guide—Pat Tynan offers hour-long guided town walks departing from the TI (€6; mid-March–Oct Mon–Sat at 10:30, 12:15, 15:00, and 16:30, Sun at 11:15 and 12:30; Nov–mid-March Sat only at 10:30, 12:15, and 15:00; mobile 087-265-1745).

SIGHTS

▲**Kilkenny Castle**—Dominating the town, this castle is a stony reminder that the Anglo-Norman Butler family controlled Kilkenny for 500 years. Tours

start with a 12-minute video explaining how the wooden fort built here by Strongbow in 1172 evolved into a 17th-century château. Now restored to its later Victorian splendor, the castle's highlight is the beautiful family-portrait gallery, which puts you face-to-face with the wealthy Butler family ghosts. Tours start running 30 minutes after the castle opens for the day and fill fast; they are first-come, first-served, and can be booked only for the same day (€5.30, covered by Heritage Card, daily June–Aug 9:30–19:00, April–May 10:30–17:00, Sept 10:00–18:30, Oct–March 10:30–12:45 & 14:00–17:00, tel. 056/772-1450).

The **Kilkenny Design Centre,** across the street from the castle in grand old stables, is full of local crafts and offers handy cafeteria lunches upstairs (April–Dec Mon–Sat 10:00–19:00, Sun 11:00–19:00; Jan–March Mon–Sat 10:00–19:00, closed Sun; www .kilkennydesign.com).

St. Canice's Cathedral—This 13th-century cathedral is early-English Gothic, rich with stained glass, medieval carvings, and

Kilkenny

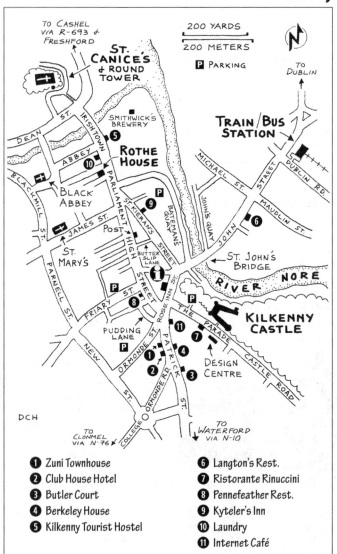

1. Zuni Townhouse
2. Club House Hotel
3. Butler Court
4. Berkeley House
5. Kilkenny Tourist Hostel
6. Langton's Rest.
7. Ristorante Rinuccini
8. Pennefeather Rest.
9. Kyteler's Inn
10. Laundry
11. Internet Café

floors paved in history. Check out the model of the old walled town in its 1641 heyday (€4, €6 combo-ticket with tower, €7 combo-ticket with Rothe House; June–Aug Mon–Sat 9:00–18:00, Sun 14:00–17:00; April, May, and Sept Mon–Sat 10:00–13:00 & 14:00–17:00, Sun 14:00–17:00; Oct–March Mon–Sat 10:00–13:00 & 14:00–16:00, Sun 14:00–16:00; tel. 056/776-4971, www.cashel.anglican .org/cances.shtm). The 100-foot-tall round **tower,** built as part of a long-gone pre-Norman church, recalls the need for a watchtower and refuge. The fun ladder-climb to the top affords a grand view of the countryside (€3, €6 combo-ticket with cathedral).

Rothe House—This well-preserved Tudor merchant's house expanded around interior courtyards as the prosperous family grew. The museum, which also serves as the County Kilkenny genealogy center, runs a 15-minute video giving a glimpse of life here in Elizabethan times (€4, €7 combo-ticket with St. Canice's Cathedral; April–Oct Mon–Sat 10:30–17:00, Sun 15:00–17:00; Nov–March Mon–Sat 10:30–16:45, closed Sun; Parliament Street, tel. 056/772-2893).

SLEEPING

$$$ Zuni Townhouse is an elegant splurge, with 13 boutique-chic rooms sporting colorfully angular furnishings above a fashionable restaurant. Ask about two-night weekend breaks and midweek specials that include a four-course dinner (Sb-€70–140, Db-€120–170, Tb-€180–255, parking in back, 26 Patrick Street, tel. 056/772-3999, fax 056/775-6400, www.zuni.ie, info@zuni.ie).

$$$ Club House Hotel is perfectly central. Originally a gentlemen's sporting club, it comes with old-time Georgian elegance; a palatial, well-antlered breakfast room; and 35 large, comfy bedrooms (Sb-€70–90, Db-€140–160, 10 percent discount with this

Kilkenny

Sleep Code

(€1 = about $1.30, country code: 353, area code: 056)
S = Single, **D** = Double/Twin, **T** = Triple, **Q** = Quad, **b** = bathroom, **s** = shower only. All of these places include breakfast and accept credit cards.

   To help you easily sort through these listings, I've divided the rooms into three categories, based on the price for a standard double room with bath:

   $$$ Higher Priced—Most rooms €130 or more.
   $$ Moderately Priced—Most rooms between €80–130.
   $ Lower Priced—Most rooms €80 or less.

book in 2008, Patrick Street, tel. 056/772-1994, fax 056/777-1920, www.clubhousehotel.com, clubhse@iol.ie).

$$$ Butler Court, across the street and uphill from the Club House Hotel, is Kilkenny's best lodging value. Ever-helpful Yvonne offers 10 modern rooms behind cheery yellow walls (Sb-€60–110, Db-€100–140, Tb-€160–180, accessible to wheelchair users, continental breakfast in room, Patrick Street, tel. 056/776-1178, fax 056/779-0767, www.butlercourt.com, info@butlercourt.com).

$$ Berkeley House, with 10 rooms across the street and downhill from the Club House Hotel, is small, affordable, and comfortable (Db-€90–120, Tb-€120–150, 5 Lower Patrick Street, tel. 056/776-4848, fax 056/776-4829, www.berkeleyhousekilkenny.com, berkeleyhouse@eircom.net).

$ Kilkenny Tourist Hostel, filling a fine Georgian townhouse in the town center, offers cheap beds, a friendly family room, a well-equipped members' kitchen, and a wealth of local information (dorm bed-€16–17, D-€42, Q-€76, cash only, laundry service-€5, 2 blocks from cathedral at 35 Parliament Street, tel. 056/776-3541, www.kilkennyhostel.ie, info@kilkennyhostel.ie).

EATING

Langton's serves quality Irish dishes under a Tiffany-skylight expanse (€12–15 lunches, €16–25 dinners, daily 8:00–22:30, 69 John Street, tel. 056/776-5133), while **Ristorante Rinuccini** provides your classy, candlelit Italian fix (€10–16 lunches, €19–28 dinners, daily 12:00–14:30 & 17:30–22:30, €28 three-course early-bird special before 19:00, 1 The Parade, tel. 056/776-1575).

Zuni is a stylish splurge, offering international cuisine (Mon–Wed 12:30–14:30 & 18:00–21:00, Thu–Sat 12:30–14:30 & 18:30–21:30, Sun 13:00–15:00 & 18:00–21:00, €23 two-course and €28 three-course early-bird specials before 19:30 every night but Sat, weekend reservations smart, 26 Patrick Street, 056/772-3999).

Pennefeather Restaurant, above the Kilkenny Book Centre, is good for a quick, light lunch (Mon–Fri 9:00–17:30, Sat 9:00–17:00, closed Sun, 10 High Street, tel. 056/776-4063).

Kyteler's Inn serves basic pub grub in a timber-and-stone atmosphere. Visit their fun 14th-century cellar and ask about their witch (Mon–Sat 12:00–21:00, Sun 12:00–20:00, 27 St. Kieran's Street, tel. 056/772-1064). Try a pint of Smithwick's in its hometown.

TRANSPORTATION CONNECTIONS

From Kilkenny by Train to: Dublin (4/day, 2 hrs), **Waterford** (4/day, 45 min).

By Bus to: Dublin (7/day, 2 hrs), **Waterford** (2/day, 1 hr), **Tralee** (3/day, 5 hrs), **Galway** (6/day, 4.5 hrs).

Rock of Cashel

Rising high above the fertile Plain of Tipperary, the Rock of Cashel—worth ▲▲▲—is one of Ireland's most historic and

evocative sights. Seat of the ancient kings of Munster (c. A.D. 300–1100), this is where St. Patrick baptized King Aengus in about A.D. 450. Strategically located and perfect for fortification, the Rock was fought over by local clans for hundreds of years. Finally, in 1101, clever Murtagh O'Brien gave the Rock to the Church. His seemingly benevolent donation increased his influence with the Church, while preventing his rivals, the powerful McCarthy clan, from regaining possession of the Rock. As Cashel evolved into an ecclesiastical center, Iron Age ring forts and thatch dwellings gave way to the majestic stone church buildings enjoyed by visitors today.

Cost and Hours: €5.30, families-€11.50, covered by Heritage Card, daily early June–mid-Sept 9:00–19:00; mid-March–early June and mid-Sept–mid-Oct 9:00–17:30; mid-Oct–mid-March 9:00–16:30; last entry 45 minutes before closing. Parking will cost you €3 (buy parking ticket at machine inside lot, display on dashboard).

Orientation: At the base of the Rock and next to the parking lot, you'll see WCs (none up on Rock) and the Bru Boru Cultural Centre (see page 121); you may want to visit the center to learn more about the Rock before you ascend.

It's a steep 100-yard walk up to the Rock itself. On this 200-foot-high outcrop of limestone, the first building you'll encounter is the 15th-century Hall of the Vicars Choral, housing the ticket desk, a tiny museum (with an original 12th-century high cross dedicated to St. Patrick and a few replica artifacts), and a 20-minute video (2/hr, shown in the hall's former dormitory). You'll also find a round tower, an early Christian cross, a delightful Romanesque chapel, and a ruined Gothic cathedral, all surrounded by my favorite Celtic-cross graveyard. Bring a coat for the deceptively cool conditions on the high, windy, exposed Rock.

Crowd-Beating Tips: Summer crowds flock to the Rock (worst June–Aug 11:00–15:00). Try to plan your visit for early or late in the day. If you're here at a peak time, tour the Rock first and save the movie, museum, and Hall of the Vicars Choral for the end of your visit, when the tourist tide has receded. Otherwise, see the movie and museum first.

Tours: Call ahead for the tour schedule (included in entry price, 45 min, tel. 062/61437). Otherwise, set your own pace with the tour I've outlined below.

SELF-GUIDED TOUR

Exploring the Rock of Cashel

• *Follow this tour counterclockwise around the Rock. To start the tour, climb the stairs opposite the ticket desk.*

❶ **Hall of the Vicars Choral:** This is the youngest building on the Rock (early 1400s). It housed the minor clerics appointed to sing during cathedral services. These vicars—who were granted nearby lands by the archbishop—lived comfortably here, with a large fireplace and white, lime-washed walls (to reflect light and act as a natural disinfectant). Window seats gave the blessedly literate vicars the best light to read by. The furniture is original, but the oak timber roof is a reconstruction, built to medieval specifications using wooden dowels instead of nails. The large wall tapestry, showing King Solomon with the Queen of Sheba, contains intentional errors—to remind viewers that only God can create perfection. The vicars, who formed a sort of corporate body to assist the bishop with local administration, used a special seal to authorize documents such as land leases. You can see an enlarged wooden copy of the seal (hanging above the fireplace), depicting eight vicars surrounding a seated organist. It was a good system—until some of the greedier vicars duplicated the seal for their own purposes, forcing the archbishop to curtail its use.

• *Go outside the hall and find...*

❷ **St. Patrick's Cross:** St. Patrick baptized King Aengus at the Rock of Cashel around A.D. 450. Legend has it that St. Patrick, intensely preoccupied with the holy ceremony, accidentally speared the foot of the king with his crosier staff while administering the baptismal sacrament. But the pagan king stoically held his tongue until the end of the ceremony, thinking this was part of the painful process of becoming a Christian.

This 12th-century cross, a stub of its former glory, was carved to celebrate the handing over of the Rock to the Church 650 years after St. Patrick's visit. Typical Irish high crosses use a ring around the cross' head to support its arms and to symbolize the sun (making Christianity more appealing to the sun-worshipping Celts). But instead, this cross uses the Latin design: The weight of the arms is supported by two vertical beams on each side of the main shaft, representing the two criminals who were crucified beside

Rock of Cashel

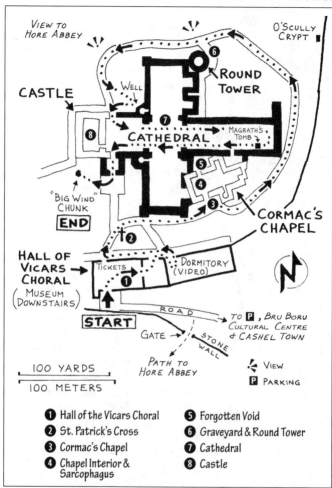

VIEW TO HORE ABBEY

O'SCULLY CRYPT

⑥ ROUND TOWER

CASTLE

WELL

⑦

⑧   CATHEDRAL   → MAGRATH'S TOMB

⑤

④

"BIG WIND" CHUNK

END

⑬ ⑫

③   CORMAC'S CHAPEL

HALL OF VICARS CHORAL →

TICKETS

DORMITORY (VIDEO)

①

(MUSEUM DOWNSTAIRS)

START

ROAD

GATE →

TO 🅿, BRU BORU CULTURAL CENTRE & CASHEL TOWN

STONE WALL

PATH TO HORE ABBEY

VIEW

🅿 PARKING

|——— 100 YARDS ———|
|——— 100 METERS ———|

N

1 Hall of the Vicars Choral
2 St. Patrick's Cross
3 Cormac's Chapel
4 Chapel Interior & Sarcophagus
5 Forgotten Void
6 Graveyard & Round Tower
7 Cathedral
8 Castle

Christ (today only one of these supports remains).

On my first visit, 25 years ago, the original cross still stood here. But centuries of wind and rain slowly eroded away important detail, so the cross was moved into the adjacent museum and replaced by this replica.

• *Turn your back on St. Patrick's Cross, and walk about 100 feet slightly uphill along the gravel path beside the cathedral. Roughly opposite the far end of the Hall of the Vicars Choral is the entry to...*

❸ Cormac's Chapel: As the wild Celtic Christian church was reined in and reorganized by Rome 850 years ago, new architectural influences from continental Europe began to emerge on the

remote Irish landscape. This small chapel—Ireland's first and finest Romanesque church, consecrated in 1134 by King Cormac MacCarthy—reflects this evolution. Travel in your imagination back to the 12th century, when this chapel and the tall round tower (described below) were the only stone structures on the Rock.

The "new" Romanesque style reflected the ancient Roman basilica floor plan. Its columns and rounded arches created an overall effect of massiveness and strength. Romanesque churches were like dark fortresses with thick walls, squat towers, few windows, and minimal decoration. Irish stone churches of this period (like the one at Glendalough in the Wicklow Mountains) were simple rectangular buildings with no ornate stone carving at all.

Tradition says that the chapel's easy-to-cut sandstone was quarried 12 miles away, and the blocks were passed from hand to hand back to the Rock. The two square towers resemble those in Regensburg, Germany, further suggesting that well-traveled medieval Irish monks brought back new ideas from the Continent.

• The modern, dark-glass chapel door (always unlocked) is a recent addition to keep out nesting birds. Enter the chapel (remembering to close the door behind you) and let your eyes adjust to the low light.

❹ Chapel Interior: Just inside the chapel is an empty stone **sarcophagus.** Nobody knows for sure whose body once lay here (possibly the brother of King Cormac MacCarthy). The damaged front relief is carved in the Scandinavian Urnes style. Vikings raided Ireland, intermarried with the Irish, and were melting into Irish society by the time this chapel was built. Some scholars interpret the relief design (a tangle of snakes and beasts) as a figure-eight lying on its side, looping back and forth forever, symbolizing the eternity of the afterlife.

With your back to the sarcophagus, let your eyes wander around the chapel interior. You're standing in the **nave,** lit by the three windows (partially blocked by the later cathedral) in the wall behind you. Overhead is a round vaulted ceiling with support ribs. The strong round arches support not only the heavy stone roof, but also the (unseen) second-story scriptorium chamber, where monks once carefully copied manuscripts.

The **chancel arch,** studded with fist-sized heads, framed the altar (now gone). The lower heads are more grotesque, while those nearing the top become serene as they climb closer to God. The arch is off-center in relation to the nave, symbolic of Christ's head drooping to the side as he died on the cross.

Walk into the chancel and look up at the ceiling, examining the faint **frescoes,** a labor of love from 850 years ago. Frescoes are rare in Ireland because of the perpetually moist climate. (Mixing pigments into wet plaster worked better in dry climates like Italy.) Once vividly colorful, then fading over time, these frescoes were further damaged during the Reformation. Such ornamentation was considered vain by Protestants, who piously whitewashed over them. These surviving frescoes were discovered under multiple whitewash layers during painstaking modern restoration. The rich blue color came from lapis lazuli, an expensive gemstone imported from Asia.

• *Walk through the other modern, dark-glass doorway (don't let the birds in), opposite the door you used to enter the chapel. You'll find yourself in a...*

❺ Forgotten Void: This enclosed space (roughly 30 feet square) was created when the newer cathedral was wedged between the older chapel and the round tower. Once the main entrance into the chapel, this forgotten doorway is crowned by a finely carved tympanum decorating the arch above it. It's perfectly preserved because the huge cathedral shielded it from the elements. The large lion (symbol of St. Mark's gospel) is being hunted by a centaur (half-man, half-horse) archer wearing a Norman helmet (essential conehead attire in the late Middle Ages).

As you exit the chapel (turning left), take a look at the more exposed and weathered tympanum outside, above the south entrance. The carved bloated "hippo" is actually a bull, part of St. Luke's apocalyptic vision.

• *Tiptoe through the tombstones around the east end of the cathedral to the base of the round tower.*

❻ Graveyard and Round Tower: This graveyard still takes permanent guests—but only those put on a waiting list by their ancestors in 1930. A handful of these chosen few are still alive, and once they're gone, the graveyard will be considered full. The 20-foot-tall shaft at the edge of the graveyard, marking the O'Scully family crypt, was once crowned by an elaborately carved Irish high cross—destroyed during a lightning storm in 1976.

Look out over the **Plain of Tipperary.** Called the "Golden Vale," its rich soil makes it Ireland's most prosperous farmland. In St. Patrick's time, it was covered with oak forests. A path leads to the ruined 13th-century **Hore Abbey** in the fields below (free, always open and peaceful). The abbey is named for the Cistercian monks who wore simple gray robes, roughly the same color as hoarfrost (the ice crystals that form on morning grass).

Gaze up at the **round tower,** the first stone structure built on the Rock after the Church took over in 1101. The shape of these towers is unique to Ireland. Though you might think towers like this were chiefly intended as a place to hide in case of invasion, they were instead used primarily as bell towers and lookout posts. (Enemies could smoke out anyone inside the tower, and with enough warning, monks were better off

concealing themselves in the countryside.) The tower stands 92 feet tall, with walls over three feet thick. The doorway, which once had a rope ladder, was built high up not only for security, but also because having it at ground level would have weakened the foundation of the top-heavy structure. The interior once contained wooden floors connected by ladders, and served as safe storage for the monks' precious sacramental treasures. The tower's stability is impressive when you consider its age, the winds it has endured, and the shallowness of its foundation (only five feet under present ground level).

Continue walking around the cathedral's north transept, noticing the square holes in the exterior walls. During construction, wooden scaffolding was anchored into these holes. On your way to the cathedral entrance, in the corner where the north transept joins the nave, you'll pass a small **well.** Without this essential water source, the Rock could never have withstood a siege, and would not have been as valuable to clans and clergy. In 1848, a chalice was dredged from the well, likely thrown there by fleeing medieval monks intending to survive a raid. They didn't make it. (If they had, they would have retrieved the chalice.)

• *Now enter the...*

❼ **Cathedral:** Traditionally, the choir of a church (where the clergy celebrate Mass) faces east, while the nave (where the congregation stands) stretches off to the west. Because this cathedral was squeezed between the pre-existing chapel, round tower, and drinking well, the builders were forced to improvise—giving it an extra-long choir and a cramped nave.

Built between 1230 and 1290, the church's pointed arches and high, narrow windows proclaim the Gothic style of the period (and let in more light than earlier Romanesque churches). Walk under the central bell tower and look up at the rib-vaulted **ceiling.** The hole in the middle was for a rope used to ring the church bells. The wooden roof is long gone. When Lord Inchiquin (Oliver Cromwell's general) attacked the town of Cashel in 1647, hundreds of townsfolk fled to the sanctuary of this cathedral and held out. Inchiquin packed turf around the exterior and burned it down, massacring those inside.

Rock of Cashel

Ascend the **terraces** at the choir end of the cathedral, where the main altar once stood. Stand on the gravestones (of the 16th-century rich and famous) with your back to the open east wall (where the narrow windows have crumbled away) and look back down toward the nave. The right wall of the choir is filled with graceful Gothic windows, while the solid left wall hides Cormac's Chapel (which would have blocked any sunlight). The line of stone supports on the left wall once held the long, wooden balcony where the vicars sang. Closer to the altar, high on the same wall, is a small, rectangular window called the "leper's squint"—which allowed unsightly lepers to view the altar during Mass without offending the congregation.

The grand **wall tomb** on the left contains the remains of archbishop Miler Magrath, the "scoundrel of Cashel," who lived to be 100. From 1570 to 1622, Magrath was the Protestant archbishop of Cashel who simultaneously profited from his previous position as Catholic bishop of Down. He married twice, had lots of kids, confiscated the ornate tomb lid here from another bishop's grave, and converted back to Catholicism on his deathbed.

• *Walk back down to the far end of the nave and exit the cathedral on the left, through the porch entrance.*

❽ **Castle:** Back outside, stand beside the huge chunk of wall debris and try to picture where it might have fit in the ruins above. This end of the cathedral was converted into an archbishop's castle in the 1400s (shortening the nave even more). Looking high into the castle's damaged top floors, you can see the bishop's residence chamber and the secret passageways that were once hidden in the thick walls. Lord Inchiquin's cannons weakened the structure during the 1647 massacre, and in 1848, a massive storm (known as "Night of the Big Wind" in Irish lore) flung the huge chunk next to you from the ruins above.

In the mid-1700s, the Anglican Church transferred cathedral status to St. John's in town, and the archbishop abandoned the drafty Rock for a more comfortable residence, leaving the ruins that you see today.

SIGHTS

Near the Rock of Cashel

Bru Boru Cultural Centre—Nestled below the Rock of Cashel parking lot, next to the statue of the three blissed-out dancers, this center adds to your understanding of the Rock in its wider historical and cultural context. The highlight of the Sounds of History museum downstairs is the exhibit showing the Rock's gradual evolution from ancient ring fort to grand church ruins—projected down onto a large disc that visitors gather around.

Those headed for Dingle's great traditional music scene will enjoy the surprisingly good 15-minute film introduction to Irish traditional music in the small museum theater (€5, June–Sept Tue–Sat 9:00–22:30, closed Sun–Mon; Oct–May Mon–Fri 9:00–17:00, closed Sat–Sun; cafeteria, tel. 062/61122).

If you stay overnight in Cashel, consider taking in a performance of the Bru Boru musical dance troupe in the center's large theater (€18, €48 with dinner, mid-June–mid-Sept Tue–Sat at 21:00).

Town of Cashel—The huggable town at the base of the Rock affords a good break on the long drive from Dublin to Dingle (**TI** open daily 9:30–17:30; Nov–mid-March closed Sat–Sun, tel. 062/62511). The Heritage Centre, next door to the TI, presents a modest six-minute audio explanation of Cashel's history around a walled town model.

SLEEPING

(€1 = about $1.30, country code: 353, area code: 062)
If you spend the night in Cashel, you'll be treated to views of the ruins beautifully illuminated at night.

$$$ Legends Guesthouse has seven pleasant rooms (some with views of the floodlit ruins) above a friendly restaurant in a convenient location near the base of the Rock (Sb-€50–90, Db-€100–140, Tb-€120–150, non-smoking, parking, The Kiln, tel. 062/61292, www.legendsguesthouse.com, info@legendsguesthouse.com).

$ Rockville House, with six fine rooms, is close to the Rock (Sb-€39, Db-€52–60, Tb-€75–90, parking behind, Dominic Street, tel. 062/61760).

$ Abbey House, a bit farther toward town, has five comfortable rooms cheerily tended to by Ellen Ryan (Sb-€50, D-€60, Db-€70, Dominic Street, tel. & fax 062/61104, teachnamainstreach @eircom.net).

$ Cashel Lodge, well kept and a step above most other hostels, is housed in an old stone grain warehouse behind the rock near the Hore Abbey (dorm beds-€17.50, Db-€55–60, Tb-€65–70, camping spots-€8/person, laundry service-€10, Dundrum Road

R-505, tel. 062/61003, fax 062/62797, www.cashel-lodge.com, info@cashel-lodge.com).

EATING

Grab a soup-and-sandwich lunch at tiny **Granny's Kitchen** (next to the parking lot at the base of the Rock) or at snug **King Cormac's** (a block away, near the base of the road up to the Rock).

For a splurge dinner, consider the classy **Chez Hans** (two-course €27.50 early-bird menu before 19:15, otherwise €25–37 entrées, Tue–Sat 18:00–22:00, closed Sun–Mon, in an old church a block below the Rock, tel. 062/61177). The same folks also run the cheaper **Chez Hans Café** up the street, serving lunch until closing (€11–16 meals, Tue–Sat 12:00–17:30, closed Sun–Mon).

Legends Restaurant offers good dinners with great night-time views of the lit-up Rock (daily 12:00–19:00, The Kiln, behind hedge beside main parking lot, tel. 062/61292).

TRANSPORTATION CONNECTIONS

Cashel has no train station; the closest one is 13 miles away in the town of Thurles.

From Cashel by Bus to: Dublin (6/day, 3 hrs), **Kilkenny** (3/day, 2.5 hrs), **Waterford** (6/day, 2 hrs).

Rock of Cashel

WATERFORD AND COUNTY WEXFORD

The best overnight stop in southeast Ireland is the historic Viking and Norman beachhead town of Waterford. From here, you can explore the varied sights of County Wexford. Throughout your travels, you'll see evidence of the region's Norman roots in its high concentration of family names with old Norman (French) prefixes: De Berg, De Lacy, Devereux, Fitzgilbert, Fitzsimmons, Fitzgerald, and so on.

Waterford

The oldest city in Ireland, Waterford was once more important than Dublin. Today, while tourists associate the town's name with its famous crystal, locals are quick to remind you that the crystal is named after the town, and not vice versa. That said, Waterford is a plain, gray, workaday town. Pubs outnumber cafés, and freighters offload cargo at the dock. It's a dose of gritty Ireland, with fewer leprechauns per capita than other Irish destinations. Wandering the back streets, you're reminded that until a couple of generations ago, Ireland was one of the poorest countries in Western Europe.

Planning Your Time

A day is more than enough time for Waterford. Visit the crystal factory, located on the south edge of town, on your way in or out to avoid the midday crowds (the TI at the factory has a free visitor's guide with a town map). In Waterford, your best activity is the historic walk (at 11:45 or 13:45 in peak season, see "Tours" on page 126), followed by a visit to the Waterford Museum of Treasures and

Reginald's Tower. To feel the pulse of contemporary Waterford, hang out on the town's pedestrian square and stroll through its big, modern shopping mall.

ORIENTATION

(area code: 051)

Waterford's main drag runs along its ugly harbor, where you'll find the bus station and easy parking lots (€5.50/24 hrs, pay at automated station before driving out gate). All recommended accommodations and sights (except the Waterford Crystal Factory tour) are within a 10-minute walk of the harbor. Both museums and the TI are on the harborfront. The stubby two-story Victorian clock tower marks the middle of the harbor. It's also the start of the pedestrian Barronstrand Street, which runs a block inland to the town square.

Tourist Information

The TI is inside the old brick granary warehouse on Merchant's Quay (July–Aug Mon–Fri 9:15–18:00, Sat 10:00–18:00, Sun 11:00–17:00; April–June and Sept–Oct Mon–Fri 9:00–18:00, Sat 10:00–18:00, closed Sun; Nov–March Mon–Sat 9:15–17:00, closed Sun; tel. 051/875-823). As with all Irish TIs, it's basically a shop with a counter where clerks tell you about places that they endorse (i.e., get money from).

City Pass Ticket: If you're visiting all three participating town sights (Waterford Museum of Treasures-€7, Reginald's Tower-€2.10, and Waterford Crystal Factory-€9.50), you'll save €6.90 in admissions by buying the €11.70 City Pass Ticket (sold at TI and each sight).

Helpful Hints

Internet Access: Handy **Voyager Internet** is on the waterfront at 85 Parade Quay (€3.50/30 min, Mon–Sat 10:00–21:00, Sun 14:00–18:00, tel. 051/843-843).

Post Office: It's on Parade Quay (Mon–Fri 9:00–17:30, Sat 9:00–13:00, closed Sun).

Laundry: Snow White launderette is at 61 Mayor's Walk (Mon–Sat 9:30–13:30 & 14:30–18:00, closed Sun, tel. 051/858-905).

Dinner Show: On Thursday evenings in summer, Dooley's Hotel hosts a musical show on the experience of Irish emigrants in America (see page 131).

Taxis: Consider **Street Cabs Ltd.** (117 Parade Quay, tel. 051/877-778). **Rapid Cabs** operates local taxis (tel. 051/858-585) and **Rapid Express** offers coaches to Dublin's airport (tel. 051/872-149).

TOURS

▲▲Waterford Historic Walking Tour—Jack Burtchaell and his partners lead informative hour-long historical town walks that meet at the Waterford Museum of Treasures (behind TI) every day at 11:45 and 13:45 (just show up, pay €7 at the end, mid-March–mid-Oct only, tel. 051/873-711). The tour—really the most enjoyable thing to do in Waterford—is an entertaining walk from the TI to Reginald's Tower, giving you a good handle on the story of Waterford.

SIGHTS

In Waterford
Cathedral of the Holy Trinity—In 1793, the English king granted Ireland the Irish Relief Act, which, among other things, allowed the Irish to build Catholic churches and worship publicly. With Catholic France (30 million) threatening Britain (8 million) on one side, and Ireland (6 million) stirring things up on the other, the king needed to take action to lessen Irish resentment.

Allowed new freedom, the Irish built this interesting cathedral in 1796. It's Ireland's first Catholic post-Reformation church, and its only Baroque church. The building was funded by wealthy Irish wine merchants from Cadiz, Spain. Among its treasures are 10 Waterford Crystal chandeliers (free, daily 8:00–19:00).

Nearby: The cathedral faces **Barronstrand Street,** which leads from the clock tower on the harborfront to the pedestrian-friendly **town square.** The street separates the medieval town (on your left when the river is behind you) from the 18th-century city (on your right). A river once flowed here—part of the town's natural defenses just outside the old wall. The huge **shopping center** that dominates the old town was built right on top of the Viking town. In fact, the center is built over a church dating from 1150, which you can see at the bottom of the escalator (next to the kiddie rides).

▲Reginald's Tower—This oldest part of the oldest town in Ireland is named after Regnall, the first Viking leader of Waterford, who built a tower here in A.D. 914, and later invaded Jorvik (York, England). Dating from 1003, the tower you see today was once the most important corner of the town wall. The tower is supposedly Ireland's oldest intact building, and its first made with mortar. Inside, you'll see a display

Waterford

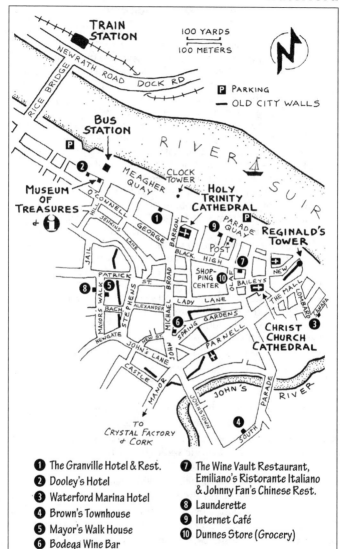

1. The Granville Hotel & Rest.
2. Dooley's Hotel
3. Waterford Marina Hotel
4. Brown's Townhouse
5. Mayor's Walk House
6. Bodega Wine Bar
7. The Wine Vault Restaurant, Emiliano's Ristorante Italiano & Johnny Fan's Chinese Rest.
8. Launderette
9. Internet Café
10. Dunnes Store (Grocery)

Waterford's History

Arriving in 850, Vikings first established Waterford as their base for piracy. Waterford was a perfect spot for launching their ships, since it's located at the gateway to the largest natural navigation system in Ireland. From here, raiders could sail 50 miles into Ireland, an island with no towns, just scattered monastic settlements and small gatherings of clans—perfect for the Vikings' plan of rape, pillage, and plunder.

Later, the Vikings decided to "go legal." They turned to profiteering, setting up shop in an established trading base they named Vandrafjord, or "safe harbor"—eventually called Waterford—Ireland's first permanent town. It was from this base that the Norsemen invaded England.

In the 12th century, a deposed Irish king invited the Normans over from England, hoping to use their muscle to regain his land from a rival clan. The great warrior knight Strongbow came...and never left, beginning Ireland's long and troublesome relationship with the English. In 1170, Strongbow married the Gaelic princess Aoife in the Gothic church that was once where Waterford's Christ Church Cathedral stands today. With this marriage, Strongbow was granted the title of King of Leinster, planting England's first roots in Ireland.

But for the English, Waterford has often proved to be a tough nut to crack. During Oliver Cromwell's "scorched earth" campaign of 1649–1650, when his forces decimated Ireland, Waterford was the only Irish city to withstand his sieges.

of medieval coins, old city models, a few Viking artifacts, and a short video (€2.10, covered by City Pass Ticket and Heritage Card, includes guided tour any time upon request—ask for the 1-hour version, which adds a historic walk around the block to French's Church; daily June–Sept 10:00–18:00, Oct–May 10:00–17:00, last entry 30 min before closing, tel. 051/304-220).

The statue outside (in the middle of the street) is of Thomas Francis Meagher, whose short hell bent-for-leather life involved him in precarious adventures from Tasmania to Nicaragua to Montana.

▲▲Waterford Museum of Treasures—With the help of hand-held audioguides, this museum presents a grand sweep through the history of Ireland as seen from Waterford. After an elevator ride to the top, you'll work your way down through three floors of intriguingly displayed artifacts, spiced with fiery characters such as Norman warlord Strongbow and Waterford-born action hero Thomas Francis Meagher (see sidebar on next page). It's housed, along with the TI, in an old stone grain warehouse where the original Waterford Crystal works stood (€7, covered by City

Thomas Francis Meagher
(1823–1867)

Waterford's favorite son had a short but amazing life. Born to the town's conservative mayor, Meagher joined Daniel

O'Connell's nonviolent movement to repeal the Act of Union with Britain. Impatient with the slow-moving political process, he joined the radical Young Irelander movement, becoming an inspiring speaker. He went to France in 1848 and returned with the first Irish tricolor flag—a gift from the French that represented the Catholics (green), the Protestants (orange), and peaceful coexistence between the two (white). Involved in a failed uprising, Meagher was sentenced to hang, but his sentence was commuted to life in prison in Tasmania. In 1852, Meagher escaped Tasmania via an American whaling ship and sailed to New York, where he eventually became a lawyer. After a trip to Nicaragua (to study the feasibility of building a canal or railway across the isthmus), he returned to New York to fight in the American Civil War. Meagher was made a Union general, raising a regiment of Irish immigrants, and famously leading them into battle at Antietam and Fredericksburg. After the war, he became the first governor of the Montana territory. At age 44, Thomas Francis Meagher fell off a riverboat and drowned in the Missouri River. His body was never found.

Pass Ticket; April–Sept Mon–Sat 9:30–18:00, Sun 11:00–18:00; Oct–March Mon–Sat 10:00–17:00, Sun 11:00–17:00; last entry 1 hour before closing, handy cafeteria in back, tel. 051/304-500).

Christ Church Cathedral—The Protestant cathedral, with 18th-century Georgian architecture, is the fourth church to stand here. Look for the exposed Gothic column six feet below today's floor level, a remnant from an earlier church where the Norman conqueror Strongbow was married (see "Waterford's History," page 128).

Wander over to the macabre tomb of 15th-century mayor James Rice, which bears a famous epitaph: "I am what you will be, I was what you are, pray for me." To emphasize the point, he requested that his body be dug up one year after his death (1482), and his partially decomposed remains be used to model his likeness, now seen on the tomb's lid...complete with worms and frogs (free, €3 donation requested, daily 10:00–17:00, tours at 11:30 and 15:00).

Near Waterford

▲▲▲**Waterford Crystal Factory**—With a tradition dating back to 1783, Waterford is the largest and one of the most respected glass-

works in the world. Its fine hour-long tours take visitors through the entire production process, offering a close-up look at many of the plant's 1,600 employees hard at work.

Your visit goes like this: While you ride a bus to one end of the factory, your guide orients you. You then see a huge furnace—where the dipping, blowing, and shaping takes place—which has been burning nonstop for 30 years (it's powered by natural gas, piped in 90 miles from Kinsale). Next is the etching demonstration, shown by workers who make the art of crystal blowing and cutting look easy (after their five-year apprenticeship). Each glass piece goes through more than 30 sets of hands before it's ready for sale. Waterford proudly sells no flawed factory seconds, smashing and re-melting about a third of the pieces if quality control detects even tiny blemishes. (Workers are paid by the successful piece.) The tour finishes with an opportunity to actually meet a cutter, see his diamond-bladed wheel in action, and ask questions. Afterwards, you land in the glittering salesroom, surrounded by hard-to-pack but easy-to-ship temptations. Before leaving, go upstairs above the gift shop to see the copies of famous sports trophies (they make backups of their most important commissions...just in case).

Cost and Hours: €9.50, covered by City Pass Ticket, daily March–Oct 8:30–18:00, Nov–Feb 9:00–17:00. A handy TI is next to the front desk.

Tours: The 60-minute tours run March–Oct daily beginning at 8:30—last tour leaves at 16:15 sharp; Nov–Feb Mon–Fri, tours begin at 9:00, last tour at 15:15 sharp, no tours Sat–Sun. Tours are liveliest weekdays before 15:30. Except for a skeleton crew working for the benefit of the tours, the factory is quiet after 16:00 and on weekends. Sidestep crowds by coming early and avoiding the after-noon rush. If arriving late, call to confirm tour times (tel. 051/332-500, www.waterfordvisitorcentre.com).

Getting There: The factory is conveniently located on the N-25 Cork road about two miles south of the city center. There are easy city bus connections from the waterfront.

Waterford

Sleep Code

(€1 = about $1.30, country code: 353, area code: 051)
S = Single, **D** = Double/Twin, **T** = Triple, **Q** = Quad, **b** = bathroom,
s = shower only. Unless otherwise noted, breakfast is included
and credit cards are accepted.

To help you easily sort through these listings, I've divided
the rooms into three categories, based on the price for a standard double room with bath:

$$$ **Higher Priced**—Most rooms €120 or more.
 $$ **Moderately Priced**—Most rooms between €70–120.
  $ **Lower Priced**—Most rooms €70 or less.

SLEEPING

Waterford is a working-class city. Cheap accommodations are
fairly rough. Fancy accommodations are venerable old places facing the water.

$$$ The Granville Hotel is Waterford's top, most historic
hotel, grandly overlooking the center of the harborfront. The place
is plush, from its Old World lounges to its extravagant rooms
(Sb-€80–90, Db-€95–180, Tb-€145–200, ask about "corporate dis-
counts," Meagher Quay, tel. 051/305-555, fax 051/305-566, www
.granville-hotel.ie, stay@granville-hotel.ie).

$$$ Dooley's Hotel, a more modern business-class place with
big motel-style rooms on the harbor, can be less expensive (Sb-€80–
129, Db-€140–198, Tb-€195–240, often discounted much lower,
Merchant's Quay, tel. 051/873-531, fax 051/870-262, www.dooleys
-hotel.ie, hotel@dooleys-hotel.ie). They also host "An Emigrant's
Tale," a song, dance, and storytelling show about Irish-American
life at 20:45 on Thursdays (€13, €27 with dinner, June–mid-Sept).

$$$ Waterford Marina Hotel has large, comfortable
rooms and very little personality (Sb-€80–90, Db-€108–180,
Canada Street, parking, tel. 051/856-600, fax 051/856-605, www
.waterfordmarinahotel.com, info@waterfordmarinahotel.com).

$$ Brown's Townhouse is a charming, Victorian-style, six-
room place where guests share one big, homey breakfast table. It's
on a quiet, residential street a 10-minute walk from the city center
(Sb-€50–70, Db-€100–120, Qb-€170–190, 10 percent discount for
stays of 2 or more nights, Internet access, parking, 29 South Parade,
tel. 051/870-594, fax 051/871-923, www.brownstownhouse.com,
info@brownstownhouse.com, Siobhan and Gerry McConnell).

$ Mayor's Walk House is a well-worn, grandmotherly place
that takes you right back to the 1950s. Bob and Jane Hovenden rent

four economical yet pleasant rooms (S-€29, D-€52, T-€78, cash only, 12 Mayor's Walk, tel. & fax 051/855-427, www.mayorswalk .com, mayorswalkbandb@eircom.net).

EATING

For something livelier than tired pub grub, consider three good restaurants (wine bar, Italian, and Chinese) that share a tiny street behind Reginald's Tower. All are small, popular, and serve an early-bird special (two or three courses for €17–23 before 19:00).

The Wine Vault—a cellar wine shop by day—offers decent European cuisine and seafood with a nice selection of wines. Its 18th-century cellar is good for romantic candlelit dinners (Mon–Sat 12:30–14:30 & 17:30–22:30, closed Sun, tel. 051/853-444); you're welcome to climb into the wine cellar below the restaurant. Located next door, and lively with locals, are **Emiliano's Ristorante Italiano** (Tue–Sun 12:30–14:30 & 17:00–22:00, closed Mon, tel. 051/820-333) and **Johnny Fan's Chinese Cuisine and Seafood** (Mon–Sat 12:30–14:30 & 17:00–23:30, Sun 13:00–15:00 & 18:00–23:00, tel. 051/879-535).

The relaxed **Bodega** is my favorite wine bar, run by laid-back Cormac in a warm-glow Mediterranean atmosphere (daily 12:00–22:00, 54 John Street, tel. 051/844-177).

The carvery at **The Granville Hotel** is your easiest lunch option, given its central location (daily 12:30–14:30, otherwise good bar food daily 10:30–19:00, Meagher Quay).

Pub Grub and Music: Waterford's staple food seems to be pub grub. Several typical pubs serve dinner in the city center. For your musical entertainment, just wander around, read the notices, and follow your ears. You'll find plenty of live action on George Street, Barronstrand Street, and Broad Street.

Supermarket: **Dunnes Store** in the shopping center is your best grocery option (Mon–Wed and Sat 9:00–19:00, Thu–Fri 9:00–21:00, Sun 12:00–18:00).

TRANSPORTATION CONNECTIONS

From Waterford by Train to: Dublin (6/day, 3 hrs), **Kilkenny** (4/day, 45 min), **Rosslare** (2/day, 1.5 hrs).

By Bus to: Cork (13/day, 2.25 hrs), **Kilkenny** (2/day, 1 hr), **Rosslare** (5/day, 1.25 hrs), **Wexford** (5/day, 1 hr). Waterford bus station info: tel. 051/879-000.

County Wexford

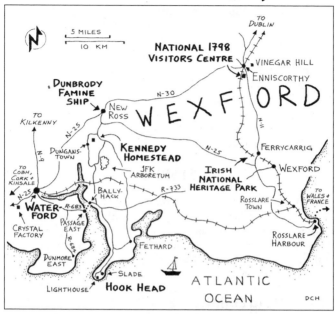

County Wexford

The southeast corner of Ireland, peppered with pretty views and historic sites, is easily accessible to drivers as a day trip from Waterford. While most of the sights are mediocre, five worth considering are within an hour's drive of Waterford.

The dramatic Hook Head Lighthouse—capping an intriguing and remote peninsula—comes with lots of history and a great tour. The Kennedy Homestead is a pilgrimage site for Kennedy fans. The *Dunbrody* Famine Ship in New Ross gives a sense of what 50 days on a "coffin ship" with dreams of "Americay" must have been like. The Irish National Heritage Park in Wexford is a Knott's Berry Farm...circa the Stone Age. And the National 1798 Visitors Centre at Enniscorthy explains the roots of the Irish struggle for liberty.

Planning Your Time

New Ross, Enniscorthy, and Wexford are each less than 30 minutes apart, connected by fast roads. The Kennedy Homestead is a 10-minute drive from New Ross, and the lighthouse is a 45-minute trip to the end of the Hook Peninsula. All are well signposted and easy to find. Connecting Dublin with Waterford, you could visit many of these sights in a best-of-County Wexford day en route.

Cty Wexford

On a quick trip, the sights are not worth the trouble by public transit. If you'll be spending the night, Enniscorthy and New Ross are blue-collar towns (with decent hotels and B&Bs) that provide a good glimpse of Ireland.

If connecting Waterford to Hood Head, use the car-ferry shortcut from Passage East to Ballyhack (€8, 5-min crossing, runs continuously, daily April–Sept 7:00–22:00, Oct–March 7:00–20:00). To reach the ferry from Waterford, go west on the N-25 Cork road. Before you reach the Waterford Crystal Factory, turn left (south) on R-684 toward Dunmore, and then branch left (east) on R-683 to Passage East.

SIGHTS

If you plan on visiting more than one of these Wexford sights—the Hook Head Lighthouse, *Dunbrody* Famine Ship, or Irish National Heritage Park—take advantage of the "Southeast Explorer" pass discount coupons, which offer 20 percent off each sight (ask for it at the first sight you visit). The coupons do not cover the Kennedy Homestead or 1798 Centre.

▲Hook Head Lighthouse

This is the oldest operating lighthouse in Northern Europe. According to legend, St. Dubhan arrived in the sixth century, and

discovered the bodies of ship-wrecked sailors. Dismayed, he and his followers began tending a fire on the headland to warn future mariners. What you see today is essentially a structure from the 12th century, built by the Normans, who first landed five miles up the east coast (at Baginbun Head, in 1169). They established Waterford Harbor—a commercial beachhead for the rich Irish countryside they intended to conquer. This beacon assured them safe access.

Today's lighthouse is 110 feet tall, and looks modern on the outside. (It was automated in 1996, and its light can be seen for 23 miles out to sea.) But it's 800 years old, built on a plan inspired by the lighthouse of Alexandria in Egypt—one of the seven wonders of the ancient world.

Since it's a working lighthouse, it can be toured only with a guide or escort. Fine 30-minute tours leave about hourly. When you're inside—seeing the lighthouse's black-stained, ribbed, vaulted ceilings and stout, 10-foot-thick walls—you can almost feel the presence of the Benedictine monks who tended this coal-burning beacon for the Normans. Climbing 115 steps through four levels rewards you with a breezy, salt-air view from the top.

Oliver Cromwell arrived here to secure the English claim to this area. He considered his two options, and declared he'd take strategic Waterford "by Hook or by Crooke." Hook is the long peninsula with the lighthouse. Crooke is a little village on the other side (just south of Passage East).

Cost, Hours, Services: €5.50, March–Oct daily 9:30–17:00, tours roughly hourly depending on demand, Nov–Feb tours Sat–Sun only, last tour usually at 16:00, call to check tour times before driving out (tel. 051/397-055, www.thehook-wexford.com).

There's a decent cafeteria and a shop with fliers explaining other sights on the peninsula. Kids-at-heart can't resist climbing out on the rugged rocky tip of the windy Hook Head.

▲Kennedy Homestead

Patrick Kennedy, JFK's great-grandfather, left Ireland in 1858. Distant relatives have turned his property into a little museum/shrine for Kennedy pilgrims. Physically, it's not much: A barn and a wing of the modern house survive from 1858. JFK dropped in by helicopter in June of 1963, a few months before he was assassinated. You'll view two short videos: five minutes of Kennedy's actual visit to the farm and a 16-minute newsreel tracing the events of his 1963 trip through Ireland (both fascinating if you like Kennedy stuff).

After the videos, you're led on a 15-minute tour by Patrick Grennan, a distant Kennedy relative whose grandmother hosted the tea here for JFK. You're then free to peruse the barn, lined with Kennedy-in-Ireland memorabilia that details the history of the dynasty. While it's just a private home, anyone interested in the Kennedys will find it worth driving the treacherous, narrow lane to see.

Cost, Hours, Location: €4, daily July–Aug 10:00–17:00, May–June and Sept 11:30–16:30; by appointment after hours, in slow times, and Oct–April (no big deal, as it's their home); tel. 051/388-264, www.kennedyhomestead.com. It's four miles south of New Ross near Dunganstown (look for sign off R-733, long one-lane road). Don't confuse the Kennedy Homestead with the nearby JFK Arboretum. The arboretum is lovely if you like trees and plants. It's a huge park with 4,500 species of trees and a grand six-county view—but no Kennedy history.

▲▲*Dunbrody* Famine Ship

Permanently moored on a river in the tiny port of New Ross, this ship was built as a re-creation of similar vessels full of countless hungry Irish who sailed to America. The *Dunbrody* is a full-scale

Cty Wexford

reconstruction of a 19th-century three-masted bark built in Quebec in 1845. It's typical of the trading vessels that originally sailed empty to America to pick up goods; during the famine, they found that they could make a little money on the westward voyage. Extended families camped out for 50 days on bunk beds no bigger than a king-size mattress. Often, boats like this would arrive in America with only 50 percent of their original human cargo. Those killed by Potato Famine fever were dumped overboard, and the ships gained their morbid moniker: "coffin ships."

After a 10-minute video about the building of the vessel, you'll follow an excellent guide through the ship, encountering a couple of grumpy passengers who tell vivid tales about life aboard. Roots-seekers are welcome to peruse the computerized file of a million names of immigrants who sailed from 1846 through 1865.

Cost, Hours, Location: €7, daily April–Oct 9:00–18:00, Nov–March 10:00–17:00, 45-min tours go 2/hr, last tour leaves 1 hour before closing (tel. 051/425-239, www.dunbrody.com). The *Dunbrody* is in New Ross, near the Kennedy Homestead. Parking is easy and free on Sundays, but during work hours, you'll need to feed the parking meters (€1/hr) in the lot.

▲Irish National Heritage Park

This 35-acre wooded park, which contains an 1857 tower commemorating local boys killed in the Crimean War, features replicas of buildings from each era of Irish history. Ireland's countless ancient sights are generally unrecognizable ruins—hard to re-create in your mind. This park is intended to help out. You'll find buildings and settlements illustrating life in Ireland from the Stone Age through the 12th-century Norman Age. As a bonus, you'll see animal skin–clad characters doing their prehistoric thing—gnawing on meat, weaving, making arrowheads, and so on.

Your visit begins with a 12-minute video followed by a 90-minute tour. During 13 stops, the guide explains various civilizations. The highlight is a monastic settlement from the age when Europe was dark, and Ireland was "the island of saints and scholars." While you can wander around on your own, the place is a bit childish (there's nothing actually old here), and only worthwhile if you take the included tour.

Cost, Hours, Location: €7.50, daily 9:30–18:30, until 17:30 in winter, last entry 90 minutes before closing, tours go hourly (tel. 053/912-0733, www.inhp.com). It's clearly signposted on the west end of Wexford—you'll hit it before entering town on the N-11 Enniscorthy road.

National 1798 Visitors Centre

Located in Enniscorthy, this museum creatively tells the story of the rise of revolutionary thinking in Ireland, which led to the ill-fated rebellion of 1798. Enniscorthy was the crucial Irish battle-ground of a populist revolution (inspired by the American and French Revolutions). The town witnessed the bloodiest days of the doomed uprising. The material is compelling for anyone intrigued by the struggles for liberty, but there's little more here than video clips of reenactments and storyboards on the walls.

Leaving the center, look east across the Slaney River, which divides Enniscorthy, and you'll see a hill with a stumpy tower on it. This is Vinegar Hill. The tower is the old windmill that once flew the green rebel flag. Drive to the top for the views that the rebels had of the surrounding British forces. The doomed rebels desperately tried to hold the high ground, with no shelter from the merciless British artillery fire.

Cost, Hours, Location: €7; April–Oct Mon–Fri 9:30–18:00, Sat–Sun 12:00–17:00; Nov–March Mon–Fri until 16:00, closed Sat–Sun; last entry one hour before closing (tel. 053/923-7596, www.iol.ie/~98com). Enniscorthy is 12 miles north of Wexford town. The National 1798 Visitors Centre is the town's major sight and is well signposted (follow the brown *Aras 98 Centre* signs).

Cty Wexford

KINSALE AND COBH

County Cork, on Ireland's south coast, is fringed with historic port towns and scenic peninsulas. The typical tour-bus route here includes Blarney Castle and Killarney—places where most tourists wear nametags. A major mistake many travelers make is allowing destinations into their itineraries simply because they're famous (in a song or as part of a relative's big-bus-tour memory). If you have the misfortune to spend the night in Killarney, you'll understand what I mean. The town is a sprawling line of green Holiday Inns littered with pushy shoppers looking for three-leaf clovers.

Rather than kissing the spit-slathered Blarney Stone, spend your time in County Cork enjoying the bustling, historic maritime towns of Kinsale and Cobh.

Planning Your Time

Kinsale makes a great home base for enjoying the County Cork coast. From Kinsale, you can wade through the salty history of Cobh. Travelers approaching this region from Waterford can easily visit Ardmore and the Old Midleton Whiskey Distillery. Those departing this region for the Ring of Kerry or Dingle can stop by Blarney Castle and Macroom en route.

Kinsale

While nearby Cork is the biggest town in southern Ireland, Kinsale (15 miles south) is actually more historic and certainly cuter: It's delightful to visit. Thanks to the naturally sheltered bay barbed

Kinsale and Cobh

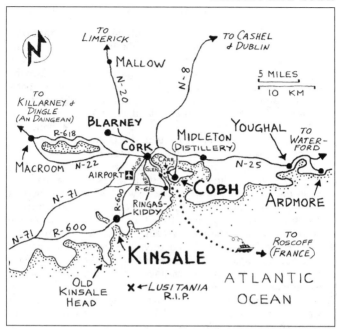

by a massive 17th-century star fort, you can submerge yourself in maritime history, from the Spanish Armada to Robinson Crusoe to the *Lusitania*. Apart from all the history, Kinsale has a laid-back Sausalito feel with a touch of wine-sipping class.

Planning Your Time

Kinsale is worth two nights and a day. The town's two tiny museums open at 10:00 and will occupy you until the 11:15 town walking tour. After lunch at the Fishy Fishy Café, head out to Charles Fort for great bay views and insights into British military life in colonial Ireland. On the way back, stop for a pint at the Bulman Bar. Finish the day with a good dinner and live music in a pub. Those on the blitz tour can give Kinsale five hours—see the fort, wander the town, and have a nice lunch—before driving on.

ORIENTATION

(area code: 021)

Kinsale, because of its great natural harbor, is older than Cobh (Cork's harbor town). While the town is prettier than the actual harbor, the harbor was its reason for being. Today Kinsale is a wealthy resort of 2,200 residents. The town's long and skinny old

Kinsale's History

Kinsale's remarkable harbor has made this an important port since prehistoric times. The bay's 10-foot tide provided a natural shuttle service for Stone Age hunter-gatherers: They could ride it, at two miles per hour twice a day, the eight miles up and down the River Bandon. In the Bronze Age, when people discovered that it takes tin and copper to make bronze, tin came from Cornwall and copper came from this part of Ireland. From 500 B.C. to A.D. 500, Kinsale was a rich trading center. The result: Lots of Stonehenge-type monuments are nearby. The best is Drombeg Stone Circle (a one-hour drive west, just off R-597 Glandore Road).

Kinsale's importance peaked during the 16th, 17th, and 18th centuries, when sailing ships ruled the waves, turning maritime countries into global powers. Kinsale was Ireland's most perfect natural harbor and the gateway to both Spain and France—potentially providing a base for either of these two powers in cutting off English shipping. Because of this, two pivotal battles were fought here in the 17th century: in 1601 against the Spanish, and in 1690 against the French. Two great forts were built to combat these threats from the Continent. England couldn't rule the waves without ruling Kinsale.

To understand the small town of Kinsale, you need to understand the big picture: Around 1500, the pope gave the world to Spain and Portugal. With the Reformation breaking Rome's lock on Europe, maritime powers such as England were ignoring the pope's grant. This was important because trade with the New World and Asia brought huge wealth in spices (necessary for curing meat), gold, and silver. England threatened Spain's New World piñata, and Ireland was Catholic. Spain had an economic and a religious reason to defend the pope and Catholicism. The showdown between Spain and England for mastery of the seas (and control of all that trade) was in Ireland. The excuse: to rescue the dear Catholics of Ireland from the treachery of Protestant England (as if democracy and not oil were the rationale for the modern conflict in the Middle East).

So the Irish disaster unfolded. The powerful Ulster chieftains Hugh O'Neill and Red Hugh O'Donnell and their clans had been

center is part modern marina and part pedestrian-friendly medieval town—an easy 15-minute stroll from end to end.

Tourist Information

The TI is as central as can be, at the head of the harbor across from the bus stop (July–Aug Mon–Sat 9:15–19:00, Sun 10:00–17:00; March–June and Sept–Nov Mon–Sat 9:30–17:30, closed Sun; shorter hours Dec–Feb; tel. 021/477-2234, www.kinsale.ie). It has a on a roll in their battle against the English. With Spanish aid, they figured they could actually drive the English out of Ireland. In 1601, the Spanish Armada dropped off 5,000 soldiers, who established a beachhead in Kinsale. After the ships left, the Spaniards were pinned down in Kinsale by the English commander (who, breaking with martial etiquette, actually fought in the winter). Virtually the entire Irish fighting force left the north and marched through a harsh winter to the south coast, thinking they could liberate their Spanish allies and win freedom from England.

The numbers seemed reasonable (10,000 Englishmen versus 5,000 Spaniards as 5,000 Irish clansmen approached). The Irish attacked on Christmas Eve in 1601. But, holding the high ground around fortified and Spanish-occupied Kinsale, a relatively small force of English troops kept the Spaniards hemmed in, leaving the bulk of the English force to outnumber and rout the fighting Irish. (Today's visitors will be reminded of this crucial battle as they wander past pubs with names like "The 1601" and "The Spaniard"—see pub sign at left.)

The Irish resistance was broken and its leaders fled to Europe (the "flight of the Earls"). England made peace with Spain and began the "plantation" of mostly Scottish Protestants in Ireland (the seeds of today's Troubles in Ulster). England ruled the waves and it ruled Ireland. The lesson: Kinsale is key. England eventually built two huge, star-shaped fortresses to ensure control of the narrow waterway, a strategy it would further develop in later fortifications built at Gibraltar and Singapore.

Kinsale's maritime history continued. Daniel Defoe used the real-life experience of Scottish privateer Alexander Selkirk, who departed from Kinsale in 1703 and was later marooned alone on a desert island, as the basis for his book *Robinson Crusoe*. And it was just 10 miles offshore from Old Kinsale Head that the passenger liner *Lusitania* was torpedoed by a German submarine in 1915, killing 1,200 and sparking America's entry into World War I.

Kinsale

free town map and brochures outlining a world of activities in the vicinity.

Arrival in Kinsale

Since Kinsale doesn't have a train station, you'll arrive by bus (the stop is at the Sea View gas station on Pier Road at the south end of town) or by car. Park your car and enjoy the town on foot. While Kinsale's windy medieval lanes are narrow and congested, parking is fairly easy. There's a big lot at the head of the harbor behind the TI (highway robbery at €2/hr, €12/day, overnight 18:00–9:00 is €10 extra). Use the big, safe, free parking lot across the street from St. Multose Church at the top of town, a three-minute walk from most recommended hotels and restaurants. Parking on the street requires a disk, except when it's free: before 10:30, after 18:00, or on Sunday (purchase disk at a newsstand such as Boland's, on corner of Emmet Place and Pierce Street, €0.60/hr, 2-hour maximum 10:30–18:00). The outlying streets, a five-minute stroll from all the action, have wide-open parking.

Helpful Hints

Banking: The two banks in town are **Allied Irish Bank** on Pearse Street and **Bank of Ireland** on Emmett Street (both open Mon 10:00–17:00, Tue–Fri 10:00–16:00, closed Sat–Sun).

Internet Access: Your best bet is **Computer Services,** near the Olde Bakery on Lower O'Connell Street (daily 10:00–20:00, can transfer photos from memory cards to CDs).

Post Office: It's on Pearse Street (Mon–Fri 9:00–17:30, Sat 9:00–13:00, closed Sun).

Laundry: The **Kinsale Launderette** washes and dries in a day, but it gets my vote for the most expensive laundry in Ireland (€15 minimum per load, no self-service, Mon–Fri 9:00–18:00, Sat 9:00–17:00, closed Sun, Market Street, tel. 021/477-2875). Don't let them take you to the cleaners—if possible, wait to do it in another town.

Bike Rental: **Murphy's** rents bikes from a handy spot next to the SuperValu (€10/day, Mon–Sat 9:30–18:00, closed Sun but arrangements can be made for pick-up or drop-off, shorter hours in winter, tel. 021/477-2703). Paths good for biking or walking stretch around the harbor. For the best short-and-scenic route, bike past Charles Fort and two miles along the harbor to its mouth. Get other suggestions from the bike-rental shop.

Taxi: Kinsale Cabs has regular cab service and minibuses available (Market Square, tel. 021/477-2642 or 021/470-0100).

TOURS

▲▲**Don Herlihy's Historic Town Walk**—To understand the important role Kinsale played in Irish, English, and Spanish history, join Don Herlihy or Barry Moloney on a fascinating 90-minute walking tour (€7, daily March–mid-Nov at 11:15, no reservation necessary, meet outside TI, private tours possible, tel. 021/477-2873). Both guides are a joy to hear, as they creatively bring to life Kinsale's place in a wide sweep of history and make the stony sights more than just buildings. Collections for the tour happen at the end, giving anyone disappointed in the talk an easy escape midway through. This walk is Kinsale's single best attraction.

Ghost Walk Tour—This is not just any ghost tour; it's more Monte Python–style slapstick comedy than horror. Two actors (Brian and David) weave funny stunts and stories into a loose history of the town, offering an entertaining 90 minutes of fun on Kinsale's after-dark streets (€10, May–Sept Mon–Fri at 21:00, leaves from Tap Tavern, mobile 087-948-0910). You'll spend the first 15 minutes in the back of the Tap Tavern—time to finish your drink and get to know some of the group. This tour doesn't overlap with the more serious historic town walk described above.

SIGHTS

Kinsale Town Wander—Stroll the old part of town. The medieval walled town's economy was fueled by the harbor, where ships came to be stocked. The old walls defined the original town and created a small fortified zone following what is now O'Connell Street and Main Street. The windy Main Street traces the original coastline. Walking this, you'll see tiny lanes leading to today's harbor. These originated as piers—just wide enough to roll a barrel down to an awaiting ship. The wall detoured inland to protect St. Multose Church, which dates from Norman times (back when worshippers sharpened their swords on the doorway of the church—check it out). After the James and Charles Forts were built in the 1600s, the wall became obsolete—and also boxed in the town, preventing further expansion. The townspeople later disassembled the wall and used its ready-cut stones to build out the piers in the harbor.

What seems like part of the old center was actually built later on land reclaimed from the harbor. The town sits on the floor of a natural quarry, with easy-to-cut shale hills ideal for a ready supply of fill. Notice the mudflats in the harbor at low tide. Clear-cutting of the once-plentiful oak forest upriver (for ship-building and barrel-making) hastened erosion and silted up the harbor. By the early 1800s—when British ships needed lots of restocking for the Napoleonic Wars—Kinsale's port was slowly dying, and nearby Cobh's deepwater port took over the lion's share of shipping.

▲▲Charles Fort—Kinsale is protected by what was Britain's biggest star-shaped fort—a state-of-the-art defense when artillery made the traditional castle obsolete. The British occupied it until

Kinsale

Kinsale

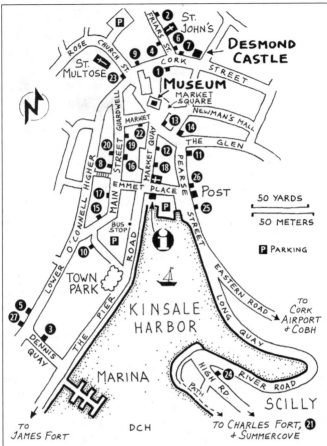

1 The Old Presbytery B&B
2 Friar's Lodge
3 Chart House B&B
4 Cloisters B&B
5 The Olde Bakery B&B
6 San Antonio B&B
7 The Sea Gull B&B
8 Kinsale Arms
9 Fishy Fishy Shop
10 Fishy Fishy Café
11 Café Blue
12 Cucina Café
13 Patsy's Corner
14 Mother Hubbard's

15 The Little Skillet
16 Hoby's Restaurant
17 Max's Wine Bar
18 Jim Edward's Steak & Seafood
19 Muddy Maher's Pub
20 Cobra Tandoori
21 To Bulman Bar & Rest.
22 An Seanachai Pub
23 The Tap Tavern
24 Spaniard Inn
25 Super Valu Supermarket
26 Bike Rental
27 Computer Services (Internet)

Kinsale

Irish independence in 1922. Its interior buildings were torched in 1923 by anti-treaty IRA forces to keep it from being used by Free State troops during the Irish Civil War. Guided 45-minute tours (which depart on the hour—confirm at entry)  engross you in the harsh daily life of the 18th-century British soldier. Before or after your tour, peruse the exhibits in the barracks and walk the walls.

For a coffee, beer, or meal nearby, stop by the Bulman Bar (see "Eating," below) in Summercove, where the road runs low near the water on the way back to town. And to actually see how easily the forts could bottle up this key harbor, stop for the grand harbor view at the high point on the road back into town (above Scilly, just uphill from the Spaniard pub).

Cost, Hours, Location: €3.70, covered by Heritage Card, daily mid-March–Oct 10:00–18:00, Nov–mid-March 10:00–17:00, last entry 45 min before closing, half a mile south of town in Summercove, tel. 021/477-2263.

James Fort—Older, overgrown, and filling a peaceful park, James Fort is Kinsale's other star fort, guarding the bay opposite Charles Fort. Built in the years just after the famous 1601 battle, this fort is more ruined, less interesting, and less visited than Charles Fort. Its satellite blockhouse sits below the fort at the water's edge opposite Summercove and controlled a strong chain that could be raised to block ships from reaching Kinsale's docks.

Easily accessible by car or bike, it's two miles south of town along Pier Road on the west shore of the bay (cross bridge and turn left; you'll dead-end at Castle Park Marina, where you can park or leave your bike). It's up the hill behind the Dock pub. From the fort, a popular, scenic 40-minute walk goes around the James Fort Headland.

▲Desmond Castle—This 15th-century fortified Norman customs house has had a long and varied history. It was the Spanish armory during Spain's 1601 occupation of Kinsale. Nicknamed "Frenchman's Prison," it served as a British prison and once housed 600 prisoners of the Napoleonic Wars (not to mention earlier American Revolutionary War prisoners captured at sea—who were treated as rebels, not prisoners, and chained to the outside of the building as a warning to any rebellion-minded Irish). In the late 1840s, it was a famine-relief center. Today the evocative little ruin comes with a scant display of its colorful history, as well as the modest two-room Museum of Wine, highlighting Ireland's little-known connection to the international wine trade. In the Middle Ages, Kinsale was renowned for its top-quality wooden casks. Developing strong trade links with Bordeaux, local merchants traded their dependable empty casks for casks full of wine. Later, Kinsale became a "designated wine port" for tax collection purposes.

Cost, Hours, Location: €3, covered by Heritage Card, mid-April–Oct daily 10:00–18:00, last entry 17:15, tours given on request, closed Nov–mid-April, Cork Street, tel. 021/477-4855.

▲**Kinsale Regional Museum**—In the center of the old town, traffic circles the old town market, which later became a courthouse and is now the Regional Museum. Drop by at least to read the fun 1788 tax code for all Kinsale commercial transactions (outside at the front door). The modest museum is worth a quick visit for its fun mishmash of domestic and maritime bygones. It also gives a good perspective on the controversial *Lusitania* tragedy. Kinsale had maritime jurisdiction over the waters 10 miles offshore, where the luxury liner was torpedoed in 1915. Hearings were held here in the courthouse shortly afterward to investigate the causes of the disaster—which helped propel America into World War I—and to paint the German Hun as a bloodthirsty villain. Claims by Germany that the *Lusitania* was illegally carrying munitions seem to have been borne out by the huge explosion and rapid sinking of the vessel. But perhaps even more interesting, in the side room, is the boot of the 8-foot 3-inch Kinsale giant, who lived here in the late 1700s.

Cost, Hours, Location: €2.50, Wed–Sat 10:30–17:30, Sun 14:00–17:30, closed Mon–Tue, Market Square, tel. 021/477-7930.

SLEEPING

Kinsale is a popular place in summer for yachters and golfers (who don't flinch at paying $300 for 18 holes out on the exotic Old Head of Kinsale Golf Course). It's wise to book your room in advance. I've listed peak-season prices. These places are all within a five-minute walk of the town center.

$$$ The Old Presbytery is a fine, quiet house a block outside the commercial district, with a goofy floor plan, plush lounge, and 10 pleasant rooms. Listed in most guidebooks, it has lots of American guests. The breakfasts are a delight, the rooms are stocking-feet cozy, and Noreen McEvoy runs the place with a passion for excellence (Db-€110, bigger Db-€150, biggest Db-€170, family Qb-€180, 2 Qb suites with no breakfast-€170, 10 percent discount with cash and this book in 2008, free Internet access and Wi-Fi, private parking, 43 Cork Street, tel. 021/477-2027, www.oldpres.com, info@oldpres.com).

Sleep Code

(€1 = about $1.30, country code: 353, area code: 021)
S = Single, **D** = Double/Twin, **T** = Triple, **Q** = Quad, **b** = bathroom,
s = shower only. Unless otherwise noted, breakfast is included
and credit cards are accepted.

To help you easily sort through these listings, I've divided
the rooms into three categories, based on the price for a standard double room with bath:

$$$ Higher Priced—Most rooms €110 or more.
$$ Moderately Priced—Most rooms between €65–110.
$ Lower Priced—Most rooms €65 or less.

$$$ Friar's Lodge is a newly built shingled hotel, perched
up the hill past St. John's Catholic church. What its 18 spacious
rooms lack in Old World character, they make up for in modern,
dependable quality (Sb-€80, Db-€90–140, Tb-€150–160, Qb-
€190, Wi-Fi access, private parking, Friar Street, tel. 021/477-7384,
fax 021/477-4363, www.friars-lodge.com, mtierney@indigo.ie).

$$$ Chart House B&B is a luxurious Georgian home rent-
ing a tidy little single and three grand, sumptuous doubles. It's a
block off the harbor at the marina end of the old town. This non-
smoking, quiet, and well-run place is top-end in every respect—
high ceilings, chandeliers, and a plush living room (Sb-€40–45,
Db-€120, deluxe Db-€170, 10 percent discount for paying cash,
easy parking, 6 Dennis Quay, tel. 021/477-4568, fax 021/477-7907,
www.charthouse-kinsale.com, charthouse@eircom.net, Mary
O'Connor).

$$$ Cloisters B&B, run by Mairead Ryan, has four prim
and clean rooms and a friendly atmosphere (Sb-€55, Db-€90–110,
Tb-€130, tel. 021/470-0680, www.cloisterskinsale.com, info
@cloisterskinsale.com).

$$ The Olde Bakery B&B makes you feel at home, with six
quilt-bedded rooms, two friendly dogs, and a cozy breakfast at the
kitchen table cooked up by Tom and Chrissie Quigley (D-€70,
Db-€80, cash only, non-smoking, laundry service available, 56
Lower O'Connell Street, tel. 021/477-3012, www.theoldebakery
.com, theoldebakery@oceanfree.net).

$$ San Antonio B&B is a 200-year-old house with five rooms
and a funky budget feel, lovingly looked after by owner Jimmie
Conron. He occasionally plays with other musicians at local pubs
(Sb-€50, Db-€75, Tb-€110, cash only, tel. 021/477-2341).

$$ The Sea Gull, perched up the hill right next to Desmond
Castle, offers six retro-homey rooms run by Mrs. Mary O'Neill,

Kinsale

who also runs The Tap Tavern down the hill (S-€40, Db-€75, Tb-€100, 10 percent discount with this book in 2008, cash only, Cork Street, tel. 021/477-2240, marytap@iol.ie).

$$ Kinsale Arms is a run-down, old-time place offering nine cheap, spartan, and last-resort rooms in the center of town (Db-€60–70, small rooms with smaller double beds, no twins, 55 Main Street, tel. 021/477-2233).

EATING

Back in the 1990s, when Ireland was just getting its cuisine act together, Kinsale was the island's self-proclaimed gourmet capital.

While good restaurants are commonplace in Irish towns today, Kinsale is still a delight at mealtime. Local competition is fierce, and restaurants offer creative and tempting menus. With so many options in the ever-changing scene, it's worth a short stroll to assess your options. Reservations can be smart, especially if eating late or on a weekend.

Lunch

Cafés: The Fishy Fishy Shop and the Fishy Fishy Café are *the* places for good seafood lunches.

Meals at the **Fishy Fishy Shop** are like eating in a fish market, surrounded by the day's catch and a pristine stainless-steel kitchen. Marie and her white-aproned staff hustle wonderful steaming plates of beautifully presented seafood to eager customers (€15–20 meals, cash only, daily 12:00–16:00 for lunch only, across from church on Guardwell Street, tel. 021/470-0415). Look at the lobster tank and ponder this: Several years ago, a soft-hearted, fat-walleted Buddhist tourist bought up the entire day's supply of live lobster (worth over €600) and set them free in the bay. They've refilled the tank since.

Fishy Fishy Café is bigger with more spacious seating (indoor, balcony, and terrace). It offers the same good prices and wonderful menu with slightly longer hours (Tue–Fri 12:00–20:00, Sat–Mon 12:00–16:30, no reservations taken, Pier Road, tel. 021/470-0415).

Other inviting cafés are **Café Blue** (open daily, at Blue Haven Hotel on Pearse Street, with lots of old-time town photos) and **Cucina Café** (open daily, on Market Street).

Cheap and Cheery Lunches: Try **Patsy's Corner,** packed with happy locals, or the breakfast hangout, **Mother Hubbard's.**

Both are near Market Square and serve sandwiches, baguettes, or salads with coffee for under €10. Or, gather picnic supplies at the **Super Valu** supermarket (Mon–Sat 8:30–21:00, Sun 10:00–21:00, Pearse Street).

Good Dinners in the Old Center

The Little Skillet feels intimate, with tasty food and a romantic, rough-stone-and-timber atmosphere. You'll find all the old-time Irish favorites with traditional Irish music, fresh and seasonal veggies, and absolutely no French fries (€20 entrées, daily 12:00–14:30 & 18:00–22:30, €25 three-course early-bird meal before 19:30, Main Street, tel. 021/477-4202).

Hoby's Restaurant, another well-established favorite for seafood and duck, offers modern cuisine in a quiet, candlelit room. It's popular with people from Cork coming down for a romantic night out (€27.50 three-course dinners, daily 18:00–22:00, Main Street, tel. 021/477-2200).

Max's Wine Bar has a respected French chef who concocts international cuisine. Both the presentation and interior are fancy (lunch 12:30–15:00, dinner 18:30–22:00, closed Tue, €22 three-course early-bird meal before 19:30, Main Street, tel. 021/477-2443).

Several other candlelit wine-bar restaurants vie for your attention along the gently curving Main Street. **Jim Edward's Steak & Seafood** keeps eaters happy in both the bar and the restaurant. Choose between the restaurant's candlelit maritime ambience (€20–30 meals, dinner only) or simpler food in the no-nonsense bar (€12–19 meals). Arrive early or wait. While cheaper and less gourmet than other Kinsale eateries, it's a high-energy place that's clearly a local family favorite for its decent steaks, seafood, and vegetables (bar daily 12:30–22:00, restaurant daily 18:00–22:00, Market Quay, tel. 021/477-2541).

Muddy Maher's Pub is one of several pubs with decent kitchens serving casual €8 lunches and €10–15 dinners in a funky atmosphere (daily 12:00–15:00 & 18:00–21:00, Main Street, tel. 021/477-4602). Many pubs follow dinner with live music.

Ethnic: Walk around the old-town block for a full array of inviting ethnic eateries. **Cobra Tandoori** is good for tasty Punjabi/Indian cuisine (€11 plates, daily 16:00–23:30, 69 Main Street, tel. 021/477-7911).

Fine Food Near Charles Fort

Bulman Bar and Restaurant serves seafood with seasonal produce. The mussels are especially tasty; on a balmy day or evening, diners take a bucket and a beer out to the seawall. This is the only real way to eat on the water in Kinsale (€10 lunches, €22–26 meals upstairs in fancy restaurant, daily 12:30–21:30, 200 yards toward

Kinsale from Charles Fort in hamlet of Summercove, tel. 021/477-2131). The pub, strewn with fun decor and sporting a big fireplace, is also good for a coffee or beer after your visit to the fort.

Without a car (and weather permitting), enjoy Kinsale's best 45-minute stroll back into town with great harbor views on the Scilly Walk paved pedestrian trail (trailhead on left after you climb from Bulman Bar 200 yards up steep road toward town, look for stone steps and old black iron turnstile).

Live Pub Music

Kinsale's pubs are packed with atmosphere and live music (though not always traditional Irish). Rather than target a certain place, simply walk the area between Guardwell, Pearse Street, and the Market Square. Pop into each pub that has live music, and then settle in your favorite. Several of the pubs wind deep into buildings. On a Thursday night, I found six places with live music thriving at 23:00 along this proposed loop. **An Seanachai** (SHAN-ah-key) means "storyteller" in Gaelic, but it's now known for its music (Main Street). **The Tap Tavern** has music on Thursday nights (just below St. Multose Church).

Irish music purists will be rewarded if they take the five-minute taxi ride (€7 one-way) out to the **Bulman Bar** near the base of Charles Fort. This is Kinsale's best pub for traditional Irish music sessions (Tue, Thu, Sun at 21:30, Wed folk session at 21:30, get there well before 21:00 to ensure a seat, see above, tel. 021/477-2131). Otherwise, get your trad fix at the tiny **Spaniard Inn,** a 10-minute walk out to the Scilly peninsula across the harbor from town. Its eye-catching golden walls fill the center of a hairpin turn on the crest of the peninsula (Wed at 21:30, you'll stand all night unless you arrive by 20:30, tel. 021/477-2436).

TRANSPORTATION CONNECTIONS

Like many worthwhile corners of Ireland, Kinsale is not accessible by train. The closest train station is in Cork, 15 miles north. But buses run frequently between Kinsale (stop is at Sea View gas station on Pier Road, south end of town) and Cork's bus station (10/day, 45 min, €6 one-way, €10 round-trip).

In Cork, the bus station and train station are a 10-minute walk apart. Cork's bus station (corner of Merchant's Quay and Parnell Place) is on the south bank of the Lee River, just over the nearest bridge from Cork's train station (north of the river on Lower Glanmire Road).

By Bus from Cork to: Dublin (6/day), **Galway** (12/day), **Tralee** (8/day), and **Kilkenny** (9/day). Bus info: tel. 021/450-8188.

Cobh

If your ancestry is Irish, there's a good chance that this was the last Irish soil your ancestors had under their feet. Cobh (cove) was the major port of Irish emigration in the 19th century. Of the six million Irish who have emigrated to America, Canada, and Australia since 1815, nearly half left from Cobh.

The first steam-powered ship to make a transatlantic crossing departed from Cobh in 1838—cutting the journey time from 50 days to 18. When Queen Victoria came to Ireland for the first time in 1849, Cobh was the first Irish ground she set foot on. Giddy, the town renamed itself "Queenstown" in her honor. It was still going by that name in 1912, when the *Titanic* made its final fateful stop here before heading out on its maiden (and only) voyage. To celebrate their new independence from British royalty in 1922, locals changed the name back to its original Irish name: Cobh.

ORIENTATION

Cobh sits on a large island in Cork harbor. The town's inviting waterfront is colorful yet salty, with a playful promenade. The butcher's advertisement reads, "Always pleased to meet you and always with meat to please you." Stroll past the shops along the water. Ponder the *Lusitania* memorial on Casement Square and the modest *Titanic* memorial nearby on Pearse Square. A hike up the hill to the towering Neo-Gothic St. Colman's Cathedral rewards you with a fine view of the port.

Tourist Information: The TI is in the Old Yacht Club on the harbor (Mon–Fri 9:30–17:30, Sat–Sun 13:00–17:00, tel. 021/481-3301, www.cobhharbourchamber.ie). You can buy parking disks here or in local shops (€0.50/hr, 2-hour maximum parking anywhere in Cobh).

Post Office: It's on the waterfront opposite the *Lusitania* memorial (Mon–Fri 9:00–17:30, Sat 9:00–13:00, closed Sun).

TOURS

"Titanic Trail" Tours—Michael Martin leads 75- to 90-minute walking tours of Cobh that give you unexpected insights into the tragic *Titanic* voyage, Spike Island (Ireland's Alcatraz), and Cobh's maritime history (€9.50, includes free pint in pub at end of tour,

Cobh

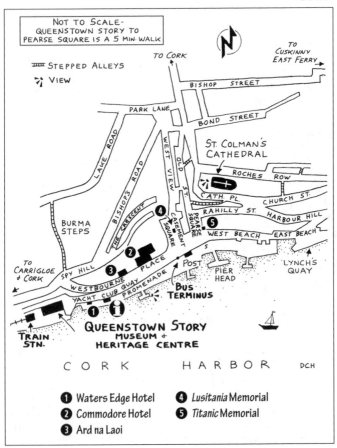

NOT TO SCALE-
QUEENSTOWN STORY TO
PEARSE SQUARE IS A 5 MIN. WALK

▥ STEPPED ALLEYS
↗ VIEW

TO CORK
TO CUSKINNY EAST FERRY

BISHOP STREET
PARK LANE
BOND STREET
LAKE ROAD
BISHOPS ROAD
WEST VIEW ST.
OLD ST.
ST. COLMAN'S CATHEDRAL
ROCHES ROW
CATH. PL.
CHURCH ST.
RAHILLY ST.
HARBOUR HILL
THE CRESCENT
BURMA STEPS
❹ LUSITANIA MEMORIAL
CASEMENT SQUARE
PEARSE SQUARE
❺
WEST BEACH
EAST BEACH
TO CARRIGLOE & CORK
SPY HILL
❷
❸
PLACE
POST
PIER HEAD
LYNCH'S QUAY
WESTBOURNE
YACHT CLUB QUAY
PROMENADE
BUS TERMINUS
TRAIN STN.
❶
ℹ
QUEENSTOWN STORY
MUSEUM & HERITAGE CENTRE

C O R K   H A R B O R   DCH

❶ Waters Edge Hotel   ❹ *Lusitania* Memorial
❷ Commodore Hotel   ❺ *Titanic* Memorial
❸ Ard na Laoi

daily at 11:00, June–Aug also at 14:00, meet at Commodore Hotel, call ahead to confirm tour times in winter, private tours available, tel. 021/481-5211 or mobile 087-276-7218, www.titanic.ie, info @titanic.ie).

SIGHTS

▲**The Queenstown Story**—Cobh's major sightseeing attraction, filling its harborside Victorian train station, is an earnest attempt to make the city's emigration and history interesting. The topics—the famine, Irish emigration, Australia-bound prison ships, the sinking of the *Lusitania,* and the ill-fated voyage of the *Titanic*—are fascinating enough to make this museum a worthwhile stop. But the museum itself, while kid-friendly, is weak on actual historical artifacts. It reminds me of a big, interesting history picture book with the pages expanded and tacked on the wall (€6.60, daily May–Oct 10:00–18:00, Nov–April 10:00–17:00, last entry 1 hour before closing, tel. 021/481-3591).

Those with Irish roots to trace can use the Heritage Centre's genealogy search service (www.cobhheritage.com, info @cobhheritage.com).

SLEEPING

(€1 = about $1.30, country code: 353, area code: 021)
The following listings are all centrally located near the harbor, less than a five-minute walk from the Queenstown Story.

$$$ Waters Edge Hotel, located 50 yards from the Queenstown Story, has 18 bright, modern rooms and a pleasant harbor-view restaurant (Sb-€75–110, Db-€120–180, Tb-€130–200, Yacht Club Quay, tel. 021/481-5566, www.watersedgehotel.ie, info@watersedgehotel.ie).

$$$ Commodore Hotel is a grand 150-year-old historic landmark. This place was once owned by the wealthy German Humbert family, who opened it up to *Lusitania* refugees after the 1915 sinking. Its high-ceilinged rooms creak with Victorian character (Sb-€70–92, Db-€95–138, Tb-€200–210, Westbourne Place, tel. 021/481-1277, fax 021/481-1672, www.commodorehotel .ie, commodorehotel@eircom.net).

$$ Ard na Laoi is a friendly place with five modest rooms (Sb-€45–50, Db-€68, Tb-€99, Westbourne Place, tel. 021/481-2742).

TRANSPORTATION CONNECTIONS

By Car: Driving to Cobh from Cork or Waterford, leave N-25 about eight miles east of Cork, following little R-624 over a bridge, onto the Great Island, and directly into Cobh.

Kinsale to Cobh is 25 miles, takes an hour, and involves catching a small ferry. Leave Kinsale north on R-600 toward Cork. Just south of Cork and its airport, go east on R-613. You will be following little *car-ferry* signs, but they ultimately take you to the wrong ferry (Ringaskiddy—to France). After you hit N-28, take R-610 to Monkstown and then Glenbrook, where a (poorly signposted) shuttle ferry takes you to Carrigloe on the Great Island (5 min, daily 7:00–22:00, €4). Once on the island, turn right and drive a mile or two into Cobh. In Cobh, follow the *Heritage Centre* signs to The Queenstown Story, where you'll find easy parking right at the museum (buy parking disks at nearby TI, €0.50/hr, 2-hour maximum).

Cobh

By Plane: Cork Airport has become an increasingly handy entry point into (or exit point from) Ireland. Located four miles south of Cork city (on N-27/R-600 to Kinsale, a 30-min drive away), it offers connecting flights from London Heathrow on Aer Lingus, London Stansted on Ryanair, and Edinburgh on Aer Arann. More distant connections can be made from Frankfurt, Amsterdam, Paris, Prague, and Málaga (tel. 021/431-3131, www.corkairport.com).

To sleep near Cork Airport, consider **$$$ Radisson Cork Airport** (Db-€129 Mon–Thu, €110 Fri–Sun, best prices if booked online, tel. 021/494-7500, www.radissonsas.com).

More Sights in and near County Cork

These sights are convenient stops when connecting Kinsale and Cobh with Waterford (to the east) or the Ring of Kerry (to the west).

Between Waterford and Kinsale

If you're driving from Waterford (previous chapter) to Cobh and Kinsale, you can easily visit these sights just off N-25 (listed roughly from east to west).

Ardmore—This funky little beach resort, with a famous ruined church and round tower, is a handy stop (just west of Youghal, 3 miles south of N-25 between Waterford and Cobh). A couple of buses run daily from Ardmore to Cork and Tue–Fri 12:00–20:00 to Waterford.

This humble little port town is just a line of pastel houses that appear frightened by the sea. Its beach claims (very modestly) to be "the most swimmable in Ireland." The beachside **TI**, housed in an alien spacecraft, has a flier laying out a historic walk (June–Aug Mon–Fri 9:30–17:30, Sat 10:00–17:00, closed Sun, shorter hours off-season, tel. 024/94444).

The town's historic claim to fame: Christianity came to Ireland here first (thanks to St. Declan, who arrived in A.D. 416—15 years before St. Patrick). As if to proclaim that feat with an 800-year-old exclamation mark, one of Ireland's finest examples of a round tower stands perfectly intact, 97 feet above an evocative graveyard and a ruined church (noted for the faint remains of some early Christian carvings on its west facade). You can't get into the tower—the entrance is 14 feet off the ground.

Sleeping in Ardmore (area code: 024): **$$ Duncrone B&B** has four vividly colorful rooms run by Jeanette Dunne (Sb-€38–45, Db-

€70, Tb-€90, a half-mile outside of town, up past the round tower, tel. 024/94860, www.duncronebandb.com, info@duncronebandb .com). **$$$ Round Tower Hotel,** a sedate, traditional place, is a safe bet in town (Sb-€60, Db-€110, on R-673 leading west out of town, tel. 024/94494, www.irelandhotels.com).

▲**Old Midleton Distillery**—Sometime during your Ireland trip, even if you're a teetotaler, you'll want to tour a whiskey distillery. Of the three major distillery tours (this one, Jameson in Dublin, and Bushmills in Northern Ireland), the Midleton experience is the most interesting. After a 10-minute video, you'll walk with a guide through a great old 18th-century plant on a 45-minute tour; see

waterwheel-powered crankshafts and a 31,000-gallon copper still—the largest of its kind in the world; and learn the story of whiskey. Predictably, you finish in a tasting room and enjoy a free, not-so-wee glass. The finale is a Scotch/Irish whiskey taste test. Your guide will take two volunteers for this. Don't be shy—raise your hand like an eager little student and enjoy an opportunity to taste the different brands.

Cost, Hours, Location: Tour-€9.75, daily 9:00–18:00 year-round, last tour at 17:00, 2/hr in summer, 3/day in winter (tel. 021/461-3594, www.whiskeytours.ie). It's 12 miles east of Cork in Midleton, about a mile off N-25, the main Cork–Waterford road. There's easy parking—just drive right into the distillery lot. A cafeteria is on site.

Between Kinsale and Killarney

If you're driving between Kinsale and the Ring of Kerry (see next chapter), you can easily visit these sights (listed from east to west).
Blarney Stone and Castle—The town of Blarney is of no importance, and the 15th-century Blarney Castle is an empty hulk (with no effort at making it meaningful or interesting). It's only famous as the place of tourist pilgrimage, where busloads line up to kiss a stone on its top rampart and get "the gift of gab." The stone's origin is shrouded in myth (it was either brought back from the Holy Land by crusaders, or perhaps was part of Scotland's royal Stone of Scone). The best thing about this lame sight is the opportunity to watch a cranky man lower lemming tourists over the edge, belly up and head back, to kiss the stone while his partner snaps a photo—which will be available for purchase back at the parking lot. After a day of tour groups mindlessly climbing up here to perform this ritual, the stone is literally slathered with spit and lipstick.

The tradition goes back to the late 16th century, when Queen Elizabeth I was trying to plant loyal English settlers in Ireland to tighten her grip on the rebellious island. She demanded that the Irish clan chiefs recognize the crown, rather than the clan chiefs, as the legitimate titleholder of all lands. One of those chiefs was Cormac MacCarthy, Lord of Blarney Castle (who was supposedly loyal to the queen). He was smart enough never to disagree with the Queen—instead, he would cleverly avoid acquiescing to her demands by sending a never-ending stream of lengthy and deceptive excuses, disguised with liberal doses of flattery (while subtly maintaining his native Gaelic loyalties). In

her frustration, the Queen declared his endless words nothing but "blarney." Walking back, you'll cross a stream littered with American pennies—as if the good-luck fairy can change them into euros.

While the castle is unimpressive, the gardens are beautiful, well kept, and picnic-worthy (if you are there anyway). There are even some hints of Ireland's pre-Christian past on the grounds; you can see dolmens beside the trail in the forested Rock Close.

Cost, Hours, Location: €8, Mon–Sat 9:00–18:30, Sun 9:30–17:30, later in peak season, shorter hours in winter, free parking lot, helpful TI, tel. 021/438-5252, www.blarneycastle.ie. It's five miles northwest of Cork, the major city in south Ireland. Looking for shopping galore? Adjacent Blarney Woolen Mills has it all (right next to the castle parking lot).

Macroom—This colorful, inviting market town is a handy stop between Cork and Killarney. The ghostly gateway of its ruined castle (once owned by the father of the William Penn who founded Pennsylvania) overlooks its entertaining main square, where you'll find plenty of parking. The Irish civil war saga *The Wind that Shakes the Barley* (released in 2006) was filmed in this area. Macroom makes for an excellent coffee or lunch stop midway between Cork and Killarney. The Next Door Café, next to Castle Hotel, serves a good, fast lunch.

More Sights

KENMARE AND THE RING OF KERRY

It's no wonder that, since Victorian times, visitors have been attracted to this dramatic chunk of Ireland. Mysterious ancient ring forts stand sentinel on mossy hillsides. A beloved Irish statesman maintained his ancestral estate here, far from 19th-century power politics. And early Christian hermit monks left a lonely imprint of their devotion, in the form of simple stone dwellings atop an isolated rock crag far from shore...a holy retreat on the edge of the then-known world.

Today, it seems like every tour bus in Ireland makes the ritual loop around the scenic Ring of Kerry, using the bustling and famous tourist town of Killarney as a springboard. I prefer to skip Killarney (useful only for its transportation connections). Instead, home-base in the tidy town of Kenmare and circle the much-loved peninsula cleverly—entirely missing the convoy of tour buses.

Kenmare

Cradled in a lush valley, this charming little town (known as Neidín, or "Little Nest," in Gaelic) hooks you right away with its rows of vividly colored shop fronts and go-for-a-stroll atmosphere. Its fresh appearance won it Ireland's "Tidy Town" award in 2000, and the nearby finger of the gentle sea feels more like a large lake (called the Kenmare River, just to confuse things). Far from the assembly-line tourism of Killarney town, Kenmare (rhymes with "chair") also makes a great launchpad for enjoying the sights along the road around the Iveragh (eev-er-AH) Peninsula—known to shamrock-lovers everywhere as The Ring of Kerry.

Planning Your Time

All you need in compact Kenmare is one night and a couple of hours to wander the town. Check out the Heritage Centre (in the back rooms of the TI) to get an overview of the region's history. Visit the Kenmare Lace and Design Centre (above TI, entry next door) to get a close look at its famously delicate lace. Hands-on access to an ancient stone circle is just a five-minute walk from the edge of town. Finish up by taking a peek inside Holy Cross Church to see the fine ceiling woodwork. Call it an early night to get a crack-of-dawn start on the Ring of Kerry in the morning.

ORIENTATION

(area code: 064)

Carefully planned Kenmare is shaped like an "X." The X makes two triangles. The upper (northern) triangle contains the town

square (colorful markets Wed and Fri in summer), with the adjacent TI and Heritage Centre, as well as a cozy park. The lower (southern) triangle contains three one-way streets busy with shops, lodgings, and restaurants. Use the tall Holy Cross Church spire to get your bearings (next to the northeast parking lot, public WCs across the street).

Tourist Information: The helpful TI is on the town square (July–Aug daily 9:00–19:00, May–June and Sept Mon–Sat 9:00–18:00, Sun 10:00–18:00, closed Oct–April, tel. 064/41233).

Helpful Hints

Banking: Bank of Ireland faces the town square, and **Allied Irish Bank** takes up the corner of Henry and Main streets (both open Mon 10:00–17:00, Tue–Fri 10:00–16:00, closed Sat–Sun).

Internet Access: Live Wire is handy for mobile-phone and digital-photo needs, as well as email access (€2/30 min for Internet access, Mon–Sat 10:00–21:00, Sun 11:00–19:00, shorter hours off-season, just off Main Street on Rock Street, tel. 064/42714).

Post Office: It's on Henry Street, at the intersection with Shelbourne Street, and has Internet access (Mon–Fri 9:00–17:30, Sat 10:00–13:00, closed Sun).

Laundry: O'Shea's Cleaners and Launderette is the only option in town (Mon–Fri 8:30–18:00, Sat 9:30–17:30, closed Sun, a mile north of town on N-71 in Kenmare Business Park, tel. 064/41394).

Kenmare's History: Axes, Xs, Nuns, and Lace

Bronze Age people (2000 B.C.), attracted to this valley for its abundant game and fishing, stashed their prized axe heads and daggers in hidden hoards. Nearly 4,000 years later (in 1930), a local farmer from the O'Sullivan clan pried a bothersome boulder from one of his fields and discovered it to be a lid for a collection of rare artifacts that are now on display in the National Museum in Dublin (the "Killaha hoard"). The O'Sullivans (Gaelic for "descendants of the one-eyed") were for generations the dominant local clan, and you'll still see their name on many Kenmare shop fronts.

Oliver Cromwell's bloody Irish campaign (1649) subdued Ireland but never reached Kenmare. However, Cromwell's chief surveyor, William Petty, knew good land when he saw it and took a quarter of what is now County Kerry as payment for his valuable services, marking the "lands down" on maps. His heirs, the Lansdownes, created Kenmare as a model 18th-century estate town and developed its distinctive "X" street plan. William Petty-Fitzmaurice, the first Marquis of Lansdowne and landlord of Kenmare, became the British Prime Minister who negotiated the peace that ended the American War of Independence in 1783.

Sister Margaret Cusack, a.k.a. Sister Mary Francis Clare, lived in the town from 1862 to 1881, becoming the famous Nun of Kenmare. Her controversial religious life began when she decided to become an Anglican nun after her fiancé's sudden death. Five years later, she converted to Catholicism, joined the Poor Clare order as Sister Mary Francis Clare, and moved with the order to Kenmare. She became an outspoken writer who favored women's rights and lambasted the tyranny of the landlords during the famine. She eventually took church funds and attempted to set herself up as abbess of a convent in Knock. Her renegade behavior led to her leaving the Catholic faith, converting back to Protestantism, writing an autobiography, and lecturing about the "sinister influence of the Roman Church."

After the devastation of the Great Potato Famine (1845–1849), an industrial school was founded in Kenmare to teach trades to destitute youngsters. The school, run by the Poor Clare sisters, excelled in teaching young girls the art of lacemaking. Inspired by lace created earlier in Italy, Kenmare lace caught the eye of Queen Victoria and became much coveted by Victorian society. Examples of it are now on display in the Victoria and Albert Museum (London), the Irish National Museum (Dublin), and the US National Gallery (Washington, D.C.).

Bike Rental: Finnegan's Corner rents bikes for €15 per day (up to 24 hours if you like), and has route maps and advice on maximizing scenery and minimizing traffic (July–Aug Mon–Sat 10:00–20:00, Sept–June until 18:00, closed Sun, leave ID for deposit, office in gift shop at 37 Henry Street, across from post office, tel. 064/41083).

Parking: The town's two largest public parking lots (free overnight) cling to the two main roads departing town to the north (otherwise free street parking is allowed for 2 hours).

Taxi: Try **Murnane Cabs** (mobile 087-236-4353) or **Kenmare Koach and Kab** (mobile 087-248-0800).

TOURS

Finnegan's Guided Coach Tours—This company runs a variety of local day tours, departing from the TI at 10:00 and returning by 17:00. While this is little more than a scenic joyride, the tour guide gives a fun, anecdotal narration and generally makes three rest stops and one sightseeing stop (route depends on day: Ring of Kerry on Mon, Wed, and Fri; Ring of Beara on Tue; Glengarrif and Garnish Island on Thu; €25 for any tour, reserve a day in advance, can book private tours for small groups with enough notice, tel. 064/41491, mobile 087-248-0800, www.kenmarecoachandcab.com).

SIGHTS AND ACTIVITIES

Heritage Centre—This museum, in the back rooms of the TI, consists of a series of storyboards and a model of the planned town. A 20-minute visit here explains the nearby ancient stone circle, as well as the history of Kenmare's lacemaking fame and feisty, troublemaking nun (free, May–Sept Mon–Sat 9:00–18:00, Sun 10:00–18:00, closed Oct–April, tel. 064/41233).

Kenmare Lace and Design Centre—A single large room (above the TI) displays the delicate lacework that put Kenmare on the modern map. From the 1860s until World War I, the Poor Clare convent at Kenmare became the center of excellence for Irish lacemaking. Inspired by antique Venetian lace, but creating their own unique designs, nuns taught needlepoint lacemaking as a trade to girls in a region struggling to get back on its feet in the wake of the catastrophic famine. Queen Victoria commissioned five pieces of lace in 1885, and by the end of the century, tourists began visiting Kenmare on their way to Killarney just for a peek at the

Kenmare

Kenmare

1. Lansdowne Arms Hotel
2. Sallyport House
3. Hawthorn House & Kenmare Failte Hostel
4. Willow Lodge
5. Whispering Pines B&B
6. Waters Edge B&B
7. Kenmare Lodge Hostel
8. To Parknasilla Hotel
9. The Purple Heather & Packies Restaurants
10. Café Mocha
11. Supermarket
12. The Lime Tree Rest.
13. Mulcahy's Wine Bar
14. Horse Shoe Pub & Rest.
15. P.F. McCarthy's Pub & Rest.
16. Crowley's Pub
17. Foley's Pub
18. Davitt's Pub
19. Internet Café
20. Bike Rental
21. Launderette
22. To Star Sailing (Boat Rental)
23. To River Valley Riding Stables

lace. Nora Finnegan, who runs the Centre, usually has a work in progress to demonstrate the complexity of fine lacemaking to visitors (free; May–mid-Oct Mon–Sat 10:15–13:00 & 14:15–17:30, closed Sun; mid-Oct–April Mon–Sat 10:30–13:30, closed Sun; tel. 064/42978).

Ancient Stone Circle—Of the 100 stone circles that dot southwest Ireland (Counties Cork and Kerry), this is one of the biggest and most accessible (5-min walk from TI, free and always open). It's over 3,000 years old, and it may have been used both as a primitive calendar and a focal point for rituals. The circle has a diameter of 50 feet and consists of 15 stones ringing a large center boulder (probably a burial monument). Experts think that this stone circle (like most) functioned as a celestial calendar—it tracked the position of the setting sun to determine the two solstices (in June and Dec), which mark the longest and shortest days of the year.

Getting There: From the city center, face the TI, turn left, and walk 200 yards down Market Street, passing a row of cute 18th-century houses on your right. Beyond the row of houses, veer right through an unmarked modern gate mounted in stone columns, and continue 50 yards down the paved road. You'll see the circle on your right.

Holy Cross Church—Finished in 1864, this is Kenmare's grand Catholic church. It's worth visiting to see the ornate wooden ceiling with 10 larger-than-life angels (carved in Germany's Black Forest).

Horseback Riding—River Valley Riding Stables offers day treks for all levels of experience through beautiful hill scenery in the Roughty River Valley (€25/hr, discounts for groups, open long hours, located about 7 miles east of Kenmare off R-569 near Kilgarvan, tel. 064/85360, rivervalleystables@hotmail.com).

Boating and Hiking—Star Sailing rents boats, offers sailing lessons, and organizes hill walks. Hop on a small two-person sailboat (€50/hr) or canoe (€35/hr), kick around in a kayak (€20/hr), or take sailing lessons. Phone ahead to reserve boats or ask about hikes (located 5 miles southwest of Kenmare on R-571 on Beara Peninsula, courtesy shuttle can pick you up in Kenmare, tel. 064/41222, www.staroutdoors.ie; adjacent Con's Restaurant is open daily 12:00–21:00).

Golfing—Another way to experience Ireland's 40 shades of green is to splurge on a scenic day on the links. The Kenmare Golf Club is right on the edge of town (greens fees Mon–Fri €50, Sat–Sun €55, on R-569 toward Cork, tel. 064/41291). Or try the Ring of Kerry Golf and Country Club (€80 greens fees, 4 miles west of town on N-70, pre-booking advisable on weekends, tel. 064/42000, www.ringofkerrygolf.com).

NIGHTLIFE

Music in Pubs

Wander the entire Kenmare town triangle and stick your head in wherever you hear something you like. Music usually starts at 21:30 (although some pubs have early 18:30 sessions—ask at the TI) and ranges from Irish traditional sessions to sing-along strummers. **Crowley's** is an atmospheric little shoebox of a pub with an unpretentious clientele. **Foley's** jug-stacked window invites you in for a folksy songfest. Across the street, **Davitt's** competes for your ears. The **Landsdowne Arms Hotel** (see below) sponsors live traditional sessions, too.

SLEEPING

In Kenmare

$$$ Lansdowne Arms Hotel is the town's venerable grand hotel, with generous public spaces. This centrally located, 200-year-old historical landmark rents 26 large, crisp rooms (Sun–Fri: Sb-€100, Db-€150, Tb-€225; Sat: Sb-€110, Db-€170, Tb-€235; most rooms non-smoking, music in pub until late on Fri–Sat, parking, corner of Main and Shelbourne Streets, tel. 064/41368, fax 064/41114, www.lansdownearms.com, info@lansdownearms.com).

$$$ Sallyport House, an elegantly quiet house filled with antique furniture, has been in Helen Arthur's family for generations. Ask her to point out the foot-worn doorstep that was salvaged from the local workhouse and built into her stone chimney (Sb-€120, Db-€150–180, Tb-€210–225, closed Nov–mid-March, cash only, no kids, non-smoking, parking, 5-min walk south of town before crossing Our Lady's Bridge, tel. 064/42066, fax 064/42067, www.sallyporthouse.com, port@iol.ie).

Sleep Code

(€1 = about $1.30, country code: 353, area code: 064)
S = Single, **D** = Double/Twin, **T** = Triple, **Q** = Quad, **b** = bathroom, **s** = shower only. Breakfast is included; credit cards are accepted unless otherwise noted.

To help you easily sort through these listings, I've divided the rooms into three categories, based on the price for a standard double room with bath:

$$$ Higher Priced—Most rooms €100 or more.
  $$ Moderately Priced—Most rooms between €65–100.
   $ Lower Priced—Most rooms €65 or less.

Kenmare

$$$ Hawthorn House is a fine, modern, freestanding house with a lounge, a warm and classy hostess, and eight comfy rooms sporting fine woodwork courtesy of Mr. O'Brien, who's also a carpenter. Its quiet residential location is just a block from all the pub and restaurant action (Db-€90–100, Tb-€120–140, Qb-€140, may be cheaper when slow, ample parking, Shelbourne Street, tel. 064/41035, www.hawthornhousekenmare.com, info @hawthornhousekenmare.com, Mary and Noel O'Brien).

$$ Willow Lodge feels American-suburban, with a chatty and friendly hostess renting seven comfortable rooms on the main road at the edge of town (Sb-€60–90, Db-€95, Tb-€130–135, cash only, non-smoking, parking, 100 yards beyond Holy Cross Church, tel. 064/42301, www.willowlodgekenmare.com, willowlodgekenmare@yahoo.com, Gretta Gleeson-O'Byrne).

$$ Whispering Pines B&B rents five rooms with traditional Irish hospitality in a 1960s-style suburban Irish house (Sb-€60, Db-€76–84, Tb-€110, cash only, at the edge of town down Henry Street on the Bantry Road to Bellheight, tel. 064/41194, wpines @eircom.net, John and Mary Fitzgerald).

$ Waters Edge B&B is a new building isolated on a forested hillside a mile south of town and overlooking the estuary. It has four clean, colorful rooms and a kid-pleasing backyard (Sb-€45, Db-€64, Tb-€80, cash only, non-smoking, parking, tel. 064/41707, mobile 087-413-4235, watersedgekenmare@gmail.com). To get here, drive south over Our Lady's Bridge, stay on the road (bearing left), look for the sign, and turn into the driveway on the right. Go a couple hundred yards up the bumpy paved road, then at the end of the white wall (on left), turn right onto the gravel lane and drive a hundred yards to the dead-end.

$ Kenmare Fáilte Hostel (fawl-chuh) maintains 40 budget beds in a well-kept, centrally located building with more charm than most hostels (dorm beds-€16 in rooms without bath, €4 more in rooms with shower, D-€40, Db-€48, T-€54, Tb-€62, Q-€68, Qb-€80, closed Nov–March, Shelbourne Street, tel. 064/42333, fax 064/42466, www.kenmare.eu/failtehostel, failtefinn@eircom.net).

$ Kenmare Lodge Hostel is a practical, no-frills place renting comfortable beds in modern dorms, right in the town center on a quiet side street (€15 per bed in 6- to 10-bed dorms, Db-€50, three family rooms, kitchen, ample and modern bathrooms, Main Street, tel. 064/40662, kenmarehostel@eircom.net). It's run by Paul, who works at the Fuji Imaging shop next door—which functions as the reception area for the hostel.

Sleeping in Luxury out on the Ring of Kerry

$$$ Parknasilla Hotel is a 19th-century luxury hotel lost in 300 plush acres of a subtropical park overlooking the wild Atlantic

Ocean. The tranquility combined with the old-fashioned service and Victorian elegance makes this a good stop for anyone interested in luxuriating on the Ring of Kerry. Originally an old railroad hotel for Romantic Age tourists, in recent decades it's been a ritual splurge for Irish families (Db-€200 without breakfast, croquet, 19th-century diversions, park walks, see website for details and their complex pricing scheme, tel. 1-850-383-848, www.parknasillahotel.ie).

EATING

This friendly little town offers plenty of quality choices. If dining, make a reservation or get a table early, as many finer places book up later in the evening during the summer. Pub dinners are a good value and easier on the budget, but pubs close their kitchens earlier than restaurants.

Lunch

Soup-and-sandwich lunch options abound. **The Purple Heather** makes great salads and omelets (€8–15 meals, Mon–Sat 11:00–19:00, closed Sun, Henry Street, tel. 064/41016). **Café Mocha** is a basic €4 sandwich shop (Mon–Fri 9:00–17:30, Sat–Sun 10:00–17:00, on the town square, tel. 064/42133). **Super Valu** supermarket is a good place to stock up for a Ring of Kerry picnic (Mon–Thu 8:00–20:00, Fri 8:00–21:00, Sat 8:00–19:00, Sun 9:00–17:00, Main Street).

Dinner

The Lime Tree Restaurant occupies the former Lansdowne Estate office, which gave more than 4,000 people free passage to America in the 1840s. These days, it serves delicious, locally caught seafood dishes in a modern yet cozy dining hall. It's wise to reserve ahead (€21–25 meals, April–Oct daily 18:30–22:00, closed Nov–March, Shelbourne Street, tel. 064/41225).

Packies is a popular bistro with a leafy, low-light interior and cottage ambience serving traditional cuisine with French influence. Their seafood gets rave reviews (€20–30 meals, Tue–Sat 18:00–22:00, closed Sun–Mon, reservations wise, Henry Street, tel. 064/41508).

Mulcahy's Wine Bar has a jazz-mellowed, elegant ambience and creatively presented gourmet dishes. Chef Bruce Mulcahy's "fusion cuisine" is inspired by his travels, with Indian, Japanese, and American influences, and there's always a good vegetarian entrée (€18–28 meals, daily 18:00–22:00, reservations smart, 36 Henry Street, tel. 064/42383, mobile 087-236-4449).

Horse Shoe Pub and Restaurant, specializing in steak and

Kenmare

spare ribs, somehow turns rustic farm-tool decor into a romantic candlelit sanctuary (€15–25 meals, daily 17:00–22:00, Main Street, tel. 064/41553).

P. F. McCarthy's Pub and Restaurant, which feels like a sloppy saloon, serves reasonable salad or sandwich lunches and filling dinner fare. Their barbecued-ribs meal (€14) is a fine value (€13–24 meals, Tue–Sat 12:00–15:00 & 17:00–21:00, Mon lunch only, closed Sun, 14 Main Street, tel. 064/41516).

TRANSPORTATION CONNECTIONS

Kenmare has no train station (the nearest is in Killarney, 20 miles away) and only a few bus connections (www.buseireann.ie). Most buses transfer in Killarney (described later in this chapter).

From Kenmare by Bus to: Killarney (5/day, 45 min), **Tralee** (4/day, 2 hrs), **Dingle** (3/day, 3.25 hrs, change in Tralee or Killarney), **Kinsale** (3/day, 5 hrs), **Dublin** (3/day, 7.5 hrs).

Near Kenmare

These two attractions are near Kenmare, at the eastern (inland) end of the Ring of Kerry. If you're approaching the region from Kinsale and Cobh, drive through Killarney and visit Muckross House the day before you make the big Ring of Kerry loop (described on page 169). This plan allows you to get an early start from Kenmare and helps you avoid all the bus traffic on the Ring.

Killarney

Killarney is a household word among American tourists. And it seems to be on every big-bus tour itinerary. Springing from the bus and train station of this thriving regional center are a few colorful streets lined with tourist-friendly shops and restaurants. Killarney's suburbs sprawl with vast hotels that, except for their weather, feel more like Nebraska than Ireland. Killarney's elegant Neo-Gothic church stands tall as if to say the town existed and mattered long before tourism. But then you realize it dates from 1880...just about when Romantic Age tourism here peaked. For non-shoppers, Killarney's charm is its location at the doorstep of Killarney National Park. And for any tour organizer, it's the logical jumping-off point for excursions around the famous Ring of Kerry peninsula.

If you're traveling in the region without a car, you'll have to stop here. The Killarney bus and train stations flank the big, modern Killarney Outlet Centre mall. (In some touristy parts of Ireland like this one, every other shopping center is called an "outlet"—implying factory-direct values.) With layover time between connections, you can walk straight out from the front of the mall for five minutes, and check out Killarney's shop-lined High Street and New Street.

TRANSPORTATION CONNECTIONS

From Killarney Around the Ring of Kerry: Bus Éireann drives the loop around the Ring of Kerry from Killarney—suitable for a quick peek. While it generally stops only long enough to pick up and drop off travelers en route, there is a 50-minute stop in Sneem (€21, daily June–mid-Sept, departs the Killarney bus station at 13:15 and returns to Killarney at 17:40, no reservation needed). You can catch this same bus from Tralee at 11:50, returning to Tralee by 18:45 (€23).

By Bus to: Kenmare (5/day, 45 min), **Tralee** (16/day, 1.5 hrs), **Dingle** (6/day, 2.5 hrs, change in Tralee), **Shannon Airport** (6/day, 3.5 hrs), **Dublin** (5/day, 6 hrs, change in Limerick). The bus station has a left-luggage desk. For bus schedules, call 01/836-6111 or visit www.buseireann.ie.

By Train to: Tralee (9/day, 45 min), **Cork** (5/day, 1.5 hrs), **Waterford** (2/day, 3 hrs), **Dublin** (7/day, 3.5 hrs). For train schedules, call 01/836-6222 or visit www.irishrail.ie.

To Muckross House: There's no bus service. You can hike, rent a bike, hire a horse buggy, or catch a cab (€12).

Muckross House

Perhaps the best Victorian stately home you'll see in Ireland, Muckross House (built in 1843) is magnificently set at the edge of

Killarney National Park, adjacent to a fascinating open-air farm museum.

Getting There: Muckross House is conveniently located for a break on the long ride from Cork or Cashel to Dingle or Kenmare. From Killarney, follow signs to *Kenmare*, where you'll find Muckross House three miles

south of town. As you approach from Killarney, you'll see a small parking lot two miles before the actual parking lot. This is used by horse-and-buggy bandits to hoodwink tourists into thinking they have to pay to clip-clop to the house. Giddy-up on by and you'll find a big, safe, and free parking lot right at the mansion.

Cost and Hours: €5.75 for house, €8.65 includes house and old farms, covered by Heritage Card. House open daily 9:00–17:30,

July–Aug until 19:00, shorter hours in winter, last entry 1 hour before closing; farms open May–Sept only; tel. 064/31440.

Tours: Be sure to take the 45-minute guided tour that gives meaning to the house (included with admission, offered regularly throughout the day). If you don't take the tour, talk to the docents stationed in several of the rooms.

❷ Self-Guided Tour: This regular stop on the tour-bus circuit includes several sights in one: the mansion, a set of traditional farms showing rural life in the 1930s, a fine garden idyllically set on a lake, and an information center for the national park. The poignant juxtaposition of the magnificent mansion and the humble farmhouses illustrates in a thought-provoking way the vast gap that once separated rich and poor in Ireland.

Muckross House takes you back to the Victorian period—the 19th-century boom time, when the sun never set on the British Empire, and the Industrial Revolution (born in England) was chugging the world into the modern age. Of course, Ireland was a colony back then, with big-shot English landlords. During the Great Potato Famine of 1845–1849, most English gentry lived very well—profiting off the export of their handsome crops to lands with greater buying power—while a third of Ireland's population starved. You can read the Muckross House lord's defense on page 43 of the fine souvenir book.

Muckross House feels lived-in (it was, until 1933). Its fine Victorian furniture is cluttered around the fireplace under Waterford Crystal chandeliers and lots of antlers. You'll see Queen Victoria's bedroom (ground floor, since she was afraid of house fires). They spent a couple of years preparing for her visit in 1861, but she stayed only three nights.

The house exit takes you through an information center for Killarney National Park, with a relaxing 15-minute video on "Ireland's premier national park," featuring lots of geology, flora, and fauna (free, shown on request).

The **garden** is a hit for those with a green thumb, and a €1.50 guide booklet makes the nature trails interesting. A bright, modern cafeteria (with indoor/outdoor seating) faces the garden. The adjacent crafts shop shows weaving and pottery in action.

Muckross Traditional Farms gives the Muckross stop a little heft. It consists of six different farmhouses showing off life in the 1930s. Several farms come with a person ready to feed you a little home-baked bread and reminisce about the old days. The

farms are strung along a mile-long road with an old bus shuttling those who don't want to hike (free, 4/hr).

For those interested in Irish farm life from the 1920s until electricity arrived in 1955, this is a great experience—but only if you engage the attendants in conversation. Each farm is staffed by a Kerry farmer who enjoys telling tales of life on the farm in the old days. They actually remember 1955, when electricity first came. They'd pull on their rubber Wellington boots for safety and nervously "switch it on." Poor farmers could only afford electricity with the help of money from relatives in America. They'd have one bulb hanging from the ceiling and, later, one plug for a hot pot. Every table had a Sacred Heart of Jesus shrine above it. The plug went directly below it. No one dreamed of actually heating the house with electricity. Children slept six to a bed: "three up and three down...feet in your face." You'll learn what happened when you had the only radio in the area, and how one flagstone on the mud floor was enough for the fiddler and dancer to set the beat. Probe with your questions...get personal.

From Muckross House to Kenmare: As you drive south on N-71, Torc Waterfall is a couple of miles past Muckross House (a 10-min walk from the parking lot, through one of the oldest oak forests in Ireland). Driving farther, you pass Black Valley, which separates you from a ridge with the highest point in Ireland (3,600 feet). The scenic pullout called Ladies View is worth a stop. Going over Moll's Gap (WCs beside parking lot), you descend into Kenmare.

Ring of Kerry

The Ring of Kerry (the Iveragh Peninsula) has been the perennial breadwinner of Irish tourism for decades now. Lassoed by

a winding coastal road (the Ring), this mountainous, lake-splattered region comes with breathtaking scenery and the highest peak in Ireland. While a virtual fleet of big, tourist-laden buses circles it each day, they all stay together and seem to stop at the same handful of attractions. Therefore, if you avoid those places at rush hour, the Ring feels remarkably unspoiled and dramatically isolated. Clever motorists, armed with a good map and a reliable alarm clock, can sidestep the crowds and enjoy one of the most rewarding days in Ireland.

Planning Your Time

More than twice the size of the Dingle Peninsula (see next chapter) and backed by a muscular tourism budget that promotes every sight as a "must-see," the Iveragh Peninsula can seem overwhelming. Be selective and don't let them pull the turf over your eyes.

By Car: You can explore the Ring (primarily on N-70) in one satisfying day. Travelers linking overnights in Kinsale and Dingle can insert a night between them in Kenmare (a good base for enjoying the best of the Ring of Kerry). If visiting Muckross House, go there in the afternoon before arriving in Kenmare, to save all of the following day for the Ring.

Tackling the Kinsale-to-Dingle drive plus the Ring of Kerry, all in the same day, is doable—but you add about 2.5 hours of driving beyond the actual Ring, meaning you have little time to stop and enjoy anything.

If you're considering a boat trip out to the desperately remote and evocative island of Skellig Michael (described on page 181), you'll need to add another day to allow for an overnight in the Portmagee area...and hope for good weather.

By Public Transportation: You have three options for seeing the Ring of Kerry without a car, none of which is as enjoyable as driving the loop yourself: minibus tour from Kenmare (see page 160); big-bus tour from Killarney (TI tel. 064/31633); or public bus from Killarney (see page 167).

Driving the Ring of Kerry (Made Less Scary)

On a one-day visit to the Ring, I'd leave Kenmare by 8:30 and head clockwise (against the prevailing tour-bus traffic). Allow time for stops at Staigue Ring Fort (45 min) and Derrynane House (1 hour), and get to Waterville before noon. To entirely miss the chain of tour buses, which slithers (like a python swallowing a pig) counterclockwise around the Ring, get to Waterville by 10:30; shortly after that, leave the main drag for the Skellig Ring (which has a road too narrow for big buses). By the time you rejoin the main route, the python is long gone. On the last half of the route, there are two more hour-long stops: the Skellig Experience Centre and another two big ring forts. For a stop-by-stop description of this route, see my self-guided driving tour on page 172.

The only downside of going against all the bus traffic is that, on this narrow Ring road, buses have the right-of-way. There are lots of scenic-view pullouts, and it will be up to you to back up to the nearest wide spot in the road to let

The Ring of Kerry vs. the Dingle Peninsula

If I had to choose one spot to enjoy the small-town charm of traditional Ireland, it would be Dingle and its history-laden scenic peninsula. But the Ring of Kerry—a much bigger, more famous, and more touristed peninsula just to its south—is also great to visit. If you go to Ireland and don't see the famous Ring of Kerry, your uncle Pat will never forgive you. Here's a comparison to help with your itinerary planning.

Both peninsulas come with a scenic loop drive. Dingle's is 30 miles. The Ring of Kerry is 120 miles. Both loops come with lots of megalithic wonder. Dingle's prehistory is more intimate, with numerous little evocative stony structures. The Ring of Kerry's prehistory shows itself in three massive ring forts—far bigger than anything on Dingle.

Dingle town is the perfect little Irish burg—alive with traditional music pubs, an active fishing harbor, and the sturdy cultural atmosphere of a Gaeltacht. You can easily spend three fun nights here. In comparison, Kenmare (the best base for the Ring of Kerry loop) is pleasant but forgettable. Those spending a night on the west end of the Ring of Kerry find a rustic lack of charm in Portmagee (the base for a cruise to Skellig Michael).

Near Dingle, the heather- and moss-covered Great Blasket Island and the excellent Great Blasket Centre offer insights into the storytelling traditions and simple lives of hardy fisherfolk who—until 50 years ago—lived just off the tip of the Dingle Peninsula. Off the tip of the Ring of Kerry, Skellig Michael—a brutally rugged and remote chunk of rock in the Atlantic, with evocative medieval stone ruins of its long-gone hermit monks—is a world-class sight. But the Skellig Experience Centre near Portmagee on the mainland is unimpressive compared with Dingle's Great Blasket Centre.

Muckross House, with its fascinating open-air farmhouse museum and beautiful lake views of Killarney National Park, is on the eastern side of the Ring of Kerry. But it's also an efficient and natural stop for those driving between Kinsale and Dingle—so you can see it regardless of which scenic peninsula drive you take.

Both regions are beyond the reach of the Irish train system and require a car or bus service to access. Both offer memorable scenery, great restaurants, warm B&B hospitality, and similar prices. The bottom line: With limited time, choose Dingle. If you have a day or two to spare, the Ring of Kerry is also a delight.

a less-nimble bus get through a tight curve. But with an early start, you can avoid these hassles: On my last circuit, I got to Waterville by 11:00, from where I slipped happily into the bus-free Skellig Ring...and didn't have to pass a single bus all day.

Smart drivers equip themselves with a good map before driving the Ring of Kerry loop. If you don't have one already, pick up the *Ordnance Survey Atlas* (€12.50, sold in most TIs and bookstores in Ireland). The *Fir Tree Aerial* series makes a useful map that covers both the Iveragh (Ring of Kerry) and Dingle Peninsulas, giving you a bird's-eye feel for the terrain (€8, sold in many TIs and bookstores in County Kerry).

The flat, inland, northeastern section of the Ring, from Killarney to Killorglin on N-72, is entirely skippable. Note that gas in Kenmare is cheaper than out on the Ring.

SELF-GUIDED DRIVING TOUR

The Ring of Kerry

Here's a sightseeing tip sheet for my preferred clockwise route, kilometer by kilometer. If you do any exploring, you'll likely get hopelessly off, but the kilometer references still help—just do the arithmetic to know how far various stops are from each other. Several of these stops are explained in far greater detail later in this chapter, in the same order that they're listed here.

0 km: Leave Kenmare.

17.6 km: On the right is Glacier Lake, with a long, smooth limestone "banister" carved by a glacier 10,000 years ago.

22.8 km: Parknasilla Hotel—a posh 19th-century hotel—is a great stop for tea and scones (described on page 164).

26 km: Visit the town of Sneem (described below).

40.4 km: Turn off for Staigue Ring Fort (described below).

41.5 km: On the left, enjoy great views of the Beara Peninsula beyond a ruined hospital with IRA ties (it was funded around 1910 by a local English woman sympathetic to the Irish Republican cause). No one wants to touch these ruins today, out of fear of "kicking up a beehive."

43.5 km: Carroll's Cove has a fine beach with some of the warmest water in Ireland, grand views of Kenmare Bay, a local trailer park, and "Ireland's only beachside bar."

46.4 km: Take the turn-off for Derrynane House (Home of Daniel O'Connell, described below).

50.4 km: Enjoy brilliant views for the next two kilometers to Coomikista Pass.

52.4 km: The Coomikista Pass lookout point (700-foot altitude) offers grand views in both directions.

54.5 km: Watch for fine views of Skellig Islands.

Ring of Kerry

TO TRALEE

KERRY AIRPORT

N-22

FARRAN-
FORE

KILLARNEY

MUCKROSS
HOUSE +
FARM

TORC
WATERFALL

TO
CORK

KILLORGLIN

N-72

R-561

KILLARNEY
NATL. PARK

LADIES
VIEW

MOLLS
GAP

KENMARE

PENINSULA

TO
GLENGARRIFF

DINGLE
(AN DAINGEAN)

DINGLE PENINSULA

INCH

DINGLE BAY

GLENCAR

IVERAGH PENINSULA

N-70

KELLS

LISSATINNIG
BRIDGE

N-71

N-70

R-568

SNEEM

RIVER

PARKNASILLA
HOTEL

BEARA

BLASKET
ISLANDS

LEACANABUAILE
+ CAHERGAL
RING FORTS

CAHER-
SIVEEN

WATERVILLE

COOMA-
KESTA PASS

STAIGUE
FORT

CASTLE-KENMARE

CAHER-
DANIEL

COVE

SKELLIG
EXPERIENCE
CENTRE

VALENTIA
ISLAND

R-565

SKELLIG
RING

R-567

BALLIN-
SKELLIGS

DERRYNANE
HOUSE

PORTMAGEE

COOMAN-
ASPIC
PASS

SMALL
SKELLIG

SKELLIG
MICHAEL

KILLARNEY NATL. PARK

5 MILES

10 KM

"RING OF KERRY"
RECOMMENDED
DRIVING ROUTE

OTHER ROADS

KILLARNEY NATL. PARK

Ring of Kerry

The Ring Forts of Kerry

The Ring of Kerry comes with three awe-inspiring prehistoric ring forts—among the largest and best-preserved in all of Ireland. Staigue Fort (near the beginning of my recommended, clockwise Ring route) is most impressive and in a desolate setting, with a small museum a couple of miles away, at the base of the access road. The two others—Cahergal and Leacanabuaile, side-by-side just north of Cahersiveen  (closer to the end of the Ring, after Valentia Island)—are easier to visit and plenty evocative. Each ring fort is about a 2.5-mile (4-km) side-trip off the main drag. If you're trying to beat the tour-bus convoy, Staigue Fort is problematic because it eats up morning time before the buses have passed you. The Cahersiveen ring forts are your last stop in the Ring of Kerry, when bus traffic is of no concern.

All of these ring forts have the same basic features. The circular drystone walls were built sometime between 500 B.C. and A.D. 300 without the aid of mortar or cement. About 80 feet across, with walls 12 feet thick at the base and up to 20 feet high, these brutish structures would have taken a hundred men six months

56.4 km: Notice the ruins of famine villages on both sides of the road.

59.6 km: In the town of Waterville, you'll see a sculpture of Charlie Chaplin on the left. Waterville is also home to Butler Arms Hotel—a fine stop for tea and scones in their Charlie Chaplin room (with lots of photos of the silent film icon and his young wife frolicking as they lived well in Ireland).

65 km: After rejoining the main road and turning left, cross the small bridge that's locally famous for salmon fly-fishing. Take the first left (R-567) for the Skellig Ring loop (follow brown *Skellig Ring* signs through Ballinskelligs, and then scenically to Portmagee). At this point, you've left the big bus route.

75 km: St. Finan's Bay lies about halfway around, with a pleasant little picnic-friendly beach (but no WCs). Just before the bay is the small Skelligs Chocolate Factory (free samples and a fun visit).

83 km: You reach Portmagee, a small port town and jumping-off point for boats to Skellig Islands (described on page 181).

to complete. Expert opinion is divided, but most believe that the people who built them would have retreated here at times of  tribal war. As this was a time when civilization was morphing from nomadic hunter-gathers to settled farmers, herders used these forts. They likely brought their valuable cattle inside to protect them from ancient rustlers. Other experts see the round design as a kind of amphitheater, where local clan chieftains would have gathered for important meetings or rituals. However, the ditch surrounding the outer walls of Staigue Fort suggests a defensive, rather than ceremonial, function. Without written records, we can only imagine the part these awe-inspiring piles of finely stacked stones played in ancient dramas.

There is such a wealth of prehistoric sights in southwest Ireland because this region had copper mines. The Bronze Age wouldn't have been the Bronze Age without copper, which was melted together with tin to make bronze for better weapons and tools (2000 to 500 B.C.). The many circles reflect the affluence that the abundance of copper brought to the region.

83.2 km: Cross the bridge to the Skellig Experience Centre (described below). You've entered Valentia Island, its name hinting at medieval trading connections with nearby Spain—which lies due south.

91.2 km: At the church in Knightstown, turn left for the Knightstown Heritage Museum (described below).

93 km: Return to the main road and go through Knightstown to the tiny ferry (€5/car, goes constantly, 2-kilometer trip).

95 km: Leaving the ferry, rejoin N-70 (the main Ring of Kerry route), turning left for the town of Cahersiveen. In Cahersiveen, you can detour a few kilometers to two impressive stone ring forts, Cahergal and Leacanabuaile (described below).

100 km: Return to N-70 at Cahersiveen and follow signs for *Glenbeigh* and *Killorglin*. Enjoy views of Dingle town (you can see the harbor and Ersk Tower) and Inch Beach.

The rest of the loop is the least scenic. At Killorglin, you've seen all there is to see. From here, go either to Dingle (left) or to Kenmare/Killarney/Kinsale (right).

Sneem

Sneem is inundated by tour buses daily from 14:00 to 16:00. The rest of the day, Sneem is peaceful and laid-back. This humble town has two entertaining squares. The Irish joke, "As we're in Kerry, the square on the east side is called South Square and the one on the west is called North Square." On the first (South) square, you'll see a statue of Steve "Crusher" Casey, the local boy who reigned as world champion heavyweight wrestler (1937–1947). Across from that, the Celtic Weave China shop is the only place other than Tiffany & Co. in New York City where you can buy this fine woven china (reportedly a favorite of Jackie Onassis). A sweet little peat-toned waterfall gurgles under the bridge connecting the two Sneem squares. The North Square features a memorial to former French president Charles de Gaulle's visit (he came here for two weeks of R&R during the tumultuous days in 1969, when students were revolting in Paris). Locals call it "da gallstone."

Staigue Fort

This ring fort is worth a stop on your way around the Ring. Before seeing the fort (which is always open and free), visit the exhibition centre (tiny museum, detailed fort model, 10-minute film, drop €1 in the donation box, Easter–Sept daily 10:00–21:00, closed Oct–Easter, tel. 066/947-5127, coffee shop and WCs). While viewing the imposing pile of stone, read "The Ring Forts of Kerry" sidebar.

The fort is 2.5 miles (4 km) off the main N-70 road up a tiny rural access lane (look for signs just after the hamlet of Castle Cove).

Derrynane House

This is the home of Daniel O'Connell, Ireland's most influential pre-independence politician, whose tireless nonviolent agitation gained equality for Catholics 175 years ago. The coastal lands of the O'Connell estate that surround Derrynane House are now a national historic park. A visit here is a window onto a man who not only liberated Ireland from the last oppressive anti-Catholic penal laws, but who also first developed the idea of a grass-roots movement, organizing on a massive scale to achieve political ends without bloodshed (see sidebar).

Getting There: Just outside the town of Derrynane, pick up a handy free map of the estate from the little TI inside the brown

Ring of Kerry

Daniel O'Connell
(1775–1847)

Born in Cahersiveen and elected in Ennis as the first Catholic member of the British Parliament, O'Connell was the hero of Catholic emancipation in Ireland. Educated in France at a time when the anti-Catholic penal laws limited schooling for Irish Catholics in Ireland, he witnessed the carnage of the French Revolution. Upon his return to Ireland, he saw more bloodshed during the futile Rebellion of 1798. He chose law as his profession and reluctantly killed a man who challenged him to a duel. Abhorring all this violence, O'Connell dedicated himself to peacefully gaining equal rights for Catholics in an Ireland dominated by a wealthy Protestant minority. He formed the Catholic Association with a one-penny-per-month membership fee and quickly gained a huge following (especially among the poor) with his persuasive speaking skills. Although Catholics weren't allowed to hold office, he ran for election to Parliament anyway and won a seat in 1828. His unwillingness to take the anti-Catholic Oath of Supremacy initially kept him out of Westminster, but the moral force of his victory caused the government to give in and concede Catholic emancipation the following year. Known as "the Liberator," O'Connell was making progress toward his next goal of repealing the Act of Union with Britain when the Potato Famine hit in 1845. O'Connell died two years later in Genoa on his way to Rome, but his ideals lived on: His Catholic Association was the model for political organization to the Irish who later emigrated and rose within American big-city political "green machines."

Wave Crest market (TI open mid-March–mid-Oct daily 9:00–20:00, closed mid-Oct–mid-March, tel. 066/947-5188; market is a great place to buy a picnic). One mile after the market, take a left and follow the signs into Derrynane National Historic Park.

Cost and Hours: €2.90, covered by Heritage Card; May–Sept Mon–Sat 9:00–18:00, Sun 11:00–19:00; April and Oct Tue–Sun 13:00–17:00, closed Mon; Nov–March Sat–Sun 13:00–17:00, closed Mon–Fri; last entry 45 min before closing, tel. 066/947-5113.

⊙ Self-Guided Tour: Navigate the house's quirky floor plan with the laminated guide from the front desk. Ask about the next scheduled 20-minute audiovisual show, which fleshes out the highlights of O'Connell's turbulent life and makes the contents of the house more interesting.

In the exhibition room downstairs is a glass case containing the pistols that were used in O'Connell's famous duel. Beside them are his black gloves, one of which he always wore on his right hand when he went to Mass (out of remorse for the part it played in taking a man's life). The drawing room upstairs is lined with family portraits and contains his ornately carved chair with tiny harp strings and wolfhound collars made of gold. On a wall in the upstairs bedroom is a copy of O'Connell's famous speech imploring the Irish not to riot when he was arrested. The coach house (out back) shows off the enormous grand chariot that carried O'Connell through throngs of joyous Dubliners after his release from prison in 1844. He added the small chapel wing to the house in gratitude to God for his prison release.

Portmagee

Just a short row of snoozy buildings lining the bay, Portmagee is the best harbor for boat excursions out to the Skellig Islands (see page 181). It's a quiet village with a handful of B&Bs, two pubs, a bakery, a market, and no ATMs. On the rough harborfront, a slate memorial to sailors lost at sea from here reads, "In the nets of God may we be gathered."

A 100-yard-long bridge connects Portmagee to gentle Valentia Island, where you'll find the Skellig Experience Centre (on the left at the Valentia end of the bridge; see next page). A public parking lot is at the Portmagee end of the bridge, with award-winning WCs (no kidding: Irish Toilet of the Year 2002 runner-up plaque proudly displayed). The first transatlantic cable (for telegraph communication) was laid from Valentia Island in 1866 (see page 180). The tiny post office hides inside O'Connell's Market (Mon–Fri 9:00–17:30, Sat 9:00–13:00, closed Sun).

SLEEPING

(€1 = about $1.30, country code: 353, area code: 066)
$$$ Moorings Guest House feels like a small hotel, with 17 rooms, a pub and a fine restaurant downstairs, and the most convenient location in town, 50 yards from the end of the pier (Db-€80–130, Tb-€120–150, Qb-€160–190, tel. 066/947-7108, fax 066/947-7220, www.moorings.ie, moorings@iol.ie, Gerard and Patricia Kennedy).

$$ Portmagee Heights B&B is a modern, solid slate home at the edge of town renting five hotel-like rooms (Db-€70–80, Tb-€120, 10 percent discount with this book in 2008—mention when you book, on the road into town, tel. 066/947-7251, www.portmageeheights.com, stay@portmageeheights.com, Monica Hussey).

$$ Beach Cove B&B offers four comfortable, fresh, and lovingly decorated rooms in splendid isolation four miles south of Portmagee, over lofty Coomanaspic ridge, beside the pretty beach at St. Finan's Bay. Charming Bridie O'Connor will arrange a boat trip out to the Skelligs for you. Her adjacent cottage out back has two double rooms and a kitchen, making it ideal for families (Sb-€45–50, Db-€66–70, Tb-€99–105, tel. 066/947-9301, mobile 087-202-1820, www.stayatbeachcove.com, beachcove@eircom.net). Bridie's husband, Jack, happens to be the head coach of the Kerry football team...a very important person in this part of Ireland.

EATING

These options all line the waterfront (between the pier and the bridge to Valentia Island).

The Moorings is an expensive restaurant with great seafood caught literally just outside its front door (€18–29 dinners, Tue–Sun 18:00–22:00, closed Mon, reservations smart, tel. 066/947-7108).

The **Bridge Bar,** next door, does traditional pub grub but stops serving food a bit early. Call ahead to check on their traditional music and dance schedule (€12–17 meals, daily 12:00–20:30, live music Tue, Fri, and Sun nights, tel. 066/947-7108).

The **Fisherman's Bar** is less pretentious, with more locals and cheaper prices (€10–18 meals, daily 12:00–21:00, tel. 066/947-7103).

Picnic Supplies: **O'Connell's Market** is the only grocery (Mon–Sat 9:00–21:30, Sun 10:00–18:00). **Skellig Mist Bakery** can make basic lunch sandwiches to take on Skellig boat excursions (daily 9:00–17:00, tel. 066/947-7250).

Valentia Island

These two sights are on Valentia Island, across the bridge from Portmagee.

Skellig Experience Centre

Whether or not you're actually sailing to Skellig Michael (described below), this little center (with crude exhibits and a 15-minute audiovisual show) explains it well—both the story of the monks and the natural environment (€5, daily July–Aug 10:00–19:00, until 18:00 in spring and fall, closed entirely mid-Nov–mid-March, last entry 1 hour before closing, call ahead outside of peak season as hours may vary, on Valentia Island beside bridge linking it to Portmagee, tel. 066/947-6306, www.skelligexperience.com).

The Skellig Experience Centre arranges two-hour **boat trips,**

Communication in Ireland: Tetrapods to Lindbergh

Many Irish paleontologists believe the first fish slithered out of the water here on four stubby legs 385 million years ago, onto what would become the Isle of Saints and Scholars. Over time, those tetrapods evolved. Irish scribes—living in remote outposts like the Skellig Islands just off this coast—kept literate life alive in Europe through the

darkest depths of the so-called "Dark Ages." In fact, around the year 800, Charlemagne imported monks from this part of Ireland to be his scribes. Evolution, literacy, communication. Just over a thousand years later, in the mid-19th century, Paul Julius Reuter—who provided a financial news service in Europe—couldn't get his pigeons to fly across the Atlantic. So he relied on ships coming from America to drop a news capsule overboard as they rounded this southwest corner of Ireland. His boys would wait in their little boats with nets to "get the scoop." They say Europe learned of Lincoln's assassination (1865) from a capsule tossed over a boat here. The first cables were laid across the Atlantic from here to Newfoundland, giving the two hemispheres telegraphic communication. Queen Victoria got to be the first to send a message—greeting American president Andrew Johnson in 1866. Marconi achieved the first wireless transatlantic communication from this corner of Ireland to America in 1901. And in 1927, when Charles Lindbergh ushered in the age of transatlantic flight, this was the first bit of land he saw. Today, driving under the 21st-century mobile phone and satellite tower crowning a hilltop above Valentia Island while gazing out at the Skellig Islands, a traveler marvels at the progress in communication—and the part this remote corner of Ireland played in it.

circling both Skellig Michael and Little Skellig (without actually putting people ashore on them)—ideal for those who want a close look without the stair climb and vertigo that go with an actual visit to the island (€20, sailing daily about 15:00 and returning by 17:00, weather permitting, depart from Valentia Island pier 50 yards below the Skellig Experience Centre).

Knightstown Heritage Museum

The humble Valentia schoolhouse, built in 1861, houses an equally humble but interesting little museum highlighting the quirky things of historic interest on Valentia Island. You'll see a 19th-century schoolroom and learn about tetrapods (those first fish to climb onto land—which locals claim happened here). You'll also follow the long story of the expensive, frustrating, and heroic battle to lay telegraph cable across the Atlantic, which finally succeeded in 1866 when the largest ship in the world connected this tiny island of Valentia with Newfoundland. This project was the initiative of the Atlantic Telegraph Company, which later became Western Union. These local stories are told with intimate black-and-white photos and typewritten pages (€3, April–Sept daily 10:30–18:00, closed Oct–March). If interested in those tetrapods, the actual "first footprints" are a 15-minute drive from here, on a rugged bit of rocky shoreline a 10-minute hike below a parking lot (free, always viewable, get details locally).

Cahergal and Leacanabuaile Ring Forts

Crowning bluffs in farm country, 2.5 miles (4 km) off the main road at Cahersiveen, these two windy and desolate forts are each different and worth a look. You'll hike a few hundred yards from the tiny parking lot (free, always open, no museum). Just beyond the Cahersiveen town church at the tourist office, turn left, cross the narrow bridge, turn left again, and follow signs for ancient forts—you'll see the huge stone structures in the distance. For all the details, see "The Ring Forts of Kerry" on page 174.

Skellig Michael

A trip to this jagged, isolated pyramid—the Holy Grail of Irish monastic island settlements—rates as a truly memorable ▲▲▲ experience. After visiting Skellig Michael a hundred years ago, Nobel Prize–winning Irish author George Bernard Shaw called it "the most fantastic and impossible rock in the world."

Rising seven miles offshore, the Skelligs (Gaelic for "splinter") are two gigantic slate-and-sandstone rocks crouched aggressively on the ocean horizon. The larger of the two, Skellig Michael, is over 700 feet tall and a mile around, with a tiny cluster of abandoned beehive huts clinging near its summit like stubborn barnacles. The smaller of the two, Little Skellig, is home to a huge colony of gannets (like a large, graceful seagull with a six-foot wingspan), protected by law from visitors setting foot on shore.

Skellig Michael (dedicated to the archangel) was first inhabited by sixth-century Christian monks. Inspired by earlier hermit monks in the Egyptian desert, they sought the purity of isolation to get closer to God. Neither Viking raids nor winter storms could dislodge them as they patiently built a half-dozen small stone igloo-like dwellings and a couple of tiny oratories. Their remote cliff-terrace perch is still connected to the sea 600 feet below by an amazing series of rock stairs. Viking Olav Trygvasson, who later became King of Norway and introduced Christianity to his country, was baptized here in 956.

Chiseling the most rudimentary life out of solid rock, the monks lived a harsh, lonely, disciplined existence for over 500 years. They collected rainwater in cisterns and lived off fish and birds. To supplement their meager existence, they gathered bird eggs and feathers to trade with passing boats for cereals, candles, and animal hides (used for clothing and for copying scripture). They finally moved their holy community ashore to Ballinskelligs in the early 1100s.

Since you'll have only a few hours to explore the island, begin by climbing the seemingly unending series of stone stairs to the monastic ruins (600 vertical feet of uneven stone stairs with no handrails). Save most of your photographing for the way down. Those who linger too long below risk missing the enlightening 20-minute free talk among the beehive huts given by guides who camp on the island

from April through October. Afterward, poke your head into some of the huts and try to imagine the dark, damp, and devoted life of a monk here over 1,000 years ago. After rambling through the ruins, you can give in to photo frenzy as you wander back down the stairs.

The two lighthouses on the far side of the island are now automated, and access to them has been blocked off. There are no WCs or modern shelters of any kind on Skellig Michael.

If you visit between late April and early August, you'll be surrounded by fearless rainbow-beaked puffins, which nest here in underground burrows. Their bizarre swallowed cooing sounds like a distant chainsaw. These portly little birds live off fish, and divers have reported seeing them 20 feet underwater in pursuit of their prey.

Your return boat journey usually includes a pass near Little Skellig, which looms like an iceberg with a white coat of guano—courtesy of the 20,000 gannets that circle overhead like feathered confetti. Although these large birds have six-foot wing spans, they suddenly morph into sleek darts when pursuing a fish, piercing the water from over 100 feet above. You're also likely to get a glimpse of gray seals lazing on rocks near the water's edge.

Getting to Skellig Michael: To book a boat trip from Portmagee, contact **Murphy Sea Cruise** (€40, office across from O'Connell's Market, tel. 066/947-7156, mobile 087-234-2168 or 087-645-1909, www.esatclear.ie/~skelligsrock, murphyseacruise @esatclear.ie), **Joe Roddy** (tel. 066/947-4268 or mobile 087-120-9924, www.skelligstrips.com), or **Brendan Casey** (tel. 066/947-2437).

Warning: Landing on Skellig Michael is highly weather-dependent. If the seas are too choppy, the boats cannot safely put people ashore on the concrete island pier (a bit like jumping off a trampoline onto an ice rink). Excursions are scheduled to run daily from Easter to late September, but experienced boat captains say they are able to put visitors ashore roughly five days out of seven in an average summer week.

Your best bet is to reserve a room near Portmagee that fits your itinerary, then call a few days in advance to make a boat reservation. Keep your fingers crossed for good weather. Contact the boat operator on the morning of departure to get the final word. If the seas are too rough, he can tell from Portmagee and will make a decision that morning whether or not to go (rather than taking passengers halfway out, then aborting).

Boat trips normally depart Portmagee at 10:30, sail for an hour, leave you ashore from 11:30 until 14:00, and get you back into Portmagee by 15:00 (with plenty of time to drive on to Dingle). There is a total fleet of 15 small boats (from Portmagee, Ballinskelligs, Waterville, and Valentia Island) that have permits

Skellig Michael

to land on Skellig Michael. Each boat can carry a dozen passengers. This limits the number of daily visitors and minimizes the impact on the sensitive island ecosystem.

Bring your camera, a sandwich lunch (easy to buy at Skellig Mist Bakery in Portmagee—see page 179), water, sunscreen, rain gear, and comfortable hiking shoes for rocky terrain.

DINGLE PENINSULA

An Daingean

The Dingle Peninsula, the westernmost tip of Ireland, offers just the right mix of far-and-away beauty, ancient archaeological wonders, and isolated walks and bike rides—all within convenient reach of its main town. Dingle town is just large enough to have all the necessary tourist services and a steady nocturnal beat of Irish folk music.

Although crowded in summer, it still feels like the fish and the farm really matter in Dingle. Forty fishing boats sail from here, tractor tracks dirty the main drag, and a faint whiff of peat fills the nighttime streets.

For 30 years, my Irish dreams have been set here on this sparse but lush peninsula, where locals are fond of saying, "The next parish over is Boston." There's a feeling of closeness to the land in Dingle. When I asked a local if he was born here, he thought for a second and said, "No, it was about six miles down the road." When I told him where I was from, a far-away smile filled his eyes, and he looked out to sea and sighed, "Ah, the shores of Americy." I asked his friend if he'd lived here all his life. He said, "Not yet."

Dingle feels so traditionally Irish because it's part of the Gaeltacht, a region where the government subsidizes the survival of the Irish language and culture. While English is always there, the signs, menus, and songs come in Gaelic. Children carry hurling sticks to class, and even the local preschool brags "ALL Gaelic."

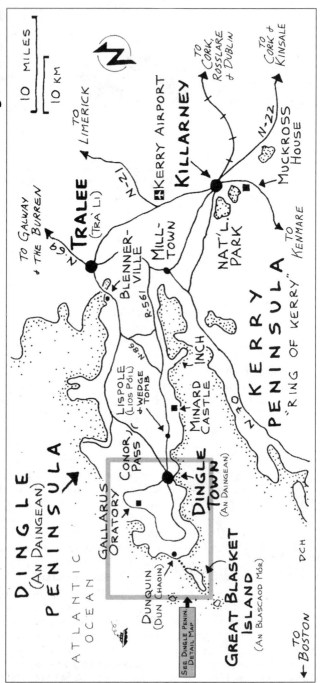

Dingle Town

Of the peninsula's 10,000 residents, 1,500 live in Dingle town. Its few streets, lined with ramshackle but gaily painted shops and pubs, run up from a rain-stung harbor always busy with fishing boats and leisure sailboats. Traditionally, the buildings were drab gray or whitewashed. Thirty years ago, Ireland's "tidy town" competition prompted everyone to paint their buildings in playful pastels.

It's a peaceful town. The courthouse (1832) is open one hour a month. The judge does his best to wrap up business within a half-hour. During the day, you'll see teenagers—already working on ruddy beer-glow cheeks—roll kegs up the streets and into the pubs in preparation for another night of music and *craic* (fun conversation and atmosphere).

Planning Your Time

For the shortest visit, give Dingle two nights and a day. It takes six to eight hours to get there from Dublin, Galway, or the boat dock in Rosslare. By spending two nights, you'll feel more like a local on your second evening in the pubs. You'll need the better part of a day to explore the 30-mile loop around the peninsula by bike, car, or tour bus (see "Dingle Peninsula Circular Tour," page 209). To do any serious walking or relaxing, you'll need two or three days. It's not uncommon to find Americans slowing way, way down in Dingle town.

Dingle's season peaks in July and August and really dies off-season. If you're traveling during the summer months, it's wise to reserve your B&B in advance. I've generally listed hours for the tourist season (April–Sept). Hours may be longer in July and August, and most places cut way back or shut down entirely from October to March.

ORIENTATION

(area code: 066)
Dingle—extremely comfortable on foot—hangs on a medieval grid of streets between the harborfront (where the Tralee bus stops) and Main Street (three blocks inland). Nothing in town is more than a 10-minute walk away. Street numbers are used only when more than one place is run by a family of the same name. Most locals know most locals, and people on the street are fine sources of information. Remember, locals love their soda bread, and tourism provides the butter. You'll find a warm and sincere welcome.

Dingle

Dingle or An Daingean?

There's been a controversy lately over the name of this town and peninsula. Being a Gaeltacht, the entire region gets subsidies from the government (which supports the survival of the traditional Irish culture and language). A precondition of this financial support is that towns use their Irish (Gaelic) name. But Dingle (which is An Daingean in Irish—pronounced "on DANG-un") has voted down this dictate from Dublin. Dingle has become so wealthy from the tourist trade that it sees its famous name as a trademark, and doesn't want to become "the cute tourist town with the unpronounceable name formerly known as Dingle." Therefore, while many road signs identify the town only as "An Daingean," local businesses, all tourist information, and nearly all people—locals and tourists alike—still refer to it as Dingle.

For the sake of clarity, in this book I'll follow the local convention: Dingle instead of "An Daingean," Great Blasket Island instead of "An Blascaod Mór," and so on. But for ease of navigation, I'll also include the place's Irish name in parentheses. For a complete list of these bilingual place names, see the sidebar on page 208.

Tourist Information

The TI is a privately owned, for-profit business—little more than a glorified shop with a green staff who know the town, but not much about the rest of the peninsula (July–Aug Mon–Sat 9:00–18:00, Sun 10:00–17:00, less off-season, on Strand Street by the water, tel. 066/915-1188). For more knowledgeable help, drop by the Mountain Man shop (on Strand Street, see "Dingle Activities," in "Helpful Hints" below) or talk to your B&B host.

Dingle Area

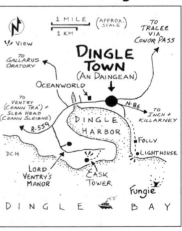

Helpful Hints

Before You Go: The local website (www.dingle-peninsula.ie) lists festivals and events.

Crowds: Crowds trample Dingle's charm throughout July and August. The absolute craziest times are during the Dingle Races (second weekend in Aug), Dingle Regatta (third weekend in Aug), and the Blessing of the Boats (end of Aug and beginning of Sept). The first Mondays in May, June, and August are bank holidays, giving Ireland's workers three-day weekends—and ample time to fill up Dingle. The town's metabolism (prices, schedules, activities) rises and falls with the tourist crowds, so October through April is sleepy.

Money: Two banks in town, both on Main Street, offer the same rates (Mon 10:00–17:00, Tue–Fri 10:00–16:00, closed Sat–Sun) and have cash machines. The TI happily changes cash and travelers checks at mediocre rates. Expect to use cash (rather than credit cards) to pay for most peninsula activities.

Internet Access: Dingle has three places to get online (the first two charge about €4/hr and are open daily 10:00–22:00, and the third is free): **Dingle Internet Café** (on Main Street), **The Old Forge Internet Café** (at Holy Ground), and the **old library** (Green Street, its two free terminals are usually busy but you can drop by and reserve a 40-minute slot anytime).

Post Office: It's on Main Street near Benners Hotel (Mon–Fri 9:00–17:30, Sat 9:00–13:00, closed Sun).

Laundry: While there is no self-service laundry in Dingle, two full-service places offer same-day wash and dry: **Dingle Cleaners** (€12 for up to 14 pounds, Mon–Sat 9:30–18:00, closed Sun, beside Moran's Market and gas station, tel. 066/915-0680, Kay) and **Niolann Laundromat** (€10 for a big load, Mon–Fri 9:00–17:30, closed Sat–Sun, off Green Street in Dick Mack's yard, tel. 066/915-1837).

Bike Rental: Bike-rental shops abound, renting 18-speed hybrids for around €10 day. The cheapest is at **Eileen Collins B&B** (€8/day, Greys Lane—see "Sleeping," page 199), or try Paddy's **Bike Hire** (€10/day or €3 more for 24 hrs, €12 for better bikes, daily 9:00–19:00, on Dykegate next to Grapevine Hostel, tel. 066/915-2311). **Foxy John's** (Green Street), **Mountain Man** (no helmets), and the **Ballintaggert Hostel** also rent bikes. If you're biking the peninsula, get a bike with skinny street tires, not slow and fat mountain-bike tires. Plan on leaving €20 plus a driver's license or passport as a security deposit.

Taxi: Try Diarmuid Begley (mobile 087-250-4767), Sean with S.O.L. Cabs in Dingle (mobile 087-660-2323), or Tom Kearney out in Dunquin (mobile 087-933-2264).

Parking: If you're not staying overnight (i.e., parking at your B&B), then use the waterfront parking lot extending west from the TI (€1/hr, pay at meter in lot and display on dashboard, daily 8:00–18:00).

Dingle Activities: The **Mountain Man,** a hiking shop run by local guide Adrian Curran, is a clearinghouse for information on hiking, biking, horseback riding, climbing, peninsula tours, and trips to the Blasket Islands (the shop is the Dingle town

Dingle's History

The wet sod of Dingle is soaked with medieval history. In the darkest depths of the Dark Ages, peace-loving, bookish monks fled the chaos of the Continent and its barbarian raids. They sailed to the drizzly fringe of the known world—places like Dingle. These monks kept literacy alive in Europe. Charlemagne, who ruled much of Europe in the year 800, imported Irish monks to be his scribes.

It was from this peninsula that the semi-mythical explorer-monk, St. Brendan, is said to have set sail in the sixth century in search of a legendary western paradise. Some think he beat Columbus to North America by nearly a thousand years (see page 195).

Dingle was a busy seaport in the late Middle Ages. Dingle and Tralee (covered later in this chapter) were the only walled towns in Kerry. Castles stood at the low and high ends of Dingle's Main Street, protecting the Normans from the angry and dispossessed Irish outside. Dingle was a gateway to northern Spain—a three-day sail due south. Many 14th- and 15th-century pilgrims left from Dingle for the revered Spanish church in Santiago de Compostela, thought to house the bones of St. James.

In Dingle's medieval heyday, locals traded cowhides for wine. When Dingle's position as a trading center waned, the town faded in importance. In the 19th century, it was a linen-weaving center. Until 1970, fishing dominated, and the only visitors were scholars and students of old Irish ways. In 1970, the movie *Ryan's Daughter* introduced the world to Dingle. The trickle of Dingle fans has grown to a flood as word of its musical, historical, gastronomical, and scenic charms—not to mention its friendly dolphin—has spread.

contact for the Dunquin–Blasket Islands boats and shuttle-bus rides to the harbor—see "Blasket Islands," page 218). Give them a call a few days ahead of time to see which guided, scenic, mountain day-hikes are scheduled (daily July–mid-Sept 9:00–21:00, mid-Sept–June 9:00–18:00, just off harbor at Strand Street, tel. 066/915-2400, www.themountainmanshop.com).

Travel Agency: Maurice O'Connor at **Galvin's Travel Agency** can book plane tickets, as well as boat rides to France (Mon–Fri 9:30–18:00, Sat 9:30–17:00, closed Sun, John Street, tel. 066/915-1409).

Farmers Market: On most Fridays (10:00–14:00), local farmers gather near the roundabout to sell their fresh produce and homemade marmalade.

SELF-GUIDED WALK

▲Dingle Introductory Historical Walk

This quick 10-stop circle through town gives you a once-over-lightly overview and good orientation (see route—outlined in gray—on page 201).

1. Start at the **roundabout,** which replaced the big bridge over the town river in the 1980s. Step out on the tiny pedestrian bridge (toward the bay) with the black wrought-iron railing. This was the original train line coming into Dingle (the westernmost train station in all of Europe from 1891 to 1953). The train picked up fish with the wild claim that its cargo would be in London markets within 24 hours. The tracks ran right along the harborfront. All the land beyond the old buildings you see today has been reclaimed from the sea. As you look inland, the building on the left with the slate siding was the typical design for 19th-century weatherproofing. The radio tower marks the police station.

2. Cross the roundabout and walk 20 yards along the river up "The Mall" to the two stubby red-brick **pillars** marking the entry to the police station. These pillars are all that remains of the 19th-century British Constabulary, which afforded a kind of Green Zone for British troops when they tried to subdue the local insurgents here. It was burned in the Civil War. The present building dates from 1938.

3. The big white **crucifix** across the street is a memorial to heroes who died in the 1916 Uprising. Note that it says in the people's language, "For honor and glory of Ireland, 1916 to 19." The date is unfinished until Ireland is united and free. Except for one hunger striker, the names listed are of patriots executed by the English.

4. At the *Russels B&B* sign, take 15 paces up the driveway to see an old stone etched with a cross sitting atop the fence. This marks the place of a **Celtic holy well,** indicating this was a sacred spot for people here 2,000 years ago. Across the street, enjoy the fine landscaping work of Jim from the Captain's House B&B.

5. Just beyond Jim's riverside garden (opposite the monastery) is another much-honored spot: the distribution center for **Guinness.** From this warehouse, pubs throughout the peninsula are stocked with beer. The wooden kegs have been replaced by what locals fondly call "iron lungs."

6. Farther up and across the street is the 19th-century **courthouse.** Once a symbol of British oppression, today it's a laid-back place where on the last Friday of each month, the roving County Kerry judge drops by to adjudicate cases (mostly domestic disputes and drunken disorderliness).

7. The next intersection is the "Small Bridge." Continuing straight takes you to the scenic Conor Pass. Turn left into the

commercial heart of the town, up **Main Street.** The old stage-coach from Tralee ended at Dingle's first hotel, Benners (with its Georgian facade and door surviving). Across the street is the church. Since the 13th century, a church has stood here (just inside the medieval wall). Today it's Anglican on Sundays, and filled with great traditional music several nights a week (schedule on gate, see "Folk Concerts" on page 199). Farther uphill on the Benners side, a storefront is plastered with newspaper clippings dealing with the contentious An Daingean/Dingle name issue (see sidebar on page 188).

8. At the first intersection, take a left on Green Street. Pop into the beautiful, modern Catholic church. The convent behind it shows off its delightful **Díseart windows** (described below under "Sights and Activities"). Wander in the backyard to check out the peaceful nuns' cemetery, with its white-painted iron crosses huddling peacefully together under a big oak tree. Just past the church, the driveway to the priest's home leads past the "Trinity Tree," a three-part tree trunk carved by a Chilean (well described by a panel).

9. Green Street leads past lots of inviting boutiques, estates agents (showing the high price of houses here), and the library. The **library,** a gift from the Carnegie Foundation, has a shelf of tourist-information books, a small exhibit (in the foyer and upstairs) about the local patriot Thomas Ashe and the Blasket Island writers, and the best historic photos you'll find in town, decorating its walls with images of 19th-century Dingle. Green Street continues to the Strand, where a right takes you to the harbor.

10. The **harbor** was built on land reclaimed (with imported Dutch expertise) in 1992. The string of old stone shops facing the harbor was the loading station for the narrow-gauge railway that hauled the fish from Dingle to Tralee until 1953. Walk out to the end of the breakwater—newly paved and illuminated at night. The Eask Tower on the distant hill is a marker that was built in 1847 during the famine as a make-work project. In pre-radar days, it helped ships locate Dingle's hidden harbor. The fancy mansion across the harbor is Lord Ventry's 17th-century manor house (see "Dingle Peninsula Circular Tour," page 209). Near the dolphin statue, you'll find an office that serves as a clearinghouse for the various boat excursions.

SIGHTS AND ACTIVITIES

▲▲**The Harry Clark Windows of Díseart**—Just behind Dingle's St. Mary Church stands St. Joseph's Convent and Díseart (dee-SHART), containing a beautiful Neo-Gothic chapel built in 1884. The sisters of this order, who came to Dingle in 1829 to educate local girls, worked heroically during the famine. During Mass in the chapel, the Mother Superior would sit in the covered stall in the rear, while the sisters—filling the carved stalls—chanted in response.

The chapel was graced in 1922 with 12 windows—the work of Ireland's top stained-glass man, Harry Clark. Long appreciated only by the sisters, these special windows—showing six scenes from the life of Christ—are now open to the public. The convent has become a center for sharing Christian Celtic culture and spirituality (€3.50, Mon–Fri 9:30–13:00 & 14:00–17:00, closed Sat–Sun, tel. 066/915-2476, www.diseart.ie).

Enjoy a quick orientation by the attendant followed by a 15-minute recorded narration explaining the chapel and its windows. The scenes (clockwise from the back entrance) are: the visit of the Magi, the Baptism of Jesus, "Let the little children come to me," the Sermon on the Mount, the Agony in the Garden, and Jesus appearing to Mary Magdalene. Each face is lively and animated in the imaginative, devout, medieval, and fun-loving style of Harry Clark, whom locals talk about as if he's the kid next door.

▲**Fungie**—In 1983, a dolphin moved into Dingle Harbor and became a local celebrity. Fungie (FOON-ghee, with a hard *g*) is

now the darling of the town's tourist trade and one reason you'll find so many tour buses parked along the harbor. With a close look at Fungie as bait, tour boats are thriving. Hardy little boats motor 7 to 40 passengers out to the mouth of the harbor, where they troll around looking for Fungie. You're virtually assured of seeing the dolphin, but you don't pay unless you do (€16, kids–€8, 1-hour trips depart 10:00–19:00 depending on demand, behind TI at Dolphin Trips office, tel. 066/915-2626). To actually swim with Fungie, rent wetsuits at Brosnan's B&B (Cooleen Street, tel. 066/915-1967) and catch the early-morning 8:00–10:00 trip (€50 includes boat trip and wetsuit—unless you've packed your own). As Fungie is getting on in years, locals admit that he doesn't come up as often as he used to.

▲**Oceanworld**—The aquarium offers a little peninsula history, 300 different species of fish in thoughtfully described tanks, and the easiest way to see Fungie the dolphin...on video. Walk through the tunnel while fish swim overhead. You'll see local fish as well as a colorful Amazon collection. The aquarium's mission is to teach, and you're welcome to ask questions. The petting pool is fun. Splashing attracts the rays, which are unplugged (€11, families-€30, daily July–Aug 10:00–20:30, May–June and Sept 10:00–18:00, Oct–April 10:00–17:00, cafeteria, just past harbor on west edge of town, tel. 066/915-2111, www.dingle-oceanworld.ie).

▲Short Harbor Walk from Dingle—For an easy stroll along the harbor out of town (and a chance to see Fungie, 90 min round-trip), head east from the roundabout past the Esso station. Just after Bambury's B&B, take a right, following signs to Skelligs Hotel, and go left at the Irish Coast Guard station on the bay. At the beach, climb the steps over the wall and follow the seashore path to the mouth of Dingle Harbor (marked by a tower—some 19th-century fat cat's folly). Ten minutes beyond that is a light-house. This is Fungie's neighborhood. If you see tourist boats out, you're likely to see the dolphin. The trail continues to a dramatic cliff.

Horseback Riding—Dingle Horse Riding takes out beginners (€30/hr for a trail ride) and experienced riders on two-hour (€55),

four-hour (€95), and six-hour (€135) excursions (manager James offers readers of this book a 10 percent discount in 2008, call ahead to book, follow Main Street out of Dingle, turn right at sign, tel. 066/915-2199, www .dinglehorseriding.com). Long's Horseriding Centre is farther out on the peninsula at Ventry—an easy stop for bikers or drivers doing the Slea Head loop (€30–40/hr, a variety of rides for all levels, short rides often depart at 10:00, call to book a trip, tel. 066/915-9034, mobile 087-225-0286, www .longsriding.com). In either case, beach rides are only for advanced riders, and all horses come with English-style saddles (no horns to hang on to).

Dingle World of Leisure—This is a health club for adults and a good rainy-day option for kids, offering bowling, arcade games, a swimming pool (open swim 14:00–18:00 only), and a children's indoor playground (daily July–Sept 11:00–23:00, Oct–June 11:00–20:00, just off John Street, tel. 066/915-0660, www.dwol.eu).

Dingle Pitch & Putt—With 18 wildly scenic holes (ranging from 30 to 70 meters in length) overlooking the harbor on a lush green point a 10-minute walk out of town, this is a delight (€6 includes gear, April–Oct daily 10:00–20:00, closed Nov–March, over bridge take first left and follow signs, Milltown, tel. 066/915-2020).

The Voyage of St. Brendan

It has long been part of Irish lore that St. Brendan the Navigator (A.D. 484–577) and 12 followers sailed from the southwest of Ireland to the "Land of Promise" (what is now North America) in a *currach*—a wood-frame boat covered with oxhide and tar. According to a 10th-century monk who poetically wrote of the journey, St. Brendan and his crew encountered a paradise of birds, were attacked by a whale, and suffered the smoke of a smelly island in the north before finally reaching their Land of Promise.

The legend and its precisely described locations still fascinate modern readers. A British scholar of navigation, Tim Severin, re-created the entire journey from 1976 to 1977. He and his crew set out from Brendan Creek in County Kerry in a *currach*. The prevailing winds blew them to the Hebrides, the Faeroe Islands, Iceland, and finally to Newfoundland. While this didn't successfully prove that St. Brendan sailed to North America, it did prove that he could have.

St. Brendan fans have been heartened by an intriguing archaeological find in Connecticut. Called the "Gungywamp," the site includes a double circle of stones and a beehive-like chamber built in the same manner as the stone *clochans* huts on the Dingle Peninsula. The Gungywamp beehive chamber has been carbon-dated to approximately A.D. 600. Outside the chamber, a stone slab is inscribed with a cross that resembles the unique style of the Irish cross.

According to his 10th-century biographer, "St. Brendan sailed from the Land of Promise home to Ireland. And from that time on, Brendan acted as if he did not belong to this world at all. His mind and his joy were in the delight of heaven."

Golf—Located out west, near the tip of the Dingle peninsula in the town of Ballyferriter (Baile an Fheirtearaigh, 9 miles from Dingle town), Ceann Sibéal/Dingle Links offers a round of golf in a hard-to-beat setting (€40–85 green fees, open daily, tel. 066/915-6255, www.dinglelinks.com).

East of Dingle Town

▲**Minard Castle**—Three miles southwest of the town of Annascaul (Abhainn an Scail), off the Lispole (Lios Póil) Road, is the largest fortress on the peninsula. Built by the Knights of Kerry in 1551, Minard Castle was destroyed by Cromwell in about 1650. With its corners undermined by Cromwellian explosives, it looks ready to split—it's no longer safe to enter this teetering ruin.

From the outside, look for the faint scallop in the doorway, the symbol of St. James. Medieval pilgrims would stop here before making a seafaring pilgrimage from Dingle to St. James' tomb at Santiago de Compostela in northern Spain. Imagine the floor plan of the castle: ground floor for animals and storage; main floor with fireplace; then living-quarters floor; and, on top, the defensive level.

The setting is dramatic, with the Ring of Kerry across the way and Storm Beach below. The beach is notable for its sandstone boulders that fell from the nearby cliffs. Grinding against each other in the wave and tidal action, the boulders eroded into cigar-shaped rocks. Pre-Christian Celts would carry them off and carve them into ogham stones to mark clan boundaries (for more on ogham stones, see page 217).

Next to the fortress, look for the "fairy fort," an Iron Age fort from about 500 B.C.

▲**Puicin Wedge Tomb**—While pretty obscure, this is worth the trouble for its evocative setting. Above the hamlet of Lispole (Lios Póil) in Doonties, park your car and hike 10 minutes up a ridge. At the summit is a pile of rocks made into a little room with one of the finest views on the peninsula. Beyond the Ring of Kerry you may just make out the jagged Skellig Rock, noted for its sixth-century monastic settlement (see page 181).

Inch Strand—This four-mile sandy beach, shaped like a half-moon, was made famous by the movie *Ryan's Daughter*. It's rated a "Blue Flag" beach for its clean water and safe swimming (usually has a lifeguard in summer).

SHOPPING

Dingle is a petri dish of capitalism, with boutiques and charming shops popping up all the time to meet the rising demand of all the tourists and its newly affluent residents. Shoppers enjoy plenty of options, as many fine Dingle shops show off local craftsmanship. The **West Kerry Craft Guild**—a co-op selling the work of 15 local artists—is a delight even if you're just browsing. The prices here are good since you're buying directly from the artists (daily June–Aug 10:00–18:00, Sept–May 11:00–17:00, 18 Main Street, tel. 066/915-2976). The **Niamh Utsch Jewelry** shop on Green Street is much respected for its unique work. **Dingle Crystal,** also on Green Street, features Sean Daly and his Waterford-trained crystal-cutting skills. Sean prides himself on his deeper, sharper

Dingle

design cuts (cutting demonstrations daily, tel. 066/915-1550, www
.dinglecrystal.ie). **Lisbeth Mulcahy Weaver,** filled with traditional
but stylish woven wear, is also the Dingle sales outlet of the well-
known potter from out on Slea Head (Mon–Fri 9:00–18:00, Sat
10:00–18:00, Sun 11:00–18:00, Green Street, tel. 066/915-1688).

NIGHTLIFE

▲▲▲Music in Dingle Pubs

Traditional pub music is Dingle town's best experience. Even if
you're not into pubs, take a nap and then give these a whirl. Dingle
is renowned among traditional musicians as a place to get work
("€40 a day, tax-free, plus drink"). The town has piles of pubs.
There's music every night and rarely a cover charge. The scene is
a decent mix of locals, Americans, and Germans. Music normally
starts around 21:30, and the last call for drinks is "half eleven"
(23:30), sometimes later on weekends. For a seat near the music,
arrive early. If the place is chockablock, power in and find breath-
ing room in the back. By midnight, the door is usually closed and
the chairs are stacked. For more information, see "Traditional Irish
Music" on page 27 in the Introduction.

While two pubs, the **Small Bridge Bar** (An Droichead Beag)
and **O'Flaherty's,** are the most famous for their good beer and

folk music, make a point to wander the town and follow your
ear. Smaller pubs may feel a bit
foreboding to a tourist, but be
rest assured that people—locals as
well as travelers—are out for the
craic. Irish culture is very accessible in the pubs; they're like highly
interactive museums waiting to be
explored. But if you sit at a table, you'll be left alone. Stand or sit
at the bar and you'll be engulfed in conversation with new friends.
Have a glass in an empty, no-name pub and chat up the publican.
Pubs are no longer smoky, but can be stuffy and hot, so leave your
coat home. The more offbeat pubs are more likely to erupt into
leprechaun karaoke.

Pub Crawl: The best pub crawl start is along Holyground
Street to **O'Flaherty's.** Quietly intense owner Fergus O'Flaherty,
a fixture since my first visit to Dingle, sings and plays a half-dozen
different instruments during nightly traditional music sessions. His
domain has a high ceiling and is dripping in old-time photos and
town memorabilia—it's touristy but lots of fun. Moving up Strand
Street, find lively **Murphy's,** offering ballads and traditional music
nightly. A few doors farther down, **John Benny Moriarty's** has

dependably good traditional music sessions, with John himself joining in on accordion when he's not pouring pints.

Then head up Green Street. **Dick Mack,** across from the church, is nicknamed "the last pew." Until recently, this was a tiny leather shop by day, expanding into a pub at night. Today Dick Mack keeps the old leather-shop ambience but sells only drinks, with several rooms, a fine snug (private booth, originally designed to allow women to drink discreetly), reliably good beer, and strangely fascinating ambience. Notice the Hollywood-type stars on the sidewalk recalling famous visitors. The pub was established in 1899 by Dick Mack (who was the master of the westernmost train station in Europe), whose mission was to provide "liquid replenishment" to travelers. The grandson of the original Dick Mack runs the place today. A painting in the window shows Dick Mack II with the local gang.

Green Street climbs to Main Street, where two more Dick Mack–type places are filled with locals deep in conversation (but no music): **Foxy John's** (a hardware shop by day) and **O Currain's** (across the street, a small clothing shop by day).

A bit higher up Main Street is **McCarthy's Pub,** a smoke-stained relic. It's less touristy and has occasional traditional music sessions on its little stage. Wander down Main Street. **The Dingle Pub** is well established as *the* place for jaunty, shanty-type folk singing rather than the churning traditional beat of an Irish folk session. At the bottom of Main Street, **Small Bridge Bar** offers live music nightly. It's popular for good reason. While the tourists gather around the music, poke around the back and do an end run around the wall, which leads to a window nook actually closest to the musicians.

After Hours: The pubs close up around midnight. That's when people who are just warming up head up the Conor Pass Road to the **Hillgrove Lounge** (€5 cover, only place open after pub hours). Some like to hang out at **Rob Roys,** munching a bag of greasy curry-cheese fries and watching the late-night migration. It's quite a scene.

Off-Season: From October through April, the bands play on, though at fewer pubs: Small Bridge Bar (live music nightly), John Benny Moriarty's (Mon, Wed, Thu), McCarthy's (Fri, Sat), and Murphy's (Sat).

Music Shops: Danlann Gallery sells musical instruments and woodcrafts (Mon–Fri 10:00–18:00, later in summer, "flexible" on weekends, owner makes violins, Green Street). **Siopa Ceoil** is enthusiastically run by Michael Herlihy, who offers *bodhrán* (traditional drum) lessons for €15 (or gives you a quick and dirty lesson for free), sells advance tickets to the St. James Church concert (€12, see below), and is an encyclopedia of Irish music knowledge

(Mon–Sat 9:30–19:00, Sun 14:00–19:00, shorter hours off-season, Main Street, tel. 066/915-2618, www.siopaceoil.ie).

Other Nightlife

▲▲**Folk Concerts**—Top local musicians offer a quality evening of live, acoustic, classic Irish music in the fine little St. James' Church on Main Street (€12 advance purchase, €15 at the door; Mon, Wed, and Fri at 19:30, May–Sept only; mobile 087-284-9656, see sign on church gate or drop by the TI, Murphy's Ice Cream shop, or Siopa Ceoil music shop for details or to book a ticket). If you're not a night owl (music in pubs doesn't begin until 21:30) or prefer not to be packed into a pub with the distractions of conversation, then this is your best opportunity to hear Irish traditional music in a more controlled environment.

Blue Zone Jazz and Pizza Bar—Climb the stairs to enter a totally different nightlife zone—the only real mellow ambience in town, where Patrick Juillet brings a splash of French attitude to Dingle. A wonderful gourmet chef, he applies his cooking genius to pizzas (Tue–Sun from 18:00 until very late, closed Mon, no cover, lots of live music, Green Street, tel. 066/915-0303). Warning: Patrick is very political (anti-Bush).

Cinema—Dingle's great little theater is The Phoenix on Dykegate. Its film club (50–60 locals) meets here Tuesdays year-round at 20:30 for coffee and cookies, followed by a film at 21:00 (€6 for film, anyone is welcome). The leader runs it almost like a religion, with a sermon on the film before he rolls it. The regular film schedule for the week is posted on the door.

SLEEPING

In or near the Town Center

$$$ **Greenmount House** sits among chilly palm trees in the countryside at the top of town. A five-minute hike up from the town center, this guest house commands a fine view of the bay and mountains. John and Mary Curran run one of Ireland's best B&Bs, with two fine rooms (Db-€110), three superb rooms (Db-€140), and seven sprawling suites (Db-€170) in a modern building with lavish public areas and breakfast in a solarium (reserve in advance, most rooms at ground level, parking, top of John Street, tel. 066/915-1414, fax 066/915-1974, www.greenmount-house.com, info@greenmount-house.com).

$$$ **Bambury's Guesthouse,** big and modern with views of grazing sheep and the harbor, rents 12 airy, comfy rooms (Db-€110–130, less off-season, family deals; coming in from Tralee it's on your left on Mail Road, 2 blocks before Esso station; tel. 066/915-1244, fax 066/915-1786, www.bamburysguesthouse.com,

Sleep Code

(€1 = about $1.30, country code: 353, area code: 066)
S = Single, **D** = Double/Twin, **T** = Triple, **Q** = Quad, **b** = bathroom, **s** = shower only. Prices vary with the season, with winter cheap and August tops. Breakfast is included unless otherwise noted. Many places only accept cash.

To help you easily sort through these listings, I've divided the rooms into three categories, based on the price for a standard double room with bath:

$$$ Higher Priced—Most rooms €100 or more.
  $$ Moderately Priced—Most rooms between €60–100.
    $ Lower Priced—Most rooms €60 or less.

info@bamburysguesthouse.com).

$$$ Barr Na Sraide Inn, central and hotel-like, has 26 comfortable rooms (Sb-€60, Db-€110, Tb-€150, family deals, self-service laundry, bar, parking, past McCarthy's pub, Upper Main Street, tel. 066/915-1331, fax 066/915-1446, www.barrnasraide.com, barrnasraide@eircom.net).

$$$ Benners Hotel was the only hotel in town a hundred years ago. It stands bewildered by the modern world on Main Street, with sprawling public spaces and 52 abundant, overpriced rooms (Db-€200 July–Aug, €160 May–June and Sept, €150 Oct–April, discounts on website, tel. 066/915-1638, fax 066/915-1412, www.dinglebenners.com, info@dinglebenners.com).

$$$ Alpine Guest House looks like a Monopoly hotel, but that means it's comfortable and efficient. Its 14 spacious, bright, and fresh rooms come with wonderful views of sheep and the harbor, a cozy lounge, a great breakfast, and friendly owners (Db-€110, Tb-€130, less off-season, 10 percent discount with this book through 2008, strictly non-smoking, easy parking, Mail Road, tel. 066/915-1250, fax 066/915-1966, www.alpineguesthouse.com, alpinedingle@eircom.net, Paul). Driving into town from Tralee, you'll see this a block uphill from the Dingle roundabout and Esso station.

$$ Captain's House B&B is a shipshape place in the town center, fit for an admiral, with eight classy rooms, peat-fire lounges, a stay-a-while garden, and a magnificent breakfast in the conservatory. Mary, whose mother ran a guest house before Dingle was discovered, loves her work and is very good at it (Sb-€60, Db-€90–100, great suite-€140–160, The Mall, tel. 066/915-1531, fax 066/915-1079, captigh@eircom.net, Jim and Mary Milhench).

Dingle Accommodations and Services

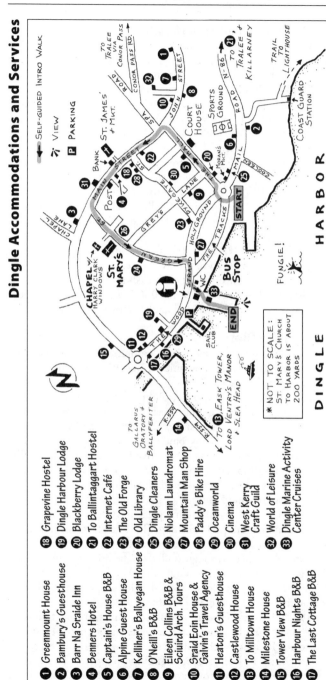

- ① Greenmount House
- ② Bambury's Guesthouse
- ③ Barr Na Sraide Inn
- ④ Benners Hotel
- ⑤ Captain's House B&B
- ⑥ Alpine Guest House
- ⑦ Kelliher's Ballyegan House
- ⑧ O'Neill's B&B
- ⑨ Eileen Collins B&B & Sciuird Arch. Tours
- ⑩ Sraid Eoin House & Galvin's Travel Agency
- ⑪ Heaton's Guesthouse
- ⑫ Castlewood House
- ⑬ To Milltown House
- ⑭ Milestone House
- ⑮ Tower View B&B
- ⑯ Harbour Nights B&B
- ⑰ The Last Cottage B&B
- ⑱ Grapevine Hostel
- ⑲ Dingle Harbour Lodge
- ⑳ Blackberry Lodge
- ㉑ To Ballintaggart Hostel
- ㉒ Internet Café
- ㉓ The Old Forge
- ㉔ Old Library
- ㉕ Dingle Cleaners
- ㉖ Niolann Laundromat
- ㉗ Mountain Man Shop
- ㉘ Paddy's Bike Hire
- ㉙ Oceanworld
- ㉚ Cinema
- ㉛ West Kerry Craft Guild
- ㉜ World of Leisure
- ㉝ Dingle Marine Activity Center Cruises

$$ Kelliher's Ballyegan House is a big, plain building with six fresh, comfortable rooms on the edge of town and great harbor views (Db-€75, Tb-€110, cash only, non-smoking, parking, Upper John Street, tel. 066/915-1702, Hannah and James Kelliher).

$$ O'Neill's B&B is homey and friendly, with six decent rooms on a quiet street at the top of town (Db-€70–80, family deals, cash only, strictly non-smoking, parking, John Street, tel. 066/915-1639, oneills@godingle.com, Mary O'Neill).

$$ Eileen Collins' B&B, which takes up a quiet corner in the town center, is run by the same Collins family that does archaeological tours of the peninsula (see "Sciuird Archaeology Tours," page 218). They offer fine rooms, cheap bike rental (€8/day), great prices, and a homey friendliness (Db-€76, tel. 066/915-1606, Kirrary House on Avondale Road, collinskirrary@eircom.net, Eileen Collins).

$$ Sraid Eoin House offers four modest but pleasant top-floor rooms above Galvin's Travel Agency (Db-€75–80, Tb-€112–120, 10 percent discount with cash and this book in 2008, John Street, tel. 066/915-1409, fax 066/915-2156, sraideoinhouse@hotmail.com, friendly Kathleen and Maurice O'Connor).

Beyond the Pier

These accommodations are a 10–15-minute walk from Dingle's town center. They tend to be quieter, since they are farther from the late-night pub scene.

$$$ Heaton's Guesthouse, big, peaceful, and American in its comforts, is on the water just west of town at the end of Dingle Bay—a five-minute walk past Oceanworld on The Wood. The 16 thoughtfully appointed rooms come with all the amenities (Db-€138, suite Db-€190, less off-season, creative breakfasts, parking, The Wood, tel. 066/915-2288, fax 066/915-2324, www.heatonsdingle.com, heatons@iol.ie, Cameron and Nuala Heaton).

$$$ Castlewood House is a palatial refuge playfully competing with Mom and Dad Heaton's place next door. Each of its 12 tasteful rooms has unique furnishings. The breakfast room and patio have wonderful views of Dingle Harbor (Sb-€125, Db-€160, Tb-€195, rates guaranteed through 2008 if you mention this book when making your reservation, parking, The Wood, tel. 066/915-2788, fax 066/915-2110, www.castlewooddingle.com, castlewoodhouse@eircom.net, Brian and Helen Heaton).

$$$ Milltown House is a plush and rambling four-star guest house with 10 rooms on a large estate across the estuary from town. It comes with grand harbor views, perfect peace, and enough charm to keep Robert Mitchum happy, as he called it home during the filming of *Ryan's Daughter* (Db-€160, occasional discounts when slow, strictly non-smoking, plush public spaces, memorable conservatory for breakfast with a view, tel. 066/915-1372, fax 066/915-1095, www.milltownhousedingle.com, info @milltownhousedingle.com).

$$ Milestone House, a 15-minute walk out of town, has warmly decorated rooms, great views of Dingle Harbor, an ancient boundary stone in the front yard, and wonderful breakfasts. Friendly Barbara Carroll is a font of sightseeing tips (Sb-€55, Db-€80, Tb-€120, Qb-€150, parking, tel. & fax 066/915-1831, www .milestonedingle.com, milestonedingle@eircom.net).

$$ Tower View B&B is a big, bright-yellow modern home just outside of town on a lovely wooded lot. This kid-friendly mini-farm, with pettable animals, rents eight fine rooms (Sb-€60, Db-€70–90, Tb-€105, Qb-€140, just past the roundabout on the west side of town on High Road, tel. 066/915-2990, www.towerviewdingle .com, towerviewdingle@eircom.net).

$$ Harbour Nights B&B weaves together a line of old row houses to create a 14-room guest house. Facing the harbor, it's run by a youthful couple (Sb-€50, Db-€80, Tb-€105, just past the aquarium on The Wood, tel. 066/915-2499, mobile 087-686-8190, www.harbournightsguesthouse.com, info@dinglebandb.com, Sèan and Kathleen).

$ The Last Cottage B&B is a good budget bet with three old-fashioned rooms in a 1909 Council House on the harbor at the far edge of town. This time warp—almost like a museum—is modest, unpretentious, and comfortably cluttered (D-€55, The Wood, tel. 066/915-1469, www.dinglelastcottage.page.tl, mholderied@gmail .com, Elvis fan Margaret Holderied).

Hostels and Dorms

$ Grapevine Hostel is clean and friendly, quiet yet very centrally located, with a cozy fireplace lounge and a fine members' kitchen. Each four- to eight-bed dorm has its own bathroom. Dorms are generally coed, but there can be a girls-only room on request (28 beds, €16–18 per person, Db-€42, open all day, Dykegate Lane, tel. 066/915-1434, www.grapevinedingle.com, hostel@grapevinedingle .com, run by Siobhan—sheh-vahn).

$ Dingle Harbour Lodge is a big, modern hotel on the edge of town. You have the feeling of being a guest in a comfy hotel—including a fancy hotel-style breakfast—without the fancy prices (Db-€60–80, Tb-€85–100, family rooms, up a long driveway off The Wood near the aquarium, tel. & fax 066/915-1577, www .dingleharbourlodge.com, harbourlodge@eircom.net).

$ Blackberry Lodge is your last resort—extremely basic, run-down, and low-energy, but cheap and central (€15 dorm beds, €20 per person in private rooms, The Mall, tel. 066/915-0500, mobile 087-614-1803, dinglebudgetacc@yahoo.com).

$ Ballintaggart Hostel, a backpackers' complex, is housed in a stylish old manor house used by Protestants during the famine as a soup kitchen (for those hungry enough to renounce Catholicism). It comes complete with laundry (€8), a classy study, a family room with a fireplace, and a resident ghost (138 beds, €15 in 10-bed dorms, €20 beds in Qb, Db-€70, 4- to 6-person family room-€65–80, no breakfast but there's a kitchen, a mile east of town on Tralee Road, tel. 066/915-1454, fax 066/915-2207, www .dingleaccommodation.com, info@dingleaccommodation.com). Ask the Tralee bus to drop you here before arriving in Dingle. A taxi into Dingle costs €6.

EATING

The Only Cheap Meal in Dingle: Picnic

The **Super Valu** supermarket/department store, at the base of town, has everything and stays open late (Mon–Sat 8:00–21:00, Sun 8:00–19:00, daily until 22:00 in July–Aug). Smaller groceries, such as **Centra** on Main Street (Mon–Sat 8:00–21:00, Sun 8:00–18:00), are scattered throughout the town. Consider a grand-view picnic out on the end of the newer pier (as you face the harbor, it's the pleasure-boat pier on your right). There are picnic tables on the harbor side of the roundabout, and benches along the busy harborfront. The best take-away pizza is at Novecento (across from the Small Bridge Pub on Main Street; also listed below, under "Inexpensive Dingle Dinners"). The Chinese eatery on Green Street also does take-away.

Dining in Dingle

All of these restaurants are good, but I've listed them in the order of my personal preference.

Chart House Restaurant serves contemporary cuisine in a sleek, well-varnished dining room. Settle back into the shipshape, lantern-lit, harborside ambience. The menu is shaped by what's fresh and seasonal. The chef, who has a Tuscan connection and a passion for South African wines, is committed to always offering a good vegetarian entrée (€19–28 dinners, June–Sept daily 18:30–22:00, Oct–May closed Tue, at roundabout at base of town, reservations wise, tel. 066/915-2255, Jim McCarthy).

Out of the Blue Seafood-Only Restaurant is *the* local choice for just plain great fresh fish. The interior is bright and elegantly simple. The menu—not printed, but on a chalkboard—is dictated literally by what the fishermen caught that morning. If they're closed, you know there was a storm and the fishermen couldn't go out. The €10–15 lunches and heartier €21–30 dinners are artfully presented, with a touch of nouveau cuisine and certainly no chips

Dingle

Dingle Restaurants and Pubs

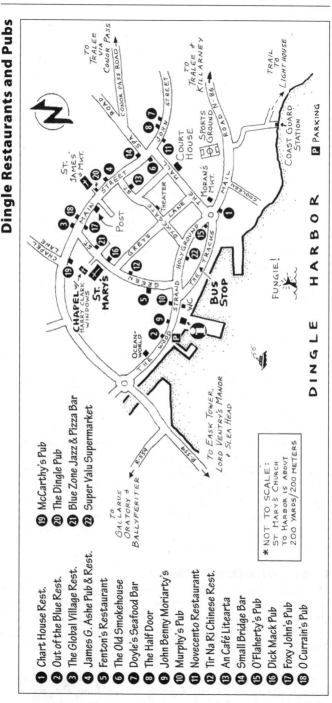

1 Chart House Rest.
2 Out of the Blue Rest.
3 The Global Village Rest.
4 James G. Ashe Pub & Rest.
5 Fenton's Restaurant
6 The Old Smokehouse
7 Doyle's Seafood Bar
8 The Half Door
9 John Benny Moriarty's
10 Murphy's Pub
11 Novecento Restaurant
12 Tir Na Ri Chinese Rest.
13 An Café Litearta
14 Small Bridge Bar
15 O'Flaherty's Pub
16 Dick Mack Pub
17 Foxy John's Pub
18 O Currain's Pub

19 McCarthy's Pub
20 The Dingle Pub
21 Blue Zone Jazz & Pizza Bar
22 Super Valu Supermarket

* NOT TO SCALE:
ST MARY'S CHURCH
TO HARBOR IS ABOUT
200 YARDS/200 METERS

(daily 12:30–15:00 & 18:30–21:30, closed Wed and after a storm, some outdoor picnic-table seating, reservations smart, just past the TI, facing the harbor on The Waterside, tel. 066/915-0811).

At **The Global Village Restaurant,** Martin Bealin concocts his favorite dishes, with inspiration gleaned from his travels around the world. He has a passion for making things from scratch and giving dishes a creative twist. No chips, no deep-fat-fried anything. It's an eclectic, healthy, fresh seafood-eaters' place (€25 dinners, good salads, early-bird special 17:30–19:00, open June–Sept Wed–Mon 17:30–22:00, closed Tue and through the winter, top of Main Street, tel. 066/915-2325, mobile 087-917-7700).

James G. Ashe Pub and Restaurant, an old-fashioned joint, is popular with locals for its nicely presented, top-quality, traditional Irish food and seafood at good prices. Try their beef-and-Guinness stew (€10–15 lunches, €15–25 dinners, lunch served 12:00–15:00, dinner 18:00–21:00, closed Sun, Main Street, tel. 066/915-0989).

Fenton's is good for seafood meals with a memorable apple-and-berry-crumble dessert (€22–32 main courses, €25 two-course and €30 three-course early-bird specials before 19:00, open Tue–Sun 18:00–21:30, closed Mon, reservations smart, on Green Street down the hill below the church, tel. 066/915-2172, mobile 087-248-2487). They have a delightful garden section out back.

The Old Smokehouse, serving happy locals in a rustic woody setting, offers good meals for a bit less money, with fresh Dingle Bay fish and fresh vegetables (€16–27 dinner plates daily 17:30–21:30, corner of Main Street and The Mall, tel. 066/915-1061).

John Street Splurges: Two of Dingle's long-established top-notch restaurants stand side by side at the top of the town (on John Street), satisfying diners with €40 meals: **Doyle's Seafood Bar** (more famous, with excellent seafood and service, tel. 066/915-1174) and **The Half Door** (heartier portions, also open for lunch Mon–Sat 12:30–14:00, tel. 066/915-1600). While elegant, the dining rooms at these restaurants feel a bit congested. Both have the same dinner hours (Mon–Sat 18:00–21:30, closed Sun), offer an early-bird special (two-course meal-€26, roughly 18:00–19:00), and recommend reservations.

Inexpensive Dingle Dinners

While the top-end restaurants are charging €20–30, you can eat well for €10 in Dingle's pubs and ethnic eateries. Fancy restaurants serve early-bird specials from 18:00 to 19:00. Many "cheap and cheery" places close at 18:00. Most pubs stop serving food around 21:00 (to make room for their beer-drinkers). Anyone will serve tap water for free. Here are some ideas:

John Benny Moriarty's is a waterfront pub dishing up traditional Irish fare with a relatively cozy interior. John, the proprietor, hopes people will come here for dinner, and stay for a drink and enjoy his nightly live music (€10–12 hearty dinner plates, food daily 12:30–21:30, music after 21:30, The Pier).

Murphy's Pub is a favorite for good, sloppy pub grub with an extensive and kid-friendly menu and lots of fries (€11–14 plates, daily 12:00–21:00, at 21:00 the restaurant makes way for beer and music, 30 yards from John Benny Moriarty's on The Strand, tel. 066/915-1450).

Novecento Restaurant, "where Irish soul meets Italian character," is your best bet for Italian food, with a spacious hardwood and candlelit interior and an appealing menu (€10 pastas, Thu–Tue 18:00–23:00, only pizza until 19:00, closed Wed, no lunch, John Street, tel. 066/915-2584). They have a more casual pizza and pasta place a block away, on Main Street (Mon–Fri 12:00–14:00 & 16:00–21:30, closed Sat–Sun).

Tir Na Ri Chinese Restaurant serves what you'd expect in relatively plush ambience (€11–15 plates, Mon–Fri 12:30–14:30 & 17:00–23:00, Sat–Sun 17:00–23:00, also take-away, Green Street, tel. 066/915-0803).

An Café Litearta, a likeable eatery hidden behind an inviting bookstore, serves tasty soup and sandwiches to a good-natured crowd of Gaelic speakers (daily 10:00–18:00, Dykegate Street, tel. 066/915-2204).

On the Slea Head Loop

The Stone House Restaurant offers good meals in a great atmosphere. It's a good choice for those looking for an out-of-the-way dinner and a 20-minute scenic drive. It's right across the road from the Dunbeg fort at kilometer 12.5 on the "Dingle Peninsula Circular Tour" (see page 209). Its outdoor picnic tables come with vast sea views (open Wed–Mon 12:30–15:30 for €11–15 lunches and 18:30–21:30 for €18–25 dinners, closed Tue, dinner reservations essential, tel. 066/915-9970, Deirdre).

TRANSPORTATION CONNECTIONS

Tralee (Tra' Li), 30 miles from Dingle, is the region's transportation hub (with the nearest train station to Dingle). All bus trips make connections in Tralee.

From Dingle by Bus to: Galway (5/day, 6.5 hrs), **Dublin** (3/day, 8 hrs), **Rosslare** (2/day, 9 hrs), **Tralee** (5/day, 75 min, €9 one-way, €15 round-trip); fewer departures on Sundays. Most bus trips out of Dingle require at least one or two (easy) transfers. Dingle has no bus station and only one bus stop, on the waterfront behind the Super Valu supermarket (bus info tel. 01/836-6111 or Tralee station at 066/712-3566, Tralee train info tel. 066/712-3522).

Dingle

All Roads Lead to An Daingean

The western half of the Dingle Peninsula is part of the Gaeltacht, where locals speak the Irish (Gaelic) language. In an effort to ward off English-language encroachment, all place names on road signs were controversially changed to Irish-only in the spring of 2005. For ease of understanding I've used the English names in this book, but you'll need this listing to navigate the peninsula's signs.

While the signs are changing, old habits die hard: Many businesses in Dingle town are keeping easy-to-pronounce "Dingle" in their names (to make things simpler for tourists), and most locals—both here and elsewhere in Ireland—still refer to this region as Dingle.

As you travel along Slea Head Drive (known as Cean Sleibhethe in Irish), you can refer to this cheat sheet of the most useful destination names. Remember that there's a complete translation of all Irish place names in the Gazetteer section at the back of the *Ordnance Survey Road Atlas*.

English Name	Irish (Gaelic) Name	Pronounced
Dingle	*An Daingean*	on DANG-un
Ventry	*Ceann Tra'*	k'yown (rhymes with crown) thraw
Slea Head	*Ceann Sleibhe*	k'yown SHLAY-veh
Dunquin	*Dun Chaoin*	doon qween
Blasket Islands	*Na Blascaodai*	nuh BLAS-kud-ee
Great Blasket Island	*An Blascaod Mór*	on BLAS-kade moor
Ballyferriter	*Baile an Fheirtearaigh*	BALL-yuh on ERR-ter-ig
Reasc Monastery	*Mainistir Riaisc*	MON-ish-ter REE-isk
Gallarus	*Gallaras*	GAHL-russ
Kilmalkedar	*Cill Mhaoil-cheadair*	kill moyle-KAY-dir
Annascaul	*Abhainn an Scail*	ow'en on skahl
Lispole	*Lios Póil*	leesh pohl
Tralee	*Tra' Li*	traw lee

For more information, see "Transportation Connections" in Tralee, page 225.

By Car: Drivers choose two roads into town: the easy southern route or the much more dramatic, scenic, and treacherous Conor Pass (see "Transportation Connections" in Tralee, page 225). It's 30 miles from Tralee either way.

By Air: Kerry Airport, at Killarney, is a 45-minute, €60 taxi ride away (4 flights/day to Dublin). For more on this airport, see the end of this chapter.

Dingle Peninsula Circular Tour

A sight worth ▲▲▲, the Dingle Peninsula loop trip is about 30 miles (47 km) long and must be driven in a clockwise direction. It's easy by car, or it's a demanding four hours by bike—if you don't stop. Cyclists should plan on an early start (preferably by 9:00) to allow for enough sightseeing and lunch/rest time.

While you can take the basic guided tour of the peninsula (see "Tours," page 218), the self-guided tour described below makes it unnecessary. A fancy map is also not necessary with my instructions. I've provided distances to help locate points of interest. Just like Ireland's speed-limit signs, Ireland's car speedometers and odometers have gone 100 percent metric in recent years. I've given distances below in kilometers so you can follow along with your rental-car odometer. Most Irish odometers give distances to tenths of a kilometer.

If you're driving, check your odometer at Oceanworld, as you leave Dingle (ideally, reset your odometer to zero—usually you can do this by holding down the button next to it). Even if you get off track or are biking, you can subtract the kilometers listed below to figure out distances between points. To get the most out of your circle trip, read through this entire section before departing. Then go step by step (staying on R-559 and following the brown *Ceann Sleibhe/Slea Head Drive* signs). Roads are very congested mid-July to late August.

The Dingle Peninsula is 10 miles wide and runs 40 miles from Tralee to Slea Head. The top of its mountainous spine is Mount Brandon—at 3,130 feet, the second-tallest mountain in Ireland

Dingle Peninsula Circle Tour

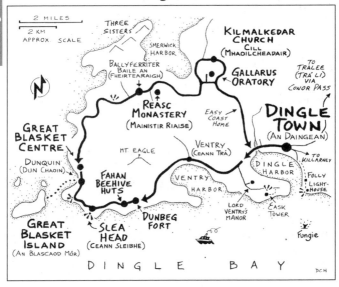

(after a nearby peak above Killarney that's almost 500 feet higher). While only tiny villages lie west of Dingle town, the peninsula is home to 500,000 sheep.

SELF-GUIDED TOUR

Leave Dingle town west along the waterfront (0.0 km at Oceanworld). Driving out of town, on the left you'll see a row of humble "two up and two down" flats from a 1908 affordable housing government initiative. Today, even these little places would cost more than €250,000.

0.5 km: There's an eight-foot tide here. The seaweed was used to make formerly worthless land arable. (Seaweed is a natural source of potash—organic farming before it was trendy.) Across the Milltown River estuary, the fancy Milltown House B&B (with flags) was Robert Mitchum's home for a year during the filming of *Ryan's Daughter*. (Behind that is an extremely scenic pitch & putt range—described on page 194.) Look for the narrow mouth of this blind harbor (where Fungie frolics), and the Ring of Kerry beyond that. Dingle Bay is so hidden that ships needed the tower (1847) on the hill to find its mouth.

0.7 km: At the roundabout, turn left over the bridge. The hardware-store building on the right was a corn-grinding mill in the 18th century. You'll pass the junction where you'll complete this circular tour later.

1.3 km: The Milestone B&B is named for the stone pillar (*gallaun* in Gaelic) in its front yard. This may have been a prehistoric grave or a boundary marker between two tribes. The stone goes down as far as it sticks up. The peninsula, literally an open-air museum, is dotted with more than 2,000 such monuments dating from the Neolithic Age (4000 B.C.) through early-Christian times. Another stone pillar stands in the field across the street, in the direction of the yellow manor house of Lord Ventry (in the distance). Its function today: cow scratcher.

Lord Ventry, whose family came to Dingle as post–Cromwellian War landlords in 1666, built this mansion in about 1750. Today it houses an all-Gaelic boarding school for 140 high-school girls.

As you drive past the Ventry estate, you'll pass palms, magnolias, and exotic flora introduced to Dingle by Lord Ventry. The Gulf Stream is the source of the mild climate (it never snows), which supports subtropical plants. Consequently, fuchsias—imported from Chile and spreading like weeds—line the roads all over the peninsula and redden the countryside June through September. More than 100 inches of rain a year gives this area its "40 shades of green."

The old red-sandstone and slate-roof cottages along the roadside housed Ventry estate workers in the 1840s.

4.6 km: Stay off the "soft margin" as you enjoy views of Ventry Bay, its four-mile-long beach (to your right as you face the water), and distant Skellig Michael, which you'll see all along this part of the route. Skellig Michael—an island jutting up like France's Mont St. Michel—contains the rocky remains of a sixth-century monastic settlement (see page 181). Next to it is a smaller island, Little Skellig—a breeding ground for gannets (seagull-like birds with six-foot wingspans). In 1866, the first transatlantic cable was laid from nearby Valentia Island to Canada's Newfoundland (see sidebar on page 180). It was in use until 1965. Mount Eagle (1,660 feet), rising across the bay, marks the end of Ireland.

In the town of Ventry—or Ceann Tra'—Gaelic is the first language. Ventry is little more than a bungalow holiday village today. Urban Irish families love to come here in the summer to immerse their kids in the traditional culture and wild nature. A large hall at the edge of the village is used as a classroom where big-city students come on field trips to learn the Gaelic language. Just past the town, a lane leads left to a fine beach and mobile-home vacation community. An information board explains the history, geology, and bird life of this bay. The humble trailer park has no running water or electricity. Locals like it for its economy and proximity to the beach. From here, a lane also leads inland to Long's Horseriding Centre (described on page 194).

5.2 km: The bamboo-like rushes on either side of the road are the kind used to make the local thatched roofs. Thatching, which nearly died out because of the fire danger, is more popular now that anti-flame treatments are available. It's not the cheap alternative, however; it's expensive to pay the few qualified craftsman thatchers that remain in Ireland. Black-and-white magpies fly.

8.6 km: The Irish football (GAA) star Paidi O Se (Paddy O'Shea) is a household name in Ireland. He won eight all-Ireland football titles for Kerry as a player. He then trained the Kerry team for many years, and he now runs the pub on the left (also notice the tiny grocery on the right; easy beach access from here).

9.2 km: The plain blue cottage hiding in the trees 100 yards off the road on the left (view through the white gate, harder to see in summer when foliage is thickest) was kept cozy by Tom Cruise and Nicole Kidman during the filming of *Far and Away*. Just beyond are fine views of the harbor and Dingle's stone tower.

10.7 km: *Taisteal go Mall* means "go slowly"; there's a red-colored, two-room schoolhouse on the right (20 students, two teachers). During the summer, it's used for Gaelic courses for kids from the big cities. On the left is the small Celtic and Prehistoric Museum, a quirky private collection of prehistoric artifacts collected by a retired busker named Harris (€4, family-€12, daily 10:00–17:30, tel. 066/915-9191).

11.1 km: The circular mound (that looks like an elevated hedge) on the right is a late-Stone Age ring fort. In 500 B.C., it was a petty Celtic chieftain's headquarters, a stone-and-earth stockade filled with little stone houses. These survived untouched through the centuries because of superstitious beliefs that they were "fairy forts." While this site is unexcavated, recent digging has shown that people have lived on this peninsula since well before 4000 B.C.

11.7 km: Look ahead up Mount Eagle at the patchwork of stone-fenced fields.

12.5 km: Dunbeg Fort, a series of defensive ramparts and ditches around a central *clochan*, is open to tourists—though it's ready to fall into the sea. There are no carvings to be seen, but the small *(beg)* fort *(dun)* is dramatic (€3, daily 9:30–19:00, May–Aug until 20:00, descriptive handout, includes 15-minute video giving a bigger picture of the prehistory of the peninsula in the restaurant across the street). Forts like this are the most important relics left from Ireland's Iron Age (500 B.C.–A.D. 500).

Along the road, you'll see a new stone-roofed house built to blend in with the landscape and the region's ancient rock-slab architecture (A.D. 2000). It's the Stone House Restaurant, serving good lunches (daily 12:30–15:30, also open for dinner 18:30–21:30, see page 207). A traditional *currach* boat (see page 215) is permanently dry-docked in the parking lot.

12.6 km: Just 50 yards up the hill is a cottage abandoned by a family named Kavanaugh 150 years ago, during the famine. With a few rusty and chipped old artifacts and good descriptions, it provides an evocative peek into the simple lifestyles of the area in the 19th century (€3, family-€10, May–Sept daily 9:30–18:00, closed Oct–April, tel. 066/915-6241).

13.4 km: A group of beehive huts, or *clochans,* is a short walk uphill (€2, daily 9:30–19:00, WC). These mysterious stone igloos, which cluster together within a circular wall, are a better sight than the similar group of beehive huts a mile down the road. Look over the water for more Skellig views.

Farther on, you'll ford a stream. There has never been a bridge here; this bit of road—nicknamed the "upside-down bridge"—was designed as a ford.

14.9 km: Pull off to the left at this second group of beehive huts. Look downhill at the rocky field—in the movie *Far and Away,* that's where Lord Ventry evicted (read: torched) peasants from their cottage. Even without Hollywood, this is a bleak and godforsaken land. Look above at the patches of land slowly made into farmland by the inhabitants of this westernmost piece of Europe. Rocks were cleared and piled into fences. Sand and seaweed were laid on the clay, and in time it was good for grass. The created land, if at all tillable, was generally used for growing potatoes; otherwise it was only good for grazing. Much has fallen out of use now. Look across the bay at the Ring of Kerry in the distance, and ahead at the Blasket Islands (Na Blascaodai).

16.1 km: At Slea Head (Ceann Sleibhe)—marked by a crucifix, a pullout, and great views of the Blasket Islands (described on page 218)—you turn the corner on this tour. On stormy days, the waves are "racing in like white horses."

16.9 km: Pull into the little parking lot (at *Dun Chaoin* sign) to view the Blasket Islands and Dunmore Head (the westernmost point in Europe) and to review the roadside map (which traces your route) posted in the parking lot. The scattered village of Dunquin (Dun Chaoin) has many ruined rock homes abandoned during the

famine. Some are fixed up, as this is a popular place these days for summer homes. You can see more good examples of land reclamation, patch by patch, climbing up the hillside. Mount Eagle was the first bit of land Charles Lindbergh saw after crossing the Atlantic on his way to Paris in 1927. Villagers here were as excited as he was—they had never seen anything so big in the air. About a kilometer down a road on the left, a plaque celebrates the 30th anniversary of the filming of *Ryan's Daughter*. From here, a trail leads down to a wild beach.

19.3 km: The Blasket Islands' residents had no church or cemetery on the island. This was their cemetery. The famous Blascaod storyteller Peig Sayers (1873–1958) is buried in the center. At the next intersection, drive down the little lane that leads left (100 yards) to a small stone marker (hiding in the grass on the left) commemorating the 1588 shipwreck of the *Santa María de la Rosa* of the Spanish Armada. Below that is the often-tempestuous Dunquin Harbor, from where the Blasket Islands ferry departs. Island farmers—who on a calm day could row across in 30 minutes—would dock here and hike 12 miles into Dingle to sell their produce.

19.4 km: Back on the main road, follow signs to the *Ionad An Blascaod Mór* (Great Blasket Centre). You'll pass a village school from 1914 (its two teachers still teach 18 students, grades one through six).

22.3 km: Leave the Slea Head Road left for the Great Blasket Centre (good cafeteria, described on page 220).

23.1 km: Back at the turnoff, head left (sign to *Louis Mulcahy Pottery*).

24.5 km: Passing land that was never reclaimed, think of the work it took to pick out the stones, pile them into fences, and bring up sand and seaweed to nourish the clay and make soil for growing potatoes. Look over the water to the island aptly named the "Sleeping Giant"—see his hand resting happily on his beer belly.

24.9 km: Grab the scenic pull-out. The view is spectacular. Ahead, on the right, study the top fields, untouched since the planting of 1845, when the potatoes didn't grow, but rotted in the ground. The faint vertical ridges of the potato beds can still be seen—a reminder of the famine (easier to see a bit later). Before the

Currach **Boats**

A *currach* is the traditional fishing boat of the west coast of Ireland—lightweight and easy to haul. In your Dingle travels,

you'll see a few actual *currach* boats—generally retired and stacked where visitors can finger them and ponder the simpler age when they were a key part of the economy. They were easy to make: Cover a wooden frame with canvas (originally cowhide) and paint with tar—presto. When transporting sheep, farmers would lash each sheep's pointy little hooves together and place it carefully upside-down in the *currach*—so it wouldn't puncture the frail little craft's canvas skin.

famine, 40,000 people lived on this peninsula. After the famine, the population was so small that there was never again a need to farm so high up. Today, only 10,000 live on the peninsula.

Coast downhill. The distant hills are crowned by lookout forts built back when Britain expected Napoleon to invade.

The lousy farmland on both sides of the straight stretch of road was stripped of seven feet of peat (turf) in the 19th century. While the land here provided a lot of warmth back then...it provides no food today.

30 km: The town of Ballyferriter (Baile an Fheirtearaigh), established by a Norman family in the 12th century, is the largest on this side of Dingle. The pubs serve grub, and the old schoolhouse is a museum (€2.50, May–Sept daily 10:00–18:00, closed Oct–April, tel. 066/915-6333). The early-Christian cross next to the schoolhouse looks real. Tap it...it's fiberglass—a prop from *Ryan's Daughter*.

31.4 km: At the T-junction, signs direct you left to *An Daingean* (Dingle, 11 km). Go left, via *Gallaras* (and still following *Ceann Sleibhe/Slea Head Drive*). Take a right over the bridge, following signs to *Gallaras*.

32 km: Just beyond the bridge, you'll pass the Tigh Bhric pub and market (great pub-grub lunches, tel. 066/915-6325). Five yards before the sign to *Mainistir Riaise* (Reasc Monastery), detour right up the lane. After 0.3 km (up the unsigned turnout on your right), you'll find the scant remains of the walled Reasc Monastery (dating from the 6th–12th centuries, free, always open). The inner wall divided the community into sections for prayer and business (cottage industries helped support the monastery). In 1975, only the stone pillar was visible, as the entire site was buried. The layer of black tar paper marks where the original rocks stop and the excavators' reconstruction begins. The stone pillar is Celtic (c. 500 B.C.). When the Christians arrived in the fifth century, they didn't throw out the Celtic society. Instead, they carved a Maltese-type cross over the Celtic scrollwork. The square building was an oratory (church—you'll see an intact oratory at the next stop). The round buildings would have been *clochans*—those stone igloo–type dwellings. One of the cottage industries operated by the monastery was a double-duty kiln. Just outside the wall (opposite the oratory, past the duplex *clochan,* at the bottom end), find a stone hole with a passage facing the southwest wind. This was the kiln—fanned by the wind, it was used for cooking and drying grain. Locals would bring their grain to be dried and ground, and the monks would keep a 10 percent tithe. With the arrival of the Normans in the 12th century, these small religious communities were replaced by relatively big-time state and church governments.

32.8 km: Return to the main road, and continue to the right.

34.6 km: At the big hotel (Smerwick Harbor), turn left following the sign to *Gallaras* (Gallarus Oratory).

35.6 km: At the big building (with *camping* sign), go right and follow the sign for the oratory, where you'll find a small tourist center with a coffee shop, WC, and video theater. For €3 you get a worthwhile 17-minute video overview of Dingle Peninsula's historic sights (daily May–Sept 9:00–21:00, Oct–April 9:00–19:00, tel. 066/915-5333). Note that the actual stone church—described below—is free (a small parking lot  200 yards farther up the tiny lane is actually closer to the sight). This tourist reception zone is the business initiative of a man who simply owns the land; you can skip it to save the €3 and just see the old church.

The Gallarus Oratory, built about 1,300 years ago, is one of Ireland's best-preserved early-Christian churches (see photo above). Shaped like an upturned boat, its finely fitted drystone walls are still waterproof. Notice the holes once used to secure covering at the door, and the fine alternating stonework on the corners.

From the oratory, return to the main road and continue, following the brown *Ceann Sleibhe/Slea Head Drive* sign.

37.7 km: Turn right at the fork and immediately take a right (at the blue shop sign) at the next fork. Here you leave the Slea Head Drive and head for Dingle (10 km away).

39.5 km: The ruined church of Kilmalkedar (Cill Mhaoil-cheadair, on the left) was the Norman center of worship for this end of the peninsula. It was built when England replaced the old monastic settlements in an attempt to centralize their rule. The 12th-century Irish Romanesque church is surrounded by a densely populated graveyard (which has risen notice-

ably above the surrounding fields over the centuries). In front of the church, you'll find the oldest medieval tombs, a stately early-Christian cross (substantially buried by the rising graveyard and therefore oddly proportioned), and a much older ogham stone. This stone, which had already stood here 900 years when the church was built, is notched with the mysterious Morse code–type ogham script used from the third to seventh centuries. It marked a grave, indicating this was a pre-Christian holy spot. The hole was drilled through the top of the stone centuries ago as a place where people would come to seal a deal—standing on the graves of their ancestors and in front of the house of God, they'd "swear to God" by touching thumbs through this stone. You can still use this to renew your marriage vows (free, B.Y.O. spouse). The church fell into ruin during the Reformation. As Catholic worship went underground until the early 19th century, Kilmalkedar was never rebuilt.

40.2 km: Continue uphill, overlooking the water. You'll pass another "fairy fort" (Ciher Dorgan) on the right dating back to 1000 B.C. (free, go through the rusty "kissing gate"). The bay stretched out below you is Smerwick Harbor. In 1580 a force of 600 Italian and Spanish troops (sent by the pope to aid a rebellion against the Protestant English) surrendered at this bay to the English. All 600 were massacred by the English forces, who included Sir Walter Raleigh.

41.7 km: At the crest of the hill, enjoy a three-mile-long coast back into Dingle town (sighting, as old-time mariners did, on the Eask Tower).

46.3 km: *Tog Bog E* means "take it easy." At the T-junction, turn left. Then turn right at the roundabout.

47.5 km: You're back in Dingle town. Well done.

Dingle

TOURS

▲▲**Sciuird Archaeology Tours**—Sciuird (SCEW-erd, Irish for "excursion") tours are offered by a father–son team with Dingle history—and a knack for sharing it—in their blood. Tim Collins, a retired Dingle police officer, and his son Michael give serious 2.5-hour minibus tours (€20, departing at 10:30 and 14:00, depending upon demand). Drop by the Eileen Collins' B&B (at Dykegate and Grey's Lane) or call 066/915-1606 to put your name on the list. Call early. Tours fill quickly in summer. Off-season (Oct–April), you may have to call back to see if the necessary six people signed up to make a bus go. While skipping the folk legends and the famous sights, your guide will drive down tiny farm roads (the Gaelic word for road literally means "cow path"), over hedges, and up ridges to hidden Celtic forts, mysterious stone tombs, and forgotten castles with sweeping seaside views. The running commentary gives an intimate peek into the history of Dingle, and their sound system allows you to hear clearly, no matter where you sit. Dress for the weather. In a gale storm with horizontal winds, Tim kept telling me, "You'll survive it."

More Minibus Tours—Moran's Tour, which does a quickie minibus tour around the peninsula, offers meager narration and a short stop at the Gallarus Oratory (€18 to Slea Head, normally May–Sept at 10:00 and 14:00 from Dingle TI, 2.5 hrs; Moran's is at Esso station at roundabout, tel. 066/915-1155, mobile 087-275-3333). There are usually enough seats, though it's best to book a day ahead. But if no one shows up, consider a private Moran taxi trip around the peninsula (€75 for 4 people, cabbie narrates 2.5-hour ride).

Dingle Marine Activity Center Cruises—Dingle Marine Eco Tours offers a 2-hour birds-and-rocks boat tour of the peninsula. The guided tour sails either east toward Minard Castle or west toward the Blasket Islands (€35, runs April–Sept only, departs at 16:00 weather permitting, office around corner from TI, mobile 086-285-8802).

Blasket Islands

This rugged group of six islands (Na Blascaodai) off the tip of Dingle Peninsula seems particularly close to the soul of Ireland. The population of Great Blasket Island (An Blascaod Mór), home to as many as 160 people, dwindled until the government moved the last handful of residents to the mainland in 1953. Life here was hard. Each family had a cow, a few sheep, and a plot of potatoes. They cut their peat from the high ridge and harvested fish from the sea. There was no priest, pub, or doctor. Because they were not entirely dependent upon the potato, they survived the famine relatively unscathed. These people formed the most traditional Irish community of the 20th century—the symbol of ancient Gaelic culture.

A special closeness to an island—combined with a knack for vivid storytelling—is inspirational. From this primitive but proud fishing/farming community came three writers of international repute whose Gaelic work—basically tales of life on Great Blasket Island—is translated into many languages. You'll find *Peig* (by Peig Sayers), *Twenty Years a-Growing* (Maurice O'Sullivan), and *The Islander* (Thomas O'Crohan) in shops everywhere.

The island's café and hostel have closed down, and today Great Blasket is little more than a ghost town overrun with rabbits on a peaceful, grassy, three-mile-long poem.

Getting to the Blasket Islands

From Dunquin (Dun Chaoin): The 40-passenger Blasket Islands ferry runs hourly from Dunquin, at the tip of Dingle Peninsula; in summer, it goes every half-hour, depending on weather and demand (€30 round-trip, 10 percent cheaper if booked at Dingle harbor office, April–Sept 10:00–17:00, no boats Oct–March, ferry tel. 066/915-6422 or 066/915-4864). There's also a scenic 2.5-hour Blasket Island circuit cruise from Dunquin Harbor. Dunquin has a fine hostel (tel. 066/915-6121).

From Dingle Town (An Daingean): In summer, a fast 12-passenger boat called the *Peig Sayers* runs between Dingle town and the Blasket Islands. The ride (which may include a quick look at Fungie the dolphin) traces the spectacular coastline all the way

to Slea Head, in a boat designed to slice expertly through the ocean chop. The tricky landing at Great Blasket Island's primitive little boat ramp makes getting off a challenge, and landing at all impossible in a storm (€35 same-day round-trip, departs from the marina pier in Dingle at

9:00, 11:00, 13:00, and 15:00, includes 35-min ride with free time to explore island, call Mary at tel. 066/915-1344 or mobile 087-672-6100). Another, larger boat with a smoother ride, the *Loch an Iasc*, offers a similar service from Dingle town, as well as three-hour eco-tours for those interested in puffins, dolphins, and seals (€35 round-trip, €40 for eco-tour, call Tom at tel. 066/915-1640 or mobile 086-254-7512).

SIGHTS

Note that this sight isn't on the Blasket Islands, but on the mainland facing the islands. It's an essential stop before visiting the islands—or a good place to learn about them without making the crossing (fits neatly with the "Dingle Peninsula Circular Tour," described above).

▲▲**Great Blasket Centre (Ionad An Blascaod Mór)**—This state-of-the-art Blascaod and Gaelic heritage center gives visitors the best look possible at the language, literature, and way of life of Blasket Islanders. The building's award-winning design mixes interpretation and the surrounding countryside. Its spine, a slopping village lane, leads to an almost sacred view of the actual island. Don't miss the exceptional 20-minute video (shows on the half-hour), then hear the sounds, read the poems, browse through old photos, and gaze out the big windows at those rugged islands... and imagine. Even if you never got past limericks, the poetry of these people—so pure and close to each other and nature—will have you dipping your pen into the cry of the birds (€3.70, covered by Heritage Card, Easter–Oct daily 10:00–18:00, July–Aug until 19:00, closed Nov–Easter, fine cafeteria, well signposted on the Slea Head Drive near Dunquin/Dun Chaoin, tel. 066/915-6444).

Tralee

While Killarney is the tour-bus capital of County Kerry, Tralee (Tra' Li) is its true leading city. Except for the tourist complex around the TI and during a few festivals, Tralee feels like a bustling Irish town. A little outdoor market combusts on The Square (Thu–Sat).

The famous Rose of Tralee International Festival, usually held in mid-August, is a celebration of arts and music, culminating in the election of the Rose of Tralee—the most beautiful woman at the festival. While the rose garden in the Castle Gardens surrounding the TI is in bloom from summer through October, Tralee's finest roses are going about their lives in the busy streets of this workaday town.

Dingle

ORIENTATION

(area code: 066)

For the tourist, the heart of Tralee is Ashe Memorial Hall, housing the TI and the Kerry the Kingdom museum, located near the rose garden and surrounded by the city park. Beyond the park is the Aqua Dome and steam railway that, if you were here 50 years ago, would chug-chug you to Dingle. Today, it goes only to the touristy windmill.

Tourist Information

The TI is hidden under the east end of Ashe Memorial Hall, which also houses the Kerry the Kingdom museum (TI open July–Aug Mon–Sat 9:00–19:00, Sun 10:00–18:00; May–June Mon–Sat 9:00–18:00, closed Sun; Sept–April Mon–Sat 9:15–17:00, closed Sun; also closed Sat in Jan–Feb, tel. 066/712-1288).

Arrival in Tralee

From the train and bus station (both are located in the same building, with bike rental available), the Ashe Memorial Hall is a 10-minute walk through the center of town. Exit the station right, take a near-immediate left on Edward Street, then turn right on Castle Street and left on Denny. The hall is at the end of Denny. Drivers should knock around the town center until they find a sign to the TI. Parking on the street requires a disk (€1.20/hr, sold at TI and newsstands—have them date it for you—or from exact-change machines on the street).

Helpful Hints

Post Office: It's on Edward Street (Mon–Fri 9:00–17:30, Sat 9:00–13:00, closed Sun).

Laundry: Kerin's launderette on Strand Street charges €12 for an average load (Mon–Sat 9:30–18:30, closed Sun, 103 Strand Street).

Taxis: Try **Speedy Cab** (tel. 066/712-7411) or **Behan Cab** (tel. 066/712-6296).

Day Trips from Tralee: For those without their own wheels, **Dingle** town is an easy day trip from Tralee in summer. Bus Éireann departs from the Tralee bus and train station at 9:00, putting you in Dingle at 10:15; the last bus returns from Dingle at 21:30, getting you back to Tralee at 22:45 (June–mid-Sept only). You can also take a blitz bus tour of the **Ring of Kerry:** Bus Éireann departs the Tralee bus station at 7:50, drives the N-70 ring route, and gets you back to Tralee at 13:45 (runs late June–early Sept, stops only to pick

Dingle

up and drop off). You can also connect to a similar Ring of Kerry bus loop from Killarney (see page 167).

SIGHTS AND ACTIVITIES

▲▲**Kerry the Kingdom**—This is *the* place to learn about life in Kerry. The museum has three parts: Kerry slide show, museum, and medieval-town walk. Get in the mood by relaxing for 15 minutes through the Enya-style continuous slide show of Kerry's spectacular scenery, then wander through 7,000 years of Kerry history in the museum (well described, no need for free headphones). The Irish say that when a particularly stupid guy moved from Cork to Kerry, he raised the average IQ in both counties—but this museum is pretty well done. It starts with good background on the archaeological sites of Dingle and goes right up to a video showing highlights of the Kerry football team (a fun look at Irish football—more like rugby than soccer). Good coverage is given to adventurous Annascaul native Tom Crean, who survived three Antarctic expeditions with Scott and Shackleton. The lame finale is a stroll back in time on a 1450 re-creation of Tralee's Main Street (€8; June–Aug daily 9:30–17:30; April–May and Sept–Dec Tue–Sat 9:30–17:30, closed Sun–Mon; Jan–March Tue–Fri 10:00–16:30, closed Sat–Mon; tel. 066/712-7777, www.kerrymuseum.ie). The Café Park Gate makes a handy basic lunch stop (under Ashe Memorial Hall, beside TI, same hours). Before leaving, horticulture enthusiasts will want to ramble through the rose garden in the adjacent park.

Blennerville Windmill—On the edge of Tralee, just off the Dingle road, spins a restored mill originally built in 1800. Its eight-minute video tells the story of the windmill, which ground grain to feed Britain as the country steamed into the Industrial Age (€5 gets you a one-room emigration exhibit, the video, and a peek at the spartan interior of the working windmill; April–Oct daily 10:00–18:00, closed Nov–March, tel. 066/712-1064).

A restored narrow-gauge steam railway runs hourly between Tralee's Ballyard Station (near the Aqua Dome swim center) and the windmill (€5 round-trip, June–Aug only, 15 min each way, tel. 066/712-1064). In the 19th century, Blennerville was a major port for America-bound emigrants. It was also the home port where the *Jeannie Johnston* was built. This modern-day replica of a 19th-century ship is now docked on the Liffey River in Dublin, explaining the Irish emigrant experience.

Tralee

P PARKING

100 YARDS
100 METERS

TO BALLYBUNION VIA B-556

TO **❶**, LIMERICK & COUNTY CLARE VIA N-69

BREWERY ROAD

NORTH CIRCULAR ROAD

OAK PARK RD.

TRAIN & BUS STATION

PEMBROKE

ROCK ST.

MAINE

P

❻

CHURCH

ASHE

EDWARD ST.

JOHN JOE SHEEHY ROAD

ISLAND OF GEESE

THE MALL

THE SQUARE

DOM.

Post

STRAND

HIGH

ABBEY

BANK

CASTLE ST.

❷

BOHERBEE

P

TO KILLARNEY & KERRY AIRPORT VIA N-21

❼

PRINCE'S ST.

MARY ST.

❹

❸

❺

DENNY

P

P

❶ ST. JOHN'S

MOYDERWELL

BASIN RD.

IVY TERRACE

WC

❶

← ROSE GARDEN

TOWN PARK

PRINCE'S QUAY

P

KERRY THE KINGDOM MUSEUM (ASHE MEMORIAL HALL)

■ TOWN HALL

SIAMSA TIRE THEATRE

TO **❽**

DAN SPRING ROAD

DCH

TO RING OF KERRY VIA N-70

P ● AQUA DOME

← BALLYARD STEAM RAILWAY TO WINDMILL

❶ To Meadowlands Guest House & Denton's B&B

❷ Benners Hotel

❸ Finnegan's Hostel & Cellar Restaurant

❹ The Cookery Restaurant

❺ Tesco Supermarket

❻ Super Valu Supermarket

❼ Launderette

❽ To Blennerville Windmill & Dingle

Siamsa Tíre Theatre—The National Folk Theatre of Ireland, Siamsa Tíre (shee-EM-sah TEE-rah), stages two-hour dance and theater performances based on Gaelic folk traditions. The songs are in Irish, but there's no dialogue (€25; June–Aug Mon–Sat at 8:30, no shows Sun; April–May and Sept Mon–Thu and Sat at 20:30, no shows Fri or Sun; closed Oct–March; next to Kingdom of Kerry building in park, tel. 066/712-3055, www.siamsatire.com, siamsaboxoffice@eircom.net).

Swimming—The Aqua Dome is a modern-yet-fortified swim center—the largest indoor water world in Ireland—at the Dingle end of town, near the Ashe Memorial Hall. Families enjoy the huge slide, wave pool, and other wet amusements (adults-€12, kids-€10, locker-€1, bring your own towels, July–Aug daily 10:00–22:00, shorter hours off-season, tel. 066/712-8899 or 066/712-9150).

Music and Other Distractions—Tralee has several fine pubs within a few blocks of each other (on Castle Street and Rock Street) offering live traditional music most evenings. There's greyhound racing (Fri–Sat year-round plus Tue in summer, 19:30–22:00, ten 30-second races, one every 15 min, 10-min walk from station or town center, tel. 066/718-0008). Entry to the track costs €10—plus what you lose gambling. At just about any time of day, you can drop into a betting office to check out the local gambling scene.

SLEEPING

(€1 = about $1.30, country code: 353, area code: 066)

Benners Hotel and Finnegan's accommodations are central. Meadowlands and Denton's B&B are next door to each other, a 10-minute walk north from the train station on Oakpark Road (or a €4 cab ride).

$$$ Meadowlands is a classy 58-room guest house with a bar that serves great pub meals. If you want to splurge in Tralee, do it here (Sb-€85–125, Db-€170–210, suites-€250–300, parking, Oakpark Road, tel. 066/718-0444, fax 066/718-0964, www.meadowlands-hotel.com, info@meadowlandshotel.com).

$$ Benners Hotel has 45 predictable-quality rooms in the center of town. They charge by the room, making triples and family quads a good deal (April–Sept Db/Tb/Qb-€150, a bit more on festival or holiday dates, cheaper off-season rates, some parking, Castle Street, tel. 066/712-1877, www.bennershoteltralee.com, info@bennershoteltralee.com).

$$ Denton's B&B is a tidy, modern house hosted by enthusiastic Eileen Doherty, with four comfy rooms on a busy street (Sb-€30–35, Db-€60–70, Tb-€90–105, private parking, Oakpark Road, tel. 066/712-7637, mobile 087-687-7341, www.dentontralee.com, dentonbandb@eircom.net).

$ Finnegan's Hostel, in a stately Georgian house, is a block from the TI at 17 Denny Street (€16 beds in 4-, 6-, 8-, or 10-bed dorms, Sb-€30, Db-€40, tel. 066/712-7610, www.finneganshostel.com, finneganshostel@eircom.net).

EATING

The Cookery is consistently good (€16–24 dinners Tue–Sun 17:00–22:00, closed Mon, a block off The Square, 16 Abbey Street, tel. 066/712-8833). Or try candlelit **Finnegan's Cellar** (€15–24 dinners, daily 17:30–22:30, 17 Denny Street, tel. 066/718-1400). Shop for a picnic at **Tesco,** the big grocery off The Square (Mon–Sat 8:00–22:00, Sun 10:00–20:00), or at **Super Valu** on Rock Street (Mon–Sat 8:00–22:00, Sun 8:00–19:00).

TRANSPORTATION CONNECTIONS

Day-trippers can store bags for €2.50 per day in the Fast Track office next to the ticket window beside the tracks (Mon–Fri 8:30–17:30, Sat–Sun only when trains arrive or depart, ring doorbell for service).

From Tralee by Train to: Dublin (7/day, 5/day on Sun, always via Killarney, 4 hrs, €57). Train info: tel. 066/712-3522.

By Bus to: Dingle (5/day, less off-season and on Sun, 75 min, €10 one-way, €15 round-trip), **Galway** (8/day, 4 hrs), **Limerick** (9/day, 2 hrs), **Doolin/Cliffs of Moher** (2/day, 5 hrs), **Ennis** (9/day, 3 hrs, change in Limerick), **Rosslare** (2/day, 6 hrs), **Shannon** (8/day, 2.5 hrs), **Dublin** (7/day, 6 hrs). Tralee's bus station is at the train station. Bus info: tel. 066/712-3566.

Car Rental: Duggan's Garage Practical Car Hire rents Fiat Puntos (€110/48 hrs, includes everything but gas, must be at least 25 years old, 2 blocks from train station on Ashe Street, tel. 066/712-1124, fax 066/712-7527).

Airport

Kerry Airport, a 45-minute drive or €60 taxi ride from Dingle town (just off the main road from Killarney to Tralee), offers connecting flights from **Dublin** on Aer Arann (about 4/day, www .aerarann.com), **London Stansted** on Ryanair (www.ryanair .com), and even **Hahn, Germany** (near Frankfurt) on Ryanair (tel. 066/976-4644, www.kerryairport.ie).

Dingle Route Tips for Drivers

From Tralee to Dingle: Drivers choose between the narrow, but very exciting, Conor Pass road or the faster, easier, but still narrow N-86 through Lougher and Annascaul (Abhainn an Scail). On a clear day, Conor Pass comes with incredible views over Tralee Bay and Brandon Bay, the Blasket Islands, and the open Atlantic. On the north slope, pull out at the waterfall. From here, there's a fun five-minute scramble to a dramatic little glacier-created lake. Pause also at the summit viewpoint to look down on Dingle town and harbor. While in Kerry, listen to Radio Kerry FM 97. To practice your Gaelic, tune in to FM 94.4.

Between Tralee and Galway/Burren/Doolin: The Killimer–Tarbert ferry connection allows those heading north for the Cliffs of Moher (or south for Dingle) to avoid the 80-mile detour around the Shannon River. If you're going straight to Galway, the inland Limerick route is faster. But the ferry route is more scenic and direct to the Cliffs of Moher and the Burren (hourly, 20 min, €15/carload, April–Sept departs Mon–Sat on the half-hour 7:30–21:30 going north and on the hour 7:00–21:00 going south, on Sun the first departures are 9:30 going north and 9:00 going south, Oct–March last departures at 19:00, no need to reserve, tel. 065/905-3124, www.shannonferries.com).

GALWAY

Galway feels like a boomtown—rare in Western Ireland. With 65,000 people, it's the county's main city, a lively university town, and the region's industrial and administrative center. Amid the traditional regions of Connemara and the Aran Islands, it's also a Gaelic cultural preserve.

Galway offers tourists plenty of traditional music, easy train connections to Dublin (7/day, 3 hours), and a convenient jumping-off point for a visit to the Aran Islands.

While Galway has a long and interesting history, its British overlords (who ruled until 1921) had little use for anything important to the Irish heritage. Consequently, precious little from old Galway survives. What does remain has the interesting disadvantage of being built in the local limestone, which, even if medieval, looks like modern stone construction. The city's quincentennial celebration in 1984 prompted a spirit of preservation.

What Galway lacks in sights it makes up for in ambience. Spend an afternoon just wandering its medieval streets, with their delightful mix of colorful facades, labyrinthine pubs, weather-resistant street musicians, and steamy eateries.

Blustery Galway heats up after dark, with fine theaters and a pub scene that attracts even Dubliners. Visitors mix with old-timers and students as the traditional music goes round and round.

If you hear a strange language on the streets and wonder where those people are from...it's Irish, and so are they.

Planning Your Time

Galway's sights are little more than pins on which to hang the old town. The joy of Galway is its street scene. You can see its sights

Galway's History

In 1234, the medieval fishing village of Galway went big time, when the Normans captured the territory from the O'Flaherty family. Making the town a base, the Normans invited in their Angle friends, built a wall (1270), and kicked out the Irish. Galway's Celtic name (Gaillimh) comes from an old Irish word, *gall*, which means "foreigner." Except for a small section in the Eyre Square Shopping Centre and a chunk at the Spanish Arch, that Norman wall is gone.

In the 14th century, 14 merchant families, or tribes, controlled Galway's commercial traffic, including the lucrative wine trade with Spain and France. These English families constantly clashed with the local Irish. Although the wall was built to "keep out the O's and the Macs," it didn't always work. A common prayer at the time was, "From the fury of the O'Flahertys, good Lord deliver us."

Galway's support of the English king helped it prosper. But with the rise of Oliver Cromwell in the 1600s, Galway paid for that prosperity. After sieges by Cromwell's troops (in 1651) and the Protestant King William of Orange (in 1691), Galway declined. It wasn't until the last half of the 20th century that it regained some of its importance and wealth.

in three hours, but without an evening in town, you've missed the best. Many spend three nights and two days: one for the town and another for a side-trip to the Burren, the Aran Islands, or the Connemara region (see following chapters). Tour companies make day trips to all three regions cheap and easy.

ORIENTATION

(area code: 091)

The center of Galway is Eyre Square. Within two blocks of the square, you'll find the TI, Aran boat offices, a tour pick-up point, accommodations (from the best cheap hostel beds to fancy hotels), and the train station. The train and bus station butt up against the Great Southern Hotel, a huge gray railroad hotel that overlooks and dominates Eyre Square. The lively old town lies between Eyre Square and the river. From Eyre Square, Williamsgate Street leads right through the old town (changing names several times) to Wolfe Tone Bridge. Nearly everything you'll see and do is within a few minutes' walk of this spine.

Tourist Information

The TI, located a block from the bus/train station in the ground floor of the Forster Court Hotel, has a bookshop and many booking services (June–Sept daily 9:00–17:45; Oct–May Mon–Sat 9:00–17:45, Sun 9:00–12:45; tel. 091/537-700, www.irelandwest.ie). Pick up the TI's free weekly *What's Going On* or *Galway Magazine* (€3, persistent readers will find several maps and walking tours amid the ads).

Arrival in Galway

Trains and most buses share the same station, virtually on Eyre Square (which has the nearest ATMs). The Fast Track office in the train station can store your bag (€2.50/day, Mon–Sat 7:30–18:30, Sun 10:00–18:30). To get from the station to the TI, go left on Station Road as you exit the station (toward Eyre Square), then turn right on Forster Street. Some buses from Dublin and Dublin's airport use the Forster Street Bus Park, next to the TI.

For drivers, the most central and handiest parking garage is under Jurys Inn in the town center (€1.70/hr, €20/24 hrs, Mon–Sat 9:00–1:00 in the morning, Sun 9:00–18:00). To park nearby for free, try across the bridge along the Claddagh Quay or by the Siamsa Theatre. Otherwise, you'll have to buy a pay-and-display ticket and put it on your dashboard (€1.50/hr, buy from machines on street).

Helpful Hints

Crowd Control: Expect huge crowds—and much higher prices—during the Galway Arts Festival (July 14–27 in 2008, www.galwayartsfestival.com) and Galway Oyster Festival (4 days near end of Sept, www.galwayoysterfest.com). The Galway Races are heaven for horserace lovers and hell for everyone else (biggest race is July 28–Aug 3 in 2008, with fall races Sept 8–10 and Oct 26–27, www.galwayraces.com); prices double for food and lodging, and simple evening strolls become as challenging as punt returns.

Markets: On Saturday, a fun market clusters around St. Nicholas' Church (all day, but best 9:00–12:00).

Internet Access: The **e-2008 Internet Café** is located next to the Park House Hotel (€2.10/30 min, daily 9:00–24:00, Forster Street). There are also several good places along High Street near Jurys Inn.

Post Office: You'll find it on Eglinton Street (Mon–Fri 9:00–17:30, Sat 9:00–13:00, closed Sun).

Laundry: Launderland is close to the recommended B&Bs on College Road (€8.50 drop-off, Mon–Fri 8:30–18:30, Sat

Galway

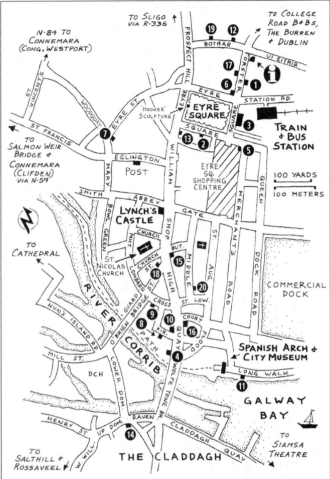

1 Park House Hotel & Internet Café
2 Skeffington Arms Hotel
3 Hotel Meyrick
4 Jurys Galway Inn
5 Kinlay House Hostel
6 Garvey's Inn
7 McSwiggan's Rest. & Pub
8 Kirwan's Lane Creative Cuisine
9 Busker Brownes
10 McDonagh's Fish-and-Chips

11 Nimmo's Wine Bar Bistro
12 Al Muretto Restaurant
13 Galway Bakery Co. (GBC)
14 Monroe's Pub
15 Taaffe's Pub
16 The Quays Pub
17 An Pucán Pub
18 Tig Coili Pub
19 Launderette
20 Bike Rental

9:00–18:00, closed Sun, Forster Court, 2-min walk up hill from TI, tel. 091/568-393).

Bike Rental: Mountain Trail rents a variety of mountain bikes (€10/day, Mon–Sat 9:30–18:00, closed Sun, Cornstore Mall, Unit 15, Middle Street, tel. 091/569-888).

TOURS

▲Hop-on, Hop-off City Bus Tours—Guided 60-minute double-decker bus tours run from the TI and Eyre Square, making nine stops, including the cathedral, Salthill, and the Spanish Arch. You can get off and explore, and hop back on later (€10, April–Sept daily 10:30–16:30, 4/day, buses usually depart every 90 min from TI on Forster Street, tel. 091/524-728 or mobile 087-679-8525).

Walking Tour—**Galway Gothic's** 90-minute tour focuses on the city's medieval folklore, mythology, gore, and ghosts (€10, April–Sept Mon–Sat at 11:00 and 15:00, departs from TI, tel. 091/568-751, mobile 087-778-2887, www.legendtours.ie).

SIGHTS

Medieval Galway's "Latin Quarter"

From the top of Eyre Square, Williamsgate Street—named for the old main gate of the Norman town wall that once stood here—is the spine of medieval Galway, leading downhill straight to the Corrib River. While the road changes names several times (William, Shop, High, and Quay Streets), it leads generally downhill and straight past these sights:

Lynch's Castle—Now the Allied Irish Bank, Galway's best late-15th-century fortified townhouse was the home of the Lynch family—the most powerful of the town's 14 tribes—and the only one of their mansions to survive. More than 80 Lynch mayors ruled Galway in the 16th and 17th centuries.

Collegiate Church of St. Nicholas—This church, located a half-block off the main street on the right, is the finest medieval building in town (1320), and is dedicated to St. Nicholas of Myra, the patron saint of sailors. Columbus is said to have worshipped here in 1477, undoubtedly while contemplating a scary voyage. Its interior is littered with obscure town history (€3 donation for admission).

A wonderful **open-air market** surrounds the church most Saturdays year-round and also on Sundays in summer.

The Quays—The pub was once owned by "Humanity Dick," an 18th-century Member of Parliament who was the original animal-rights activist. It's worth a peek inside for its lively interior. The lane just before it leads to the...

Druid Theatre—This 100-seat theater offers top-notch contemporary Irish theater. Drop by to see if anything's playing tonight (€16–25 tickets, Chapel Lane, tel. 091/568-617, www.druidtheatre .com).

Directly across the alley from the theater door (under the glass Revenue Building) are the foundations of Galway's oldest building. It was once the 13th-century hall of the Norman lord Richard DeBurgo.

Spanish Arch and City Museum—Overlooking the Corrib River, these structures make up the best remaining chunk of the old city wall. The Spanish Arch (1584), the place where Spanish ships would unload their cargo, is a reminder of Galway's former importance in trade. Fragments of old Galway are kept in the recently expanded museum (€4, May–Sept daily 10:00–13:00 & 14:00–17:00; Oct–April Wed–Sun 11:00–13:00 & 14:00–17:00, closed Mon–Tue; call to verify price and hours, tel. 091/567-641).

Corrib River Sights—At the Corrib River, you'll find a riverside park perfect for a picnic (or get take-out from the town's best chippy, McDonagh's, located across the street). Over the river (southeast of the bridge) is the modern housing project that replaced the original Claddagh in the 1930s. Claddagh (CLA-dah) was a picturesque, Gaelic-speaking fishing village with a strong tradition of independence—and open sewers. This gaggle of thatched cottages actually functioned as an independent community with its own "king" until the early 1900s.

The old Claddagh village has since disappeared, but the tradition of its popular ring (sold all over town) lives on. The Claddagh ring shows two hands holding a heart that wears a crown. The heart represents love, the crown is loyalty, and the hands are friendship. If the ring is worn with the tip of the heart pointing toward the wrist, it signifies that the wearer is married or otherwise taken. However, if the tip of the heart points toward the fingertip, it means the wearer is available.

Look at the monument (just before the bridge) given to Galway by the people of Genoa, celebrating Columbus' visit here in 1477. (That acknowledgment, from a town known in Italy for its stinginess, helps to substantiate the murky visit.) From the middle of the bridge, look up the river. The green copper dome marks the city's Cathedral of St. Nicholas (described below). Down the river is a tiny harbor with a few of Galway's famous square-rigged "hooker" fishing ships tied up and on display. Called hookers for their hook-and-line fishing, these sturdy yet graceful boats were later used for transporting turf from Connemara until improved roads and electric heat made them obsolete. Beyond that, a huge park of reclaimed land is popular with the local kids for Irish football and hurling. From there, the promenade leads to the resort town of Salthill.

More Sights in Galway

▲**Eyre Square**—On a sunny day, grassy Eyre Square is a popular hangout. In the Middle Ages, it was a field just outside the town wall. The square is named for the mayor who gave the land to the city in 1710. While still called Eyre Square, it now contains John F. Kennedy Park—established in memory of the Irish-American president's visit in 1963, a few months before he was assassinated. Though Kennedy is celebrated as America's first Irish-Catholic president, there have been several US presidents who descended from Protestant Ulster stock. Take a look at the JFK bust (near the kids' play area) commemorating his visit.

Walk to the rust-colored Quincentennial Fountain, built in 1984 to celebrate the 500th anniversary of the incorporation of the city. The sails represent Galway's square-rigged fishing ships and the vessels that made Galway a trading center so long ago. The Browne Doorway, from a 1627 fortified townhouse, is a reminder of the 14 family tribes that once ruled the town (see Lynch's Castle, listed earlier in this chapter, to get a feel for an intact townhouse). Each had a town castle—much like the towers that characterize the towns of Tuscany with their feuding noble families. So little survives of medieval Galway that the town makes a huge deal of any remaining window or crest.

The Eyre Square Shopping Centre—a busy, modern shopping mall (see the arcaded entry from the square)—leads to a piece of the old town wall that includes two reconstructed towers (and an antiques market).

▲▲**Cathedral of St. Nicholas**— Opened by American Cardinal Cushing in 1965, this is one of the last great stone churches built in Europe. The interior is a treat—mahogany pews set on green Connemara marble floors under a Canadian cedar ceiling. The acoustically correct cedar enhances the church's fine pipe

Galway Legends

Because of the dearth of physical old stuff, the town milks its legends. Here are a few you'll encounter repeatedly:

- In the 15th century, the mayor, one of the Lynch tribe, condemned his son to death for the murder of a Spaniard. When no one in town could be found to hang the popular boy, the dad—who loved justice more than his son—did it himself.
- Columbus is said to have stopped in Galway in 1477. He may have been inspired by tales of the voyage of St. Brendan, the Irish monk who is thought by some (mostly Irish) to have beaten Columbus to the New World by nearly a thousand years.
- On the main drag you'll find a pub called The King's Head. It was originally given to the man who chopped off the head of King Charles I in 1649. For his safety, he settled in Galway—about as far from London as an Englishman could get back then.

organ. Two thousand worshippers sit in the round facing the central altar. A Dublin woman carved 14 larger-than-life Stations of the Cross. The carving above the chapel (left of entry) is from the old St. Nicholas church. Explore the modern stained glass. Find the Irish holy family—with Mary knitting and Jesus offering Joseph a cup of tea. The window depicting the Last Supper is particularly creative—find the 12 apostles.

Next, poke your head into the side chapel with a mosaic of Christ's resurrection (if you're standing in the nave facing the main altar, it's on the left and closest to the front). Take a closer look at the profiled face to the right of Christ—the one looking up while praying with clasped hands. It's JFK, nearly a saint in Irish eyes at the time this cathedral was built.

Church bulletins at the doorway tell of upcoming Masses and concerts (located across Salmon Weir Bridge on outskirts of town, tel. 091/563-577).

Salmon Weir Bridge—This bridge was the local "bridge of sighs." It led from the courthouse (opposite the church) to the prison (torn down to build the church—unlikely in the US). Today the bridge provides a fun view of the fishing action. Salmon run up this river most of the summer (look for them). Fishermen, who wear waders and carry walking sticks to withstand the strong current, book long in advance to get half-day appointments for a casting spot.

Canals multiplied in this city (sometimes called the "Venice of Ireland") to power more water mills.

Outer Galway

▲Salthill—This small resort town packs pubs, discos, a splashy water park, amusement centers, and a fairground up against a fine, mile-long beach promenade. At the **Atlantaquaria Aquarium**, which features solely Irish water life, kids can help feed the big fish at 15:00, and the small fish at 16:00 (€9, Mon–Fri 9:00–17:00, Sat–Sun 9:00–18:00, touch tanks, The Promenade, tel. 091/585-100, www.nationalaquarium.ie). For beach time, a relaxing sunset stroll, late-night traditional music, or later-night disco action, Salthill hops. To get to Salthill, catch bus #1 from Eyre Square in front of the AIB bank, next to Meyrick Hotel (€1.35, runs 7:00–23:00).

Trad on the Prom—This fine traditional music and dance troupe was started by Galway-born performers who returned home after years of touring with *Riverdance*. It's a great way to enjoy live step dancing and accomplished musicians in a fairly intimate venue (€25, May–Sept, call for schedule, in Salthill Hotel, tel. 091/522-711 or mobile 087-2388-489, www.tradontheprom.com).

Dog Racing—Join the locals and cheer on the greyhounds on Thursday, Friday, and Saturday evenings from 20:00 to 22:30 (€10, barking distance from my recommended B&Bs, a 10-min walk from Eyre Square, tel. 091/562-273).

NIGHTLIFE

▲Traditional Irish Music in Pubs—Galway, like Dingle and Doolin, is a mecca for good Irish music (nightly 21:30–23:30). But unlike Dingle and Doolin, this is a university town (enrollment: 12,000), and many pubs are often overrun with noisy students. Still, the chances of landing a seat close to a churning band surrounded by new Irish friends are good any evening of the year. Touristy and student pubs are found and filled along the main drag down from Eyre Square to the Spanish Arch, and across Wolfe Tone Bridge along William Street West and Dominick Street. Across the bridge, start at **Monroe's,** with its vast, music-filled interior (live music nightly at 21:30, set-dancing Tue at 21:30, Dominick Street, tel. 091/583-397). Several other pubs within earshot also feature almost-nightly traditional music.

Pubs known for Irish music along the main drag include **Tig Coili** (sessions Mon–Sat at 18:00 and 21:00, Sun at 14:00 and 21:00, intersection of Main Guard Street

and High Street, tel. 091/561-294), **Taaffe's** (nightly music sessions at 17:00 and 21:30, Shop Street, across from St. Nicholas Church, tel. 091/564-066), and **The Quays** (traditional music Mon–Thu at 21:30, Fri–Sun at 17:00, young scene, Quay Street, tel. 091/568-347).

An Pucán Pub, a cauldron of music and beer drinking with an older crowd—including lots of tourists—is worth a look (music nightly at 22:00, sometimes traditional, just off Eyre Square on Forster Street, tel. 091/561-528).

SLEEPING

There are three price tiers for most beds in Galway: high season (Easter–Oct), off-season, and charge-what-you-like festivals and race weekends (see "Crowd Control," page 229). I've listed high-season rates. B&Bs simply play the market. If you're on a tight budget, call around and see where the best prices are. All B&Bs include a full fried breakfast. For locations, see the map on page 230.

Hotels
For a fancy hotel, Park House Hotel offers the best value. For a budget hotel, go to Jurys. For cheap beds, hit the hostel.

$$$ Park House Hotel, a plush, business-class hotel, is ideally located a block from the train station and Eyre Square. Its 84 spacious rooms come with all the comforts you'd expect (Db-€150–185 is the "corporate rate" you should get most of the year, ask if there's a discount, Sun night is slow and rooms can rent for Db-€118, elevator, good restaurant, free garage, helpful staff, Forster Street, tel. 091/564-924, www.parkhousehotel.ie, parkhousehotel @eircom.net).

$$$ Skeffington Arms Hotel, which feels more Irish (and a bit smokier) than the Park House or Jurys, escapes most of the

---

Sleep Code

(€1 = about $1.30, country code: 353, area code: 091)
S = Single, **D** = Double/Twin, **T** = Triple, **Q** = Quad, **b** = bathroom, **s** = shower only. All of these places accept credit cards.

To help you easily sort through these listings, I've divided the rooms into three categories, based on the price for a standard double room with bath:

  $$$ Higher Priced—Most rooms €120 or more.
   $$ Moderately Priced—Most rooms between €60–120.
    $ Lower Priced—Most rooms €60 or less.

tour-group scene because it has only 23 rooms. Centrally located on Eyre Square, it's furnished in a dark-wood Victorian style (Db-€109–200, online discounts, pub downstairs, Eyre Square, tel. 091/563-173, fax 091/561-679, www.skeffington.ie, reception @skeffington.ie).

$$$ Hotel Meyrick, filled with palatial Old World elegance and 99 rooms, marks the end of the Dublin–Galway train line and the beginning of Galway. Since 1845, it has been Galway's landmark hotel...JFK stayed here in 1963 when it was the Great Southern (Db-€165–180, some discounts during slow times, best rates by booking online, breakfast-€15 extra, sauna, at the head of Eyre Square, tel. 091/564-041, fax 091/566-704, www .hotelmeyrick.ie).

$$$ Garvey's Inn, with 18 comfortable but occasionally smoky rooms right across from the station, offers the best price on Eyre Square. Mrs. Garvey adds a personal touch that bigger places can't offer (Sb-€60–70, Db-€120–140, above a great pub, tel. 091/562-224, fax 091/562-526, www.garveysinn.com, info @garveysinn.com).

$$ Jurys Galway Inn has 130 American-style rooms in a modern hotel, centrally located where the old town hits the river. The big, bright rooms have two double beds and huge modern bathrooms. You'll pay the same per room whether it's for a single, a couple, three adults, or a family of four (€100–122 Mon–Thu, or €135–145 Fri–Sun depending on season, breakfast-€12, elevator, lots of tour groups, 3 non-smoking floors, parking-€10, Quay Street, tel. 091/566-444, fax 091/568-415, US tel. 800-423-6953, www.jurysinn.com, jurysinngalway@jurysdoyle.com).

$ *Hostel:* Kinlay House is a no-nonsense place just 100 yards from the train station, with 220 beds (1–8 beds per room) in bare, clean, and simple rooms, including 15 doubles/twins. Easygoing people of any age feel welcome here, but if you want a double, book well ahead—several months in advance for weekends (dorm bed-€16–24, Sb-€35–50, Db-€54–62, Internet access, elevator, self-service kitchen, launderette, baggage storage, on Merchants Road just off Eyre Square, tel. 091/565-244, fax 091/565-245, www .kinlaygalway.ie, info@kinlaygalway.ie).

B&Bs

Drivers following city-center signs into Galway pass by a string of B&Bs just after the greyhound-racing stadium. These are about an eight-minute walk from Eyre Square (from the station, walk up Forster Street, which turns into College Road). All six of the listings are lined up like battleships on College Road. Although there are other B&Bs on this road, my favorites are the ones where the owner lives on site (and their pride of ownership shows). The Petra

Galway B&Bs

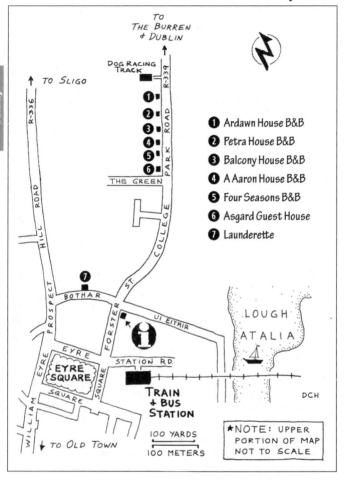

TO THE BURREN & DUBLIN

DOG RACING TRACK

TO SLIGO

R-336

R-339

HILL ROAD

COLLEGE PARK ROAD

THE GREEN

COLLEGE ST.

BOTHAR

FORSTER ST.

UI EITHIR

PROSPECT

EYRE SQUARE

EYRE SQUARE

STATION RD.

EYRE SQUARE

WILLIAM

TRAIN + BUS STATION

LOUGH ATALIA

DCH

100 YARDS
100 METERS

↓ TO OLD TOWN

1 Ardawn House B&B
2 Petra House B&B
3 Balcony House B&B
4 A Aaron House B&B
5 Four Seasons B&B
6 Asgard Guest House
7 Launderette

★NOTE: UPPER PORTION OF MAP NOT TO SCALE

Galway

House and Four Seasons B&B are the best values. For locations, see the map above.

$$$ Ardawn House is a classy B&B with nine comfortable rooms (Sb-€70–90, Db-€80–150, Qb-€160, Wi-Fi, College Road, near stadium on right, tel. 091/568-833, fax 091/563-454, www .galway.net/pages/ardawn-house, ardawn@iol.ie, Mike and Breda Guilfoyle).

$$ Petra House, a peaceful-feeling brick building, rents six great rooms, including a family room. The owners, Joan and Frank Maher, keep everything lovingly maintained. Breakfasts are a highlight (Sb-€50–75, Db-€80–100, Tb-€120–140, elegant sitting room, Wi-Fi, next door to Ardawn House—listed above,

29 College Road, tel. & fax 091/566-580, www.galway.net/pages /petra-house, petrahouse@eircom.net).

$$ Four Seasons B&B is well kept, with seven inviting rooms hosted by Eddie and Helen Fitzgerald (Sb-€50–75, Db-€80–100, Tb-€120–140, Qb-€110–160, parking, 23 College Road, tel. 091/564-078, fax 091/569-765, www.galway.net/pages/fourseasons, 4season@gofree.indigo.ie).

$$ Balcony House B&B rents eight pleasant rooms (Db-€70–100, Tb-€105–140, Qb-€140–160, 27 College Road, tel. 091/563-438, www.aaabalconyhouse.com, info@aaabalconyhouse .com). Teresa Coyne provides treats in your room on arrival.

$$ Asgard Guest House offers eight restful rooms and an appealing glass-atrium breakfast room (Sb-€45–60, Db-€70–90, Tb-€90–120, Qb-€140–160, 21 College Road, tel. 091/566-855, www.galway.net/pages/asgard, asgard@eircom.net, Veronica or Geraldine).

$$ A Aaron House B&B maintains 14 modest rooms, including two in a duplex out back that make a handy family quad (Sb-€50–60, Db-€90–100, Tb-€90–150, Qb-€110–160, 25 College Road, tel. 091/563-315, fax 091/563-732, www.galway.net/pages /aaaron, aaaron@indigo.ie, Ena Burke).

Salthill

$$ Carraig Beag B&B, the classiest, friendliest, and most peaceful of all, is a big brick home on a residential street a block off the beach, just beyond the resort town of Salthill. Catherine Lydon, with the help of her husband, Paddy, rents six big, bright, fresh, and comfy rooms with a welcoming living room and a communal breakfast table (Sb-€55–70, Db-€70–95, family room-€100–135, closed Nov–March; 8-min drive from Galway, follow the beach past Salthill, take second right after the golf course on Knocknacarra Road and go 2 blocks to 1 Burren View Heights; tel. 091/521-696, www.dirl.com/galway/salthill/carraig-beag.htm, thelydons@eircom.net). Take bus #2 (€1.35, 3/hr) from Eyre Square (picks up in front of Skeffington Arms pub) to the Knocknacarra stop at the B&B's doorstep, or you can catch bus #37 from Corrib Centre by Roches Store (€1.35). Catherine can arrange for daytour pickups at her place.

EATING

This college town is filled with colorful, inexpensive eateries. People everywhere seem to be enjoying their food. Each of these places is at the bottom of the old town, within a block or two of Jurys Inn. For locations, see the map on page 230.

Kirwan's Lane Creative Cuisine, considered Galway's best restaurant, is a dressy place where reservations are required (€16–22 lunches, €24–30 dinners, daily 12:30–16:00 & 18:00–22:00, no lunch on Sun, on Kirwan's Lane a block from Jurys Inn, tel. 091/568-266).

Busker Brownes has three eateries in a sprawling spot popular for its good, cheap food. Enter on Cross Street for the restaurant and walk to the back for better seating, or enter on Kirwan's Lane for the ground-floor pub; the third section is upstairs from the pub (€10–25 meals, daily 10:30–21:30, Sunday jazz session at noon, Cross Street and Kirwan's Lane, tel. 091/563-377).

McDonagh's Fish-and-Chips is a local favorite. It has a fast, cheap section and a classier restaurant. If you're determined to try Galway oysters, remember that they're in season September through April only. Other times you'll eat Pacific oysters—which doesn't make much sense to me (€10 lunch, €15–25 in restaurant, Mon–Sat 12:00–15:00 & 17:00–22:00, chipper open Sun 17:00–22:00 but restaurant closed, 22 Quay Street, tel. 091/565-001).

Nimmo's Wine Bar Bistro lurks peacefully in an old stone warehouse behind the Spanish Arch with terrific €9 fish soup and a diverse wine list. The candlelit ambience is great even for a cup of coffee (€15–26 meals, daily 18:00–22:30, closed Mon off-season, Long Walk Street, tel. 091/561-114).

McSwiggan's, with a downstairs pub and upstairs restaurant, is a maze of wooden stairways, brick walls, and hidden alcoves, serving hearty traditional Irish meals (€11–18 lunches, €14–22 dinners, daily 11:30–22:30, Eyre Street, tel. 091/568-917).

Al Muretto serves friendly Italian trattoria-style meals, just a five-minute walk toward town from my College Road B&B listings (€12–23 meals, €20 three-course early-bird specials, daily 12:30–23:00, facing Bothar 50 yards up from corner with Forster, tel. 091/561-996).

The **Galway Bakery Company (GBC)** is a popular, basic place for a quick Irish meal (€9–14 meals in ground-floor cafeteria, pricier restaurant upstairs, daily 8:00–22:00, 7 Williamsgate Street, near Eyre Square, tel. 091/563-087).

Supermarket: **Dunne's** is accessed through the Eyre Square Shopping Centre or around the corner at tiny Castle Street, off the pedestrian Williamsgate Street (Mon–Sat 9:00–18:30, Thu–Fri until 21:00, Sun 12:00–18:00, supermarket in basement). Lots of smaller grocery shops are scattered throughout town.

Medieval Banquet in Kinvarra: If you have a car, consider a **Dunguaire Castle medieval banquet** in Kinvarra, a 30-minute drive south of Galway (see page 253). The 17:30 banquet can be done very efficiently as you're driving into or out of Galway (B&Bs can accommodate late arrivals if you call).

TRANSPORTATION CONNECTIONS

From Galway by Train to: Dublin (7/day, 3 hrs). For **Belfast, Tralee,** and **Rosslare,** you'll change in or near Dublin. Train info: tel. 091/561-444.

By Bus to: Ennis (14/day, 1.25 hrs), **Doolin** (4/day, 2 hrs), **Cliffs of Moher** (2/day in summer, 1.5 hrs, €15 round-trip), **Limerick** (14/day, 2 hrs), **Rosslare** (2/day, 6.5 hrs), **Belfast** (4/day, 7 hrs), **Dublin** (14/day, 3.5 hrs; also see Citylink, below). Bus info: tel. 091/562-000, www.buseireann.ie.

Citylink (tel. 091/564-164, www.citylink.ie) runs cheap and fast bus service from Galway's Forster Street Bus Park to **Dublin** (arriving at Bachelor's Walk, a block from Tara Street DART Station; 15/day, 3–3.5 hrs, €14), **Dublin Airport** (14/day, 3.5 hrs, €19), and **Shannon Airport** (5/day, 1.5 hrs).

By Car: For ideas on driving from Galway to Derry or Portrush in Northern Ireland, see "Between Galway and Derry" on page 282 for sights in the Republic of Ireland, and "For Drivers: Northern Ireland Sights Between Derry and Galway" on page 343 for sights in Northern Ireland.

COUNTY CLARE
AND THE BURREN

Those connecting Dingle in the south with Galway in the north can entertain themselves along the way by joyriding through the fascinating landscape and tidy villages of County Clare. Ennis, the major city of the county, with a medieval history and a market bustle, is a workaday Irish town ideal for anyone tired of the tourist crowds. The dramatic Cliffs of Moher overlooking the Atlantic offer tenderfeet a thrilling hike. The Burren is a unique, windblown limestone wasteland that hides an abundance of flora, fauna, caves, and history. For your evening entertainment, you can join a tour-bus group in a castle for a medieval banquet in Kinvarra or meet up with traditional Irish music enthusiasts from around Europe for tin whistling in Doolin.

Planning Your Time

By **train** and **bus,** your gateways to this region are Ennis from the south and Galway from the north (consider a tour from Galway; see "Bus Tours of the Burren," on the next page).

By **car,** the region can be an enjoyable daylong drive-through or a destination in itself. None of the sights has to take much time. But do get out and walk a bit.

If driving from Dingle to Galway, I'd recommend this day plan rather than the main road via Limerick: Drive north from Tralee via Listowel to catch the Tarbert–Killimer car ferry (avoiding Limerick traffic and the

County Clare and the Burren

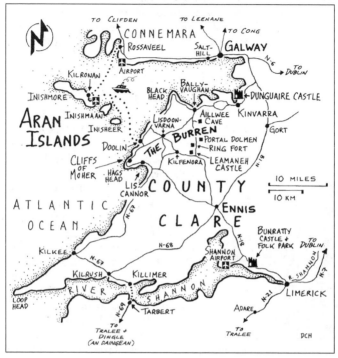

80-mile/90-minute drive around the Shannon estuary; see "Dingle Route Tips for Drivers" at the end of the Dingle chapter), then drive the coastal route to the Cliffs of Moher for an hour break. The scenic drive through the Burren, with a couple of stops and a tour of the caves, takes about two hours. There's a 17:30 medieval banquet at Dunguaire Castle near Kinvarra (just 30 min south of Galway, see Kinvarra section below).

Tips: Visit an ATM in Ennis, Galway, or Lahinch before you enter this region (there are no ATMs in Doolin, Lisdoonvarna, Kilfenora, or Ballyvaughan). Skip the **Bunratty Castle and Folk Museum.** I'd leave this most commercial and least lively of all European open-air folk museums to the jet-lagged, big-bus American tour groups (located just a potty stop from the Shannon Airport, past Limerick on the road to Ennis).

Bus Tours of the Burren

Two Galway-based companies—Lally and O'Neachtain—run all-day tours of nearby regions (€23–31). Tours of the Burren do a loop south of Galway, covering Kinvarra, Aillwee Cave, Poulnabrone Dolmen, and the Cliffs of Moher. Tours go most days from about 10:00 to 17:30 (departing from in front of Kinlay House on Merchant's Road in Galway, call to confirm exact itinerary: Lally tel. 091/562-905, www.lallytours.com; O'Neachtain tel. 091/553-188, www.oneachtaintours.com). Drivers take cash only; to pay with a credit card, book at Galway's TI.

Cliffs of Moher

A visit to the Cliffs of Moher (pronounced "more"), a ▲▲▲ sight, is one of Ireland's great natural thrills. For five miles, the dramatic cliffs soar as high as 650 feet above the Atlantic.

You'll find the **TI** in the new visitors center—a stonework hobbit-hole building tucked into the grassy knoll across the street from the parking lot (May–Sept daily 8:30–20:30, closed Oct–April, tel. 065/708-6141). The new center charges an €8 "facilities charge," basically a parking fee, although access to the cliffs is still technically free. Be careful—many people try to avoid the facilities charge by parking illegally on the narrow, shoulder-less road, and then walking to the cliffs (a risk not worth the €8 they save). If you're without wheels, you can get here by bus from Galway (2/day in summer, 1.5 hrs, €15 round-trip).

The new visitors center was built in a concentric-circle layout with local stone. Upstairs is the Long Dock restaurant (which serves coffee and substantial cafeteria-style meals until 19:00); a photo diorama showing aerial views of the cliffs and underwater photos of local marine life; and the toilets, where you can enjoy a huge panoramic photo of the cliffs on the stall doors as you wait in line. Downstairs is a small café, a gift shop, and the new Atlantic Edge exhibit.

The €4 exhibit focuses mainly on natural and geological history, native bird and marine life, and virtual interactive exhibits aimed at children (often occupied by adults). You may even learn why the cliffs are always windy. A small theater with an IMAX-style screen shows "The Ledge," a film following a gannet who's a Jonathan Livingston wannabe, as he flies along the cliffs and then dives underwater, encountering puffins, seals, and even a humpback whale along the way.

After leaving the center, walk 200 yards to the cliff's edge and along the wall of the local Liscannor slate. Notice the squiggles made by worms, eels, and snails long ago when the slate was still mud on the seafloor. O'Brien's Tower, built in 1853, marks the highest point of the cliffs (tower closed to visitors during refurbishment—current plans are to turn it into a gift shop).

After years of easy public access to the cliffs, numerous fatal accidents have prompted the hiring of "rangers," who are there ostensibly to answer your questions, but whose main purpose is to keep people from getting too close to the cliff edge. The upside is that they lead guided tours up to three times a day in the summer (ask at visitors center for details). If you happen to be at the cliffs early or late, you can still try for the thrill of a creep to the edge. Read the warning, consider the risk (wind gusts can be sudden, strong, and fatal), then climb over the slate barrier and down onto the stone platform. If you're a risk-taking fool, belly out and take a peek over the ledge. You'll find yourself in a dramatic world where the only sounds are the waves, the wind, the gulls, and your stomach signaling frantically for help. There's a particularly peaceful corner of the platform over on the far right. On the far left, watch the birds play in the updrafts. In the distance, on windy days, the Aran Islands can be seen wearing their white necklace of surf.

Before leaving the area, drivers could take 10 minutes to check out the holy well of St. Bridget, located beside the tall column about a half-mile (1 km) south of the cliffs on the main road to Liscannor. In the short hall leading into the hillside spring, you'll find a treasure of personal and religious memorabilia left behind by devoted visitors seeking cures and blessings. The simple gray column outside was a folly erected 150 years ago by a local landlord with money and ego to burn.

ST BRIDGET'S WELL

Cruises: To get a different perspective of the cliffs (looking up instead of down), you can cruise along their base between Doolin and Liscannor. **Cliffs of Moher Cruises** makes the 75-minute voyage past sea stacks and crag-perching birds. Boats depart from the main pier in Doolin (same dock as Aran Islands boat) or from Liscannor (find the dock by following signs for Cliffs of Moher cruises near Vaughan's Pub). A free shuttle bus takes you back to whichever port you departed from (€22, runs daily April–Oct, 3/day from Doolin, 1/day from Liscannor, weather and tides permitting, call or go online to check sailing schedule and to reserve, tel. 065/707-5949, mobile 087-245-3239, www.mohercruises.com).

Doolin

This town is a strange phenomenon. Many tourists go directly from Paris or Munich to Doolin. It's on the tourist map for its traditional music. A few years ago, this was a mecca for Irish musicians. They came together here to jam before a few lucky aficionados. But now the crowds and the foreigners are overwhelming the musicians, and the quality of music is not as reliable. Still, as Irish and European music-lovers alike crowd the pubs, the *bodhrán* beat goes on.

Doolin has plenty of accommodations and a Greek-island-without-the-sun ambience. The "town" is just a few homes and shops strung out along a valley road from the tiny harbor. Locals generally divide the town into an Upper Village and Lower Village. The Lower Village is the closest thing to a commercial center.

Doolin is famous for three pubs, all featuring Irish folk music: Nearest the harbor, in the Lower Village, is **O'Connor's Pub** (tel. 065/707-4168). A mile farther up the road, the Upper Village straddles a bridge with the other two destination pubs, **McGann's** (tel. 065/707-4133) and **McDermott's** (tel. 065/707-4328). Music starts in the pubs between 21:30 and 22:00, finishing around midnight. Get there before 21:00 if you want a place to sit, or pop in later and plan on standing. On my last trip, I hit Doolin on a mediocre music night. The *craic* is fine regardless. Pubs serve decent dinners before the music starts. (**Dial-A-Cab** is a handy service for folks without wheels wanting to link a night of fun in Doolin with a bed in Lisdoonvarna; mobile 086-812-7049 or 087-290-2060.)

The **Michael Russell Heritage Centre** in Doolin may eventually become a museum of traditional music. For now, some *ceilidh* dances are held here. Ask at a pub if anything's scheduled.

From Doolin, you can hike or bike (rentals in town) up Burren Way for three miles to the Cliffs of Moher. (Get advice locally on the trail condition and safety.) Doolin also offers boat cruises along the Cliffs of Moher (see above).

Doolin Activity Lodge offers a handy grab-bag of services, including accommodations (see next page); an Internet café (€3/30 min, daily 8:00–22:00, 4 terminals); a launderette (drop-off only, pick up clothes in 6 hours, no self-service, same hours as café); and bike rental (€15/day, daily 8:00–22:00, shorter hours off-season, leave passport or credit card number as deposit). The staff can also recommend horseback, hiking, and fishing options.

County Clare

Sleep Code

(€1 = about $1.30, country code: 353, area code: 065)
S = Single, **D** = Double/Twin, **T** = Triple, **Q** = Quad, **b** = bathroom,
s = shower only. Breakfast is included and credit cards are
accepted unless otherwise noted.

To help you easily sort through these listings, I've divided
the rooms into categories, based on the price for a standard
double room with bath:

$$$ **Higher Priced**—Most rooms €70 or more.
 $$ **Moderately Priced**—Most rooms between €50–70.
  $ **Lower Priced**—Most rooms €50 or less.

SLEEPING

$$$ Harbour View B&B is a fine modern house with six rooms,
a mile from the Doolin fiddles, overlooking the valley. Kathy
Normoyle keeps the guests' living room stocked with games and
serves home-baked bread from her mom's house out back (Sb-
€55–60, Db-€76–80, Tb-€105, larger family-room deals, includes
classy breakfast, on main road halfway between Lisdoonvarna and
Cliffs of Moher, next to Statoil gas station, tel. 065/707-4154, fax
065/707-4935, www.harbourviewdoolin.com, clarebb@eircom.net).

$$$ Doolin Activity Lodge is a modern compound of four
stone buildings with 22 bright, airy, good-value rooms (Sb-
€40–60, Db-€70–90, Tb-€105–135, Qb-€140–180, located about
halfway between Upper and Lower villages, tel. 065/707-4888,
fax 065/707-4877, www.doolinlodge.com, info@doolinlodge.com).
The lodge offers handy amenities (see opposite page) and a pizza/
pasta **restaurant** (open mid-May–mid-Sept only, Tue–Sun 18:00–
22:00, closed Mon).

$ Doolin Hostel, right in Doolin's Lower Village, caters cre-
atively to the needs of backpackers in town for the music (dorm
bed-€16, Db-€44, Tb-€60, Qb-€90, Lower Village, tel. & fax
065/707-4006, www.doolinhostel.com, josephine@doolinhostel
.com).

EATING

My favorite restaurant is **Bruach na haille,** next door to McGann's
pub in the Upper Village. Its decor is simple but its seafood is excellent (€15–20 dinners, Mon–Sat 18:00–22:00, Sun 10:00–16:00, tel.
065/707-4120).

TRANSPORTATION CONNECTIONS

From Doolin by Bus to: Galway (4/day, 2 hrs), **Ennis** (2/day, 1–1.5 hrs).

By Ferry to the Aran Islands: The boats from Doolin to the Aran Islands (described in the next chapter) can be handy, but they often are canceled or run late. Even a balmy day can be too windy (or the tide can be too low) to allow for a sailing from Doolin's crude little port. If you're traveling by car and have time limits, don't risk sailing from Doolin. Without a car, you can travel on from the Aran Islands to  Galway by the bigger boats, so Doolin might work for you. But it's a longer trip to Inishmore, so consider an overnight stay on the islands. If you do have a car, note that parking is free beside the pier (even overnight).

There are three ferry companies in Doolin with similar schedules competing hard for your business. Although they all promise to get you to Inishmore in under an hour, every one of my crossings in the past five years has included a stop on Inisheer en route, making the actual crossing time about 1.5 hours. **Aran Doolin Ferries** has been at it longest (to Inishmore: €20 one-way, €38 same-day round-trip, 2/day, 1.5 hrs, leaving at 10:00 and 13:00, returning at 11:30 and 16:00; to Inisheer: €15 one-way, €25 same-day round-trip, 5/day, 30 min, leaving every 1.5 hrs, 10:00–17:30; tel. 065/707-4455, www.doolinferries.com). **Doolin Ferry** offers similar schedules and prices (tel. 065/707-5555, www.doolinferry.com). And the **Jack B** is your third option (tel. 065/707-5949, mobile 087-245-3239, www.mohercruises.com). No matter which company you choose, it's smart to phone a day or two ahead to confirm schedules and prices.

Lisdoonvarna

This town of 1,000 was known for centuries for its spa and its matchmakers. Today it's pretty sleepy, except for a couple of weeks in September during its Matchmaking Festival (www.matchmakerireland.com, which inspired the 1997 film *The Matchmaker*. The bank is only open one day a week. Still, it's more of a town than Doolin and, apart from festival time, less touristy. Lisdoonvarna has good traditional music in its pubs. I'd stay here, rather than in Doolin, and commute.

Sleeping in Lisdoonvarna (area code: 065): $$$ Ballinsheen House perches on a hill with five tastefully decorated rooms and a pleasant, glassed-in breakfast terrace (Sb-€40–48, Db-€60–74, Tb-€90–118, Qb-€120, parking, 5-min walk north of town on N-67 Galway Road, tel. 065/707-4806, mobile 087-992-0390, www.ballinsheenhouse.com, ballinsheenhouse@hotmail.com, Mary Gardiner).

$$ Marchmont B&B rents two large, twin/family rooms and two small doubles in a fine old house (Db-€60–65, on N-67 Galway Road near main square, just past post office, tel. 065/707-4050, Eileen Barrett).

$$ St. Enda's B&B is an old-fashioned whitewashed place, with four modest rooms, run for the last 56 years by proper proprietress Mary Finn (Sb-€47–51, Db-€64–70, non-smoking, parking, 2-min walk north of town on N-67 Galway Road, tel. 065/707-4066, stendasbb@eircom.net).

The Burren

Literally the "rocky place," the Burren is just that. This 10-square-mile limestone plateau, a ▲▲ sight, is so barren a disappointed

Cromwellian surveyor of the 1650s described it as "a savage land, yielding neither water enough to drown a man, nor a tree to hang him, nor soil enough to bury him." But he wasn't much of a botanist, because the Burren is a unique ecosystem, with flora that has managed to adapt since the last Ice Age 10,000 years ago. It's also rich in prehistoric and early Christian sites. This limestone land is littered with more than 2,000 historic locations, including about 500 Iron Age stone forts. The first human inhabitants of the Burren came about 6,000 years ago, began cutting down trees, and are partially responsible for the stark landscape we see today.

Sightseeing the Burren: The drive from Kilfenora to Ballyvaughan offers the best quick swing through the historic Burren.

Kilfenora (five miles southeast of Lisdoonvarna) is a good starting point. Its hardworking, community-run **Burren Centre** shows an intense 12-minute video explaining the geology and botany of the region, and then ushers you into its enlightening museum exhibits (€6, June–Aug daily 9:30–18:00, mid-March–May and Sept–Oct daily 10:00–17:00, closed Nov–mid-March, tel.

The Burren

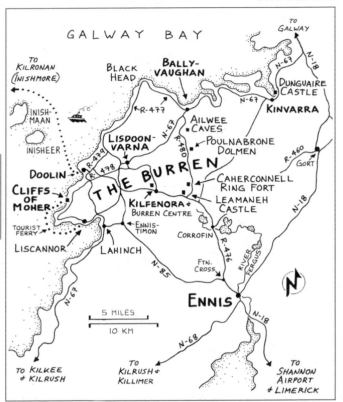

GALWAY BAY

TO GALWAY

TO KILRONAN (INISHMORE)

BLACK HEAD

BALLY-VAUGHAN

DUNGUAIRE CASTLE

KINVARRA

N-18

N-67

INISH-MAAN

R-477

AILWEE CAVES

N-67

INISHEER

LISDOON-VARNA

R-480

POULNABRONE DOLMEN

R-460

GORT

R-479

R-478

THE BURREN

CAHERCONNELL RING FORT

DOOLIN

CLIFFS OF MOHER

KILFENORA + Burren Centre

LEAMANEH CASTLE

N-18

TOURIST FERRY

ENNIS-TIMON

CORROFIN

R-476

LISCANNOR

LAHINCH

N-85

FTN. CROSS

RIVER FERGUS

N

ENNIS

N-18

5 MILES

10 KM

N-67

N-68

TO KILKEE & KILRUSH

TO KILRUSH & KILLIMER

TO SHANNON AIRPORT & LIMERICK

County Clare

065/708-8030, www.theburrencentre.ie). You'll see copies of a fine eighth-century golden collar and ninth-century silver brooch (now in Dublin's National Museum). The ruined church next door has a couple of 12th-century crosses, but isn't much to see. Mass is still held in the church, which claims the pope as its bishop. Kilfenora, as the smallest and poorest diocese in Ireland, was almost unable to function after the Great Potato Famine, so in 1866 Pope Pius IX supported the town as best he could—by personally declaring himself its bishop.

For lunch in Kilfenora, consider the cheap and cheery **Burren Centre Tea Room** (daily 9:30–17:30) or the more atmospheric **Vaughan's Pub.** If you're spending the night in County Clare, make an effort to join the locals at the fun set-dancing gettogethers run by the Vaughans in the Barn Pub adjacent to their regular pub (€4, Thu and Sun at 21:30, tel. 065/708-8004).

Leamaneh Castle, a ruined shell of a fortified house, is not open to anyone these days. From the outside, you can see how

Botany of the Burren in Brief

The Burren is a story of water, rock, geological force, and time. It supports the greatest diversity of plants in Ireland. Like nowhere else, Mediterranean and Arctic wildflowers bloom side by side in the Burren. It's an orgy of cross-pollination that attracts more insects than Doolin does music-lovers—even beetles help out. Limestone, created from layers of coral, seashells, and mud, is the bedrock of the Burren. (The same formation resurfaces 10 miles or so out to sea to form the Aran Islands.)

Geologic forces in the earth's crust heaved up the land, and the glaciers swept it bare—dropping boulders as they receded. Rain, reacting naturally with the limestone to create a mild but determined acid, slowly drilled potholes into the surface. Rainwater cut through weak zones in the limestone, leaving crevices on the surface and Europe's most extensive system of caves below. Algae grew in the puddles, dried into a powder, and combined with bug parts and rabbit turds (bunnies abound in the Burren) to create a very special soil. Plants and flowers fill the cracks in the limestone. Grasses and shrubs don't do well here, and wild goats eat any trees that try to grow, giving tender little flowers a chance to enjoy the sun. Different flowers appear in different months, sharing space rather than competing. The flowers are best in June and July.

the 15th-century fortified tower house (the right quarter of the remaining ruin) was expanded 150 years later (the left three-quarters of the ruin). The castle evolved from a refuge into a manor, and windows became wider to allow for better views as defense became less of a priority. From the castle, turn north on R-480 (direction: Ballyvaughan). After about five miles, you'll hit the start of the real barren Burren.

The **Caherconnell (Cahercommaun) ring fort**—one of 500 or so in the area—can be seen to the left on the crest of a hill just off the road. You can park in the gravel lot and walk up to the modest visitors center for a 15-minute film (a high-tech virtual tour) followed by a quick wander through the small fort (€5, July–Aug daily 9:30–18:00, Easter–June and Sept–Oct daily 10:00–17:00, closed Nov–Easter, tel. 065/708-9999, www.burrenforts.ie).

The stretch from the ring fort north to Ballyvaughan offers the starkest scenery. Soon you'll see a 10-foot-high stone structure a hundred yards off the road to the right (east, toward an ugly gray metal barn). This is the **Poulnabrone Dolmen,** a portal tomb that looks like a stone table. Two hundred years ago, locals called this a "druids' altar." Four thousand years ago, it was a grave chamber on a cairn of stacked stones.

Wander over for a look. (It's crowded with tour buses at midday, but it's all yours early or late.)

Think like a geologist. Wander for some quiet time with the wildflowers. You're walking across a former seabed, dating from 250 million years ago when Ireland was at the equator (before continental drift nudged it north). Look for fossils—the white smudges were coral. Stones embedded in the belly of an advancing glacier ground the scratches you see in the rocks. The rounded boulders came south from Connemara, carried on a giant conveyor belt of ice, then were left behind when the melting glaciers retreated north. As you drive away from the dolmen (continuing north), look for the 30-foot-deep sinkhole beside the road on the right (a collapsed cave).

The **Aillwee Caves** are touted as "Ireland's premier show caves." I couldn't resist a look. While fairly touristy and not worth the time or money if you've seen a lot of caves, they offer your easiest look at the massive system of caves that underlie the Burren. Your guide walks you 300 yards into the plain but impressive cave, giving a serious 40-minute geology lesson. During the Ice Age, underground rivers carved countless caves such as these. Brown bears, which became extinct in Ireland a thousand years ago, found this cave great for hibernating. But the caves are a constant 50°F, and I needed my sweater (€12, €29 family ticket, open daily at 10:00, last tour at 18:30 July–Aug, otherwise 17:30, Dec–Feb call ahead for limited tours, clearly signposted just south of Ballyvaughan, tel. 065/707-7036, www.aillweecave.ie).

County Clare

Ballyvaughan

Really just a crossroads, Ballyvaughan is the closest town to the Burren and an ideal rural oasis for those intending to really explore the region.

Shane Connolly leads in-depth, three-hour guided walks through the Burren, explaining the diverse flora, geology, history, and man's role in shaping this landscape. Wear comfortable shoes for the wet, rocky fields, and prepare to meet a proud farmer who really knows his stuff (€15, daily at 10:00, call

to book and find out meeting place in Ballyvaughan, tel. 065/707-7168, http://homepage.eircom.net/~burrenhillwalks).

Sleeping in Ballyvaughan (area code: 065): $$$ Rusheen Lodge feels like an oasis on the fringe of the Burren, offering six luxurious rooms and three spotless suites, as well as a great breakfast (Sb-€65–70, Db-€90–100, suites-€130–190, tel. 065/707-7092, fax 065/707-7152, www.rusheenlodge.com, rusheen@iol.ie, Karen McGann).

Kinvarra

This tiny town, between Ballyvaughan and Galway (30 min from each), is waiting for something to happen in its minuscule harbor. It faces Dunguaire Castle, a four-story tower house from 1520 that stands a few yards out in the bay.

The **Dunguaire Castle medieval banquet** is Kinvarra's most tourist-worthy attraction. The 500-year-old Dunguaire Castle hosts a touristy but fun medieval banquet (€51, April–Oct Fri–Tue at 17:30 and 20:45, closed Nov–March, reservations tel. 061/360-

788, castle tel. 091/637-108). Warning: This company also operates banquets at Bunratty Castle (30 miles south), so be sure that you've made your reservation for the correct castle.

The evening is as intimate as 55 tourists gathered under one time-stained, barrel-vaulted ceiling can be. You get a decent four-course meal with wine (or mead if you ask sweetly), served amid an entertaining evening of Irish tales and folk songs. Remember that in medieval times, it was considered polite to flirt with wenches. It's a small and multitalented cast: One harpist and three singer/actors who serve the "lords and ladies" between tunes. The highlight is the 40-minute stage show—featuring songs and poems by local writers—that comes with dessert.

Sleeping in Kinvarra (area code: 091): $$$ Cois Cuain B&B is a small but stately house with a garden, overlooking the square and harbor of the most charming village setting you'll find. Mary Walsh rents three super-homey rooms for non-smokers (Db-€72, cash only, The Quay, tel. 091/637-119).

Ennis

This bustling market town (pop. 20,000), the main town of County Clare, provides those relying on public transit with a handy transportation hub (good connections to Limerick, Dublin, and Galway; see "Transportation Connections," page 257). Ennis is less than 15 miles from Shannon Airport (www.shannonairport .ie) and makes a good first- or last-night base in Ireland for travelers not locked into Dublin flights. It also offers a chance to wander around a workaday Irish town that is not reliant upon the tourist dollar (though not shunning it either).

Tourist Information: The TI is just off O'Connell Street Square (July–Aug daily 9:30–17:30; March–June and Sept–Dec Mon–Sat 9:30–17:30, closed Sun; Jan–Feb Mon–Fri 9:30–17:30, closed Sat–Sun; tel. 065/682-8366). Walking tours, lasting 90 minutes, depart from the TI (€8, May–Oct Wed–Mon 11:00 and 19:00, no tours Tue, mobile 087-648-3714, www.enniswalkingtours .com).

Helpful Hints

Internet Access: Coffee n Bytes is upstairs on Lower Market Street (€1.50/30 min, Mon–Fri 9:00–20:00, Sat 10:00–18:00, closed Sun).

Post Office: It's on Market Place (Mon–Fri 9:00–13:00 & 14:00– 17:30, Sat 9:00–13:00, closed Sun).

Laundry: Fergus launderette is opposite the Parnell Street parking lot (Mon–Sat 8:30–18:00, closed Sun, tel. 065/682-3122).

Parking: If you're not spending the night (i.e., parking at your B&B), parking is best in the pay-and-display lots (€1/hr, Mon–Sat 9:30–17:30, pay at meter in lot and display on dashboard, 3-hour maximum, free Sun).

Ennis

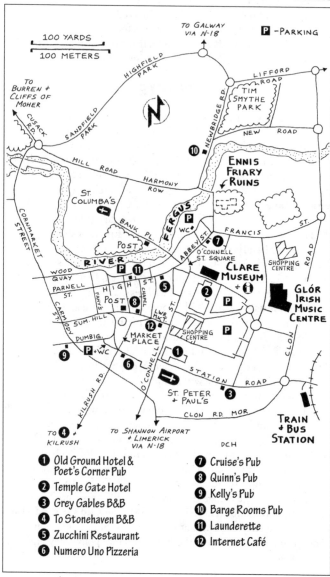

1 Old Ground Hotel & Poet's Corner Pub
2 Temple Gate Hotel
3 Grey Gables B&B
4 To Stonehaven B&B
5 Zucchini Restaurant
6 Numero Uno Pizzeria
7 Cruise's Pub
8 Quinn's Pub
9 Kelly's Pub
10 Barge Rooms Pub
11 Launderette
12 Internet Café

County Clare

Tours: Barratt Tours operate day tours by bus, departing the TI at 10:00 and returning by 17:00. On Wednesday they offer a €30 Lough Corrib cruise/Galway city tour. They also run a €27 Cliffs of Moher/Burren trip (call for schedule, tel. 061/384-700, mobile 087-237-5986, www.4tours.biz).

SIGHTS

Clare Museum—This worthwhile museum, housed in the large TI building, has eclectic displays about ancient ax heads, submarine development, and local boys who made good—from 10th-century High King Brian Boru to 20th-century statesman Eamon de Valera (free, June–Sept Mon–Fri 10:00–17:30, Sat–Sun 10:00–14:00, Oct–May closed Mon, tel. 065/682-3382, www.clarelibrary.ie).

Ennis Friary—The Franciscan monks arrived here in the 13th century, and the town grew up around their friary (like a monastery). Today, it's still worth a look, with some fine limestone carvings in its ruined walls (€1.60, sometimes includes tour, covered by Heritage Card, April–Oct daily 10:00–17:00, closed Nov–March, tel. 065/682-9100). Ask the guide to fully explain the crucifixion symbolism in the 15th-century *Ecce Homo* carving.

Glór Irish Music Centre—The town's modern theater center (*glór* is Irish for "sound") connects you with Irish culture. It's worth considering for traditional music, dance, or storytelling performances (€8–22, year-round usually at 20:00, 5-min walk behind TI, Friar's Walk, ticket office open Mon–Sat 10:00–17:00, closed Sun, tel. 065/684-3103, www.glor.ie).

Traditional Music—Live music begins in the pubs around 21:30. The best is **Cruise's** on Abbey Street, with music nightly year-round and good food (bar is cheaper than restaurant, tel. 065/682-8963). Other pubs offering traditional music are **Quinn's** on Lower Market Street (Sat year-round, tel. 065/682-8148); the rough-and-tumble **Kelly's** on Carmody Street at the intersection with Dumbiggle Road (Sat, tel. 065/682-8155); and the **Barge Rooms,** across the bridge from the friary, 100 yards up Newbridge Road (Sun at 18:00, tel. 065/682-4888). The **Old Ground Hotel** hosts live music year-round at its pub (Thu–Sun, open to anyone); though tour groups stay at the hotel, the pub is low-key and feels real, not staged.

SLEEPING

The first two listings are fancy hotels that you'll share with tour groups.

The stately, ivy-covered, 18th-century **$$$ Old Ground Hotel** has 114 rooms with a family feel (Sb-€85–115, Db-€110–150, suite-€160–200, rates vary with season, 2-night weekend stays include a dinner, at intersection of Station Road and O'Connell Street, a few blocks from station, tel. 065/682-8127, fax 065/682-8112, www.oldgroundhotel.ie, sales@oldgroundhotel.ie).

$$$ **Temple Gate Hotel** is more modern and less personal (Db from €150–180, suites-€250, rates lower off-season, 3 non-smoking floors, O'Connell Street Square, in courtyard with TI, tel. 065/682-3300, fax 065/682-3322, www.templegatehotel.com, info@templegatehotel.com).

B&Bs: $$$ **Grey Gables B&B** has 10 tastefully decorated rooms (Sb-€45, Db-€75, Tb-€100, cash only, wheelchair access, parking, on Station Road a block toward town center from station, tel. 065/682-4487, www.bed-n-breakfast-ireland.com, marykeane.ennis@eircom.net, Mary Keane).

$$$ **Stonehaven B&B** is a kid-friendly place with three comfortable rooms (Sb-€55, Db-€70, Tb-€90–95, cash only, 10-min walk from town on N-68 Kilrush Road, tel. 065/684-1775, www.stonehavenclare.com, keatinge.ennis@eircom.net, Mary Keatinge).

EATING

Zucchini is my pick for a splurge dinner, cheerful atmosphere, and central location (€17–30 meals, daily 17:00–21:30, €25 two-course and €29 three-course early-bird specials before 18:30, 7 High Street, tel. 065/686-6566). The **Old Ground Hotel** serves up hearty meals in its Poet's Corner pub (€9–11 lunches, €14–22 dinners, daily 12:00–21:00). Find basic **pub grub** at one of the places mentioned under "Traditional Music," above. Or, for an easy pub-free place for dinner, try the simple **Numero Uno Pizzeria** (Sun–Mon 17:00–23:30, Tue–Fri 12:00–23:30, closed Sat, on Old Barrack Street off Market Place, tel. 065/684-1740).

TRANSPORTATION CONNECTIONS

From Ennis by Train to: Limerick (8/day, 40 min), **Dublin** (2/day, 4 hrs). Train info: tel. 065/684-0444.

By Bus to: Galway (14/day, 1.25 hrs), **Dublin** (12/day, 4.75 hrs), **Rosslare** (4/day, 5 hrs), **Limerick** (12/day, 1 hr), **Doolin/ Lisdoonvarna** (2/day, 1–1.5 hrs), **Tralee** (9/day, 3 hrs). Bus info: tel. 065/682-4177, www.buseireann.ie.

Shannon Airport: This is the major airport in western Ireland and comes with far less stress than Dublin's overcrowded counterpart. It has direct flights to **Dublin** (2–3/day, 30 min) and **London** (6/day, 1 hr) on Ryanair (www.ryanair.com) and Aer Lingus (www.aerlingus.ie). The airport has a **TI** (daily June–Sept 6:30–19:30,

Oct–May 6:30–17:30, tel. 061/471-664, airport tel. 061/471-444, www.shannonairport.ie).

If you want to stay at the airport, consider **$$$ Park Inn Shannon Airport** (Db-€120–160, less off-season, best prices when booked online, tel. 061/471-122, www.parkinn.com).

Shannon Airport has easy bus connections to **Ennis** (nearly hourly, 45 min), **Galway** (every 2 hrs, 2 hrs), and **Limerick** (nearly hourly, 1 hr, can continue to Tralee—2 hrs, and Dingle—1.25 hrs more). Bus info: tel. 061/313-333, www.buseireann.ie.

County Clare

ARAN ISLANDS

The Aran Islands consist of three limestone islands: Inishmore, Inishmaan, and Inisheer. The largest, Inishmore (9 miles by 2 miles), is by far the most populated, interesting, and visited. The landscape of all three islands is harsh: steep, rugged cliffs and windswept rocky fields divided by stone walls. During the winter, severe gales sweep the islands; because of this, most of the settlements on Inishmore are found on its more peaceful eastern side.

There's a stark beauty about these islands and the simple lives their inhabitants eke out of six inches of topsoil and a mean sea. Precious little of the land is productive. In the past, people made a precarious living here from fishing and farming. The scoured bedrock offered little in the way of soil for farming, so it was created by the islanders—the result of centuries of layering seaweed with limestone sand. The fields are small, divided by several thousand

miles of "drystone" wall (made without mortar). Most of these are built in the Aran "gap" style, in which spaces between angled upright stones are filled with smaller stones. This allows a farmer who wants to move stock to dismantle and rebuild the walls. Nowadays, tourism boosts the local economy.

The islands are a Gaeltacht area. While the islanders speak Irish among themselves, they happily speak English for their visitors.

Many of them have direct, personal connections with close relatives in America.

Today, the 800 people of Inishmore (literally "the big island") greet as many as 2,000 visitors a day. The vast majority of these are day-trippers. They'll hop on a minibus at the dock for a 2.5-hour tour to Dún Aenghus (the must-see Iron Age fort), then spend an hour or two browsing through the few shops or sitting at a picnic table outside a pub with a pint of Guinness.

The other islands, Inishmaan and Inisheer, are smaller, much less populated, and less touristy. While extremely quiet, they do have B&Bs, daily flights, and ferry service. For most, the big island is quiet enough.

Planning Your Time

Most travelers visit Inishmore as a day trip by boat from Galway (boats from Doolin are too slow to allow time for a same-day round-trip day trip). Here's a good framework for a day trip: Leave Galway at 9:00 on the shuttle bus to Rossaveel, where you'll catch the 10:30 boat. You'll step off the boat in Kilronan around 11:15. Arrange minibus transport or rent a bike, visit Dún Aenghus, and grab a bite at a café near the base of the Dún Aenghus fort trail. Explore the island during low tide, and depart on the boat when high tides return between 16:00 and 18:00. You can squeeze an extra hour or two out of your day trip by booking an early flight over and a late flight back from Connemara Regional Airport near Rossaveel.

Staying Overnight: Travelers spending the night can savor the quiet time before and after the day-trip crowds. Here's how I'd suggest you spend the day you arrive on the island. Since most day-trippers make a beeline straight off the boat to Dún Aenghus, head the opposite direction to check out the subtle charms of the less-visited eastern end of the island. Grab a quick bite en route at the Ostan Arann hotel or the Tigh Fitz pub. Then walk to either the ruins of tiny St. Benen's Church (easy 20-minute hike one way from Tigh Fitz) or the rugged Black Fort ruins (rocky 45-minute scramble one-way from Ostan Arann). Save Dún Aenghus for later in the afternoon after the midday crowds have subsided (allow an hour at Dún Aenghus, closes at 18:00 March–Oct, off-season at 16:00, last entry 1 hour before closing). Enjoy an evening in the pubs and take a no-rush midmorning boat trip back to the mainland the next day.

On Inishmore Island: Kilronan

By far the Aran Islands' largest town, Kilronan is still just a village. Groups of backpackers wash ashore with the docking of each ferry. Minibuses, bike shops, and a few men in pony carts sop up the tourists.

Most of Kilronan huddles around the pier. There are around a dozen shops and B&Bs, about half as many restaurants, and a couple of bike-rental huts (€10/day plus €10 deposit).

A few blocks inland up the high road, you'll find the Heritage Centre (primitive Internet access upstairs, €4/30 min, daily 10:00–17:00), the best folk-music pub, a post office (Mon–Fri 9:00–13:00 & 14:00–17:30, Sat 9:00–13:00, closed Sun), and a tiny bank across from the roofless Anglican church ruins (open only on Wed 10:00–12:30 & 13:30–15:00, and same hours Thu June–Aug).

The huge SPAR supermarket, two blocks inland from the harbor, seems too big for the tiny community and has the island's only ATM. Bring cash: Some B&Bs and other businesses don't accept credit cards.

Tourist Information

Kilronan's TI is helpful, but don't rely on it for accommodations; the B&B owners who work with the TI are out of town and desperate (daily 10:00–18:00, July–Aug until 18:45, shorter winter hours, faces the harbor, tel. 099/61263). The TI will store bags for day-trippers for €1 per bag, and offers free maps of the island (though your ferry operator may have already given you one). This map is all the average day-tripper or leisure biker will need to navigate. But serious hikers who plan on scampering out to the island's craggy fringes will want to invest in the detailed black-and-white *Oileain Aran* map by Tim Robinson (€8, sold in Kilronan TI and many mainland bookstores). Public WCs are 100 yards beyond the TI on the harbor road.

Getting Around Inishmore

Just about anything on wheels functions as a taxi. A trip from Kilronan to Dún Aenghus to the Seven Churches and back to Kilronan costs €10 per person in a shared minibus. Pony carts cost about €40 for two people (€70 for 4)

Inishmore Island

for a trip to the west end of the island. Biking is great, although the terrain is hilly and there are occasional headwinds (30 min to start of trailhead up to Dún Aenghus). Cyclists should take the high road over and the low road back—fewer hills, scenic shoreline, and, at low tide, 50 seals basking in the sun. Keep a sharp lookout along the roads for handy, modern stone signposts (with distances in kilometers) that point the way to important sites. They're in Irish, but you'll be clued in by the small metal depictions of the site embedded within them.

TOURS

▲Island Minibus Tours—There can't be more than 100 vehicles on the island, and most of them seem to be minibuses. A line of buses awaits the arrival of each ferry, offering €10, 2.5-hour island tours. Chat with a few drivers to find one who likes to talk. On my

tour, I learned that 800 islanders live in 14 villages, with three elementary schools and three churches. Most islanders own a small detached field where they keep a couple of cows (sheep are too much trouble). When pressed for more information, my guide explained that

there are 400 different flowers and 19 different types of bees on the island. The tour, a convenient time-saver, zips you to the end of the island for a quick stroll in the desolate fields, gives you 10 minutes to wander through the historic but visually unimpressive Seven Churches, and then drops you off for two hours at Dún Aenghus (30 min to hike up, 30 min at the fort, 20-min hike back down, 40 min in café for lunch or shopping at drop-off point) before running you back to Kilronan. Ask your driver to take you back along the smaller coastal road (scenic beaches and sunbathing seals at low tide).

SIGHTS

▲**Aran's Heritage Centre**—This little museum, which has been closed for renovation, is scheduled to reopen in the spring of 2008. It offers a worthwhile introduction to the island's traditional lifestyle, geology, and archaeological wonders (€3.50 for museum only, €5.50 combo-ticket includes *Man of Aran* movie, April–Oct daily 10:00–17:00, July–Aug until 19:00, closed Nov–March, tel. 099/61355).

Man of Aran: This 1934 silent movie, giving a good look at traditional island life with an all-local cast, is shown at the Heritage Centre (included in €5.50 ticket to Heritage Centre, 1 hr, 4 shows/day in summer, 3 shows/day off-season). The movie features *currach*s (canoe-like boats) in a storm, shark fishing with hand-held harpoons, cultivating the fields from bare rock, and life in the early 1900s, when you couldn't rent bikes.

▲▲▲**Dún Aenghus (Dun Aonghasa)**—This is the island's block-buster sight. The stone fortress hangs spectacularly and precariously

on the edge of a cliff 300 feet above the Atlantic. The crashing waves seem to say, "You've come to the end of the world." Little is known about this 2,000-year-old Celtic fort. Its concentric walls are 13 feet thick and 10 feet high. As an added defense, the fort is ringed with a commotion of spiky stones, sticking up like lances, called a *chevaux-de-frise* (literally, "Frisian horses," named for the Frisian soldiers who used pikes like these to stop charging cavalry). Slowly, as the cliff erodes, hunks of the fort fall into the sea. Dún Aenghus doesn't get crowded until after 11:00. I enjoyed a half-hour completely alone at 10:00 in the tourist season; if you can, get there early or late (€2.10, covered by Heritage Card, daily March–Oct 10:00–18:00, Nov–Feb 10:00–16:00, guides at fort June–Aug answer questions and can sometimes give free tours if you call ahead, 5.5 miles from

Kilronan, tel. 099/61008). A small museum displays findings from recent digs and tells the story of the fort. Advice from rangers: Wear walking shoes and watch your kids closely; there's no fence between you and a 300-foot cliff overlooking the sea.

Seven Churches (Na Seacht Teampaill)—Close to the western tip of the island, this gathering of ruined chapels, monastic houses, and fragments of a high cross dates from the 8th to 11th centuries. The island is dotted with reminders that Christianity was brought to the islands in the fifth century by St. Enda, who established a monastery here. Many great monks studied under Enda. Among these "Irish apostles," who started Ireland's "Age of Saints and Scholars" (A.D. 500–900), was Columba (Colmcille in Irish), the founder of a monastery on the island of Iona in Scotland.

Kilmurvey—The island's second village sits below Dún Aenghus. With a gaggle of homes, a B&B, a great sheltered beach, and a pub, this is the place for peaceful solitude (except for the folk music in the pub).

Ancient Sites near Killeany—The quiet eastern end of Inishmore offers ancient sites in evocative settings for overnight visitors with more time, or for those seeking rocky hikes devoid of crowds. First, get a good hiking map from the Kilronan TI. Then consider a soup-and-sandwich lunch at the **Tigh Fitz** pub to fuel up either before or after a half-day spent exploring these sights on foot. Ask the folks at the pub for directions (almost always a memorable experience in Ireland).

Closest to the road, amid the dunes one mile past the Tigh Fitz pub and just south of the airport, is the eighth-century **St. Enda's Church** (Teaghlach Einne). Protected from wave erosion by a stubborn breakwater, it sits half-submerged in a sandy grave-yard, surrounded by a sea of sawgrass and peppered with tombstones. St. Enda is said to be buried here, along with 125 other saints who flocked to Inishmore in the fifth century to learn from him.

St. Benen's Church (Teampall Bheanáin) perches high on a desolate ridge opposite the Tigh Fitz pub. Walk up the stone-walled lane, passing a holy well and the stubby remains of a round tower. Then take another visual fix on the church's silhouette on the horizon, and zigzag up the stone terraces to the top. The 20-minute hike from the pub pays off with a great view. Dedicated to St. Benen, a young disciple of St. Patrick himself, this tiny 10th-century oratory is aligned north–south (instead of the usual east–west) to protect the doorway from prevailing winds.

About a five-minute walk past the

Tigh Fitz pub (heading toward the airport) you'll notice an abandoned stone pier and an adjacent, modest medieval ruin. This was **Arkin Fort,** built by Cromwell's soldiers in 1652 using cut stones taken from the round tower and the monastic ruins that once stood on the hill below St. Benen's Church. The fort was used as a prison camp for outlawed priests before they were sent by English authorities to the West Indies to be sold into slavery.

Hidden on a remote, ragged headland an hour's walk from Kilronan to the south side of the island, you'll find the **Black Fort** (Dún Duchathair). Next to Dún Aenghus, this is Inishmore's most dramatic fortification. Built on a promontory with cliffs on three sides, its defenders would have held out behind drystone ramparts, facing the island's interior attackers. Watch your step on the uneven ground, be ready to course-correct as you go, and chances are you'll have this windswept ruin all to yourself.

Pub Music—Kilronan's four pubs sporadically offer music on summer nights. Nothing is regularly scheduled, so ask at your B&B or look for posted notices on the front of the SPAR supermarket or post office. **Joe Watty's Pub,** on the high road 100 yards past the post office, sometimes has good Irish folk music. **Tigh Fitz,** one mile down the airport road, often has folk music and dancing on Fridays, Saturdays, and Sundays. The more central **Joe Mac's Pub** (next to the hostel) and the **American Bar** (next to the high cross at the base of the high road) are also possibilities.

The **Halla Ronain community center** becomes a dance hall on some Saturday nights, when from midnight to 2:00 in the morning, locals have a *ceilidh* (KAY-lee), the Irish equivalent of a hoedown. Ask at the TI to see if one is scheduled during your stay.

SLEEPING

Remember, this is a poor island. Most rooms are plain, with sparse plumbing. Only The Pier House takes credit cards.

$$$ Ostan Arann is Inishmore's first modern hotel, with a great restaurant and 22 large, well-furnished rooms, five with grand patio views of the harbor (Sb-€50–90, Db-€100–150, Db with patio €170, Tb-€190, Qb-€230, two- to three-night midweek deals, 10-min walk from pier, about 100 yards past Halla Ronain community center, tel. 099/61104, fax 099/61225, www.aranislandshotel.com, info@aranislandshotel.com).

$$$ The Pier House stands solidly a hundred yards beyond the pier, offering 12 decent rooms, a good restaurant downstairs, a dramatic setting, and sea views from most of its rooms (Db-€90–120, tel. 099/61417, fax 099/61122, www.pierhousearan.com, pierh@iol.ie).

Kilronan

1. Ostan Arann Hotel & Restaurant
2. The Pier House
3. To Man of Aran B&B
4. Clai Ban
5. Seacrest B&B
6. Kilronan Hostel & Joe Mac's Pub
7. Sean Cheibh Café
8. American Bar
9. Joe Watty's Pub
10. SPAR Supermarket & Lios Aengus Café

$$$ **Man of Aran B&B,** as classy as a thatched cottage can be, is in the peaceful countryside four miles outside of touristy Kilronan toward the western end of the island. Rooms are quiet and rustic, with fireplaces. The restaurant serves €35 meals (all-organic, with homegrown vegetables and herbs) only to overnight guests. The setting is pristine—this is where the movie was filmed over 70 years ago (S-€52, D-€74, Db-€80, cash only, reserve well in advance, 4 miles from Kilronan, bear right 100 yards after passing Kilmurvey Beach before Dún Aenghus turnoff, tel. 099/61301, fax 099/61324, www.manofarancottage.com, manofaran@eircom.net, Maura Wolf).

$$ **Clai Ban,** about the only really cheery place in town, is worth the 10-minute walk from the pier. You might be lucky enough to hear the sounds of the Hernon youngsters practicing traditional music (Sb-€50-70, Db-€60-70, Tb-€80-100, cash only,

---

Sleep Code

(€1 = about $1.30, country code: 353, area code: 099)
S = Single, **D** = Double/Twin, **T** = Triple, **Q** = Quad, **b** = bathroom,
s = shower only. Breakfast is included and credit cards are
accepted unless otherwise noted.

To help you easily sort through these listings, I've divided
the rooms into categories, based on the price for a standard
double room with bath:

$$$ **Higher Priced**—Most rooms €80 or more.
 $$ **Moderately Priced**—Most rooms between €50–80.
  $ **Lower Priced**—Most rooms €50 or less.

---

walk past bank out of town and down lane on left, tel. 099/61111,
fax 099/61423, Marion Hernon).

$$ Seacrest B&B offers six uncluttered rooms in a central
location next to the Aran Fisherman restaurant. Geraldine Faherty
manages the rooms while Tom Faherty keeps the ferries afloat
(Sb-€45, Db-€70, Tb-€80, non-smoking, tel. 099/61292, mobile
085-736-9915).

Hostel: **$ Kilronan Hostel,** overlooking the harbor near the
TI, is cheap but noisy above Joe Mac's Pub (€22–25 beds in 4- to
6-bed rooms, cash only, includes breakfast, self-service kitchen,
tel. 099/61255, www.kilronanhostel.com, kilronanhostel@ireland
.com).

EATING

There are two restaurants in Kilronan. The best is the classy **Ostan
Arann** hotel on the south fringe of town (lunch 12:30–18:00 in the
Patin Jack Bar, dinner 18:00–21:30, tel. 099/61104).

The **Pier House** operates a dependable restaurant below its
guest house (€10–20 lunches, €18–26 dinners, daily 11:00–22:00,
tel. 099/61811).

Otherwise, Kilronan's modest cafés dish up hearty soup, soda
bread, sandwiches, and tea.

Sean Cheibh ("Old Pier"), which seems to slam out more
meals than the rest of the town combined, is popular for its fish-
and-chips and great clam chowder (eat in or take out, April–mid-
Oct daily 11:00–19:00, closed mid-Oct–March, tel. 099/61228).

Lios Aengus, next door to the SPAR supermarket, does
simple lunches away from the crowds (daily 9:30–17:00, July–Aug
until 18:00, tel. 099/61030).

The **SPAR supermarket** has all the groceries you'll need

(June–Aug Mon–Sat 9:00–20:00, Sun 10:00–17:00; Sept–May Mon–Sat 9:00–18:00, closed Sun).

TRANSPORTATION CONNECTIONS

For an overview map of the region, see page 243.

By Ferry from Rossaveel: Island Ferries sail to Inishmore from Rossaveel, a port 20 miles west of Galway. The company sells tickets at the Galway TI and runs a 45-minute shuttle bus from Galway to the Rossaveel dock (3/day April–Oct, 2/day Nov–March, 40-min crossing; coming from Galway, allow 2 hrs one-way including 45-min bus ride; €25 round-trip boat crossing plus €6 round-trip for Galway–Rossaveel shuttle bus, WCs on board). Shuttle buses depart Galway (from Merchants Road in front of Kinlay House) 60 minutes before the sailing and return to Galway immediately after each boat arrives. Ferry schedule for April–Oct: from Rossaveel at 10:30, 13:00, and 18:30; from Inishmore at 8:30, 12:00, and 17:00 (plus 19:30 June–Aug). Island Ferries has three offices in Galway and one in Salthill: one at the Galway TI, another across from Kinlay House on Merchants Road, the third on Forster Street, and the fourth inside the Salthill TI (tel. 091/568-903, www.aranislandferries.com).

Aran Islands Direct, owned by the islanders, has three boats that sail to all three Aran Islands from Rossaveel. Their modern fleet is the only one with electrical stabilizers to smooth the ride on rough seas, and their schedule to Inishmore is similar to Island Ferries' (above). It's €25 from Rossaveel, plus a €6 shuttle ride that picks up at their two Galway offices: Merchants Road (near Kinlay House) and Forester Street opposite the TI (tel. 091/566-535, fax 091/534-315, www.aranislandsdirect.com, info@aranislandsdirect.com).

Drivers should go straight to the ferry landing in Rossaveel, passing several ticket agencies and pay parking lots. At the boat dock, you'll find a convenient €5-per-day lot and a small office selling tickets for Island Ferries. Check to see what's going when and for how much.

By Ferry from Doolin: This ferry is handy if you're in Doolin, but it's notorious for being canceled because of wind or tides (for specifics, see page 248).

By Plane: Aer Arann Islands, a friendly and flexible little airline, flies daily, stopping at all three islands (3/day, up to 15/day in peak season, €45 round-trip, groups of 4 or more pay €40 each, 10-min flight). These flights get booked up—reserve a day or two in advance with a credit card. Their nine-seat planes take off from the Connemara Regional Airport (not the Galway airport). It's 20 slow miles west of Galway, so allow 45 minutes for the drive,

plus 30 minutes to check in before the scheduled departure. A minibus shuttle—€6 round-trip—runs from Kinlay House on Merchants Road in Galway an hour before each flight. The Kilronan airport on Inishmore is small (baggage is transported from the plane to the "gate" in a shopping cart). A minibus shuttle travels the two miles between the airport and Kilronan, and costs €5 one-way. For reservations and seat availability, contact the airline (tel. 091/593-034, www.aerarannislands.ie).

Aran Islands

CONNEMARA AND COUNTY MAYO

If you have a car, consider spending a day exploring the wild western Irish fringe known as Connemara and straying into historic County Mayo. Gaze up at the peak of Croagh Patrick, the mountain from which St. Patrick supposedly banished the snakes from Ireland. Pass through the desolate Doo Lough valley on a road stained with tragic famine history. Bounce on a springy peat bog, and drop in at a Westport pub owned by a member of the Chieftains (a well-known traditional Irish music group). This beautiful area also claims a couple of towns—Cong and Leenane—where classic Irish movies were filmed, as well as the photogenic Kylemore Abbey.

Connemara makes an easy day trip by car from Galway. Without a car, you can take a tour from Galway or at least get to Westport by bus (see "Westport," below). Public transportation in this region is patchy, and some areas are not served at all. Trains connect Galway and Westport to Dublin, but not to each other.

Bus Tours of Connemara

Two Galway-based companies—Lally and O'Neachtain—run all-day tours of nearby regions (€23–31). Tours of Connemara include the *Quiet Man* Cottage, Kylemore Abbey, Clifden, and the "Famine Village." Tours go most days from about 10:00 to 17:30 (departing from in front of Kinlay House on Merchant's Road in Galway, call to confirm exact itinerary: Lally tel. 091/562-905, www.lallytours.com; O'Neachtain tel. 091/553-188, www.oneachtaintours.com). Drivers take cash only; to pay with a credit card, book at Galway's TI.

SIGHTS

Connemara and Mayo Loop Trip

This is a full day of driving (about 150 miles using Galway as your base). With an early start, your day will be less rushed. Those wanting to slow down and linger can sleep in Westport. These country roads, punctuated by blind curves and surprise bumps, are shared by trucks, tractors, cyclists, and sheep. Drive sanely, and bring rain gear and your sense of humor. This is rural Ireland with all the trimmings.

Take along a good map (Michelin's maps are widely sold in Ireland) and study the loop connecting these points before you start: Galway, Cong, Westport, Louisburgh, Leenane, Kylemore Abbey, and back to Galway.

Route Summary: Take N-84 north out of Galway. At Cross, take R-346 into Cong and R-345 back out again. At Neale, go north on R-334 and pick up N-84 again from Ballinrobe to Partry. Take R-330 from Partry to Westport. After lunch in Westport, go west on R-335 through Louisburgh and south through Doo Lough Valley all the way to Leenane. Pick up N-59 in Leenane and take it to Kylemore Abbey, continuing to Letterfrack and Connemara National Park. Double back from Letterfrack and take R-344 south to the junction with N-59; N-59 will take you back to Galway via Maam Cross and Oughterard.

The Tour Begins: From Galway's Eyre Square, drive north out of town on Prospect Hill Road. Follow the signs at each roundabout in the direction of Castlebar onto N-84. You'll soon be out of Galway's suburbs and crossing miles of flat bogland laced with simple rock walls. You may notice the flags on the phone poles changing colors: from burgundy and white to green and red. These are the colors of the local hurling and football teams. You've crossed the border from County Galway into County Mayo. At Cross, take R-346 into Cong. You'll pass the grand, gray gateway of Ashford Castle (on the left) as you approach the town.

Cong

Plan to spend an hour in Cong (90 min if you include the Ashford Castle grounds). Cross the small bridge and park in front of the abbey. Drop into the **TI** across from the abbey entrance for a map (March–Nov daily 10:00–18:00, July–Aug until 19:00, closed Dec–Feb, tel. 094/954-6542). There are no banks or ATMs in Cong. Public WCs are 50 yards down the street across from the *Quiet Man* cottage. That's right, pilgrim, this town is where John Wayne and Maureen O'Hara made the famous John Ford film *The Quiet Man* in 1951. The cottage's modest historical exhibits (upstairs) and film props (downstairs) are really only worth it for diehard

Connemara and County Mayo

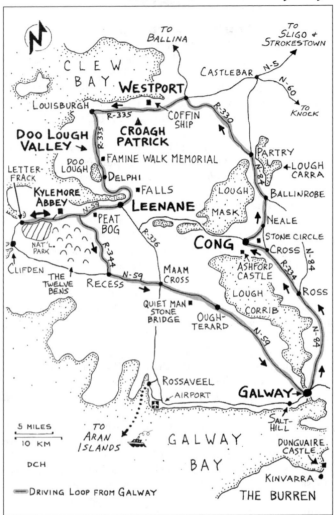

fans of the Duke (€4, mid-March–Oct daily 10:00–17:00, closed Nov–mid-March, tel. 094/954-6089). Fuel up on a cup of coffee and homemade dessert at the **Hungry Monk Café** (July–Aug daily 10:00–18:00; mid-March–June and Sept–Oct Wed–Mon 10:00–18:00, closed Tue; closed Nov–mid-March; Internet access, on Abbey Street between public WCs and TI, tel. 094/954-6866).

We're here for the ruins of **Cong Abbey** (free and always open). The abbey was built in the early 1100s, when Romanesque was going out of style and Gothic was coming in; you'll see the mixture of rounded Romanesque and pointy Gothic arch styles in the doorway. The famous Cross of Cong, which held a holy relic of what was supposedly a splinter of the True Cross, was held aloft at the front of processions of Augustinian monks during High Masses in this church. This Irish art treasure is now on display in Dublin's National Museum. Rory O'Connor, the last Irish high king, died in this abbey in 1198. After O'Connor realized he could never outfight the superior Norman armies, he retreated to Cong and spent his last years here in monastic isolation.

Take a walk through the cloister and down the gravel path behind the abbey. The forested grounds are lush, and the stream

water is incredibly clear. Cong's salmon hatchery contributes to western Ireland's reputation for great fishing. The monks fished for more than sinners. They built the modest **Monks' Fishing Hut,** just over the footbridge, right on the bank so that the river flowed underneath. They lowered a net though the floor and attached a bell to the rope; whenever a fish was netted, the bell would ring.

The next stop is...

Ashford Castle

To reach the castle from the abbey, face the Romanesque/Gothic main entrance and go left around the corner of the abbey, walk-

ing 15 minutes down the pleasant forested lane onto the grounds of the castle, which is hidden behind the trees. Garden-lovers happily pay the stiff €5 entry fee (in effect June–Aug during peak bloom, usually free rest of year) to a kid hired by the castle to patrol the bridge, so they can stroll the lakeside paradise once owned by the Guinness beer family. The renovated Victorian castle rents some of the finest rooms in all of Ireland. President Reagan stayed here in

1984, and actor Pierce Brosnan chose these grounds for his wedding reception in 2001. Many scenes from *The Quiet Man* were filmed here.

From Cong to Neale: Cong (from *conga*, Irish for "isthmus") lies between two large lakes. Departing Cong over the same bridge by which you entered, look down through the thick vegetation to see a dry canal. Built between 1848 and 1854, this canal was a famine work project that stoked only appetites. The canal, complete with locks, would have linked Lough Mask to the north with Lough Corrib to the south. But the limestone bedrock was too porous, and the canal wouldn't hold water.

Take R-345 out of Cong (left turn opposite the main stone gateway to the grounds of Ashford Castle). Heading north, you'll pass through the tiny hamlet of...

Neale

About 120 years ago, a retired army captain named Boycott was hired to manage the nearby estate of Lord Erne. But the strict captain harshly treated the tenants who worked his lands, so they united to ostracize him by deserting their jobs and isolating his estate. Over time, the agitation worked, and eventually "boycotting" became a popular tactic in labor conflicts.

From Neale to Westport: At Neale, go north on R-334, then take N-84 from Ballinrobe to Partry. At Partry, turn left off N-84 onto R-330 in the direction of Westport (the easy-to-miss turnoff is just after you pass the thatch-roofed Village Inn). Just over 200 years ago, in the countryside a few miles to your right, a French invasion force supported by locals dealt the British an embarrassing loss in the **Battle of Castlebar.** The surprised British forces were routed, and their rapid retreat is slyly remembered in Irish rebel lore as the "Castlebar races." Unfortunately for the rebels, this proved to be the last glimmer of hope for Irish victory in the uprising of 1798. The British reorganized and within weeks defeated the small force of 1,300 Frenchmen and the ill-equipped Irish rebels. The captured French soldiers were treated as prisoners of war, while the Irish rebels were executed.

Westport

On arrival in Westport, park along the Mall under the trees that line the canal-like river. This is a planned town, built in Georgian style in the late 1700s to support  the adjacent estate of Westport House (skip it for better manors at Powerscourt and Muckross). The town once thrived on the linen industry created by local Irish handlooms. But after the Act of Union with Britain in 1801, the town was unable to compete with the industrialized British linen-makers and fell into decline. The town is still pretty and a good place for a relaxed lunch and some exploration on foot.

Connemara

The **TI** is on James Street (July–Aug daily 9:00–18:00; Sept–June Mon–Fri 9:00–18:00, Sat 10:00–18:00, closed Sun; tel. 098/25711).

The **Westport Heritage Centre** gives a good overview of town history and the nearby Croagh Patrick pilgrimage tradition (€3, downstairs beneath the TI). On Tuesday and Thursday nights in July and August, 90-minute **town walks** depart at 20:00 from the clock tower at the top of Bridge Street (€6, tel. 098/26852). If you're not sleeping in Westport (i.e., parking at your B&B), free **parking** is allowed on the street for two hours; otherwise, use the pay-and-display lots for longer stays (€0.60/hr, pay at meter and display on dashboard). **Laundry** can be dropped off early at Gills and picked up late the same day (€7–9, Mon–Sat 9:00–18:30, closed Sun, James Street, tel. 098/25819).

Eating in Westport: Most of your best bets are clustered on Bridge Street. A good choice is **J. J. O'Malleys'** pub for lunch and its upstairs restaurant for dinner (€16–24 meals, daily 17:00–22:00, Bridge Street, tel. 098/27307). For a quick and easy lunch, try **O'Cee's Coffeeshop** (€9 cafeteria-style lunches, Mon–Sat 8:30–18:30, Sun 10:00–16:00, Shop Street, tel. 098/27000) or the **Stuffed Sandwich Company** (Mon–Sat 8:00–18:30, Sun 11:00–18:00, Oct–March closed Sun, Bridge Street, tel. 098/27611). Irish music fans seek out **Matt Molloy's** pub (Bridge Street, tel. 098/26655). Matt Molloy isn't just the owner of the pub—he's also a flutist for the Chieftains, the group credited with much of the resurgence of interest in Irish music worldwide over the past 30 years. The **Super Valu** market has picnic fare (Mon–Sat 8:30–19:30, Sun 10:00–18:00, Shop Street).

Sleeping in Westport (area code: 098): For those wanting extra time to explore, Westport is the best place along this route to spend a night. All of the following listings are centrally located.

Sleep Code

(€1 = about $1.30, country code: 353, area code: 098)
S = Single, **D** = Double/Twin, **T** = Triple, **Q** = Quad, **b** = bathroom, **s** = shower only. Breakfast is included and credit cards are accepted unless otherwise noted.

To help you easily sort through these listings, I've divided the rooms into categories, based on the price for a standard double room with bath:

$$$ **Higher Priced**—Most rooms €80 or more.
$$ **Moderately Priced**—Most rooms between €50–80.
$ **Lower Priced**—Most rooms €50 or less.

Westport

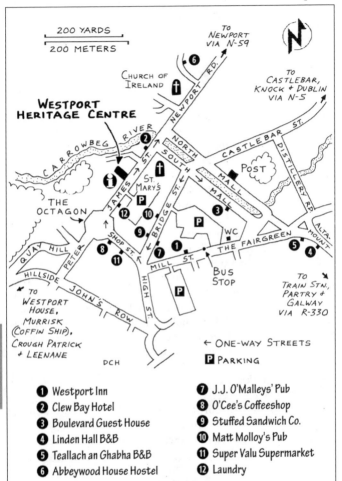

Connemara

1 Westport Inn
2 Clew Bay Hotel
3 Boulevard Guest House
4 Linden Hall B&B
5 Teallach an Ghabha B&B
6 Abbeywood House Hostel

7 J.J. O'Malleys' Pub
8 O'Cee's Coffeeshop
9 Stuffed Sandwich Co.
10 Matt Molloy's Pub
11 Super Valu Supermarket
12 Laundry

Prices vary quite a bit depending on the season.

$$$ Westport Inn has a fresh, woody feel with 34 comfortable rooms and convenient, free underground parking (Sb-€50–95, Db-€90–170, Tb-€135–255, Mill Street, tel. 098/29200, fax 098/29250, www.westportinn.ie, info@westportinn.ie).

$$$ Clew Bay Hotel is a couple of doors down from the TI, with 50 large, modern rooms with cherrywood furniture (Sb-€60–100, Db-€100–200, Tb-€195–225, James Street, tel. 098/28088, fax 098/25783, www.clewbayhotel.com).

$$ Boulevard Guest House, right on the leafy Mall, has large, tasteful rooms and a cushy lounge (Sb-€40–45, Db-€65–75,

Tb-€105, Qb-€120–140, cash only, discount for multiple-night stays, tel. 098/25138 or 087/284-4018, www.boulevard-guesthouse .com, info@boulevard-guesthouse.com, Sadie and John Moran).

$$ Linden Hall B&B has four cozy, colorful rooms (Sb-€30–50, Db-€60–90, Tb-€80–120, cash only, Altamount Street, tel. 098/27005, www.lindenhallwestport.com, lindenhall@iol.ie).

The homey **$$ Teallach an Ghabha B&B,** a couple of doors away, has four comfy, modest rooms (Db-€75, cash only, Altamount Street, tel. 098/25704).

$ Abbeywood House Hostel, behind the Church of Ireland, has seven rooms with views of Croagh Patrick (dorm beds €18–22, D-€50, cash only, includes continental breakfast, kitchen, Newport Road, tel. 098/25496, www.abbeywoodhouse.com, info @abbeywoodhouse.com).

Transportation Connections: If you want to visit Westport but lack wheels, here are your options. You can take a bus to/from **Galway** (7/day, 2 hrs), **Derry** (4/day, 5.5 hrs, change in Sligo), or **Dublin** (5/day, 5 hrs). You can also reach Dublin by train (3/day, 4 hrs).

From Westport to Murrisk by Car: Leave Westport heading west on R-335. After about five miles, as you're driving along scenic Clew Bay, you'll reach a wide spot in the road called Murrisk. Stop here. In the field on your right (opposite Campbell's Pub) is the...

Coffin Ship

This bronze ship sculpture is one of the most powerful famine memorials you'll see in Ireland. It's a "coffin ship," like those of the

1840s that carried the sick and starving famine survivors across the ocean in hope of a new life. Unfortunately, many of the ships contracted to take the desperate immigrants were barely seaworthy, no longer fit for dependable commerce. The poor were weak from starvation and vulnerable to "famine fever," which they then spread to others in the putrid, cramped holds of these awful ships. Many who lived through the six- to eight-week journey died shortly after reaching their new country. Pause a moment to look at the silent skeletons swirling around the ship's masts. Now contemplate the fact that famine still exists in the world. And before judging the lack of effective relief intervention by the British government of that time, consider the rich world's ability to ignore similar suffering today.

Across the road from the coffin ship is...

Croagh Patrick

This small mountain rises 2,500 feet above the bay. In the fifth century, St. Patrick is said to have fasted on its summit for the

40 days of Lent. It's from here that he supposedly rang his bell, driving all the snakes out of Ireland. The snakes never existed, of course, but they represent the pagan beliefs that Patrick's newly arrived Christianity replaced. Every year on the last Sunday of July, "Reek Sunday" (a "reek" is a mountain peak), more than 40,000 pilgrims hike two hours up the rocky trail to the summit in honor of St. Patrick. The most penitent attempt the hike barefoot (more than one comes down on a stretcher).

On that Sunday, Mass is celebrated throughout the day in a modest chapel on the top.

Hikers should allow three hours to reach the top and two hours to get back down (bring plenty of water, sunscreen, and rain gear). There is a WC on the summit, 30 yards below the chapel. The trail is easy to follow, but the upper half of the mountain is a steep slope of loose, shifting scree that can bang or turn exposed ankles. Both times I've climbed this, I've been glad I wore boots.

A few years ago, valuable gold deposits were discovered within Croagh Patrick. Luckily, public sentiment has kept the sacred mountain free of any commercial mining activity.

From Croagh Patrick to Doo Lough Valley: Continue on R-335. **Clew Bay** stretches out beside you, peppered with numerous humpbacked islands of glacial gravel dumped by retreating glaciers at the end of the last Ice Age. A notorious 16th-century local named Grace O'Malley (dubbed the "Pirate Queen") once ruled this bay, even earning the grudging respect of Queen Elizabeth I herself with her clever exploits. John Lennon later chose Dorinish Island to found a short-lived hippie commune. Passing through Louisburgh, you'll turn south to enter some of the most rugged and desolate country in Ireland.

Doo Lough Valley

Signs of human habitation vanish from the bogland, and ghosts begin to appear beside the road. About eight miles beyond Louisburgh, stop at the simple gray stone cross on the left. The lake ahead is Doo Lough (Irish for Black Lake), and this is the site of one of the saddest famine tales.

In the early 1800s, County Mayo's rural folk were almost exclusively dependent on the potato for food and were the hardest hit when the Potato Famine came in 1845. In the winter of 1849, about 600 starving Irish walked 12 miles from Louisburgh to Delphi Lodge, hoping to get food from their landlord, but they were turned away. On the walk back, almost 200 of them died along the side of this road. Today, the road still seems to echo with the despair of those hungry souls, and inspires an annual walk that commemorates the tragedy. Archbishop Desmond Tutu made the walk in 1988, shortly before South Africa ended its apartheid system.

From Doo Lough Valley to Leenane: Continue south on R-335. You'll get a fine view of **Aasleagh Falls** on the left. In late May, the banks below the falls explode with lush, wild, purple rhododendron blossoms. Cross the bridge after the falls, and turn right onto N-59 toward Leenane. You'll drive along Killary Harbor, an Irish example of a fjord. This long, narrow body of water was carved by an advancing glacier.

Leenane

This town is a good place for a break. The 1990 movie *The Field*, starring Limerick-born Richard Harris, was filmed here. Take a glance at the newspaper clippings about the making of the movie on the wall of **Hamilton's Pub.** While you're there, find the old photo of the British battleships that filled Killary Harbor when King Edward VII of England visited a century ago. Drop into the **Leenane Cultural Centre** (on the left as you enter town) to see interesting wool-spinning and weaving demonstrations (€3, April–Sept).

From Leenane to a Peat Bog: As you continue west on N-59, notice the rows of blue floats in Killary Harbor. They're there to mark mussel farms growing on hanging nets in the cold seawater. As you climb out of the fjord valley about five miles past Leenane, you'll pass some good areas to get a close look at a turf cut in a peat bog.

A Slog on the Bog

Walk a few yards onto the spongy green carpet. (Watch your step on wet days to avoid squishing into a couple inches of water.) Find a dry spot and jump up and down to get a feel for it. Have your companion jump; you'll feel the vibrations 15 feet away.

These bogs once covered almost 20 percent of Ireland. As the climate got warmer at the end of the last Ice Age, plants began

Ireland's Misunderstood Nomads

When you see a small cluster of trailers at the side of an Irish road, you're looking at a dying way of life. These are the Travellers, a nomadic throwback to the days when wandering craftsmen, musicians, and evicted unfortunates crowded rural Ireland. Often mislabeled as Gypsies, they have no ethnic ties to those Eastern European nomads but instead have an Irish heritage going back centuries.

There were once many more Travellers, who lived in tents and used horse-drawn carts as they wandered the countryside in search of work. Before the famine, when Irish hospitality was a given, Travellers filled a niche in Irish society. They would do odd jobs, such as repairing furniture, sweeping chimneys, and selling horses. Skilled tinsmiths, they mended pots, pans, and stills for *poitín*—Irish moonshine. (Travellers used to be called "tinkers," but they now consider this label derogatory.) Sedentary farm folk, who rarely ventured more than 20 miles from home their entire lives, depended on the roaming Travellers for news and gossip from further-flung regions. Post-famine rural depopulation and the gradual urbanization of the countryside forced this nomadic group to adapt to an almost sedentary existence on the fringes of towns.

Today, the 30,000 remaining Travellers are outsiders, usually treated with suspicion by the traditionally conservative Irish. Locals often complain that petty thefts go up when Travellers set up camp in a nearby "halting site," and that they leave their refuse behind when they depart. Travellers tend to keep to themselves, marry young, have large families, and speak their own Gaelic-based language (called Shelta, Gammon, or Cant). Attempts to settle Travellers in government housing and integrate their children into schools have met with mixed success, as poignantly shown in the 1992 movie *Into the West*.

growing along the sides of the many shallow lakes and ponds. When the plants died in these waterlogged areas, there wasn't enough oxygen for them to fully decompose. The moss built up, layer after dead layer, over the centuries, helping to slowly fill in the lakes. During World War I, this sphagnum moss was collected to use in bandages to soak up blood (it absorbs many times its weight in fluids).

Connemara

It's this wet, oxygen-starved ecosystem that has preserved ancient artifacts so well, many of which can be seen in Dublin's

National Museum. Even forgotten containers of butter, churned centuries ago and buried to keep cool, have been discovered. Since these acidic bogs contain few nutrients, unique species of carnivorous plants have adapted to life here by trapping and digesting insects. The tiny pink sundew (about two inches tall) has delicate spikes glistening with insect-attracting fluid. Take a moment to find a mossy area and look closely at the variety of tiny plants. In summer, you'll see white tufts of bog cotton growing in marshy areas.

People have been cutting, drying, and burning peat as a fuel source for over a thousand years. The cutting usually begins in April or May when drier weather approaches. You'll probably see stacks of "turf" piled up to dry along recent cuts. Pick up a brick and fondle it. Dried peat is surprisingly light and stiff. In central Ireland, there are even industrial peat cuts that were begun after World War II to fuel power stations. But in the past couple of decades, bogs have been recognized as a rare habitat, encouraging conservation efforts. Fortunately, the sweet smell of burning peat is becoming increasingly rare.

From Peat Bog to Kylemore Abbey: Continue west on N-59 and pass the junction with R-344 (direction: Recess) on the left; you'll come back to this junction on your way back to Galway. The road soon crosses a shallow lake, with a great view of Kylemore Abbey to the right. But don't stop here—you'll get a better photo from the parking lot a few hundred yards ahead. Pull into the lot and take a few minutes to enjoy the view (gate closes at 18:30).

Kylemore Abbey

This Neo-Gothic country house was built by the wealthy English businessman Mitchell Henry in the 1860s, after he and his wife had honeymooned in the area. Now they are both buried on the grounds. During World War I, refugee Benedictine nuns from Belgium took it over, and today it's an exclusive girls' boarding school. The best thing about the abbey is the view of it from the lakeshore. Tours inside are a letdown, so just enjoy its setting (overpriced at

€12 combo-ticket for abbey and gardens, daily 9:00–17:00, WCs in gift shop next to parking lot, tel. 095/41146, www.kylemoreabbey .com).

Connemara National Park

Less than five miles west of the abbey, just after passing through the town of Letterfrack (go left off N-59), this park encompasses almost 5,000 acres of wild bog and mountain scenery. The visitors center displays worthwhile exhibits of local flora and fauna, which are well explained in the 15-minute *Man and the Landscape* film that runs every half-hour. Nature-lovers may want to reverse the direction of my driving loop (and skimp on sightseeing time at other stops) in order to enjoy a two-hour walking tour with a park naturalist, departing the visitors center Monday through Friday at 10:30 in July and August. Bring rain gear and hiking shoes (visitors center-€2.90, covered by Heritage Card, mid-March–Oct daily 10:00–17:30, June–Aug until 18:30, last admission 45 min before closing, tel. 095/41054, www.heritageireland.ie).

Returning to Galway: Drive back the way you came. Turn right on R-344 (direction: Recess). Off to the right is Connemara's Twelve Bens mountains—but it's late, and we're headed for home. At the junction with N-59, turn left, and follow signs back to Galway. The tour is over.

Between Galway and Derry

Travelers continuing on to Northern Ireland (or County Donegal) should get an early start. Allow a long day for the drive from Galway to Derry (or Portrush) with these interesting stops along the way. The town of Knock is right on N-17 heading north out of Galway, while Strokestown is further east in County Roscommon. Fill up your tank just before you leave the Republic, since unleaded is at least a dollar per gallon more expensive in Northern Ireland.

Knock—In this tiny town in 1879, locals saw the Virgin Mary, St. Joseph, and St. John appear against the south gable of the church. Word of miraculous healings turned the trickle of pilgrims into a flood and put Knock solidly on the pilgrimage map. Today, you can visit the shrine. At the edge of the site, a small but interesting folk museum shows "evidence" of the healings,  photos of a papal visit, and interesting slices of traditional life.

▲▲Strokestown Park National Famine Museum—The Great Potato Famine of 1845–1849 was the bleakest period in Irish history—so traumatic that it halved the Irish population, sent desperate Irish peasants across the globe, and crystallized Irish-nationalist hatred of British rule. The National Famine Museum fills a mansion (on the former estate of the Mahon family, mentioned below) in the market town of Strokestown, 60 miles northeast of Galway. Visitors can absorb the thoughtfully done exhibits explaining how three million Irish peasants survived on a surprisingly nutritious prefamine diet of buttermilk and potatoes (12 pounds per day per average male laborer).

Major Mahon, the ill-fated landlord here during the famine, found it cheaper to fill three "coffin ships" bound for America with his evicted, starving tenants than pay the taxes for their upkeep in the local workhouse. When almost half died at sea of "famine fever," he was assassinated.

After visiting the museum, take a tour of the musty "Big House" (Mon–Fri at 11:30, 14:00, 16:00, Sat–Sun additional tour at 17:00). The tours provide insights into the gulf that divided the Protestant ascendancy and their Catholic house staff. Afterward, find the servants' tunnel—connecting the kitchen to the stable—built to avoid cluttering the Mahon family's views with unsightly common laborers (€13.50 combo-ticket for museum, house tour, and Georgian gardens, or €9 apiece, mid-March–Oct daily 10:30–17:30, tel. 071/963-3013, www.strokestownpark.ie).

Drivers connecting Westport or Galway to either Dublin or Northern Ireland can stop here en route and grab lunch in the museum café.

Connemara

NORTHERN IRELAND

NORTHERN IRELAND

The island of Ireland was once a colony of Great Britain. Unlike its Celtic cousins, Scotland and Wales, Ireland has always been distant from London—due more to its Catholicism than the Irish Sea.

Four hundred years ago, Protestant settlers from England and Scotland were strategically "planted" in Catholic Ireland to help assimilate the island into the British economy. These settlers established their own cultural toehold on the island, while the Catholic Irish held strong to their Gaelic culture.

Over the centuries, British rule has not been easy. By the beginning of the 20th century, the sparse Protestant population could no longer control the entire island. When Ireland won its independence in 1921 (after a bloody guerilla war against British rule), 26 of the island's 32 counties became the Irish Free State, ruled from Dublin with dominion status in the British Commonwealth—like Canada. In 1949 they left the Commonwealth and became the Republic of Ireland, severing all political ties with Britain.

Meanwhile, the six remaining northeastern counties (the only ones with a Protestant majority) chose not to join the Irish Free State in 1922, and remained part of the UK.

In this new political entity called Northern Ireland, the long-established Orange Order and the military muscle of the newly mobilized Ulster Volunteer Force (UVF) worked to defend the union with Britain—so their political philosophy was "Unionist." This was countered on the Catholic side by the Irish Republican Army (IRA), which wanted all 32 of Ireland's counties to be united in one Irish nation—their political goals were "Nationalist."

In World War II, the Republic stayed neutral while the North enthusiastically supported the Allied cause—winning a spot close to London's heart. After the war, the split between North and South seemed permanent, and Britain invested heavily in Northern Ireland to bring it solidly into the UK fold.

With 94 percent of the Republic of Ireland (the South) Catholic and only 6 percent Protestant, there was no question as to which group was dominant. But in the North, the Catholics,

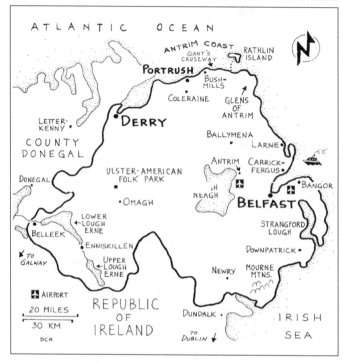

Northern Ireland

although a minority, were still a sizable 35 percent and demanded attention. Discrimination was considered necessary to maintain the Protestant status quo in the North, leading to the Troubles that have filled headlines since the late 1960s.

This isn't a fight over Protestant and Catholic religious differences—it's about whether Northern Ireland will stay part of the UK or become part of the Republic of Ireland. The indigenous Irish of Northern Ireland, who generally want to unite with Ireland, happen to be Catholic. The descendants of the Scottish and English settlers, who generally want to remain part of Britain, happen to be Protestant.

Partly inspired by Martin Luther King and the civil rights movement in America in the 1960s—beamed into Irish living rooms by the new magic of television news—the Catholic minority in Northern Ireland began to fight discrimination, advocating for better jobs and housing. Extremists polarized issues, and demonstrations, also caught on TV news, became violent. Unionists were afraid that if the island became one nation, the relatively poor Republic of Ireland would drag down the comparatively affluent North, and the high percentage of Catholics could mean repression

North'rn Ireland

Northern Ireland Almanac

Official Name: Since Northern Ireland is not an independent state, there is no official country name. Some call it Ulster, while others label it The Six Counties. Politically, it's the smallest province of the UK (the other three provinces are England, Wales, and Scotland).

Population: Northern Ireland's 1.7 million people are about 55 percent Protestant (mostly Presbyterian and Anglican) and 45 percent Catholic. English is far and away the chief language, though Gaelic (Irish) is also spoken.

Despite the country's genetic homogeneity (the largest "minority" group is 8,000 Chinese), the population is highly segregated along political, religious, and cultural lines. Roughly speaking, the eastern seaboard is more Unionist, Protestant, and of English-Scottish heritage, while the south and west (bordering Ireland) is Nationalist, Catholic, and of Irish descent. Cities are often clearly divided between neighborhoods of one group or the other. Early in life, locals learn to identify the highly symbolic (and highly charged) colors, music, and language that distinguish the cultural groups.

Latitude and Longitude: 54°N and 5°W. It's a similar latitude to the Alaskan panhandle.

Area: 5,400 square miles (about the size of Connecticut), constituting a sixth of the island. Northern Ireland includes six of the island's traditional 32 counties.

Geography: Northern Ireland is shaped roughly like a doughnut, with the UK's largest lake in the middle (Lough Neagh, 150 square miles). The terrain comprises gently rolling hills of green grass, rising to 2,800-foot Slieve Donard. The weather is temperate, cloudy, moist, windy, and hard to predict.

Biggest Cities: Belfast, the capital, has 300,000 residents. Half a million people—nearly one in three Northern Irish—inhabit the greater Belfast area. Derry (called Londonderry by Unionists) has 84,000 people.

Economy: Northern Ireland's economy is more closely tied to the UK than to the Republic of Ireland. Sectarian violence has held back growth, and the economy gets subsidies from the UK

of the Protestants. As Protestants and Catholics clashed in 1969, the British Army entered the fray. Their peacekeeping role gradually evolved into acting as muscle for the Unionist government. In 1972, a watershed year, over 500 died as combatants moved from petrol bombs to guns, and a new, more violent IRA emerged. In this most recent 39-year chapter in the struggle for an independent and united Ireland, more than 3,000 people have been killed.

and the EU. Traditional agriculture (potatoes and grain) is fading fast, though modern techniques and abundant grassland make Northern Ireland a major producer of sheep, cows, and grass seed. Modern software and communications companies are replacing old traditional manufacturing. Shipyards are rusty relics, and the linen industry is now threadbare; both are victims of cheaper labor available in Asia.

Government: Northern Ireland is not a self-governing nation, but is part of the UK, ruled from London by Queen Elizabeth II and Prime Minister Gordon Brown, and represented in Parliament by 18 elected Members of Parliament. For 50 years (1922–1972), Northern Ireland was granted a great deal of autonomy and self-governance, known as "Home Rule." The current National Assembly (108-seat Parliament)—after an ineffective five years due to political logjams—recently began to show signs of rejuvenation.

Politics are dominated, of course, by the ongoing debate between Unionists (who want to preserve the union with the UK) and the Nationalists (who want to join the Republic of Ireland). At opposite ends of this debate are two high-profile and controversial figures: the elderly firebrand Reverend Ian Paisley for the Unionists and assassination-attack survivor Gerry Adams of Sinn Fein, the political arm of the IRA. In a hopeful development in the spring of 2007, the two allowed themselves to be photographed together across a negotiation table (a moment both had once sworn would never happen) as London returned control of the government to Belfast.

Flag: The official flag of Northern Ireland is the Union flag of the UK. But you'll also see the green, white, and orange Irish tricolor (waved by Nationalists) and the Northern Irish flag (white with a red cross and a red hand at its center), which is used by Unionists (see "The Red Hand of Ulster" page 302).

North'rn Ireland

A 1985 agreement granted Dublin a consulting role in the Northern Ireland government. Unionists bucked this idea, and violence escalated. That same year, Belfast City Hall draped a huge, defiant banner under its dome, proclaiming, *Belfast Says No.*

In 1994, the banner came down. In the 1990s—with Ireland's membership in the EU, the growth of its economy, and the weakening of the Catholic Church's influence—the consequences of a united Ireland became less threatening to the Unionists. Also in 1994, the IRA declared a cease-fire, and the Protestant Ulster Volunteer Force (UVF) followed suit.

The Nationalists wanted British troops out of Ireland, while the Unionists demanded that the IRA turn in its arms. Optimists hailed the signing of a breakthrough peace plan in 1998, called the "Good Friday Accord" by Nationalists, or the "Belfast Agreement" by Unionists. This led to the emotional release of prisoners on both sides in 2000.

Recently, additional progress has taken place on both fronts. The IRA finally "verifiably put their arms beyond use" in 2005, and backed the political process. Meanwhile, British Army surveillance towers were dismantled in 2006, and the army formally ended its 38-year-long Operation Banner campaign in 2007. Major hurdles to a lasting peace persist, but the downtown checkpoints are history, and the "bomb-damage clearance sales" are over. And today, more tourists than ever are venturing north to Belfast and Derry.

Terminology

Ulster (one of Ireland's four ancient provinces) consists of nine counties in the northern part of the island of Ireland. Six of these make up Northern Ireland (pronounced "Norn Iron" by locals), while three counties remain part of the Republic.

Unionists—and the more hard-line, working-class **Loyalists**—want the North to remain in the UK. The **Ulster Unionist Party (UUP),** the political party representing moderate Unionist views, is currently led by Sir Reg Empey (after being headed for years by Nobel Peace Prize co-winner David Trimble). The **Democratic Unionist Party (DUP),** led by Reverend Ian Paisley, chooses to take a harder stance in defense of Unionism. The **Ulster Volunteer Force (UVF),** the **Ulster Freedom Fighters (UFF),** and the **Ulster Defense Association (UDA)** are the Loyalist paramilitary organizations mentioned most frequently in newspapers and on spray-painted walls.

Nationalists—and the more hard-line, working-class **Republicans**—want a united and independent Ireland ruled by Dublin. The **Social Democratic Labor Party (SDLP),** founded by Nobel Peace Prize co-winner John Hume and currently led by Mark Durkan, is the moderate political party representing Nationalist views. **Sinn Fein** (shin fayn), led by Gerry Adams, takes a harder stance in defense of Nationalism. The **Irish Republican Army (IRA)** is the Nationalist paramilitary organization (linked with Sinn Fein) mentioned most often in the press and in graffiti.

To gain more insight into the complexity of the Troubles, see the University of Ulster's informative and evenhanded Conflict Archive at http://cain.ulst.ac.uk/index.html.

Safety

Tourists in Northern Ireland are no longer considered courageous (or reckless). A United Nations study conducted in 2003 found that Northern Ireland was statistically the second safest place in the developed world (after Japan). When a local spots you with a lost look on your face, they're likely to ask, "Wot yer lookin fer?" in their distinctive Northern accent. They're not suspicious of you, but rather trying to help you find your way. You're safer in Northern Ireland than in any other part of the UK—and far safer than in most major US cities. You have to look for trouble to find it here. Just don't seek out spit-and-sawdust pubs in working-class Protestant neighborhoods and sing Catholic songs.

Tourists notice the tension mainly during the "marching season" (Easter–Aug, peaking in early July). July 12—"the Twelfth"—is traditionally the most confrontational day of the year in the North, when proud Protestant Unionist Orangemen march to celebrate their Britishness and their separate identity from the Republic of Ireland (often through staunchly Nationalist Catholic neighborhoods). Lay low if you stumble onto any big Orange parades.

Northern Ireland Is a Different Country

When you leave the Republic of Ireland and enter Northern Ireland, you are crossing an international border. Although you don't have to flash your passport, you do change stamps, phone cards, money—and your Eurailpass is no longer valid.

You won't be using euros here; Northern Ireland issues its own Ulster pound, which, like the Scottish pound, is interchangeable with the English pound (€1 = about £0.70). Some establishments near the border may take your euros, but at a lousy exchange rate. So keep any euros for your return into the Republic, and get pounds from an ATM inside Northern Ireland instead. And if you're heading to England next, it's best to change your Ulster pounds into English ones (free at any bank in Northern Ireland, England, Wales, or Scotland).

North'rn Ireland

BELFAST

Seventeenth-century Belfast was just a village. With the influx, or "plantation," of English and (more often) Scottish settlers, the character of the place changed. After the Scots and English were brought in—and the native Irish were subjugated—Belfast boomed, spurred by the success of the local linen, rope-making, and shipbuilding industries. The Industrial Revolution took root with a vengeance. While the rest of Ireland remained rural and agricultural, Belfast earned its nickname ("Old Smoke") during the time when many of the brick buildings that you'll see today were built. The year 1888 marked the birth of modern Belfast. After Queen Victoria granted city status to this boomtown of 300,000, its citizens built the city's centerpiece, City Hall.

Belfast is the birthplace of the *Titanic* (and many other ships that didn't sink). Two huge, mustard-colored cranes (the biggest in the world, nicknamed Samson and Goliath) rise like skyscrapers above the harbor. They stand idle now, but serve as a reminder of this town's former shipbuilding might.

Today, big investments from south of the border—the Republic of Ireland—are injecting quiet optimism into the dejected shipyards where the *Titanic* was built, developing the historic Titanic Quarter. Cranes are building condos along the rejuvenated Lagan riverfront.

It feels like a new morning in Belfast. It's hard to believe that the bright and bustling pedestrian zone was once a subdued, traffic-free security zone. Now there's no hint of security checks, once a tiresome daily routine. These days both Catholics and Protestants are rooting for the new Belfast Giants ice-hockey team, one of many reasons to live together peacefully.

Greater Belfast

Still, it's a fragile peace and a tenuous hope. Mean-spirited murals, hateful bonfires built a month before they're actually burned, and pubs with security gates are reminders that the island is split—and 800,000 Protestant Unionists prefer it that way.

Planning Your Time

Big Belfast is thin on sights. For most, one day of sightseeing is plenty.

Day-Trip from Dublin: On the handy, two-hour Dublin–Belfast train (cheap, £24 "day-return" tickets, can cost more Fri–Sun), you could make Belfast a day trip: 7:35–Catch the early-morning train from Dublin and arrive in Belfast at 9:45; 11:00–City Hall tour (Mon–Fri), browse the pedestrian zone, lunch, ride a shared cab up Falls Road; 15:00-side-trip to the Ulster Folk and Transport Museum; evening–Return to Dublin (last train Mon–Sat departs Belfast at 20:10 and arrives in Dublin at 22:20). Sunday's trains depart later and return earlier, compressing your already limited time in Belfast (first train departs Dublin at 10:00 and arrives in Belfast at 12:15; last train departs Belfast at 18:15

and pulls into Dublin at 20:25). Confirm train times at local stations. Note that the TI offers the Historic Belfast Walk at 14:00 on Wednesday, Friday, and Saturday, as well as summer Sundays (June–Sept). On Friday and Saturday, the St. George's Market bustles in the morning. On Saturday, the only tour of City Hall is at 14:00 and 15:00 (Oct–May only at 14:30, no tours on Sun year-round).

Staying Overnight: Belfast makes a pleasant overnight stop, with plenty of cheap hostels, reasonable B&Bs, weekend hotel deals (Fri–Sun), and a resort neighborhood full of B&Bs 30 minutes away in Bangor.

Two Days in Belfast: Choose among the Living History bus tour, Ulster Folk and Transport Museum (in nearby Cultra), Botanic Gardens, and Carrickfergus Castle. Or take a day trip to the Antrim Coast.

Two Days in Small-Town Northern Ireland: From Dublin (via Belfast), take the train to Portrush; allow two nights and a day to tour the Causeway Coast (castle, whiskey distilleries, Giant's Causeway, resort fun), then follow the Belfast-in-a-day plan above. With a third day, add Derry.

Coming from Scotland: With good ferry connections (from Stranraer or Troon in Scotland, or Liverpool in England; see "Transportation Connections" at the end of this chapter), it's easy to begin your exploration of the Emerald Isle in Belfast, then head south to Dublin and the Republic.

ORIENTATION

(area code: 028)

For the first-time visitor in town for a quick look, Belfast is pretty simple. There are three zones of interest: **central** (Donegall Square, City Hall, pedestrian shopping, TI), **southern** (Botanic Gardens, university, Ulster Museum), and **western** (working-class sectarian neighborhoods west of the freeway). Belfast's "Golden Mile"—stretching from Hotel Europa to the university district—connects the central and southern zones with many of the best dinner and entertainment spots.

Tourist Information
For Belfast

The modern TI (look for *Welcome Center* signs) has fine, free city maps and an enjoyable bookshop with Internet access (June–Sept

Mon–Sat 9:00–19:00, Sun 11:00–16:00; Oct–May Mon–Sat 9:00–17:30, Sun 11:00–16:00; 1 block north of City Hall at 47 Donegall Place, tel. 028/9024-6609, www.gotobelfast.com). City walking tours depart from the TI (see "Tours," below). For the latest on evening fun, get *The List* free at the TI or *That's Entertainment* at newsstands (50p).

For the Republic of Ireland

Traveling on to the Republic of Ireland, are ye? If it's information you'll be wanting, 'tis the place for you to go (Mon–Fri 9:00–17:00, closed Sat–Sun, 53 Castle Street, off Donegall Place, tel. 028/9026-5500, www.tourismireland.com).

Arrival in Belfast

Arriving by fast train, you'll go directly to Central Station (with ATMs and free city maps at ticket counter). From the station, a free Centerlink bus loops to Donegall Square, with stops near Shaftesbury Square (recommended hostels), the bus station (some recommended hotels), and the TI (free with any train or bus ticket, 4/hr, never on Sun; during morning rush hour, bus runs only between station and Donegall Square). Allow about £3 for a taxi from Central Station to Donegall Square, or £5 to my B&B listings in south Belfast.

Slower trains arc through Belfast, stopping at several downtown stations, including Central Station, Great Victoria Station (most central, near Donegall Square and most hotels), Botanic Station (close to the university, Botanic Gardens, and some recommended hostels), and Adelaide (near several recommended B&Bs). It's easy and cheap to connect stations by train (£1).

Helpful Hints

US Embassy: It's at Danesfort House (Mon–Fri 8:30–17:00, closed Sat–Sun, 233 Stranmillis Road, www.usembassy.org.uk).

Market: On Friday and Saturday mornings (roughly until 14:00), **St. George's Market** is a commotion of clothes, produce, and seafood (at corner of Oxford and East Bridge Streets, five blocks east of Donegall Square, tel. 028/9043-5704).

Phone Tips: To call the Republic of Ireland from Northern Ireland, dial 00-353, then the area code without its initial 0, then the local number. To call Northern Ireland from the Republic of Ireland, dial 048, then the local eight-digit number.

Internet Access: Located near the Belfast International City Hostel, **Revelations Internet Café** is at 27 Shaftesbury Square (£4/hr, Mon–Fri 8:00–22:00, Sat 10:00–18:00, Sun 11:00–19:00, tel. 028/9032-0337).

Post Office: The main Post Office, with lots of fun postcards, is at the intersection of High and Bridge Streets (Mon–Sat 9:00–17:30, closed Sun, 3 long blocks north of Donegall Square).

Laundry: Globe Launderers is at 37 Botanic Avenue (£5 self-serve, £7 drop-off service, Mon–Fri 8:00–21:00, Sat 8:00–18:00, Sun 12:00–18:00, tel. 028/9024-3956). For the B&B neighborhood south of town, the closest is **Whistle Laundry** (£6 drop-off service, Mon–Fri 8:30–18:00, Sat 8:30–17:30, closed Sun, 160 Lisburne Road, at intersection with Eglantine Avenue, tel. 028/9038-1297).

Bike Rental: McConvey Cycles is at 183 Ormeau Road (£15/24 hrs, Mon–Sat 9:00–18:00, Thu until 20:00, closed Sun, tel. 028/9033-0322, www.rentabikebelfast.com).

Getting Around Belfast

If you line up your sightseeing logically, you can do most of the town on foot.

If you're here in July or August, ask about "Day Tracker" tickets that give individuals one day of unlimited train travel anywhere in Northern Ireland for £14 (making it easy to side-trip to Bangor, the Ulster Folk and Transport Museum in Cultra, or Carrickfergus Castle). Families (up to two adults and two kids under 16) visiting in July and August get an even better deal: the £18 one-day Family Pass, valid for train and bus travel. Buy your pass at any train station in the city. Outside of July and August, buy "day return" tickets to Carrickfergus Castle, Cultra, or Bangor (always cheaper than buying two one-way tickets).

For information on trains and buses in Belfast, contact Translink (tel. 028/9066-6630, www.translink.co.uk).

By Bus: Buses go from Donegall Square East to Malone Road and my recommended B&Bs (#8A or #8B, 3/hr, £1.30, all-day pass costs £3.50 before 10:00 and £2.50 after).

By Taxi: Taxis are reasonable and should be considered. Rather than use their meters, many cabs charge a flat £3 rate for any ride up to two miles. It's £1 per mile after that. Ride a shared cab if you're going up Falls Road (explained below).

TOURS

▲**Walking Tour**—The Historic Belfast Walk takes you through the historic core of town (£6, 90 min; departs from TI at 14:00 on Wed, Fri, and Sat—June–Sept also on Sun; confirm tour times with TI, book in advance, tel. 028/9024-6609).

▲**Big Bus Tours**—**City Sightseeing** offers the Living History Tour, the best introduction to the city's recent and complicated political and social history. You'll cruise the Catholic and Protestant working-class neighborhoods, with a commentary explaining the

Belfast

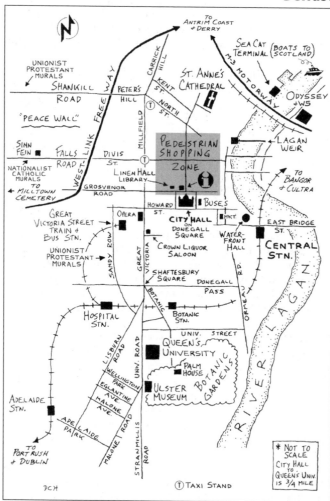

political murals and places of interest—mostly dealing with the Troubles of the last 35 years. You see things from the bus and get out only for photos (£11, 90 min, daily on the hour 10:00–16:30, fewer tours in winter—call first; depart from corner of Royal Avenue and Castle Place across from McDonald's, 2 blocks north of Donegall Square; pay cash at kiosk or on bus, or book by phone with credit card, tel. 028/9062-6888, www.city-sightseeing.com).

Minibus Tours—**Mini-Coach Travel**'s Antrim Coast Tour visits the Giant's Causeway, Dunluce Castle (photo-op only), the Carrick-a-Rede Rope Bridge, and Old Bushmills Distillery

(£20, doesn't include £5 admission to distillery, daily 9:30–17:45 depending on demand, book through and depart from Belfast International City Hostel, listed on page 308). They also have private guides (book in advance, tel. 028/9031-5333, www.minicoachni .co.uk).

Boat Tours—The Lagan Boat Company shows you shipyards on a 75-minute **Titanic Tour** cruise, narrated by a member of the Belfast Titanic Society. The tour shows off the fruits of the city's £800 million investment in its harbor, including a weir built to control the tides and stabilize the depth of the harbor (it doubles as a free pedestrian bridge over the River Lagan). The heart of the tour is a lazy harbor cruise past rusty

dry-dock gates, brought alive by the guide's proud commentary and passed-around historical photos (£8; daily sailings at 12:30, 14:00, and 15:30; fewer off-season, tel. 028/9033-0844, mobile 077-1891-0423, www.laganboatcompany.com). Tours depart from the Lagan Pedestrian Bridge and Weir on Donegall Quay. The quay is located just past the leaning Albert Clock Tower, a five-minute walk from the TI.

Bailey's Historical Belfast Pub Walk—Mixing drinks and history, these two-hour tours start at the Crown Dining Room pub and end six pubs later (£6, drinks not included except for a free shot of Baileys at tour's end; May–Oct Thu at 19:00, Sat at 16:00; book in advance, meet at pub above Crown Liquor Saloon at 46 Great Victoria Street across from Hotel Europa, tel. 028/9268-3665, www.belfastpubtours.com, Judy Crawford).

Local Guide—Ken Harper does taxi tours focusing on Catholic and Protestant neighborhoods (see below), *Titanic*-related sights, and Belfast's favorite sons—author C. S. Lewis and musician Van Morrison (£25 minimum or £6–8 per person for a 75-min tour, tel. 028/9074-2711, mobile 0771-175-7178, www.harperstaxitours.co.nr).

SIGHTS

Catholic and Protestant Neighborhoods

It will be a happy day when the sectarian neighborhoods of Belfast have nothing to be sectarian about. For a look at a couple of the original home bases of the Troubles, explore the working-class neighborhoods of Catholic Falls Road and Protestant Shankill Road or Sandy Row.

You can get tours of Falls Road or Shankill Road (see listings below), but rarely are both combined in one tour. Ken Harper is one of a new breed of Belfast taxi drivers who will give you an insightful private tour of both (see "Local Guide" under "Tours," previous page).

▲▲**Falls Road**—At the intersection of Castle and King Streets, you'll find the Castle Junction Car Park. This nine-story park-

ing garage's basement (entrance on King Street) is filled with old black cabs—and the only Irish-language signs in downtown Belfast. These shared black cabs efficiently shuttle residents from outlying neighborhoods up and down Falls Road and to the city center. This service originated more than 30 years ago at the beginning of the Troubles, when locals would hijack city buses and use them as barricades in the street fighting. When bus service was discontinued, local para-military groups established the shared taxi service. Any cab goes up Falls Road, past Sinn Fein headquarters and lots of murals, to the Milltown Cemetery (£2, sit in front and talk to the cabbie). Hop in and out. Easy-to-flag-down cabs run every minute or so in each direction on Falls Road. Twenty trained cabbies do one-hour tours (£8/person for 90 min, £10 per additional hour, cheap for a small group of up to 7 riders, tel. 028/9031-5777, www.wbta.net).

The Sinn Fein office and bookstore are near the bottom of Falls Road. The bookstore is worth a look. Page through books

featuring color photos of the political murals that decorate the buildings. Money raised here supports the families of deceased IRA members.

A sad, corrugated structure called the Peace Wall runs a block or so north of Falls Road (along Cupar Way), separating the Catholics from the Protestants in the Shankill Road area.

At the Milltown Cemetery, walk past all the Gaelic crosses down to the far right-hand corner (closest to the highway), where the IRA Roll of Honor is set apart from the thousands of other graves by little green railings. They are treated like fallen soldiers. Notice the memorial to Bobby Sands and nine other

hunger strikers. They starved themselves to death in the nearby Maze prison in 1981, protesting for political prisoner status as opposed to terrorist criminal treatment. The prison closed in the fall of 2000.

Shankill Road and Sandy Row—You can ride a shared black cab through the Protestant Shankill Road area (£20 for 1–2 people, £30 for 3–6 people, 60 min, tel. 028/9032-8775). Depart from North Street near the intersection with Millfield Road; it's not well marked, but watch where the cabs circle and pick up locals on the south side of the street.

An easier (and cheaper) way to get a dose of the Unionist side is to walk Sandy Row. From Hotel Europa, walk a block down Glengall Street, then turn left for a 10-minute walk along a working-class Protestant street. A stop in the Unionist memorabilia shop, a pub, or one of the many cheap eateries here may give you an opportunity to talk to a local. You'll see murals filled with Unionist symbolism. The mural of William of Orange's victory over the Catholic King James II (Battle of the Boyne, 1690) thrills Unionist hearts.

More Sights

▲▲**City Hall**—This grand structure, with its 173-foot-tall copper dome, dominates the town center. Built between 1898 and

1906, with its statue of Queen Victoria scowling down Belfast's main drag and the Union Jack flapping behind her, it's a stirring sight. In the garden, you'll find memorials to the *Titanic* and the landing of the US Expeditionary Force in 1942—the first stop en route to Berlin. Take the free 45-minute tour (June–Sept usually Mon–Fri at 11:00, 14:00, and 15:00, Sat at 14:00 and 15:00; Oct–May Mon–Fri at 11:00 and 14:30, Sat only at 14:30; no tours on Sun; enter at the front of the building except on Sat, when you enter at the back on the south side; call to check schedule and to reserve, tel. 028/9027-0456). The tour gives you a rundown on city government and an explanation of the decor that makes this an Ulster political hall of fame. Queen Victoria and King Edward VII look down on city council meetings. The 1613 original charter of Belfast granted by James I is on display. Its Great Hall—bombed by the Germans in 1941—looks as great as it did the day it was made.

Central Belfast

1. Hotel Europa
2. Jurys Inn
3. Granada Travelodge
4. The Morning Star Pub & Rest.
5. Kelly's Cellars
6. Crown Liquor Saloon & Dining Room
7. Caffè Metz
8. Marks & Spencer
9. Tesco Supermarket
10. Falls Road Taxi Garage
11. Shankill Road Taxi Queue

If you can't manage a tour, at least step inside, admire the marble swirl staircase, and drop into the "What's on in Belfast" room just inside the front door.

Linen Hall Library—Across the street from City Hall, the 200-year-old Linen Hall Library welcomes guests (notice the red hand above the main front door facing Donegall Square North; see "Red Hand of Ulster" sidebar, page 302). Described as "Ulster's attic," the library takes pride in being a neutral space where anyone trying to make sense of the sectarian conflict can view the Troubled

The Red Hand of Ulster

All over Belfast you'll notice a curious symbol: a red hand facing you as if swearing a pledge or telling you to halt. You'll spot it above the Linen Hall Library door, in wrought-iron fences, on old-fashioned clothes wringers (in the Ulster Folk and Transport Museum at Cultra), in Loyalist paramilitary murals, on shield emblems in the gates of Republican memorials, and even on the flag of Northern Ireland (the white flag with the red cross of St. George). It's known as the Red Hand of Ulster and it seems to pop up everywhere. Although it's more often associated with Unionist traditions, it's one of the few emblems used by both communities in Northern Ireland.

Nationalists display the red-hand-on-a-yellow-shield as a symbol of the ancient province of Ulster. It was the official crest of the once-dominant O'Neill clan (who fought tooth and nail against English rule), and today signifies resistance to British rule in these communities.

But you'll more often see the red hand in Unionist areas. They see it as a potent symbol of the political entity of Northern Ireland. The Ulster Volunteer Force chose it for their symbol in 1913 and embedded it in the center of the Northern Irish flag upon partition of the island in 1921. You'll often see the red hand clenched as a fist in Loyalist murals.

The origin of the red hand comes from a mythological tale of two rival clans that raced by boat to claim a far shore. The first clan leader to touch the shore would win it for his people. Everyone aboard both vessels strained mightily at their oars, near exhaustion as they approached the shore. Finally, in desperation, the chieftain leader of the slower boat whipped out his sword and lopped off his right hand...which he then flung onto the shore, thus winning the coveted land. Moral of the story? The fearless folk of Ulster will do *whatever* it takes to get the job done.

Images, a historical collection of engrossing political posters. It has a fine, hardbound ambience, a coffee shop, and a royal newspaper reading room (Mon–Fri 9:30–17:30, Sat 9:30–13:00, closed Sun, get free visitor's pass at entrance on Fountain Street, 17 Donegall Square North, tel. 028/9032-1707, www.linenhall.com).

Golden Mile—This is the overstated nickname of Belfast's liveliest dining and entertainment district, which stretches from the Opera House (Great Victoria Street) to the university (University Road).

The **Grand Opera House,** originally built in 1895, bombed and rebuilt in 1991, and bombed and rebuilt again in 1993, is extravagantly Victorian and *the* place to take in a concert, play, or opera (£5, guided tours Wed–Sat at 11:00; ticket office open Mon–Fri 8:30–21:00, Sat 8:30–18:00, closed Sun; on corner of Grosvenor Road and Great Victoria Street, tel. 028/9024-1919, www.goh.co.uk). **Hotel Europa,** next door, while considered the most bombed hotel in the world, feels pretty casual (listed on page 308).

Across the street is the museum-like **Crown Liquor Saloon.** Built in 1849, it's now a part of the National Trust. A wander through its mahogany, glass, and marble interior is a trip back into the day of Queen Victoria, although the privacy provided by the snugs—booths—allows for un-Victorian behavior (Mon–Sat 11:30–24:00, Sun 12:30–23:00, consider a lunch stop, see "Eating," below). Upstairs, the Crown Dining Room serves pub grub, is decorated with historic photos, and is the starting point for a pub walk (see "Tours," page 298).

▲**Ulster Museum**—While mediocre by European standards, this is Belfast's one major museum. It's closed, however, for renovation until spring 2009.

When open, the museum is free and pretty painless: Ride the elevator to the top floor and follow the spiraling exhibits downhill; there's a cheery café halfway down. You'll find an interesting *Made in Belfast* exhibit just before an arch that proclaims, "Trade is the golden girdle of the globe." The delicately worded history section is given an interesting British slant (such as the implication that the Great Famine of 1845 was caused by the Irish population doubling in 40 years—without a mention of various English contributions to the suffering). After a peek at a pretty good mummy, top things off with the *Girona* treasure. Soggy bits of gold, silver, leather, and wood were salvaged from the Spanish Armada's shipwrecked *Girona*—lost off the Antrim Coast north of Belfast in 1588 (free, likely Mon–Fri 10:00–17:00, Sat 13:00–17:00, Sun 14:00–17:00, in Botanic Gardens on Stranmillis Road, south of downtown, tel. 028/9038-3000, www.ulstermuseum.org.uk).

▲**Botanic Gardens**—This is the backyard of Queen's University, and on a sunny day, you couldn't imagine a more relaxing park setting. On a cold day, step into the Tropical Ravine for a jungle of heat and humidity. Take a quick walk through the Palm House, reminiscent of the one in London's Kew Gardens but smaller (free, Mon–Fri 10:00–12:00 & 13:00–17:00, Sat–Sun 13:00–17:00, less in winter, gardens open daily 8:00 until dusk, tel. 028/9031-4762). The Ulster Museum is on the grounds.

The Odyssey—This huge millennium-project complex offers a food pavilion and **W5**, a science center with stimulating, interactive exhibits for youngsters. Where else can a kid play a harp with laser-light strings? The name W5 stands for who, what, when, where, and why (£6.50, kids-£4.50, Mon–Sat 10:00–18:00, Sun 12:00–18:00, tel. 028/9046-7700, www.w5online.co.uk). There's also a 12-screen cinema (with IMAX) and a 10,000-seat arena where the Belfast Giants professional hockey team plays from September to April (2 Queen's Quay, 10-min walk from Central Station, tel. 028/9045-1055, www.theodyssey.co.uk).

Near Belfast

▲▲Ulster Folk and Transport Museum—This 180-acre, two-museum complex straddles the road and rail at Cultra, midway between Bangor and Belfast (eight miles east of town).

The Folk Museum, an open-air collection of 34 reconstructed buildings from all over the nine counties of Ulster, showcases the region's traditional lifestyles. After wandering through the old-town site (church, print shop, schoolhouse, humble Belfast row house, and so on), you'll head off into the country to nip into cottages, farmhouses, and mills. Most houses are warmed by a wonderful peat fire and a friendly attendant. It can be dull or vibrant, depending upon when you visit and your ability to chat with the attendants. Drop a peat brick on the fire.

The Transport Museum (downhill, over the road from the folk section) consists of three buildings. Start at the bottom and trace the evolution of transportation from 7,500 years ago—when people first decided to load an ox—to the first vertical take-off jet. The lowest building holds an intriguing section on the sinking of the Belfast-made *Titanic*. Nearby are exhibits on the Belfast-based Shorts aircraft company, which partnered with the Wright Brothers to manufacture the first commercially available aircraft in 1909. Two other buildings cover the history of bikes, cars,  and trains. The car section rumbles from the first car in Ireland (an 1898 Benz) through the "Cortina Culture" of the 1960s to the local adventures of controversial John DeLorean and a 1981 model of his car.

Cost, Hours, Location: £5.50 for Folk Museum, £5.50 for Transport Museum, £7 combo-ticket for both, £19 for families; July–Sept Mon–Sat 10:00–18:00, Sun 11:00–18:00; March–June

Mon–Fri 10:00–17:00, Sat 10:00–18:00, Sun 11:00–18:00; Oct–Feb closes daily at 16:00. Check the schedule for the day's special events (tel. 028/9042-8428, www.uftm.org.uk). Allow three hours for your visit, and expect lots of walking. Those with a car can drive from one section to the next.

From Belfast, you can reach **Cultra** by taxi (£10), bus #502 (2/hr, 30 min from Laganside Bus Centre), or train (£4 round-trip, 2/hr, 15 min, from any Belfast train station or from Bangor). Trains and buses stop right in the park, but train service is more dependable. Public-transport schedules are skimpy on Saturday and Sunday.

Carrickfergus Castle—Built during the Norman invasion of the late 1100s, this historic castle stands sentry on the shore of Belfast

Lough. William of Orange landed here in 1690, when he began his Irish campaign against deposed King James II. In 1778, the American privateer ship *Ranger* (first ever to fly the stars-and-stripes flag), under the command of John Paul Jones, defeated the more heavily armed HMS *Drake*

just offshore. These days the castle feels a bit sanitized and geared for kids, but it's an easy excursion if you're seeking a castle experience near the city (£3; April–Sept Mon–Sat 10:00–18:00, Sun 12:00–18:00; Oct–March Mon–Sat 10:00–16:00, Sun 14:00–16:00; last entry 30 min before closing, 20-min train ride from Belfast on line to Larne costs £5 round-trip, tel. 028/9335-1273).

SLEEPING

South Belfast

Many of Belfast's best budget beds cluster in a comfortable, leafy neighborhood of row houses just south of Queen's University (and the Ulster Museum, which is closed through 2009). Two train stations (Botanic and Adelaide) are nearby, and buses (£1.30) zip down Malone Road every 20 minutes. Any bus on Malone Road goes to Donegall Square East. Taxis, cheap in Belfast, take you downtown for about £3 (your host can call one).

$$$ Malone Lodge Hotel, by far the classiest listing in this neighborhood, provides slick, business-class comfort and spacious rooms in a charming environment on a quiet street (Db-£85–150, superior Db-£120–175, weekend deals, restaurant, elevator, 60 Eglantine Avenue, tel. 028/9038-8000, fax 028/9038-8088, www.malonelodgehotel.com, info@malonelodgehotel.com).

Belfast

Sleep Code

(£1 = about $2; country code: 44, area code: 028)
To call Belfast from the Republic of Ireland, dial 048 before the local 8-digit number.
S = Single, **D** = Double/Twin, **T** = Triple, **Q** = Quad, **b** = bathroom, **s** = shower only. Unless otherwise noted, breakfast is included and credit cards are accepted.

To help you easily sort through these listings, I've divided the rooms into three categories, based on the price for a double room with bath:

$$$ **Higher Priced**—Most rooms £90 or more.
$$ **Moderately Priced**—Most rooms between £50–90.
$ **Lower Priced**—Most rooms £50 or less.

$$ Camera Guest House rents 10 smoke-free rooms and has an airy, hardwood feeling throughout (S-£34–42, Sb-£48–52, Ds-£56, Db-£62, family room-£78, 44 Wellington Park, tel. 028/9066-0026, fax 028/9066-7856, camera_gh@hotmail.com, Bronagh and Peter).

$$ Malone Guest House is a crisp, stand-alone Victorian house fronting the busy Malone Road. It's homey and well run by Geraldine and Byron Quinn, who rent 13 prim rooms (Sb-£35–45, Db-£60–65, Tb-£70, 80 Malone Road, at intersection with Adelaide Park and bus stop, tel. 028/9066-9565, fax 028/9037-5090, www.maloneguesthousebelfast.co.uk, maloneguesthousebelfast @yahoo.co.uk).

$$ Windermere Guest House has 11 rooms, including several small but pleasant singles, in a large Victorian house (S-£28, Sb-£40, D-£52, Db-£55, T-£65, cash only, 60 Wellington Park, tel. 028/9066-2693, fax 028/9068-2218, www.windermereguesthouse .co.uk, windermereguesthouse@ntlworld.com).

Eglantine Avenue B&Bs: On the same quiet street (Eglantine Avenue), you'll find these two budget choices: **$$ Marine House B&B,** a grand old place with 10 high-ceilinged rooms (Sb-£45, Db-£60, Tb-£85, Qb-£100, at #30, parking, tel. & fax 028/9066-2828, www.marineguesthouse3star.com, marine30@utvinternet .co.uk) and **$ The George B&B,** with six fine, smallish rooms (S-£30, Sb-£40, Db-£50, Tb-£70, at #9, tel. 028/9068-3212, thegeorgeguesthouse@hotmail.com).

Hotels

Belfast is more of a business town than a tourist town, so business-class room rates are lower or soft on weekends (best prices booked

South Belfast

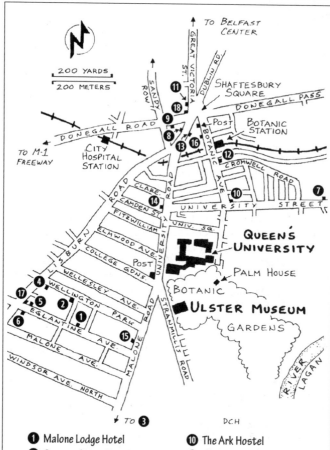

1. Malone Lodge Hotel
2. Camera Guest House
3. To Malone Guest House & Elms Village
4. Windermere Guest House
5. Marine House B&B
6. The George B&B
7. Belfast Holiday Inn Express
8. Benedicts Hotel
9. Belfast Intl. City Hostel
10. The Ark Hostel
11. Cayenne Restaurant
12. Maggie May's Restaurant
13. Bishop's Fish-and-Chips
14. Villa Italia Restaurant
15. Rain City Café
16. Globe Launderers
17. Whistle Laundry
18. Internet Café

from their websites). For the first three hotels, see the map on page 301; for the last two, see page 307.

$$$ Hotel Europa is Belfast's landmark hotel—fancy, comfortable, and central—with four stars and good weekend rates. Modern yet elegant, this place was Clinton's choice when he visited (Db-£75–210 plus £16 breakfast, President Clinton's suite-£400, 7 non-smoking floors, Great Victoria Street, tel. 028/9027-1066, fax 028/9032-7800, www.hastingshotels.com, res@eur.hastingshotels.com).

$$$ Jurys Inn, an American-style place that rents its 190 identical modern rooms for one simple price, is perfectly located two blocks from City Hall (up to 3 adults or 2 adults and 2 kids for £69–115, breakfast-£9 extra per person, 4 non-smoking floors, Fisherwick Place, tel. 028/9053-3500, fax 028/9053-3511, www.jurysinn.com, jurysinnbelfast@jurysdoyle.com).

$$ Granada Travelodge, quiet and extremely central, is a basic Jurys-style business hotel with 90 cookie-cutter rooms high on value, low on character (Db-£49–69, continental breakfast-£5, Irish breakfast-£7, a block from Hotel Europa and City Hall at 15 Brunswick Street, reservations tel. 08700-850-950 or 028/9033-3555, fax 028/9023-2999, www.travelodge.ie).

$$ Belfast Holiday Inn Express, not as central as the above hotels, offers the same basic formula (Db-£75 Mon–Thu, Db-£65 Fri–Sun, kids free, includes breakfast, 2 non-smoking floors, elevator, by Botanic Station at 106A University Street, tel. 028/9031-1909, fax 028/9031-1910, www.exhi-belfast.com, mail @exhi-belfast.com).

$$ Benedicts Hotel, with a local feel, is in a good location at the northern fringe of the Queen's University district. Its popular bar is a maze of polished wood (Sb-£65, Db-£75–85, elevator, 7–21 Bradbury Place, tel. 028/9059-1999, fax 028/9059-1990, www.benedictshotel.co.uk, info@benedictshotel.co.uk).

Hostels and Dorms

$ Belfast International City Hostel, providing the best value among Belfast's hostels, is big and creatively run, offering single and double rooms along with dorms. It's located near Botanic Station, in the heart of the lively university district and close to the center. Features include free lockers, left luggage, Internet access in lobby (£4/hr), videos, kitchen, self-serve laundry (£3.50), cheap breakfast-only cafeteria, elevator, 24-hour reception, and no curfew (beds in 6-bed dorm-£9, beds in quad-£11, S-£19, D-£26–28, Db-£37, 22–32 Donegall Road, tel. 028/9031-5435, fax 028/9043-9699, www.hini.org.uk, info@hini.org.uk). Paul, the manager of the hostel, is a veritable TI, with a passion for his work. The hostel is the starting point for Mini-Coach Travel tours (see page 297).

$ The Ark, a smaller, hipper, more youthful, and easygoing hostel, has 40 beds in the university district near Botanic Station (6- to 12-bed dorms-£10.90, a few Db-£36, kitchen, Internet access-£1.75/30 min, 44 University Street, tel. 028/9032-9626, www.arkhostel.com, info@arkhostel.com).

$ Elms Village, a huge Queen's University dorm complex, rents 1,200 basic, institutional rooms (singles only) to travelers during summer break (mid-June–early-Sept only, S-£24, Sb-£29, cheaper for students, coin-op laundry, self-serve kitchen; reception building is 50 yards down entry street, marked Elms Village on low brick wall, 78 Malone Road; tel. 028/9097-4525, fax 028/9097-4524, www.qub.ac.uk, accommodation@qub.ac.uk).

EATING

Downtown

If it's £8 pub grub you want, consider these places.

The Morning Star is woody and elegant (£9–14 restaurant dinners upstairs, £4 buffet Mon–Sat 12:00–15:00, open daily 12:00–21:00, Fri–Sat until 22:00, down alley just off High Street at 17 Pottinger's Entry, tel. 028/9023-5986).

Kelly's Cellars, with a very Irish feel, is 300 years old and hard to find—but worth it (Mon–Wed 11:30–20:00, Thu–Sat 11:30–23:00, closed Sun, live traditional music Fri–Sat nights and Sat at 15:30, 32 Bank Street, 100 yards behind Tesco supermarket, access via alley on left side when facing Tesco, tel. 028/9024-6058).

Crown Liquor Saloon, small and antique, has a mesmerizing mishmash of mosaics and shareable snugs—booths—topped with a smoky tin ceiling (Mon–Sat lunch only 11:30–15:00, Sun 12:00–17:00, 46 Great Victoria Street, across from Hotel Europa, tel. 028/9027-9901). For more on the Crown Liquor Saloon, see page 303. The **Crown Dining Room** upstairs offers dependable £7–13 meals (Mon–Sat 12:00–21:00, closed Sun, tel. 028/9027-9901, use entry on Amelia Street when the Crown Liquor Saloon is closed).

Cafés: For cafés, choose among the many popular eateries in the streets north of Donegall Square. **Caffè Metz** has a sleek, light-wood design and £6 meals, including salads (Mon–Sat 9:00–17:00, closed Sun, 12 Queen Street, at intersection with College Street, tel. 028/9024-9484).

Supermarkets: Marks & Spencer has a coffee shop serving skinny lattes, and a supermarket in its basement (Mon–Sat 8:30–19:00, Thu until 21:00, Sun 13:00–18:00, WCs on second floor, Donegall Place, a block north of Donegall Square). **Tesco,** another supermarket, is a block north of Marks & Spencer, and two blocks north of Donegall Square (Mon–Sat 8:00–19:00, Thu until 21:00, Sun 13:00–17:00, Royal Avenue and Bank Street). Picnic on the City Hall green.

Near Shaftesbury Square and Botanic Station

Cayenne is a trendy-yet-friendly restaurant refuge hiding behind Belfast's most understated exterior. It's your best bet for gourmet food—innovative global cuisine—without a snobby attitude. Owner Paul Rankin stars in the *Ready Steady Cook* weekday TV show on BBC (£15–22 meals, Mon–Fri 12:00–14:15 & 18:00–22:00, Sat 18:00–23:00, Sun 17:00–21:00; £16 three-course lunch; early-bird specials before 18:45: £16 for two courses or £20 for three courses at dinner; reservations smart on weekends; Shaftesbury Square at 7 Ascot House—look for plain, gray, blocky slab front; tel. 028/9033-1532).

Maggie May's serves hearty, simple, cheap £5–8 meals (Mon–Sat 8:00–22:30, Sun 10:00–22:30, 1 block south of Botanic Station at 50 Botanic Avenue, tel. 028/9032-2662).

Bishop's is the locals' choice for fish and chips (daily 12:00–23:30, pasta and veggie options, classier side has table service, just south of Shaftesbury Square at Bradbury Place, tel. 028/9043-9070).

Villa Italia packs in crowds hungry for linguini and *bistecca*. With its checkered tablecloths and a wood-beamed ceiling draped with grape leaves, it's a little bit of Italy in Belfast (£9–15, Mon–Fri 17:00–23:00, Sat–Sun 16:00–23:00, 39 University Road, 3 long blocks south of Shaftesbury Square, at intersection with University Street, tel. 028/9032-8356).

Rain City Café is closest to my cluster of B&B listings south of Queen's University. It's a hip grill serving tasty pasta, fish, and beef dishes. While this place has the same owners as classy Cayenne (listed above), it's cheaper, with a brighter atmosphere (£6–9 lunches, £10–15 dinners, daily 12:00–22:00, Sat–Sun brunch 10:00–16:00, near corner of Eglantine Avenue at 33–35 Malone Road, tel. 028/9068-2929).

Bangor

To stay in a laid-back seaside hometown—with more comfort per pound—sleep 30 minutes east of Belfast in Bangor (BANG-grr). It's a handy alternative for travelers who find Belfast booked up by occasional conventions. Formerly a slick Belfast seaside escape, Bangor now has a sleepy and almost residential feeling. But with elegant old homes facing its spruced-up harbor and the lack of even a hint of big-city Belfast, Bangor

has appeal. The harbor is a five-minute walk from the train station. Bangor's **TI** is at 34 Quay Street (July–Aug Mon–Fri 9:00–18:00, Sat 10:00–17:00, Sun 13:00–17:00; June and Sept closes at 17:00 Mon–Fri; Oct–May closed Sun, tel. 028/9127-0069).

Getting to Bangor

Catch the train from Belfast Central to Bangor (2/hr, 30 min, one-way-£3.80, same-day round-trip-£6.60, go to the end of the line—don't get off at Bangor West). Consider stopping en route at Cultra (Ulster Folk and Transport Museum, see listing on page 304). The journey gives you a good close-up look at the giant Belfast harbor cranes.

If day-tripping into Belfast from Bangor, get off at Belfast Central (free shuttle bus to the town center, 4/hr, not Sun) or stay on until Botanic Station for the Ulster Museum, the Golden Mile, and Sandy Row.

SLEEPING AND EATING

(**£1 = about $2, country code: 44, area code: 028**)
Sleeping in Bangor: **$$ Royal Hotel,** with 50 rooms and good weekend rates, is a fine old place right on the harbor (Db-£75 week-days, £69 Fri–Sun, view rooms are £10 pricier, 26 Quay Street, tel. 028/9127-1866, fax 028/9146-7810, www.royalhotelbangor.com, royalhotelbangor@aol.com).

$$ Hargreaves House, a homey Victorian waterfront refuge, has three cozy, smoke-free rooms (Sb-£30–35, D-£50, Db-£55, T-£55–65, 78 Seacliff Road, 10-min walk from train station, tel. 028/9146-4071, mobile 079-8058-5047, www.hargreaveshouse .com, ppeewee1@aol.com, Pauline Mendez).

$$ 108 Seacliff Road is a classy, 150-year-old Victorian house facing the water with three refined, bookshelf-lined rooms (S-£25–30, D-£48, Db-£58, non-smoking, 108 Seacliff Road, parking, 15-min walk from train station, tel. 028/9146-1077, www .bandb-bangor.co.uk, seacliff108@aol.com, Heather Bell).

Eating in Bangor: For good £7–11 meals, try **Lord Nelson Bistro** (daily 12:00–21:30, in the Marine Court Hotel facing har-bor, 18–20 Quay Street). The bar next door at the **Royal Hotel** serves £7 lunches and £8–12 dinners (daily 12:00–14:30 & 17:00–21:00). **Café Brazilia,** a popular hangout at lunch, is across from the stubby clock tower (Mon–Sat 8:30–16:30, closed Sun).

TRANSPORTATION CONNECTIONS

For updated schedules and prices for both trains and buses in Northern Ireland, check with Translink (tel. 028/9066-6630, www.translink.co.uk).

From Belfast by Train to: Dublin (8/day, 2 hrs), **Derry** (9/day, 2.25 hrs), **Larne** (hourly, 1 hr), **Portrush** (4/day, 2 hrs, transfer in Coleraine). Service is less frequent on Sundays. Train info: tel. 028/9066-6630. In July and August consider a £14 "Day Tracker" ticket, good for all-day train use in Northern Ireland (see "Getting Around," page 296).

By Bus to: Portrush (8/day, 2 hrs, £8, scenic-coast route, 2.5 hrs), **Derry** (20/day, 1.75 hrs, £9), **Dublin** (16/day, most via Dublin Airport, 3.5 hrs), **Glasgow** (2/day, 5 hrs), **Edinburgh** (2/day, 6 hrs). The Europa Bus Centre is behind Hotel Europa (Ulsterbus tel. 028/9033-7003 for destinations in Scotland and London, tel. 028/9066-6630 for destinations in Northern Ireland).

By Plane: Belfast has two airports. George Best Belfast City Airport (www.belfastcityairport.com) is a five-minute taxi ride from town (near the docks), while Belfast International Airport (www.bial.co.uk) is 18 miles west of town, connected by buses from the Europa Bus Centre behind the Europa Hotel. British Airways flies to **Glasgow** (3/day, 45 min, British Airways' Belfast office tel. 0845-606-0747, central booking tel. 0345-222-111, www .britishairways.com), and bmi British Midland flies to **London's** Heathrow Airport (8/day, tel. 0870-607-0555, www.flybmi.com).

By Ferry to Scotland: There are a number of options, ports, and companies. You can sail between Belfast and **Stranraer** on the Stena Line ferry (Mon–Sat 4/day, Sun 3/day, 1.75 hrs, £50 walk-up fare, £20 Apex 2-day advance booking fare, save more by booking online, tel. 028/9074-7747, www.stenaline.co.uk).

P&O Ferry (tel. 0870-2424-777, www.poirishsea.com) goes from **Larne** (20 miles north of Belfast, hourly trains, 1-hr trip, TI tel. 028/2826-0088) to **Cairnryan** (11/day, 1 hr, £25) or to **Troon** (2/day, 2 hrs, £30).

By Ferry to England: You can sail overnight from Belfast to **Birkenhead** (10 min from Liverpool)—with dinner and break-fast—for £35 (plus £40 for a cabin that sleeps 4) on Norfolkline Irish Sea Ferries (nightly at 22:00, 8 hrs, tel. 0870-600-4321, www .norfolkline-ferries.co.uk).

PORTRUSH AND THE ANTRIM COAST

The Antrim Coast—the north of Northern Ireland—is one of the most interesting and scenic coastlines in Ireland. Within a few miles of the Portrush train terminal, you can visit evocative castle ruins, tour the world's oldest whiskey distillery, risk your life on a bouncy rope bridge, and hike along the famous Giant's Causeway.

Homey Portrush used to be known as "the Brighton of the North." While it's seen its best days, it retains the atmosphere and architecture of a genteel, middle-class seaside resort. Portrush fills its peninsula with family-oriented amusements, fun eateries, and B&Bs. Summertime fun-seekers promenade along the tiny harbor and tumble down to the sandy beaches, which extend in sweeping white crescents on either side.

Superficially, Portrush has the appearance of any small British seaside resort, but its history and large population of young people (students from the University of Ulster at Coleraine) give the town a little more personality. Along with the usual arcade amusements, there are nightclubs, restaurants, summer theater (July–Aug) in the town hall, and convivial pubs that attract customers all the way from Belfast. At the end of the train line and just a few miles from several important sights, Portrush is an ideal base for exploring the highlights of the Antrim Coast.

Planning Your Time

You need a full day to explore the Antrim Coast, so allow two nights in Portrush. An ideal day could lace together Dunluce Castle, Old Bushmills Distillery, and the Giant's Causeway, followed by nine holes on the Portrush pitch-and-putt course.

ORIENTATION

(area code: 028)

Portrush's pleasant and easily walkable town center features sea views in every direction. On one side are the harbor and restaurants, and on the other are Victorian townhouses and vast, salty views. The tip of the peninsula is filled with tennis courts, lawn-bowling greens, putting greens, and a park.

The town is busy with students during the school year. July and August are beach-resort boom time. June and September are laid-back and lazy. Families pack Portrush on Saturdays, and revelers from Belfast crowd its hotels on Saturday nights.

Tourist Information

The TI, more generous and helpful than those in the Republic, is in the big, modern Dunluce Centre (July–Aug daily 9:00–19:00; Sept and April–June Mon–Fri 9:00–17:00, Sat–Sun 12:00–17:00; March and Oct Sat–Sun 12:00–17:00, closed Mon–Fri; closed Nov–Feb; tel. 028/7082-3333). Get the North Ireland driving map (£4), the free *Visitor Attractions* brochure, and a free Belfast map if you're Belfast-bound.

Arrival in Portrush

The train tracks stop at the base of the tiny peninsula that Portrush fills (no baggage check at station). The TI is three long blocks from the train station (follow signs down Eglinton Street and turn left at the fire station). All listed B&Bs are within a 10-minute walk of the train station see "Sleeping," page 321). The bus stop is two blocks from the train station.

Helpful Hints

Phone Tips: To call the Republic of Ireland from Northern Ireland, dial 00-353, then the area code without its initial 0, then the local number. To call Northern Ireland from the Republic of Ireland, dial 048, then the local eight-digit number.

Internet Access: Ground Coffee's coin-op machines have fast connections (daily June–Aug 9:00–22:00, Sept–May 9:00–17:00, Main Street, tel. 028/7082-5979).

Laundry: Viking Launderette charges £6/load for a full-service wash (Mon–Fri 9:00–17:30, Sat 9:00–13:00, closed Sun, Causeway Street, tel. 028/7082-2060).

Portrush

Portrush

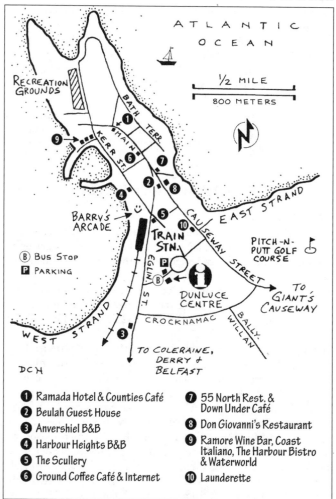

● Ramada Hotel & Counties Café
● Beulah Guest House
● Anvershiel B&B
● Harbour Heights B&B
● The Scullery
● Ground Coffee Café & Internet

● 55 North Rest. & Down Under Café
● Don Giovanni's Restaurant
● Ramore Wine Bar, Coast Italiano, The Harbour Bistro & Waterworld
● Launderette

Getting Around the Antrim Coast

By Bus: In July and August, a couple of all-day bus passes are available to help you get around the region economically. The better option is the £4.90 **Bushmills Open Topper,** connecting Portrush, Old Bushmills Distillery, and the Giant's Causeway every two hours. The £4 **Causeway Rambler**—which links Old Bushmills Distillery, the Giant's Causeway, and the Carrick-a-Rede Rope Bridge hourly—is less convenient because it doesn't include Portrush in its circuit (to get from Portrush to Bushmills, take a £7 taxi; those who want to see the Rope Bridge—along with the other sights—could consider getting both bus passes). For either pass, pick up a schedule at the TI and buy the ticket from the driver (in Portrush, the Bushmills Open Topper bus stops at Dunluce Avenue, next to public WC, a 2-min walk from TI). For more info, call Translink (tel. 028/9066-6630, www.translink.co.uk).

By Car: Distances are short and parking is easy. Don't miss the treacherous-yet-scenic coastal route down to the Glens of Antrim.

By Taxi: Groups (up to four) go reasonably by taxi, which costs only £9 from Portrush to the Giant's Causeway. A couple of companies to try are Hugh's Taxi (tel. 07702/986-110) or North West Taxi (tel. 028/7082-4446).

SIGHTS AND ACTIVITIES

Portrush

Barry's Old Time Amusement Arcade—This is a fine chance to see Northern Ireland at play (open weekends and summer only). Located just below the train station on the harbor, it's filled with candy floss (cotton candy) and little kids learning the art of one-armed bandits, 2p at a time. Get £1 worth of 2p coins from the machine and go wild, or brave the rollercoaster and bumper cars (June Mon–Fri 10:00–18:00, Sat 13:00–22:30, Sun 13:00–21:30; July–mid-Sept daily 13:00–22:30; closed mid-Sept–May).

Pitch-and-Putt at the Royal Portrush Golf Course—Irish courses, like those in Scotland, are highly sought after for their lush but dry greens in glorious settings. Serious golfers can get a tee time at the Royal Portrush, occasional home of the Senior British Open (greens fees Mon–Fri-£105, Sat–Sun-£120). Those on a budget can play the adjacent, slightly shorter Valley Course (greens fees Mon–Fri-£35, Sat–Sun-£40). Meanwhile, rookies can get a wee dose of this wonderful golf setting at the neighboring Skerry 9 Hole Links pitch-and-putt range. You get two clubs and balls for £6, and they don't care if you go around twice (daily 8:30–19:00, 10-min walk from station, tel. 028/7082-2311).

Portrush Recreation Grounds—For some easygoing exercise right in town, this well-organized park offers lawn-bowling greens (£3.50/hr with gear), putting greens, tennis courts, a great kids' play park, and a snack bar. Tennis shoes, balls, and rackets can all be rented for a low price (Easter–Sept Mon–Sat 10:00–dusk, Sun 13:00–19:00, closed Oct–Easter, tel. 028/7082-4441).

More Fun—Consider **Dunluce Centre** (kid-oriented fun zone, in same building with TI) and **Waterworld** (£4.50, pool, water-slides, bowling; Easter–Aug daily 10:00–19:00; Sept Sat–Sun 10:00–18:00, closed Mon–Fri; closed Oct–Easter; wedged between The Harbour Bistro and Ramore Wine Bar, tel. 028/7082-2001).

Antrim Coast

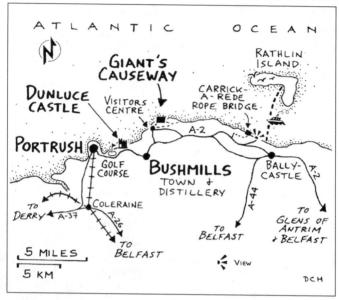

Antrim Coast

▲**Dunluce Castle**—These romantic ruins, perched dramatically on the edge of a rocky headland, are testimony to this region's turbu-

lent past. During the Middle Ages, the castle resisted several sieges. But on a stormy night in 1639, dinner was interrupted as half of the kitchen fell into the sea, taking the servants with it. That was the last straw for the lady of the castle. The countess of Antrim packed up and moved inland, and the castle "began its slow submission to the forces of nature." While it's one of the largest castles in Northern Ireland and is beautifully situated, there's precious little left to see among its broken walls.

The 16th-century expansion of the castle was financed by the salvaging of a shipwreck. In 1588, the Spanish Armada's *Girona* sank on her way home after an aborted mission against England, laden with sailors and the valuables of three abandoned sister ships. More than 1,300 drowned, and only five washed ashore. The shipwreck was excavated in 1967, and a bounty of golden odds and silver ends wound up in Belfast's Ulster Museum (closed for renovation through spring of 2009).

Castle admission includes an impromptu guided tour of the

The Scottish Connection

The Romans called the Irish the "Scoti" (meaning Pirates). When the Scoti crossed the narrow Irish Sea and invaded the land of the Picts 1,500 years ago, that region became known as Scotland. Ireland and Scotland were never conquered by the Romans, and retained similar clannish Celtic traits. Both share the same Gaelic branch of the linguistic tree.

On clear summer days from Carrick-a-Rede, the island of Mull in Scotland—only 17 miles away—is visible. Much closer on the horizon is the boomerang-shaped Rathlin Island, part of Northern Ireland. Rathlin is where Scottish leader Robert the Bruce (of *Braveheart* fame) retreated in 1307 after defeat at the hands of the English. Legend has it that he hid in a cave on the island, where he observed a spider patiently rebuilding his web

each time a breeze knocked it down. Inspired by the spider's perseverance, he gathered his Scottish forces once more and finally defeated the English at the decisive battle of Bannockburn.

Flush with confidence from his victory, Robert the Bruce decided to open up a second front against the English...in Ireland. In 1315, he sent his brother Edward over to enlist their

ruins. The tour is interesting for its effort to defend the notion of "Ulster, a place apart—facing Scotland, cut off from the rest of Ireland by dense forests and mountains..." Before you leave, poke your head into the building opposite the gift shop and check out the large castle model, which shows the joint in its fully roofed heyday (£2, April–Sept daily 10:00–18:00; off-season Mon–Sat 10:00–16:00, shorter hours Sun; last entry 30 min before closing, tel. 028/2073-1938).

▲▲**Old Bushmills Distillery**—Bushmills claims to be the world's oldest distillery. Though King James I (of Bible fame) only granted its license to distill "Aqua Vitae" in 1608, whiskey has been made here since the 13th century. Distillery tours waft you through the process, making it clear that Irish whiskey is triple distilled—and therefore smoother than Scotch whisky (distilled merely twice and minus the "e"). The 45-minute tour starts with the mash pit, which is filled with a porridge that eventually becomes whiskey. (The leftovers of that porridge are fed to the county's particularly happy cows.) You'll see thousands of oak casks—the kind used for Spanish sherry—filled with aging whiskey.

Celtic Irish cousins in an effort to thwart the English. After securing Ireland, Edward hoped to move on and enlist the Welsh, thus cornering England with their pan-Celtic nation. But Edward's timing was bad—Ireland was in the midst of famine. His Scottish troops had to live off the land and began to take food and supplies from the starving Irish. He might also have been trying to destroy Ireland's crops to keep them from being used as a colonial "breadbasket" to feed English troops. The Scots quickly wore out their welcome, and Edward the Bruce was eventually killed in battle near Dundalk in 1318.

This was the first time in history that Ireland was used as a pawn by England's enemies. Ireland was seen as the English Achilles' heel by Spain and France, who later attempted Irish invasions. The English Tudor and Stewart royalty countered these threats in the 16th and 17th centuries by starting the "plantation" of loyal subjects in Ireland. The only successful long-term settlement by the English was here in Northern Ireland, which remains part of the United Kingdom today.

It's interesting to speculate how things would be different today if Ireland and Scotland had been permanently welded together as a nation 700 years ago. You'll notice the strong Scottish influence in this part of Ireland when you ask a local a question and he answers, "Aye, a wee bit." The Irish joke that the Scots are just Irish people who couldn't swim home.

The finale, of course, is the tasting in the 1608 Bar—the former malt barn. When your guide asks for a tasting volunteer, raise your hand quick and strong. Four volunteers per tour get to taste test eight different whiskeys (Irish versus Scotch and bourbon). Everyone else gets a single glass of his or her choice. Non-whiskey enthusiasts might enjoy a cinnamon-and-cloves hot toddy. To see the distillery at its lively best, visit when the 100 workers are staffing the machinery—Monday morning through Friday noon (weekend tours see a still still). Tours are limited to 35 people and book up. In summer, call in your name to get a tour time before you arrive (£5; April–Oct daily, tours are on the half-hour from 9:30, last tour at 16:00, Sun from 12:00; Nov–March daily at 10:00, 11:00, 12:00, 13:30, 14:30, and 15:30; tel. 028/2073-1521). You can get a decent lunch in the tasting room after your tour. Look for the distillery sign a quarter mile from Bushmills town center.

▲▲**Giant's Causeway**—This four-mile-long stretch of coastline, a World Heritage Site, is famous for its bizarre basalt columns. The shore is covered with largely hexagonal pillars that stick up at various heights. It's as if the earth were offering God his choice of

37,000 six-sided cigarettes.

Geologists claim the Giant's Causeway was formed by volcanic eruptions more than 60 million years ago. As the surface of the lava flow quickly cooled, it contracted and cracked into hexagonal columns. As the rock (which looked like alligator skin) later settled and eroded, the columns broke off into many stair-like steps.

Of course, in actuality, the Giant's Causeway was made by a giant Ulster warrior named Finn MacCool who wanted to reach his love on the Scottish island of Staffa. Way back then, the causeway stretched to Scotland, connecting the two lands. Today, while the foundation has settled, the formation still extends undersea to Staffa, just off the Scottish coast. Finn's causeway was ruined (into today's "remnant of chaos") by a rival giant. As the rival fled from ferocious Finn back to his Scottish homeland, he ripped up the causeway so Finn couldn't chase him.

For cute variations on the Finn story, as well as details on the ridiculous theories of modern geologists, start your visit in the visitors center (free entry but £5 to park, daily 10:00–17:00, July–Aug until 18:00, tel. 028/2073-1855, www.nationaltrust.org.uk). A video gives a worthwhile history of the Giant's Causeway, with a regional overview (£1, 4/hr, 12 min). A gift shop and cafeteria are standing by.

A minibus (4/hr, £1 each way) zips tired tourists a half-mile directly from the visitors center to the Giant's Causeway, the highlight of the entire coast.

For a better dose of the Causeway, consider this plan: Follow the high cliff-top trail from the visitors center 10 minutes to a great viewpoint, then go 10 minutes farther to reach the Shepherd's Stairway. Zigzag down to the coast; at the T junction, go 100 yards right to the towering pipes of "the Organ." Then retrace your steps and continue left to the "Giant's Boot" for some photo fun and the dramatic point where the stairs step into the sea. Just beyond that, at the asphalt turnaround, you'll see the bus stop for a lift back to the visitors center. You could also walk the entire five-mile-long Giant's Causeway. The 75p hiking guide points out the highlights named by 18th-century guides (Camel's Back, Giant's Eye, and so on). The Causeway itself is free and always open.

Tourist Train: In summer, a quaint, narrow-gauge steam locomotive connects the Causeway to the town of Bushmills with a two-mile, 15-minute journey (£5 one-way, £6.50 round-trip, daily July–Aug, only on weekends June and Sept, tel. 028/2073-2844, www.freewebs.com/giantscausewayrailway). The train runs hourly, departing Causeway's station at the top of the hour (11:00–17:00), and leaving Bushmills station on the half-hour (11:30–17:30, on Ballaghmore Road, a 15-min walk from distillery).

▲▲**Carrick-a-Rede Rope Bridge**—For 200 years, fishermen have hung a narrow, 90-foot-high bridge (planks strung between wires)

across a 65-foot-wide chasm between the mainland and a tiny island. Today the bridge (while not the original version) still gives access to the salmon nets that are set during the summer months to catch the fish turning the coast's corner. (The complicated system is described at the gateway.) A pleasant 20-minute one-mile walk from the parking lot takes you to the rope bridge. The island affords fine views and great seabird-watching, especially during nesting season (£3 trail and bridge fee, pay at hut beside parking lot, cof-

fee shop and WCs near parking lot, March–Oct daily 10:00–18:00, July–Aug until 19:00, closed Nov–Feb, tel. 028/2076-9839, www.nationaltrust.org.uk).

If you have a car and a picnic lunch, don't miss the terrific coastal viewpoint rest area one mile steeply uphill and east of Carrick-a-Rede (on B-15 road to Ballycastle). This grassy area

offers one of the best picnic views in Northern Ireland (picnic tables but no WCs). Feast on bird's-eye views of the rope bridge, nearby Rathlin Island, and the not-so-distant Island of Mull in Scotland.

▲**Antrim Mountains and Glens**—Not particularly high (never more than 1,500 feet), the Antrim Mountains are cut by a series of large glens running northeast to the sea. Glenariff, with its waterfalls (especially the Mare's Tail), is the most beautiful of the nine glens.

SLEEPING

Portrush has decent hotels, but some B&Bs seem well worn. August and Saturday nights can be tight. Otherwise, it's a "you take half a loaf when you can get it" town. Rates vary with the view and season—probe for softness. Many listings face the sea, though sea views are worth paying for only if you get a bay window. Ask for a big room (some doubles can be very small; twins are bigger). Lounges are invariably grand and have bay-window views. All

Sleep Code

(£1 = about $2, country code: 44, area code: 028)
S = Single, **D** = Double/Twin, **T** = Triple, **Q** = Quad, **b** = bathroom,
s = shower only. Breakfast is included and credit cards are
accepted unless otherwise noted.

To help you easily sort through these listings, I've divided
the rooms into three categories, based on the price for a standard double room with bath:

$$$ **Higher Priced**—Most rooms £80 or more.
  $$ **Moderately Priced**—Most rooms between £50–80.
   $ **Lower Priced**—Most rooms £50 or less.

places listed have lots of stairs, but most are perfectly central and
within a few minutes' walk of the train station. Parking is easy.

$$$ **Ramada Hotel,** in the middle of town, has 69 modern,
nicely furnished rooms and a good restaurant. The rooms can seem
airless on warm days due to windows that only open two inches
(Db-£70–120, elevator, limited private parking, 73 Main Street,
tel. 028/7082-6100, fax 028/7082-6160, www.ramadaportrush
.com, info@ramadaportrush.com).

$$ **Beulah Guest House,** centrally located and run by cheerful Rachel Anderson, has 11 prim and smoke-free rooms (Ss-
£32–45, Db-£56–72, Tb-£80–90, parking behind, 16 Causeway
Street, tel. 028/7082-2413, www.beulahguesthouse.com, stay
@beulahguesthouse.com).

$$ **Anvershiel B&B,** with six non-smoking rooms, is a
five-minute walk from the train station. Jovial Victor Bow, who
runs the show with his wife Erna, is in the know about local golf
(Sb-£38, Db-£55, Tb-£83; 10 percent discount on a Db if you
pay in cash and stay 2 nights outside of July–Aug; Wi-Fi, park-
ing, 16 Coleraine Road, tel. 028/7082-3861, www.anvershiel.com,
enquiries@anvershiel.com).

$$ **Harbour Heights B&B** rents nine homey rooms, each
named after a different town in County Antrim. It has an inviting
guest lounge, DVD players, and a small DVD rental library (Sb-
£32, Db-£58, sea view Db-£70, family rooms, 17 Kerr Street, tel.
028/7082-2765, www.harbourheights.co.uk, harbour@heights17
.freeserve.co.uk).

EATING

Being a get-away-from-Belfast town and close to a university town (Coleraine), Portrush has more than enough chips joints. Eglinton Street is lined with cheap and cheery eateries.

The Scullery makes sandwiches and healthy wraps to take away and enjoy by the beach—or on an Antrim Coast picnic (daily 8:30–17:00, 4 Eglinton Lane, tel. 028/7082-1000).

Ground Coffee makes fresh £3 sandwiches, soup, and excellent coffee (June–Aug daily 9:00–22:00, Sept–May 9:00–17:00, Main Street, tel. 028/7082-5979). They also offer coin-op Internet access (see "Helpful Hints," page 314).

55 Down Under Cafe serves basic sandwiches with a great patio view (Mon–Tue 10:00–17:00, Wed–Sun 10:00–21:00, shorter hours off-season, 1 Causeway Street, underneath fancier 55 North restaurant run by same owners and listed below, tel. 028/7082-2811).

Counties Café dishes up dependable meals at reasonable prices (daily £6–9 lunches 12:00–14:30 and £9–16 dinners 17:00–21:00, on ground floor of the Ramada Hotel at 73 Main Street, tel. 028/7082-6100).

Don Giovanni's Italian cuisine is served in a friendly, candlelit atmosphere (£8–13 pasta dishes, daily 17:30–23:00, 9–13 Causeway Street, tel. 028/7082-5516).

Dining with Views: The best sea views are found at **55 North** (named for the local latitude), with windows on all sides. Service can be slow, but the classy pasta and fish plates are worth the wait (£8–17 entrées, daily 12:30–14:00 & 17:00–21:00, Sept–June closed Mon, 1 Causeway Street, tel. 028/7082-2811).

Harbour Road Eateries: The following four restaurants, located within 50 yards of each other (all under the same ownership and overlooking the harbor on Harbour Road), are just about everyone's vote for the best food values in town.

Ramore Wine Bar—salty, modern, and much-loved—bursts with happy eaters. They're enjoying the most inviting menu I've seen in Ireland, featuring huge meals ranging from steaks to vegetarian food. Share a decadent banoffee (banana toffee) pie dessert with a friend (£8–15 plates, daily 12:15–14:15 & 17:00–22:00, closes Sun at 21:00, tel. 028/7082-4313).

Downstairs, sharing the same building as the Ramore Wine Bar, is the energetic **Coast Italiano,** with good red wine (from £2.50/glass) as a welcome break from Guinness. Come early for a table or sit at the bar (Mon–Fri 17:00–22:00, Sat 16:00–22:30, Sun 15:00–21:30, Sept–June closed Mon–Tue, tel. 028/7082-3311).

The Harbour Bistro offers a more subdued, darker bistro ambience than the wine bar, with meals for a few pounds more

(£9–16 dinners daily 17:00–22:00, £6–9 high tea Mon–Fri 17:00–18:30, tel. 028/7082-2430).

The adjoining **Harbour Bar** has an old-fashioned pub downstairs and a plush, overstuffed, dark lounge upstairs.

TRANSPORTATION CONNECTIONS

From Portrush by Train to: Coleraine (2/hr, 12 min, sparse on Sun morning), **Belfast** (9/day, 4/day Sun, 2 hrs, transfer in Coleraine), **Dublin** (7/day, 2/day Sun, 5 hrs, transfer in Coleraine or Belfast). In July and August, consider a £14 "Day Tracker" ticket, good for all-day train use in Northern Ireland (see page 296).

By Bus to: Belfast (8/day, 2 hrs; scenic coastal route, 2.5 hrs), **Dublin** (1/day, 5.5 hrs).

Useful updated schedules and prices for both trains and buses in Northern Ireland can be obtained from Translink (tel. 028/9066-6630, www.translink.co.uk).

DERRY AND COUNTY DONEGAL

The town of Derry (or Londonderry to Unionists) is the mecca of Ulster Unionism. When Ireland was being divvied up, the Foyle River was the logical border between the North and the Republic. But, for sentimental and economic reasons, the North kept Derry, which is on the Republic's side of the river. Consequently, this predominantly Catholic city has been much contested throughout the Troubles. Still, the conflict is only one dimension of Derry; this pivotal city has a more diverse history and a prettier setting than Belfast. And with a quarter of the population (84,000), it feels more manageable to visitors.

County Donegal, to the west of Derry, is about as far-flung as Ireland gets. A forgotten economic backwater (part of the Republic but riding piggyback on the North), it lacks blockbuster museums or sights. But a visit here is more about the journey, and adventurous drivers—a car is a must—will be rewarded with a time-capsule peek into old Irish ways and uncompromisingly beautiful scenery.

Planning Your Time

Travelers heading north from Westport or Galway should get an early start (the town of Donegal makes a good lunch stop), so they can spend a couple of hours in Derry and see the essentials. In Derry, visit the Tower Museum Derry and catch some views from the town wall before continuing on to Portrush for the night.

With more time, spend a night in Derry, so you can see the powerful Bogside murals and take a walking tour around the town walls—you'll appreciate this underrated city. With two nights in Derry, consider crossing the border into the Republic

Derry

for a scenic driving loop through part of remote County Donegal (see page 346).

Derry

No city in Ireland connects the kaleidoscope of historical dots more colorfully than Derry. From leafy monastic hamlet to cannonball-battered siege survivor to Industrial Revolution sweatshop to essential WWII naval base to wrenching flashpoint of sectarian Troubles...Derry has seen it all.

The manned British army surveillance towers were taken down in 2006, and the British troops themselves finally departed in mid-2007, after 38 years in Northern Ireland. Today you can feel comfortable wandering the streets and enjoying this unique Irish city.

ORIENTATION

(area code: 028)
The Foyle River flows north, slicing Derry into eastern and western chunks. The old town walls and worthwhile sights are all on the west side. Waterloo Place and the adjacent Guildhall Square, just outside the north corner of the old city walls, are the pedestrian hubs of city activity. The Strand Road area extending north from Waterloo Place makes a comfortable home base, with the majority of lodging and restaurant suggestions within a block or two on either side. The Diamond and its War Memorial statue mark the heart of the old city within the walls.

Tourist Information
The TI sits on the riverfront and has a room-finding service, books walking tours (see "Tours," below), and gives out free city maps (July–Sept Mon–Fri 9:00–19:00, Sat 10:00–18:00, Sun 10:00–17:00; Oct–June Mon–Fri 9:00–17:00, Sat 10:00–17:00, closed Sun; 44 Foyle Street, tel. 028/7126-7284, www.derryvisitor.com).

Arrival in Derry
Derry's little end-of-the-line train station, next to the river on the east side of town, has service to Portrush, Belfast, and Dublin. Free shuttle buses to Ulsterbus station (which is on the west side of town) await each arriving train. Otherwise, it's a 15-minute walk across Craigavon Bridge to the TI, or a £3 taxi ride to Guildhall Square. The same free shuttle service leaves Ulsterbus station 15 minutes before each departing train. The Ulsterbus station is a couple minutes' walk south of Guildhall Square.

Derry is compact enough to see on foot; drivers stopping for a few hours can park at the Foyleside parking garage across from the TI (£0.80/hr, £2.20/4 hrs, Mon–Tue 8:00–19:00, Wed–Sat 8:00–23:30, Sun 12:00–19:00, tel. 028/7137-7575). Drivers staying overnight can ask about parking at their B&B or try the Quayside parking garage behind the Travelodge (£0.80/hr, £3/4 hrs, £2/hr after first 6 hours, Mon–Fri 7:30–20:00, Sat 7:30–20:30, Sun 12:30–18:30).

Helpful Hints

Phone Tips: To call the Republic of Ireland from Northern Ireland, dial 00-353, then the area code without its initial 0, then the local number. To call Northern Ireland from the Republic of Ireland, dial 048, then the local eight-digit number.

Money: Northern Bank, First Trust Bank, Ulster Bank, and Bank of Ireland cluster around Waterloo Place and Guildhall Square (all Mon–Fri 9:30–16:30, closed Sat–Sun).

Internet Access: Located inside the walls, **Claudes Café** is just north of the Diamond on Shipquay Street (£3/30 min, daily 9:00–17:00, tel. 028/7127-9379).

Post Office: The main post office is just off Waterloo Place (Mon–Fri 9:00–17:30, Sat 9:00–12:30, closed Sun, Custom House Street).

Laundry: City Clean can do a load of laundry for £7 (drop off in morning to pick up later that day, Mon–Sat 9:00–17:30, closed Sun, Waterloo Place, tel. 028/7136-1962).

Taxi: Try **Maiden City Taxi** (tel. 028/7126-1666) or **Sackville Taxi** (tel. 028/7135-4442).

TOURS

Walking Tours—You have several options for tours, each including a section of the Derry Walls. The TI runs solid 90-minute tours with a different focus depending on the day: Monday—Siege, Wednesday—Emigration, and Friday—Living History of the Troubles (£5, July–Aug Mon–Fri 11:15 and 15:15, Sept–June Mon–Fri at 14:30, no tours Sat–Sun, just show up, tel. 028/7126-7284).

Martin McCrossan and his staff lead insightful 60-minute tours of the city, departing from 11 Carlisle Road just below Ferryquay Gate (£4; daily at 10:00, 12:00, and 14:00; call to confirm schedule, tel. 028/7127-1996, mobile 077-1293-7997, www.irishtourguides.com).

Stephen McPhilemy leads private tours of his hometown, Belfast, and the North Coast—when he's not on the road guiding Rick Steves tours several months a year (tel. 028/7130-9051, mobile

Derry

078-0101-1027, stevederry@hotmail.com).

Bus Tours—City Sightseeing's double-decker bus tours are a good option on a rainy day. You'll be driven around the city in a 60-minute loop that covers the Guild Hall, city walls, political wall murals (both Bogside and Waterside), cathedrals, and shirt factories. Your ticket is good for one lap around the loop, and you stay on the bus for the duration (£8, pay driver, May–Oct daily on the hour 10:00–16:00, departs from in front of TI and beside the Guild Hall, tel. 028/7134-5335 or 028/9062-6888, www.city-sightseeing.com).

SELF-GUIDED WALKS

Though calm today, Derry is marked by years of tumultuous conflict. These two walks (each taking less than an hour) will increase your understanding of the town's history. The first walk, starting at the old city walls and ending at the Anglican Cathedral, focuses on Derry's early days. The second walking tour (page 333) helps you easily find the city's compelling murals, which document the time of the Troubles. These tours can be done separately or linked, depending on your time.

Walk the Walls

Squatting determinedly in the city center, the old city walls of Derry (built 1613–1618 and still intact, except for wider gates to handle modern vehicles) hold an almost mythic place in Irish history.

It was here in 1688 that a group of brave apprentice boys, many of whom had been shipped to Londonderry as orphans after the great fire of London in 1666, took their stand. They slammed the city gates shut in the face of the approaching Catholic forces of deposed King James II. With this act, the boys galvanized the city's indecisive Protestant defenders inside the walls.

Months of negotiations and a grinding 105-day siege followed, during which a third of the 20,000 refugees and defenders crammed into the city perished.  The siege was finally broken in 1689, when supply ships broke through a boom stretched across the Foyle River. The sacrifice and defiant survival of the city turned the tide in favor of newly crowned Protestant King William of Orange, who arrived in Ireland soon after and defeated James at the pivotal Battle of the Boyne.

To fully appreciate the walls, take a walk on top of them (free

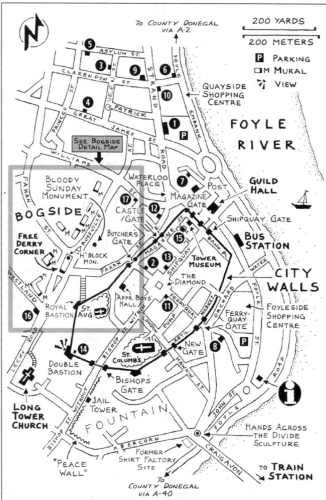

To COUNTY DONEGAL VIA A-2

200 YARDS
200 METERS

P PARKING
M MURAL
VIEW

QUAYSIDE SHOPPING CENTRE

FOYLE RIVER

SEE BOGSIDE DETAIL MAP

BLOODY SUNDAY MONUMENT

BOGSIDE

FREE DERRY CORNER

H'BLOCK MON.

WATERLOO PLACE

MAGAZINE GATE

Post

GUILD HALL

SHIPQUAY GATE

BUS STATION

CASTLE GATE

BUTCHER'S GATE

TOWER MUSEUM

THE DIAMOND

CITY WALLS

ROYAL BASTION

APPR. BOYS' HALL

FOYLESIDE SHOPPING CENTRE

FERRY-QUAY GATE

ST. AUG

NEW GATE

DOUBLE BASTION

BOGSIDE INN PUB

ST. COLUMB'S

BISHOPS GATE

JAIL TOWER

FOUNTAIN

LONG TOWER CHURCH

"PEACE WALL"

FORMER SHIRT FACTORY SITE

To COUNTY DONEGAL VIA A-40

HANDS ACROSS THE DIVIDE SCULPTURE

TO TRAIN STATION

1 Travelodge
2 Tower Hotel
3 Merchant's House B&B
4 Saddler's House B&B
5 Paddy's Palace Hostel
6 Mandarin Palace Restaurant
7 Exchange Rest. & Wine Bar
8 Fitzroy's Restaurant
9 Mange 2 Restaurant
10 Tesco Supermarket
11 Austins Dept. Store Café
12 Peadar O'Donnell's Pub
13 Internet Café
14 Verbal Arts Centre
15 Craft Village
16 Bogside Inn Pub
17 Launderette

Derry

Derry's History

Once an island in the Foyle River, Derry (from *daire,* Irish for "oak grove") was chosen by St. Colmcille (St. Columba in English) around A.D. 546 for a monastic settlement. He later banished himself to the island of Iona in Scotland out of remorse for sparking a bloody battle over the rights to a holy manuscript he had secretly copied.

A thousand years later, the English defeated the last Ulster-based Gaelic chieftains in the battle of Kinsale (1601). With victory at hand, the English took advantage of the power vacuum. They began the "plantation" of Ulster with loyal Protestant subjects imported from Scotland and England. The native Irish were displaced to less desirable rocky or boggy lands, sowing the seeds of resentment that fueled the modern-day Troubles.

A dozen wealthy London guilds took on Derry as an investment, and changed its name to Londonderry. They built the last great walled city in Ireland to protect their investment from the surrounding—and hostile—Irish locals. The walls proved their worth in 1688–1689, when the town's Protestant defenders, loyal to King William of Orange, withstood a prolonged siege by the forces of Catholic King James II. "No surrender" is still a passionate rallying cry among Ulster Unionists determined to remain part of the United Kingdom.

The town became a major port of emigration to the New World in the early 1800s. Then, when the Industrial Revolution provided a steam-powered sewing factory, the city developed a thriving shirt-making industry. The factories here employed mostly Catholic women who had honed their skills in rural County Donegal. Although Belfast grew larger and wealthier, Unionists cherished Londonderry and, in 1921, insisted that it be included in Northern Ireland when it was partitioned from the new Irish Free State (later to become the Republic of Ireland).

and open from dawn to dusk). Almost 20 feet high and at least as thick, the walls form a mile-long oval loop that you can cover in less than an hour. But the most interesting section is the half-circuit facing away from the river, starting at Magazine Gate (stairs face the Tower Museum Derry inside the walls) and finishing at Bishop's Gate.

From Magazine Gate, walk the wall as it heads uphill, snaking along the earth's contours like a mini–Great Wall of China. In the row of buildings on the left (just before crossing over Castle Gate), you'll see an arch entry into the **Craft Village,** an alley lined with a cluster of cute shops that showcase the recent economic rejuvenation of Derry (Mon–Sat 9:30–17:30, closed Sun).

• *After crossing over Butcher Gate, head to the corner of Society Street*

A bit of gerrymandering ensured that the Unionist Protestant minority maintained control of the city, despite its Nationalist Catholic majority.

Londonderry was a key escort base for US convoys headed for Britain during World War II, and dozens of German U-boats were instructed to surrender here at the end of the war. Poor Catholics—unable to find housing—took over the abandoned military barracks, with multiple families living in each dwelling. Only homeowners were allowed to vote, and the Unionist minority, which controlled city government, was not eager to build more housing that would tip the voting balance away from them. Over the years, sectarian pressures gradually built—until they reached the boiling point. Then, the ugly events of Bloody Sunday on January 30, 1972, brought worldwide attention to the Troubles (see "Touring the Murals of the Bogside," page 333).

Today, life has stabilized in Derry, and the population has increased by 25 percent in the last 30 years, to about 73,000. The modern Foyleside Shopping Centre, bankrolled by investors from Boston, was completed in 1995. The 1998 Good Friday Peace Accord has provided two-steps-forward, one-step-back progress toward peace, and the British Army withdrew in mid-2007. With a population that is 70 percent Catholic, the city has agreed to alternate Nationalist and Unionist mayors. There is a feeling of cautious optimism as Derry—the epicenter of bombs and bloody conflicts in the 1960s and 1970s—now boasts a history museum that airs all viewpoints.

(on the left) to the...

Apprentice Boys Memorial Hall: Built in 1873, it houses the private lodge and meeting rooms of an all-male Protestant organization. The group is dedicated to the memory of the original 13 apprentice boys who saved the day during the 1688 siege. Each year, on the Saturday closest to the August 12 anniversary date, the modern-day Apprentice Boys Society celebrates the end of the siege with a controversial march atop the walls. These walls are considered sacred ground for devout Unionists, who claim that many who died during the famous siege were buried within the battered walls because of lack of space.

Next, you'll pass a large, square pedestal on the right atop Royal Bastion. It once supported a column in honor of Governor

George Walker, the commander of the defenders during the famous siege. In 1973, the IRA blew up the column, which had 105 steps to the top (one for each day of the siege). The Governor's statue survived the blast and can be seen behind the Apprentice Boys Hall, down London Street and behind a protective fence.

• *Opposite the empty pedestal is the small Anglican...*

St. Augustine Chapel: Set in a pretty graveyard, it's where some believe the original sixth-century monastery of St. Columba (St. Colmcille in Irish) stood. This stretch of the walls was once a fashionable promenade walk in Victorian times.

As you walk ahead, you'll see (on the left) the site of a British Army **surveillance tower** that stood here until 2006. It was situated here for the bird's-eye view of the once-turbulent Catholic Bogside district below. Its recent dismantlement—as well as the removal of the British Army from Northern Ireland—is another positive sign in cautiously optimistic Derry.

Stop at the Double Bastion **fortified platform** that occupies this corner of the city walls. The old cannon is nicknamed "Roaring Meg" for the fury of its firing during the siege.

From here, you can see across the Bogside to the not-so-far-away hills of County Donegal in the Republic. Derry was once an island, but as the Foyle River gradually changed its course, the area you see below the wall began to drain. Over time, and especially after the Great Potato Famine (1845–1849), Catholic peasants from rural Donegal began to move into Derry to find work during the Industrial Revolution. They settled on this least desirable land...on the soggy, bog side of the city.

Directly below and to the right are Free Derry Corner and Rossville Street, where the tragic events of Bloody Sunday took place in 1972 (see "Touring the Murals of the Bogside," below). Down on the left is the 18th-century Long Tower Catholic church, named after the medieval round tower that once stood in the area (see "Long Tower Church," page 340).

• *Head to the grand brick building behind you.*

The Verbal Arts Centre: A former Presbyterian school, the center promotes the development of local literary arts in the form of poetry, drama, writing, and storytelling. Drop in for a cup of coffee in their coffeehouse and see what performances might be on during your visit (Mon–Thu 9:00–17:30, Fri 9:00–16:00, closed Sat–Sun, tel. 028/7126-6946, www.verbalartscentre.co.uk).

Continuing another 50 yards, go left around the corner and you'll reach Bishop's Gate, from which you can look down Bishop Street Without (outside the walls) and Bishop Street Within (inside the walls). The stub of another, shorter, former British Army surveillance tower peeks over your shoulder. Take a moment to look at the wall that's topped by a high mesh fence; it runs along the left side of Bishop Street Without. This is a **Peace Wall,** built to ensure the security of the Protestant enclave living behind it in the Fountain neighborhood. When the Troubles reignited more than 30 years ago, there were 20,000 Protestants living on this side of the river. Sadly, this small housing estate of

1,500 people is all that remains of that proud community today. The rest have chosen to move across the river to the Waterside district. The old brick tower halfway down the peace wall was part of the old jail that briefly held doomed rebel Wolfe Tone after the 1798 revolt against the British.

• *From Bishop's Gate, those short on time can descend from the walls and walk 15 minutes directly back through the heart of the old city, along Bishop Street Within and Shipquay Street to Guildhall Square. With more time, consider visiting St. Columb's Cathedral (page 340), the Long Tower Church (page 340), and the murals of the Bogside (described below).*

Touring the Murals of the Bogside

The Catholic Bogside area was the tinderbox of the modern Troubles in Northern Ireland. A terrible confrontation 35 years ago sparked a sectarian inferno, and the ashes have not yet fully cooled. Today, the murals of the Bogside give visitors an accessible glimpse of this community's passionate perception of those events.

Inspired by civil rights marches in America in the mid-1960s and the 1968 Prague Spring uprising, civil rights groups began to protest in Northern Ireland. Initially, their goals were to gain better housing, to secure fair voting rights, and to end employment discrimination for Catholics in the North. Tensions mounted, and clashes with the predominantly Protestant Royal Ulster Constabulary police force became frequent. Eventually, the British Army was called in to keep the peace. On January 30, 1972, a group protesting internment without trial held an illegal march through the Bogside neighborhood. They were fired upon by members of a British regiment, who claimed that snipers had fired on them first. The tragic result of the clash, now remembered as **Bloody Sunday,** caused the death of 14 civilians and led to a flood of fresh IRA volunteers.

The events are memorialized in 10 murals painted on the ends of residential flats along a 300-yard stretch of Rossville Street and Lecky Road, where the march took place. You can reach them from Waterloo Place via William Street, from the old city walls

The Bogside

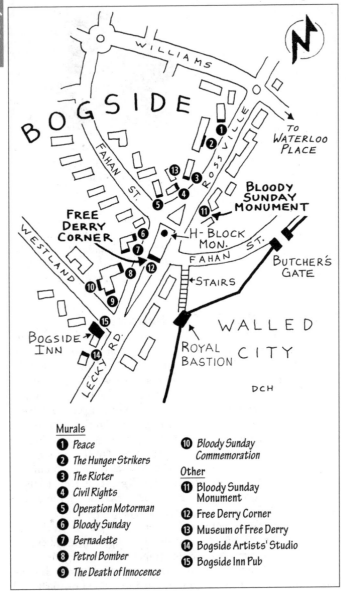

Murals
1. Peace
2. The Hunger Strikers
3. The Rioter
4. Civil Rights
5. Operation Motorman
6. Bloody Sunday
7. Bernadette
8. Petrol Bomber
9. The Death of Innocence
10. Bloody Sunday Commemoration

Other
11. Bloody Sunday Monument
12. Free Derry Corner
13. Museum of Free Derry
14. Bogside Artists' Studio
15. Bogside Inn Pub

Political Murals

The dramatic and emotional murals you'll encounter in Northern Ireland will likely be one of the enduring travel memories you'll take home with you. During the 19th century, Protestant neighborhoods hung flags and streamers each July to commemorate the victory of King William III at the Battle of the Boyne in 1690. Modern murals evolved from these colorful annual displays. With the advent of industrial paints, temporary seasonal displays became permanent territorial statements.

Unionist murals were created during the extended political debate that eventually led to the partitioning of the island in 1921, and the creation of Northern Ireland. Murals expressing opposing views in Nationalist Catholic neighborhoods were outlawed. The ban remained until the eruption of the modern Troubles, when staunchly Republican Catholic communities isolated themselves behind barricades, eluding state control and gaining freedom to express their pent-up passions. In Derry, this form of symbolic, cultural, and ideological resistance first appeared in 1969 with the simple "You are now entering Free Derry" message that you'll still see painted on the surviving gable wall at Free Derry corner.

Found mostly in working-class neighborhoods of Belfast and Derry, today's political murals have become a dynamic form of popular culture. They blur the line between art and propaganda, giving visitors a striking glimpse of each community's history, identity, and values.

at Butcher Gate via the long set of stairs extending below Fahan Street on the grassy hillside, or by the stairs leading down from the Long Tower Church. These days, this neighborhood is quiet and safe.

Two brothers and their childhood friend, all of whom grew up in the Bogside during the tragic events, began painting the murals in 1994. One of the brothers, Tom Kelly, gained a reputation as a "heritage mural" painter, specializing in scenes of life in the old days. In a surprising and hopeful development, Kelly was invited into Derry's Protestant Fountain neighborhood to work with a youth club there to paint three proud heritage murals to cover over paramilitary graffiti. You can visit their gritty studio (behind the Bogside Inn pub) to gain an understanding of the inspiration

Derry

that led to their memorable works (sporadic hours, so call first, tel. 028/7137-3842, www.bogsideartists.com).

The Bogside murals face different directions (and some are partially hidden by buildings), so they're not all visible from a single viewpoint. Plan on walking three long blocks along Rossville Street (which becomes Lecky Road) to see them all. Locals are used to visitors and don't mind if you photograph the murals.

The best place to start is from Williams Street, walking south along the right side of Rossville Street toward Free Derry Corner (described on next page). The murals will all be on your right.

The first mural you'll walk past is the most recently painted one. Finished in the summer of 2004, the colorful collage of *Peace* shows a silhouette of a dove in flight. It was inspired by a campaign of write-in suggestions for positive peacetime images from this generation of Derry city school children.

Next, *The Hunger Strikers* features two long-haired men wearing blankets. This mural represents the IRA prisoners who refused to wear the uniforms of common criminal inmates in an attempt to force the British to treat them instead as legitimate political prisoners (who were allowed to wear their own clothes).

Now look for *The Rioter*, which depicts an outgunned but

undaunted local youth behind a screen shield. He holds a stone—ready to throw—while a British armored vehicle approaches (echoing the famous Tiananmen Square photo of the lone man facing the tank).

Nearby is *Civil Rights*, showing a marching Derry crowd carrying an anti-sectarian banner. It dates from the days when Martin Luther King's successful nonviolent protest marches were being seen worldwide on TV, creating a dramatic global ripple effect. Civil rights marches—inspired into action using the same methods to combat a similar set of grievances—gave this long-suffering community a powerful new voice. In the building behind this mural, you'll find the small **Museum of Free Derry** (free, Mon–Thu 9:30–16:30, Fri 9:30–15:00, Sat–Sun 13:00–16:00, 55 Glenfada Park, tel. 028/7136-0880, www.museumoffreederry.org). Photos and a 45-minute video documentary convey the painful experience of the people of the Bogside during the worst of the Troubles.

Now cross over to the other side of Rossville Street to see the **Bloody Sunday Monument.** This small, fenced-off stone obelisk lists the names of those who died that day, most within 50 yards of this spot. Take a look at the map pedestal by the monument, which shows how a rubble barricade was erected to block the street. A 10-story housing project called Rossville Flats stood here in those days. When peaceful protests failed, and Republican youths became more aggressive, British troops feared being hit by Molotov cocktails thrown from the roof.

Cross again, this time over to the grassy median strip that runs down the middle of Rossville Street. At one end stands a granite letter *H* inscribed with the names of the 10 IRA hunger strikers who died in H-block of the Maze prison in 1981. From here, you get a good view of the *Operation Motorman* mural (at the corner of Fahan Street). In it, a soldier wields a sledgehammer, depicting the massive push by the British Army to open up the Bogside's barricaded "no-go" areas that the IRA had controlled for three years (1969–1972).

Walk down to the other end of the median strip where the white wall of **Free Derry Corner** announces "You are now enter-

ing Free Derry" (imitating a similarly defiant slogan of the time in once-isolated West Berlin). This was the gabled end of a string of houses that stood here over 30 years ago.

Cross back to the right side of the street (now Lecky Road) to see *Bloody Sunday,* in which a small group of men are carrying a body from that ill-fated march. It's based on a famous photo of Father Daly that was taken that terrible day. He waves a white handkerchief to request safe passage in order to evacuate a mortally wounded protester. The blood-stained civil rights banner was inserted under the soldier's feet for extra emphasis.

Near it is a mural called *Bernadette.* The woman with the megaphone is Bernadette Devlin McAliskey, an outspoken civil rights leader who, at age 21, became the youngest elected member of Parliament. Behind her kneels a woman supporter, banging a trash-can lid against the street in a traditional expression of protest in Republican neighborhoods. Trash-can lids were also used to warn neighbors of the approach of British patrols.

Petrol Bomber, showing a teen wearing an army-surplus gas mask, captures the Battle of the Bogside, when locals barricaded off their community, effectively shutting out British rule. The British army attempted to use tear gas and supposedly nonlethal rubber bullets to disperse hostile crowds.

In *The Death of Innocence*, a young girl stands in front of bomb wreckage. She is Annette McGavigan, a 14-year-old who was

killed on this corner by crossfire in the Bogside in 1971. She was the 100th fatality of the Troubles, which eventually took over 3,000 lives. The broken gun beside her points to the ground, signifying that it's no longer being wielded. The large butterfly above her shoulder symbolizes the hope for peace. For years, the artists left the butterfly an empty silhouette until they felt confident that the peace process had succeeded. They finally filled in the butterfly with optimistic colors in the summer of 2006.

Finally, around the corner, you'll see a circle of male faces. This mural, painted in 1997 to observe the 25th anniversary of the tragedy, is called *Bloody Sunday Commemoration* and shows the 14 victims. They are surrounded by a ring of 14 oak leaves—the symbol of Derry.

Take a few moments to walk into the **Bogside Inn** pub (facing this last mural across Westland Street) and order a beverage. This pub has been here through it all. Spend a little time examining the black-and-white news photos of Bloody Sunday and bomb damage around the city, taken during the darkest days of Derry.

Nationalist leader John Hume (Nobel Peace Prize co-winner in 1998, along with Unionist leader David Trimble) still has a house in the Bogside. He once borrowed a quote from Gandhi to explain his nonviolent approach to the peace process: "An eye for an eye leaves everyone blind."

SIGHTS

▲▲**Tower Museum Derry**—Housed in a modern reconstruction of a fortified medieval tower house that belongs to the local O'Doherty clan, this well-organized museum provides an excellent introduction to the city. Combining modern audiovisuals with historical artifacts, the displays tell the story of the city from a skillfully unbiased viewpoint, sorting out some of the tangled historical roots of Northern Ireland's Troubles.

The museum is divided into two sections: The Story of Derry (on the ground floor) and the Spanish Armada (on the four floors of the tower). Start with the Story of Derry, which explains the city's monastic origins 1,500 years ago. It moves through pivotal events, such as the 1688–1689 siege, as well as unexpected blips, including Amelia Earhart's emergency landing. Catch the thought-provoking 15-minute film in the small theater—it offers an evenhanded local perspective on the tragic events of the modern sectarian conflict, giving you a better handle on what makes this unique city tick. As you exit the small theater, scan the displays of paramilitary paraphernalia in the hallway lined with colored curbstones—red, white, and blue Union Jack colors for Loyalists; and green, white, and orange Irish tricolor for Republicans. There, you'll also find tiny notes written by IRA hunger striker Bobby Sands, which were smuggled out of the Maze prison.

The recently opened tower section holds the Spanish Armada exhibits, filled with items taken from the wreck of the *La Trinidad Valencera*. It was sunk by fierce storms nicknamed the "Protestant Winds" off the coast of Donegal in 1588 (£4 for all exhibits; July–Aug Mon–Sat 10:00–17:00, Sun 11:00–15:00; Sept–June Tue–Sat 10:00–17:00, closed Sun–Mon; Union Hall Place, tel. 028/7137-2411).

Guild Hall—This Neo-Gothic building, complete with clock tower, is the ceremonial seat of city government. It first opened

in 1890 on reclaimed lands that were once the mudflats of the Foyle River. Destroyed by fire and rebuilt in 1913, it was massively damaged by IRA bombs in 1972. In an ironic twist, Gerry Doherty, one of those convicted of the bombings, was elected as a member of the City Council a dozen years later. In November 1995, President Clinton spoke to thousands who packed into Guild Hall Square. Inside the hall are the Council Chamber, party offices, and an assembly hall featuring stained-glass windows showing scenes from Derry history. Take an informational pamphlet from the front window and explore, if civic and cultural events are not taking place inside (Mon–Fri 9:00–17:00, closed Sat–Sun, tel. 028/7137-7335).

Hands Across the Divide—Designed by local teacher Maurice Harron after the fall of the Iron Curtain, this powerful metal sculpture of two figures extending their hands to each other was

inspired by the growing hope for peace
and reconciliation in Northern Ireland
(located in a roundabout at the west end
of Craigavon Bridge).

Until recently, the Tillie and
Henderson's shirt factory (opened in
1857 and burned down in 2003) stood on
the banks of the river beside the bridge,
looming over the figures. In its heyday,
Derry's shirt industry employed over
15,000 workers (90 percent of whom
were women) in sweathouses typical of
the human toll of the Industrial Revolution. Karl Marx mentioned
this factory in *Das Kapital* as an example of women's transition
from domestic to industrial work lives.

St. Columb's Cathedral—Marked by the tall spire inside the
walls, this Anglican cathedral was built from 1628 to 1633 in a
style called "Planter's Gothic." Its construction was financed by
the same London companies that backed the Protestant plantation of Londonderry. It was the first Protestant cathedral built in
Britain after the Reformation, and the cathedral played an important part in the defense of the city during the siege. During that
time, cannons were mounted on its roof, and the original spire
was scavenged for lead to melt into cannon shot. In the entry-
way you'll find a hollow cannonball that was lobbed into the city,
containing the besiegers' surrender terms. Inside, along the nave
hangs a musty collection of battle flags and Union Jacks that once
inspired troops during the siege, the Crimean War, and World
War II. The American flag hangs among them, from the time
when the first GIs to enter the European theater in World War
II were based in Northern Ireland. Check out the small chapter-
house museum in the back of the church to see the original locks
of the gates of Londonderry and more relics of the siege (£2 donation, Mon–Sat 9:00–17:00, closed Sun, tel. 028/7126-7313, www
.stcolumbscathedral.org).

Long Tower Church—Built below the walls on the hillside above
the Bogside, this modest-looking church is worth a visit for its
stunning high altar. The name comes from a stone monastic
round tower that stood here for centuries but was destroyed for
city building materials in the 1600s. The oldest Catholic church
in Derry, it was finished in 1786, during a time of enlightened
relations between the city's two religious communities. Protestant
Bishop Hervey gave a generous-for-the-time £200 donation, and
had the four Corinthian columns shipped in from Naples to frame
the Neo-Renaissance altar (free, usually open Mon–Sat 7:30–
20:30, Sun 7:30–19:00—depending on available staff and church

functions, tel. 028/7126-2301).

Hidden outside behind the church and facing the Bogside is a simple shrine beneath a hawthorn tree. It marks the spot where outlawed Masses were secretly held before this church was built, during the infamous Penal Law period of the early 1700s. Through the Penal Laws, the English attempted to weaken Catholicism's influence by banishing priests and forbidding Catholics from buying land, attending school, voting, and holding office.

NIGHTLIFE

The **Millennium Forum** is a modern venue reflecting the city's revived investment in local culture, concerts, and plays (box office Mon–Sat 10:00–17:00, inside city walls on Newmarket Street near Ferryquay Gate, tel. 028/7126-4455, www.millenniumforum .co.uk, boxoffice@millenniumforum.co.uk).

The **Nerve Centre** shows a wide variety of art-house films (inside city walls at 7–8 Magazine Street, near Butcher Gate, tel. 028/7126-0562, www.nerve-centre.org.uk).

SLEEPING

$$$ Tower Hotel is the only hotel actually inside Derry's historic walls. It's a real splurge, with 93 modern and immaculate rooms, a classy bistro restaurant, and private basement parking (Sb-£57–99, Db-£64–110, online deals, Butcher Street, tel. 028/7137-1000, fax 028/7137-1234, www.towerhotelderry.com, reservations@thd.ie).

$$ Travelodge has 39 comfortable rooms, a great location, and a handy adjacent parking garage (Db-£50 Sun–Thu, Db-£60–85 Fri–Sat, significant online discounts if you book ahead, continental breakfast-£5, 2 non-smoking floors, 22–24 Strand Road, tel. 028/7127-1271, fax 028/7127-1277, www.travelodge.co.uk).

$$ Merchant's House, on a quiet street a 10-minute stroll from Waterloo Place, is a fine Georgian townhouse with marble fireplaces, ornate plasterwork, and a grand, colorful drawing room (S-£25–40, D-£55, Db-£60, Wi-Fi, 16 Queen Street, tel. 028/7126-9691, fax 028/7126-6913, www.thesaddlershouse.com, saddlershouse@btinternet.com, Joan and Peter Pyne).

$$ Saddler's House, run by the owners of Merchant's House, is a charming Victorian townhouse with seven rooms located a couple of blocks closer to the old town walls (Sb-£35–40, Db-£50–55, Wi-Fi, 36 Great James Street, tel. 028/7126-9691, fax 028/7126-6913, www.thesaddlershouse.com, saddlershouse @btinternet.com).

$ Paddy's Palace Hostel, located in the city center (across from a fortress-like police station), rents 40 decent beds for £11 a

Sleep Code

(£1 = about $2, country code: 44, area code: 028)
S = Single, **D** = Double/Twin, **T** = Triple, **Q** = Quad, **b** = bathroom, **s** = shower only. Breakfast is included and credit cards are accepted unless otherwise noted.

To help you easily sort through these listings, I've divided the rooms into three categories, based on the price for a standard double room with bath:

$$$ **Higher Priced**—Most rooms £80 or more.
 $$ **Moderately Priced**—Most rooms between £40–80.
  $ **Lower Priced**—Most rooms £40 or less.

night with breakfast. Look for the bright yellow "Paddy's Palace" mural on the Princes Street end of the building (4–6 beds per room, family rooms with private bathroom for up to four-£50, Internet access, laundry facilities, kitchen, nightly movies, 1 Woodleigh Terrace, Asylum Road, tel. 028/7130-9051, www.paddyspalace .com, info@paddywagontours.com, Stephen McPhilemy).

EATING

The front window of **Mange 2** declares that "cuisine is when things taste like what they are." They deliver on that promise, serving casual £5–8 lunches, filling £11–17 dinners, and a £13 three-course lunch (available 12:00–16:00) in a lighthearted atmosphere (daily 12:00–22:00, shorter hours off-season, Clarendon Street, tel. 028/7136-1222).

The **Mandarin Palace** dishes up good £8–13 Chinese dinners in a crisp dining room that faces the river (daily 16:30–23:00, buffet lunch Mon–Fri 12:00–14:00, £10 early-bird three-course deals 16:30–19:00, Queens Quay at Lower Clarendon Street, tel. 028/7137-3656).

The hip, trendy **Exchange Restaurant and Wine Bar** offers £6–8 lunches and quality £11–16 dinners with flair, in a central location near the river behind Waterloo Place (Mon–Sat 12:00–14:30 & 17:30–22:00, Sun 16:00–21:00, Queen's Quay, tel. 028/7127-3990).

Easygoing **Fitzroy's,** tucked below Ferryquay Gate, serves good £6–10 lunches and £9–14 dinners (Mon–Sat 11:00–22:00, Sun 12:00–21:00, 2–4 Bridge Street, tel. 028/7126-6211).

Austins Department Store, right on the Diamond in the center of the old city, is Ireland's oldest department store and has a top-floor café with some lofty views and £5 lunch specials

(Mon–Sat 9:30–17:30, Sun 13:00–17:00, 2–6 The Diamond, tel. 028/7126-1817).

Chat with locals in pubs that rarely see a tourist. Try **Peadar O'Donnell's** pub on Waterloo Street for Derry's best nightly traditional-music sessions (53 Waterloo Street, tel. 028/7137-2318).

Supermarkets: **Tesco** has everything for picnics and road munchies (Mon–Thu 9:00–21:00, Fri 8:30–21:00, Sat 8:30–20:00, Sun 13:00–18:00, corner of Strand Road and Clarendon Street). **Super Valu** meets the same needs (Mon–Sat 8:30–18:30, Thu–Fri until 20:30, closed Sun, Waterloo Place).

TRANSPORTATION CONNECTIONS

From Derry, it's less than an hour's drive to Portrush.

Useful updated schedules and prices for both trains and buses in Northern Ireland can be obtained from Translink (tel. 028/9066-6630, www.translink.co.uk).

From Derry by Train to: Portrush (9/day, 1 hr, change in Coleraine), **Belfast** (9/day, 2.25 hrs), **Dublin** (7/day, 5 hrs). In July and August, consider a £14 "Day Tracker" ticket, good for all-day train use in Northern Ireland (see page 296).

By Bus to: Galway (4/day, 6 hrs), **Portrush** (5/day, 1.25 hrs), **Belfast** (20/day, 1.75 hrs), **Dublin** (5/day, 4.5 hrs).

For Drivers: Northern Ireland Sights Between Derry and Galway

If you're driving into Northern Ireland from Galway, Westport, or Strokestown and don't have time to explore Donegal, consider these two interesting stops in the interior.

Belleek Pottery Visitors Centre—Just over the Northern Ireland border (30 miles northeast of Sligo) is the cute town of Belleek, famous for its pottery. The Belleek  Parian China factory welcomes visitors with a small gallery and museum (Mon–Fri 9:00–18:00, Sat 10:00–18:00, Sun 12:00–18:00, less off-season), a 20-minute video, a cheery cafeteria, and fascinating 30-minute tours of its working factory (£4, April–June and Sept Mon–Fri 9:00–18:00, Sat 10:00–18:00, Sun 14:00–18:00; longer hours July–Aug, shorter hours Oct–March, closed Sat–Sun Nov–March; call to confirm schedule and reserve a spot, tel. 028/6865-8501, www.belleek.ie). Crazed shoppers who forget to fill out a VAT tax refund form will find their financial situation looking Belleek.

▲**Ulster American Folk Park**—North of Omagh (five miles on A-5), this combination museum and folk park commemorates the many Irish who left their homeland during the hard times of the 19th century. Exhibits show life before emigration, on the boat, and in America. You'll gain insight into the origins of the tough Scots-Irish stock—think Davy Crockett (his folk were from Derry) and Andrew Jackson (Carrickfergus roots)—who later shaped America's westward migration (£5; April–Sept Mon–Sat 10:30–16:30, Sun 11:00–17:00; Oct–March Mon–Fri 10:30–15:30, closed Sat–Sun; cafeteria, tel. 028/8224-3292, www.folkpark.com).

The adjacent **Centre for Migration Studies** is handy for genealogy searches (Mon–Fri 10:30–17:00, closed Sat–Sun, tel. 028/8225-6315, www.qub.ac.uk/cms).

County Donegal

Donegal is the most remote (and perhaps the most ruggedly beautiful) county in Ireland. It's not on the way to anywhere, and it wears this isolation well. With more native Irish speakers than in any other county, the old ways are better preserved here. The northernmost part of Ireland, Donegal remains connected to the Republic by a slim, five-mile-wide umbilical cord of land on its southern coast. It's also Ireland's second-biggest county, with a wide-open "big sky" interior and a shattered-glass, 200-mile, jagged coastline of islands and inlets.

This is the home turf of St. Colmcille (St. Columba in English; means "dove of the church" in Irish), who was born here in 521. In the hierarchy of revered Irish saints, he's second only to St. Patrick. A proud Gaelic culture held out in Donegal to the bitter end, when its two famous clans (the O'Donnells and the O'Dohertys) were finally defeated by the English in the early 1600s. After their defeat, the region became know as Dun na nGall ("the fort of the foreigner"), which was eventually anglicized to Donegal.

As the English moved in, four friars (certain that Gaelic ways would be lost forever) painstakingly wrote down Irish history from Noah's Ark to their present. This labor of love became known as the Annals of the Four Masters, and without it, much of our knowledge of early Irish history and myth would have been lost. An obelisk stands in their honor in the main square of Donegal town.

The hardy people of County Donegal were famous for their quality tweed weaving, a cottage industry that has given way to modern industrial production in far-off cities. An energetic fishing fleet still churns offshore. The traditional Irish musicians of Donegal play a driving style of music with a distinctively fast and

County Donegal

County Donegal

INISHOWEN PENINSULA

NORTHERN IRELAND

DERRY

A-2
A-2
A-6
A-2

R-238

LOUGH SWILLY

R-246

N-13

LETTERKENNY

R-245

ATLANTIC OCEAN

CARRICKART

CREESLOUGH

N-56

CHURCH HILL

R-250

DUNFANAGHY

LOUGH VEAGH

R-251

HORN HEAD

GORTAHORK

GLENVEAGH NAT'L. PARK

N-56

R-251

MEEN-LARAGH

Mt. ERRIGAL

R-254

N-95

BUNBEG

DORI BEAGA

R-257

R-258

CROTHSHLI

TORY ISLAND

BLOODY FORELAND

AIRPORT

R-259

LEOS

N-56

N-95

DUNGLOW

① Grianan Aileach Ring Fort
② Newmills Corn & Flax Mills
③ Glenveagh Castle
④ Dunfanaghy Workhouse

VIEW

10 MILES

15 KM

choppy rhythm. Meanwhile, Enya (local Gweedore gal made good) has crafted languid, ethereal tunes that glide from mood to mood. Both *Dancing at Lughnasa* and *The Secret of Roan Inish* were filmed in Donegal. Today, emigration has taken its toll, and much of the trickle of tourism comes from neighboring Northern Ireland.

SIGHTS

Donegal Loop Trip

Here's my choice for a scenic mix of Donegal highlands and coastal views, organized as a daylong circuit (150 miles) for drivers based across the border in Derry. If you're coming north from Galway or Westport, you could incorporate parts of this drive into your itinerary.

Route Summary: Drive west out of Derry (direction: Letterkenny) on Buncrana Road, which becomes A-2 (and then N-13 across the border in the Republic). Follow the signs into Letterkenny, and take R-250 out the other (west) end of town. Veer right (north) onto R-251, and stay on it through Church Hill, all the way across the highlands, until you link up with N-56 approaching Bunbeg. After a couple of miles on N-56, take R-258 another four miles into Bunbeg. Depart Bunbeg going north on R-257, around Bloody Foreland, and rejoin N-56 near Gortahork. Take N-56 through Dunfanaghy (possible Horn Head mini-loop option here), and then south, back into Letterkenny. Retrace your route from Letterkenny via N-13 and A-2 back into Derry.

Helpful Hints: An early start and an Ordnance Survey map are essential. It's cheapest to top off your gas tank in Letterkenny. Consider bringing along a picnic lunch to enjoy from a scenic roadside pullout along the Bloody Foreland R-257 road, or out on the Horn Head loop. Bring your camera and remember—not all who wander are lost.

Once you cross into the Republic of Ireland, all currency is in euros, not pounds. For B&B rates, sight fees, and all other costs in Donegal, keep this exchange rate in mind: €1 = about $1.30.

The sights (listed below) along this route are well marked. Don't underestimate the time it takes to get around here, as the narrow roads are full of curves and bumps. Dogs, bred to herd sheep, dart from side lanes to practice their bluffing techniques on your car. If you average 30 miles per hour over the course of the day, you've got a very good suspension system. Folks wanting to linger at more than a couple of sights will need to slow down and consider an overnight stop in Bunbeg or Dunfanaghy (accommodations listed later in this chapter).

Donegal or Bust

Part of western County Donegal is in the Gaeltacht, where locals speak the Irish (Gaelic) language. In the spring of 2005, a controversial law was passed that erased all English place names from local road signs in Gaeltacht areas. Signs now only have the Irish-language equivalent, an attempt to protect the region from the further (and inevitable) encroachment by the English language.

Here's a cheat sheet to help you decipher the signs as you drive the Donegal loop (parts of which are in the Gaeltacht). There's also a complete translation of all Irish place names in the recommended Ordnance Survey road atlas, in the Gazetteer section in the back.

Gaelic Name	Pronounced	English Name
Letir Ceanainn	*LET-ir CAN-ning*	Letterkenny
Min an Labain	*MEEN on law-BAWN*	Churchill
Loch Ghleann Bheatha	*LOCKH thown eh-VEH-heh*	Lough (Lake) Veagh
An Earagail	*on AIR-i-gul*	Mt. Errigal
Gaoth Dobhair	*GWEE door*	Gweedore
Crothshli	*CROTH-lee*	Crolly
Bun Beag	*bun bee-OWG*	Bunbeg
Dori Beaga	*DOR-uh bee-OWG-uh*	Derrybeg
Cnoc Fola	*NOK FAW-luh*	Bloody Foreland
Gort an Choirce	*gurt on HER-kuh*	Gortahork
Dun Fionnachaidh	*doon on-AH-keh*	Dunfanaghy
Corran Binne	*COR-on BIN-eh*	Horn Head

Grianan Aileach Ring Fort

This dramatic, ancient ring fort perches on an 800-foot hill just inside the Republic, a stone's throw from Derry. It's an Iron Age

fortification, built around the time of Christ, and was once the royal stronghold of the O'Neill clan, which dominated Ulster for centuries. Its stout, drystone walls (no mortar) are 12 feet thick and 18 feet high, creating an interior sanctuary 80 feet in diameter (entry is free and unattended).

Once inside, you can scramble up the stairs built into the walls to enjoy panoramic views in all directions. Murtagh O'Brien, King of Desmond, destroyed the fort in 1101 (the same year he gave the Rock of Cashel to the Church). He had each of his soldiers carry away one stone apiece to make it tough for the O'Neill clan to find the raw materials to rebuild. What you see today is mostly a reconstruction from the 1870s. You'll see a sign for the fort posted on N-13, not far from the junction of R-239. Turn up the steep hill at the modern church with the round roof, and follow signs two miles (3 km) to the fort.

Newmills Corn and Flax Mills

Come here for a glimpse of the 150-year-old Industrial Revolution, shown high-tech Ulster style. Linen, which comes from flax, was king in this region. The 15-minute film does a nifty job of explaining the process, showing how the common flax plant ends up as cloth. Working conditions in a mill were noisy, unhealthy, and exhausting. A veteran mill worker often braved respiratory disease, deafness, lost fingers, and extreme fire danger.  For his trouble, he usually got to keep about 10 percent of what he milled.

The Corn Mill is still in working condition, but takes a skilled miller to operate it. This mill ground oats—"corn" means oats in Ireland. (What we call corn, they call maize.) The huge waterwheel, powered by the River Swilly, made five revolutions per minute and generated eight horsepower.

The entire operation could be handled by one miller, who knew every cog, lever, and flume in the joint. Call ahead to see when working mill demonstrations are scheduled; otherwise, tours last 20 minutes and are available on request (€2.90, covered by Heritage Card—see page 14, June–Sept daily 10:00–18:30, last admission 17:45, closed off-season, 5 miles west of Letterkenny on R-250, Churchill Road, tel. 074/912-5115).

Glenveagh Castle and National Park

One of Ireland's six national parks, Glenveagh's jewel is pristine Lough Veagh (Loch Ghleann Bheatha in Gaelic). The lake is three miles long, occupying a U-shaped valley scoured out of the Derryveagh mountains by powerful glaciers during the last Ice Age.

In the 1850s, this scenic area attracted the wealthy land speculator John George Adair, who bought the valley in 1857.

Right away, Adair clashed with local tenants, whom he accused of stealing his sheep. After his managing agent was found murdered, he evicted all 244 of his bitter tenants to great controversy, and set about to create a hunting estate in grand Victorian style.

His pride and joy was his country mansion, Glenveagh Castle, finished in 1873 on the shore of Lough Veagh. After his death, his widow added to the castle and introduced rhododendrons and rare red deer to the estate. After her death, Harvard art professor Kingsley Porter bought the estate, and promptly disappeared on the Donegal coast. (He's thought to have drowned.) The last owner was Philadelphia millionaire Henry McIlhenny, who filled the mansion with fine art and furniture while perfecting the lush surrounding gardens. He donated the castle to the Irish nation in 1981.

Take the 45-minute castle tour, letting your Jane Austen and Agatha Christie fantasies go wild. Antlers abound on walls, in chandeliers, and in paintings by Victorian hunting artists. A table crafted from rare bog oak (from ancient trees hundreds of years old, found buried in the muck) stands at attention in one room, while Venetian glass chandeliers illuminate a bathroom. A round pink bedroom at the top of a tower is decorated in Oriental style, with inlaid mother-of-pearl furnishings. The library displays paintings by George Russell, and has the castle's best lake views.

Afterward, stroll through the gardens and enjoy the lovely setting. A lakeside swimming pool had boilers underneath it to keep it heated. It's no wonder that Greta Garbo was an occasional guest, coming to visit whenever she "vanted" to be alone.

The castle is only accessible by 10-minute shuttle-bus rides (€2, 4/hr, depart from the park visitors center, last shuttle at 17:00). The visitors center, located beside the parking lot and tea room, explains the region's natural history. Hiking trails in the park are tempting, but beware of tiny midges that seem to want to nest in your nostrils (€2.90, covered by Heritage Card, mid March–early Nov daily 10:00–18:30, last admission 17:00, early Nov–mid March Sat–Sun only, tel. 074/913-7090).

Mount Errigal (An Earagail)

The mountain (2,400 feet) dominates the horizon for miles around. Rising from the relatively flat interior bog land, it looks taller from a distance than it is. Beautifully cone-shaped (but not a volcano), it offers a hearty nontechnical climb with panoramic views (4 hours round-trip, covering 5 miles). Hikers should ask for a weather report (frequent mists squat on the summit). The trailhead is southeast of the mountain, starting at the small parking lot right beside R-251 on the lower slope of the mountain.

Bunbeg (Bun Beag)

This modest town lies along R-257, offering a fine sandy beach. But take the trouble to seek out the quaint little hidden fishing harbor at the rocky south end of town. The harbor-access road is directly in front of you as you approach the town from the east on R-258 and pull up to the stop sign beside Tigh Bhreisleain B&B (on your right). At the dead end of the half-mile access road is a cute, watercolor-worthy harbor, with an old stone warehouse and a great guesthouse (see below).

There's an ATM at the AIB bank (on the left, going north on R-257, 100 yards past Seaview Hotel). The post office is in the back of the tiny Macaire Clocair market (Mon–Sat 9:00–17:30, Sat 9:00–13:00, closed Sun).

Turasmara operates a limited ferry service from Bunbeg harbor. It's a 90-minute voyage to the ultra-remote and rugged Tory Island (€22-round-trip, departs at 9:00 and returns at 18:00, leaves June–Sept daily—weather permitting, tel. 074/953-1340). Active travelers will enjoy the invigorating and scenic Rib Boat Excursions, which depart from Bunbeg House on the shore of cozy Bunbeg Harbor and weave among the nearby islands (€20, 45 min, daily mid-June–Aug, 10 people per boat, call for schedule, tel. 074/953-1305, www.bunbeghouse.com).

Sleeping in Bunbeg: **$$ Tigh Bhreisleain B&B** surveys the crossroads where R-257 and R-258 meet. Georgina Breslin presides over six crisp, colorful rooms with cushy carpets (Sb-€30, Db-€60, Tb-€90, cash only, non-smoking, parking, tel. 074/953-1329, fax 074/953-2625, www.bunbeg.net, breslins@bunbeg.net).

$$ Bunbeg House overlooks the snug and charming Bunbeg fishing harbor with 12 simple, spacious rooms and a tiny, inviting pub downstairs. Jean Carr knows about fun rib-boat sightseeing excursions, too (Sb-€40–45, Db-€70–80, Tb-€90–100, Qb-€120, parking, tel. 074/953-1305, fax 074/953-1420, www.bunbeghouse .com, bunbeghouse@eircom.net).

Eating in Bunbeg: Try the **Seaview Hotel Bistro,** which specializes in fish dishes (€24–28 meals, June–Sept daily 18:30–21:00, Oct–May Fri–Sat only 18:30–21:00, on R-257, tel. 074/953-1159). You'll find a fine pub dinner, plus late-evening traditional-music sessions nightly, at **Leo's Tavern,** run by Enya's dad. To get there from Bunbeg, hop on N-56 going south through the nearby hamlet of Crolly. Take a right onto R-259 (sign says *Aerphort*), and go a half-mile, following signs to Leo's, which will bring you to a jackknife—turn right and the pub will be 100 yards up on the left (Mon–Sat 13:00–20:30, Sun 13:00–15:30, tel. 074/954-8143). Groceries are sold at the **Spar Market** in nearby Derrybeg (Mon–Sat 9:00–19:30, Sun 9:00–13:30).

From Bunbeg to Derrybeg (Dori Beaga): The five miles of road heading north—as Bunbeg blends into Derrybeg (and a bit beyond)—are some of the most densely populated sections of this loop tour. Modern holiday cottages pepper the landscape in what the newly affluent Irish have come to call "Bungalow Bliss" (or "Bungalow Blight" to nature-lovers).

Bloody Foreland (Cnoc Fola)

Named for the shade of red that backlit heather turns at sunset, this scenic headland is laced with rock walls and forgotten cottage ruins. Pull off at one of the lofty roadside viewpoints and savor a picnic lunch and rugged coastal views.

Dunfanaghy Workhouse

Opened in 1845, this structure was part of an extensive workhouse compound (separating families by gender and age)—a dreaded last resort for the utterly destitute of coastal Donegal. There were once many identical compounds built across Ireland, a rigid Victorian solution to the spiraling riddle of Ireland's rapidly multiplying poor. But the system was unable to cope with the starving homeless multitudes caused by the famine.

The harsh workhouse experience is told through the true-life narrative of Wee Hannah Herrity, a wandering orphan and former resident of this workhouse. She survived the famine by taking refuge here, and died at age 90 in 1926. You'll visit three upstairs rooms where hokey papier-mâché figures relate the powerful episodes in her life (€5, April–Sept Mon–Sat 11:00–17:00, Sun 12:00–17:00; Oct–March Sat–Sun only; call to confirm winter hours, good bookstore and coffee shop, on N-56 a half-mile south of Dunfanaghy town, tel. 074/913-6540).

Dunfanaghy (Dun Fionnachaidh)

This planned town, founded by the English in the early 1600s for local markets and fairs, has a prim and proper appearance. In Dunfanaghy (dun-FAN-ah-hee), you can grab a pub lunch or some picnic fixings from the town market. Enjoy them from a scenic viewpoint on the nearby Horn Head loop drive (described later in this chapter).

The post office is at the southern end of town (Mon–Fri 9:00–17:30, Sat 9:00–13:00, closed Sun). Basic groceries are sold in the Ramsay market on the pier opposite the Muck & Muffin (Sun–Fri

8:00–16:30, Sat 8:00–20:30).

Sleeping in Dunfanaghy: **$$$ The Mill Restaurant and Accommodation** is a diamond in the Donegal rough. Susan Alcorn nurtures six wonderful rooms with classy decor, while her husband Derek is the chef in their fine restaurant downstairs (Sb-€70, Db-€95–100, Tb-€130, non-smoking, parking, tel. & fax 074/913-6985, www.themillrestaurant.com, info@themillrestaurant.com).

$$ The Whins B&B has tastefully exotic furnishings in its four prim rooms (Sb-€35–50, Db-€70, Tb-€100–105, non-smoking, parking, 10-min walk north of town, tel. 074/913-6481, www.thewhins.com, annemarie@thewhins.com, Anne-Marie Moore).

Eating in Dunfanaghy: **The Mill Restaurant and Accommodation** is gourmet all the way, specializing in memorable lamb or lobster dinners worth booking days ahead of time (€45, Tue–Sun 19:00–21:00, closed Mon, tel. 074/913-6985). **Muck & Muffin** is a simple sandwich café, great for quick, cheap lunches. It's above the pottery shop in the stone warehouse on the town square (Mon–Sat 9:30–17:00, Sun 11:00–17:00, tel. 074/913-6780).

Horn Head Loop (Corran Binne)

As you approach Dunfanaghy (if your schedule allows), take an hour and embark on a lost-world plateau drive. This heaving headland with few trees has gripping coastal views. Consult your map

and get off N-56, following the Horn Head signs all the way around the eastern lobe of the peninsula. There's less than eight miles of narrow, single-lane road out here, with very little traffic. But be alert and willing to pull over at wide spots to cooperate with other cars.

This stone-studded peninsula was once an island. Then, shortly after the last Ice Age ended, ocean currents deposited a sandy spit in the calm water behind the island. A hundred years ago, locals harvested its stabilizing dune grass, using it locally for roof thatching, and sending it abroad to Flanders for soldiers to create beds for horses during World War I. However, with the grass gone, the sandy spit was free to migrate again. It promptly silted up the harbor, created a true peninsula, and ruined Dunfanaghy as a port town.

A short spur road leads to the summit of the headland, where you can park your car and walk another 50 yards up to the abandoned lookout shelter. The views from here are dramatic, looking west toward Tory Island and south to Mount Errigal. Some may choose to hike an additional 30 minutes across the heather, to the ruins of the distant signal tower (not a castle), clearly visible near the cliffs. The trails are not maintained, but it's easy bushwhacking, offering rewarding cliff views. Navigate back to your car using the lookout shelter on the summit as a landmark.

IRELAND: PAST AND PRESENT

An old Irish proverb goes, "When God made time, he made a lot of it." Ireland is rich with history, art, and language. And the country continues to transform and grow today, building on an ever-stronger economy, searching for peace, and reexamining some of its long-held social customs.

IRISH HISTORY

Hunters, Farmers, and Mysterious Mounds (Prehistory)

Ireland became an island when rising seas covered the last land bridge (7000 B.C.), a separation from Britain that the Irish would fight to maintain for the next 9,000 years. By 6000 B.C., Stone Age hunter-fishers had settled on the East Coast, followed by Neolithic farmers (from the island of Britain). These early inhabitants left behind impressive but mysterious funeral mounds (passage graves) and large Stonehenge-type stone circles.

The Celts: Language and Legends (500 B.C.–A.D. 500)

Perhaps more an invasion of ideas than of armies, the Celtic culture from Central Europe (particularly that of the most influential tribe, called the **Gaels**) settled in Ireland, where it would dominate for a thousand years. A warrior people with over a hundred petty kings, they feuded constantly with rival clans and gathered in ring forts for protection. There were over 300 *tuatha* (clans) in Ireland, each with their own *rí* (king), who would've happily chopped the legs off of anyone who called him "petty." The island was nominally ruled by a single *Ard Rí* (high king) at the **Hill of Tara** (north of Dublin), though there was no centralized nation.

Druid priests conducted pagan, solar-calendar rituals among the megalithic stones erected by earlier inhabitants. The Celtic people peppered the countryside with thousands of Iron Age monuments. While most of what you'll see will be little more than rock piles that take a vigorous imagination to reconstruct (ring forts, wedge tombs, monumental stones, and so on), just standing next to a megalith that predates the pharaohs is evocative.

The Celtic world lives on today in the Gaelic language and in legends of Celtic warriors such as **Finn McCool**—the "Gaelic King Arthur"—who led a merry band of heroes in battle and in play. Tourists marvel at large ritual stones decorated with ogham (rhymes with "poem") script, the peculiar Celtic-Latin alphabet that used lines as letters. The **Tara Brooch** and elaborately inscribed, jewel-encrusted daggers attest to the sophistication of this warrior society (see the National Museum in Dublin, page 53).

In 55 B.C., the Romans conquered the Celts in Britain, but Ireland remained independent, its history forever skewed in a different direction—Gaelic, not Latin. The Romans called Ireland **Hibernia,** or Land of Winter; it was apparently too cold and bleak to merit an attempt at colonization. The biggest nonevent in Irish history is that the Romans never invaded. While the mix of Celtic and Roman is part of what makes the French French and the English English, the Irish are purely Celtic. Hurling, the wild Irish national pastime, goes back more than 2,000 years to Celtic days, when it was played almost as a substitute for warfare. Perhaps best described as something like airborne hockey with no injury time-outs, hurling is as central to the Irish culture as cricket is to the English, or *boules* to the French.

Christianity: Monks and Scholars (A.D. 500–800)

When Ancient Rome fell and took the Continent with it, Gaelic Ireland remained. There was no Dark Age here, and the island was a beacon of culture for the rest of Europe. Ireland (population c. 750,000) was still a land of many feuding kings, but the culture was stable.

Christianity and Latin culture arrived first as a trickle from trading contacts with Christian Gaul, then more emphatically in A.D. 432 with **St. Patrick,** who persuasively converted the sun-and-nature-worshipping Celts. (Perhaps St. Patrick had an easy time converting the locals because they had so little sun to worship.) Patrick (c. 389–461), a Latin-speaking

What's a Celt?

The Irish are a Celtic people. The Celts, who came from Central Europe, began migrating west around 1500 B.C. Over time, many settled in the British Isles and Western France. When the Angles and Saxons came later, grabbing the best land in the British Isles (which became Angle-land...or England), the Celts survived in Brittany, Cornwall, Wales, Scotland, and Ireland. Today, this "Celtic Crescent" still nearly encircles England. The word Celtic (pronounced with a hard C) comes from the Greek "Keltoi," meaning barbarian.

From about 700 B.C. on, various Celtic tribes mixed, mingled, and fought in Ireland. The last and most powerful of the Celtic tribes to enter the fray were the Gaels, who probably entered Ireland from Scotland. The Irish and Scottish language, Gaelic, is named for them. The fact that the Celts never had a written language meant that they had to pass their history, laws, and folklore down verbally from generation to generation. This may well account for the "gift of gab" attributed to today's Irish.

Celtic society revolved around warrior kings who gathered groups of families into regional kingdoms. These small kingdoms combined to make the five large provincial kingdoms of ancient Ireland (whose names survive on maps today): Leinster, Munster, Connacht, Ulster, and the Middle Kingdom (now County Meath).

For defensive purposes, these early Irish lived in small thatched huts built on manmade islands or on high ground

Christian from Roman Britain, was kidnapped as a teenager and carried off into slavery for six years in Ireland. He escaped back to Britain, then, inspired by a dream, returned to Ireland, determined to convert the pagan, often hostile Celtic inhabitants. Legends say he drove Ireland's snakes (symbolic of pagan beliefs) into the sea, and explained the Trinity with a shamrock—three leaves on one stem.

Later monks (such as **St. Columba,** 521–597) continued Christianizing the island, and foreign monks flocked to isolated Ireland. They withdrew to scattered, isolated monasteries, living in Celtic-style beehive huts, translating and illustrating (illuminating) manuscripts. Perhaps the greatest works of art of Dark Age Europe are these manuscripts, including the ninth-century **Book of Kells,** which you'll see at Dublin's Trinity College (see "Irish Art," page 371, and sight listing on page 47). Irish monks—heads shaved cross-wise from ear to ear, like the former Druids—were known surrounded by ditches and a stone or earthen wall. A strictly observed hierarchy governed Celtic societies: the king on top, followed by poets, druids (priests), doctors, legal men, skilled craftsmen, freemen, and slaves. Rarely did a high king rule the entire island. Loyalty to one's clan came first, and alliances between clans were often temporary until a more advantageous alliance could be struck with a rival clan. This fluid system of alliances ebbing and flowing across the Celtic-warrior cultural landscape meant that the Celts would never unite as a single nation.

Unlike the Celtic tribes living in Western Europe and Britain, the Celts in Ireland were never conquered by the Romans. This gives Ireland a cultural continuity and uniqueness rare in Europe. Their culture—which evolved apart from Europe—remained strong and independent for centuries. Then, in the 12th century, English dominance began leading to suppression of the Gaelic language and Celtic traditions. With Irish independence—won only in the 20th century—Irish ways are no longer threatened. The most traditional areas (generally along the west coast, such as the Dingle Peninsula) are protected as Gaeltachts. Gaeltachts (literally, places where the Gaelic language is spoken) are a kind of national park for the traditional culture. If much of Ireland's charm can be credited to its Celtic roots, you'll find that charm most vivid in a Gaeltacht.

throughout Europe as ascetic scholars.

St. Columbanus (c. 600; different from St. Columba) was one of several traveling missionary monks who helped to bring Christianity back to Western Europe, which had reverted to paganism and barbarism after Rome fell. The monks established monastic centers of learning that produced great Christian teachers and community builders. One of the monks, **St. Brendan,** may have even sailed to America (see page 195).

By 800, **Charlemagne** was importing Irish monks to help run his Frankish kingdom. Meanwhile, Ireland remained a relatively cohesive society based on monastic settlements rather than cities. Impressive round towers from those settlements still dot the Irish landscape—silent reminders of this glorious age.

Viking Invasion and Defeat (800–1100)

In 795, Viking pirates from Norway invaded, the first of many raids that wreaked havoc on the monasteries and shook Irish civilization. In two centuries of chaos, the Vikings raped, pillaged, and burned Christian churches. The Vikings prized monastic booty

Stone Circles: The Riddle of the Rocks

Ireland is home to about 250 evocative stone circles. These jaggedly sparse boulder rings are rudimentary in comparison to Britain's more famous Stonehenge. But their misty, mossy settings provide curious travelers with an intimate and accessible glimpse of the mysterious people who lived in Ireland before the arrival of the Celts.

Bronze Age Ireland (2000–600 B.C.) was populated by farming folk who had mastered the craft of smelting heated tin and copper together to produce bronze, which was used to produce more durable tools and weapons. Late in the Bronze Age, many of these primitive clannish communities also chose to put considerable time and effort into gathering huge rocks and arranging them into ceremonial circles for use in long-forgotten rituals. Many scholars believe that these circles may have been used as solar observatories, to calculate solstices and equinoxes, and to plan life-sustaining seasonal crop-planting cycles. Archaeologists have discovered a few ancient burials in the center of some circles, but their primary use seems to have been ceremonial rather than funerary. And without any written records, we can only make educated guesses as to their exact purpose.

In the Middle Ages, superstitious locals believed that the stones had been arranged by an earlier race of giants. Later Puritans thought that at least one circle was made up of petrified

such as gold chalices, silver candlestick holders, and the jeweled book covers of sacred illuminated manuscripts. Monks stood guard from their round towers to spy approaching marauders, ring the warning bells, and protect the citizens. In 841, a conquering Viking band decided to winter in Ireland, building the first permanent walled cities, Dublin and Waterford. Viking raiders slowly evolved into Viking traders, who, among other things, introduced the concept of coinage to the Irish.

Finally, **High King Brian Ború** led a Gaelic revival, defeating a mercenary Viking army allied with rebellious Leinster clans at the Battle of Clontarf (1014), near Dublin. Ború died in the battle, however, and his unified kingdom quickly fell apart. Over the centuries, Viking settlers married Gaelic gals and slowly blended in.

partiers who had dared to dance on the Sabbath. A nearby standing stone was supposed to be the frozen figure of the piper who had been playing the dance tunes.

Irish stone circles are concentrated into two main regional clusters consisting of more than a hundred circles each: central Ulster in the North (radiocarbon-dated 1500–700 B.C.) and Counties Cork and Kerry in the south (radiocarbon-dated 1000–700 B.C.). The remaining two dozen circles are scattered across central Ireland. Some circles have only recently been rediscovered after having been buried by rapidly accumulating bog growth over the centuries.

Dedicated travelers seeking stone circles (while wearing shoes impervious to grass dew and sheep doo) will find them marked in the Ordnance Survey atlas and signposted along rural Irish roads. Ask a local farmer for directions—and savor the experience.

Here are our five favorite Irish stone circles, all within a druid's dance of other destinations mentioned in this book:

Kenmare is in County Kerry, on the western fringe of Kenmare (see map on page 173).

Drombeg is in County Cork, 35 miles southwest of Kinsale, just south of the R-597 coastal road.

Glebe is in County Mayo, two miles northeast of Cong, and 100 yards south of the R-345 road to Neale.

Beltany is in County Donegal, 10 miles southeast of Letterkenny, straight south of Raphoe.

Beaghmore is in County Tyrone, 20 miles east of Omagh, north off A-505 (Cookstown Road).

Anglo-Norman Arrival (1100–1500)

The Normans were Ireland's next uninvited guests. In 1169, a small army of well-armed and fearless soldiers of fortune invaded Ireland under the pretense of helping a deposed Irish king regain

his lands. With the blessing of the only English pope in history (Adrian IV and his papal bull), a Welsh conquistador named **Strongbow** (c. 1130–1176) took Dublin and Waterford, married the local king's daughter, then succeeded his father-in-law as king of Leinster. This was the spearhead of a century-long invasion by the so-called Anglo-Normans—the French-speaking rulers of England, descended from William the Conqueror and his troops, who had invaded and conquered England a hundred years earlier at the Battle of Hastings (1066).

King Henry II of England soon followed (1171) to remind Strongbow who was boss, proclaiming the entire island under English (Anglo-Norman) rule. By 1250, the Anglo-Normans occupied three-quarters of the island, clustered in walled cities surrounded by hostile Gaels. These invaders, who were big-time administrators, ushered in a new age in which society (government, cities, and religious organizations) was organized on a grander scale. They imposed feudalism and scoffed at the old Gaelic clan system that they intended to replace. Riding on the coattails of the Normans, monastic orders (Franciscans, Augustinians, Benedictines, and Cistercians) came over from the Continent and eclipsed Ireland's individual monastic settlements, once the foundation of Irish society in the **Age of Saints and Scholars.**

But English rule was weak and distant. Preoccupied with the Hundred Years' War with France and its own internal Wars of the Roses, England "ruled" through deputized locals such as the earls of Kildare. Many English landowners actually resided in England, a pattern of absentee-landlordism that would exist for centuries. England's laws were fully enforced only in a 50-mile foothold around Dublin (**the Pale**—from the Norman-French word for "ditch"). A couple of centuries after invading, the Anglo-Normans saw their area of control shrink to only the Pale—with the rest of the island "beyond the Pale."

Even as their power eroded, the English kings considered Ireland to be theirs. They passed the **Statutes of Kilkenny** (1366), which outlawed all things Gaelic, including intermarriage with the English settlers, the Gaelic language, and the sport of hurling. In practice, the statutes were rarely enforced.

The End of Gaelic Rule (1500s)

As European powers raced to establish profitable colonies in North and South America, Ireland's location on the eastern edge of the Atlantic became more strategic. England's naval power grew to threaten Spain's monopoly on New World riches. Meanwhile, Spain viewed Ireland as England's vulnerable back door—the best place to attack. (It was similar to the USSR using Cuba to threaten the US in the early 1960s.) Martin Luther's **Reformation** split the Christian churches into Catholic and Protestant, making Catholic Ireland an even hotter potato for newly Protestant England to handle. Catholic Spain (and later France) would use their shared Catholicism with Ireland as divine justification for alliances against heretic England.

In 1534, angered by **Henry VIII** and his break with Catholicism (and taking advantage of England's Reformation chaos), the **earls of Kildare** rebelled, led by Silken Thomas. Henry crushed the revolt, executed the earls, and confiscated their land. Henry's daughter, **Queen Elizabeth I,** gave the land to colonists ("planters"), mainly English Protestants. The next four centuries would see a series of rebellions by Catholic, Gaelic-speaking Irish farmers fighting to free themselves from rule by Protestant, English-speaking landowners.

Hugh O'Neill (1540–1616), a noble angered by planters and English abuses, led a Gaelic revolt in 1595. The rebels were joined by the Spanish, who were fellow Catholics and England's archrival on the high seas. At the Battle of Yellow Ford (1598), guerrilla tactics led to an Irish victory.

But the **Battle of Kinsale** (1601) ended the revolt. The exhausted Irish, who had marched the length of Ireland in winter, arrived to help Spanish troops, who were pinned down inside the town. But the English crushed the Irish before they could join the Spanish, who then surrendered. O'Neill knelt before the conquering general, ceding half a million acres to England. Then he and other proud, Gaelic, Ulster-based nobles unexpectedly abandoned their land and sailed to the Continent (The Flight of the Earls, 1607), an event seen as the symbolic end of Gaelic Irish rule.

English Colonization and Irish Rebellions (1600s)

King James I took advantage of the Gaelic power vacuum and sent 25,000 English and Scottish planters into the confiscated land (1610–1641), making Ulster (in the northeast) the most English area of the island. The Irish responded with two major rebellions.

In 1642, with England embroiled in civil war between a Catholic king and a Protestant Parliament, Irish rebels capitalized on the instability. Tenant farmers took up pitchforks against their English landlords, slaughtering 4,000 in the **Massacre of the Planters** (1641). Irish society was split between an English-speaking landed gentry (descendants of the first Anglo-Norman invaders, called "Old English") and the local Irish-speaking landless, or nearly landless, peasantry. But with Catholicism as their common bond, the Irish forces allied with the Old English against the Protestant Parliament of **Oliver Cromwell.**

Cromwell responded by invading Ireland (1649–1650) with 20,000 men. He conquered the country—brutally. Thousands were slaughtered, priests were tortured, villages were pillaged, and rebels were sold into slavery. Most Catholic Irish landowners, given the choice of "to hell or to Connaught," were exiled to the rocky land west of the River Shannon. Cromwell confiscated 11 million acres of Catholic land to give to English Protestants. (In 1641, Catholics owned 59 percent of Ireland—by 1714 they owned 7 percent.) Cromwell's scorched-earth invasion was so harsh (the "curse of Cromwell"), it still raises hackles in Ireland.

In 1688–1689, rebels again took advantage of England's political chaos. They rallied around Catholic **King James II,** who had been deposed by Parliament in the "Glorious Revolution" of 1688 and then had fled to France. He wound up in Ireland, where he formed an army to retake the crown. In the **Siege of Londonderry,** James' Catholic army surrounded the city—but some local apprentice boys locked them out, and after months of negotiations and a 105-day standoff, James went away empty-handed.

The showdown came at the massive **Battle of the Boyne** (1690), north of Dublin. Catholic James II and his 25,000 men were defeated by the 36,000 troops of Protestant **King William III** of Orange. From this point on, the color orange became a symbol for pro-English, pro-Protestant forces.

As the 17th century came to a close, England had successfully put down every rebellion. To counter Irish feistiness, English legislation became an out-and-out attack on the indigenous Gaelic culture. The English punished the mostly Catholic nation with the **Penal Laws.** Catholics couldn't vote, hold office, buy land, join the army, play the harp, or even own a horse worth more than £5. Catholic education was banned and priests were outlawed. But the Penal Laws were difficult to enforce, and many Catholics were taught at hidden outdoor "hedge schools" and worshipped in private or at secluded "Mass rocks" in the countryside.

Protestant Rule (1700s)

During the 18th century, Ireland thrived under the English. Dublin in the 1700s (pop. 50,000) was Britain's second city, one of Europe's wealthiest and most sophisticated. It's still decorated in Georgian (Neoclassical) style, named for the English kings of the time (consecutive kings George I, II, and III, who ruled for most of the century).

But beyond the Pale surrounding Dublin, rebellion continued to brew. Over time, greed on the top and dissent on the bottom led to more repressive colonial policies. The Enlightenment provided ideas of freedom, and the Revolutionary Age emboldened the Irish masses. Irish nationalists were inspired by budding democratic revolutions in America (1776) and France (1789). The Irish say, "The Tree of Liberty sprouted in America, blossomed in France, and dropped seeds in Ireland." Increasingly, the issue of Irish independence was less a religious question than a political one, as poor, disenfranchised colonists demanded a political voice.

In Dublin, **Jonathan Swift** (1667–1745), the dean of St. Patrick's Cathedral, published his satirical *Gulliver's Travels* with veiled references to English colonialism. He anonymously wrote pamphlets advising, "Burn all that's British, except its coal."

The **Irish Parliament** was an exclusive club, and only Protestant, male landowners could be elected to a seat (only 1 percent of the population qualified). In 1782, led by **Henry Grattan** (1746–1820), the Parliament negotiated limited autonomy from England (while remaining loyal to the king) and fairer treatment of the Catholics. England, chastened by the American Revolution (and soon preoccupied by the French Revolution), tolerated a more-or-less independent Irish Parliament for two decades.

Then, in 1798, came the bloodiest Irish Rebellion. Inspired by the American and French revolutionary successes (with an "if they can do it, so can we" attitude), an idealistic band of Irish rebels rose up. The **United Irishmen** (who wanted to substitute the word "Irishman" in place of the labels Protestant or Catholic) revolted against Britain, led by **Wolfe Tone** (1763–1798), a Protestant Dublin lawyer. Tone, trained in the French Revolution, had gained French aid for the Irish cause. (Though a French naval invasion in 1796 already had failed due to a freakish "Protestant wind" that blew the ships away from Ireland's shores.) The Rebellion was marked by bitter fighting—30,000 died over six weeks—before British troops crushed the revolt.

England tried to solve the Irish problem politically by forcing

Ireland into a "Union" with England as part of a "United Kingdom" (**Act of Union**, 1801). The 500-year-old Irish Parliament was dissolved, becoming part of England's Parliament in London. Catholics were not allowed in Parliament. From then on, "Unionists" have been those who oppose Irish independence, wanting to preserve the country's union with Britain.

Votes, Violence, and the Famine (1800s)

Irish politicians lobbied in the British Parliament for Catholic rights, reform of absentee-landlordism, and for **Home Rule**—i.e., independence. Meanwhile, secret societies of revolutionaries pursued justice through violence.

Daniel O'Connell (1775–1847), known as The Liberator, campaigned for Catholic equality and for repeal of the Act of Union (independence). Having personally witnessed the violence of the French Revolution in 1789 and the 1798 United Irishman

Rebellion, O'Connell chose peaceful, legal means. He was a charismatic speaker, drawing half a million people to one of his "monster meeting" demonstrations at the Hill of Tara (1843). But any hope of an Irish revival was soon snuffed out by the biggest catastrophe in Irish history: the famine.

The **Great Potato Famine** (1845–1849) was caused by a fungus *(Phytophthora infestans)* that destroyed Ireland's main food crop. Roughly a million people starved to death or died of related diseases (estimates range between 500,000 and 1.1 million). Another one to two million emigrated—most to America, and others to Canada and Australia.

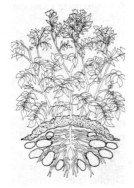

The poorest were hardest hit. Potatoes were their main food source, and any other crops were far too expensive—grown by tenant farmers on their landlords' land to pay the rent and destined for export. (If this makes you mad at the English landlords, consider today's US ownership of land in Central America, where the landlord takes things one step beyond by not growing the local staple at all. He devotes all the land to more profitable cash crops for export, and leaves the landless farmer no alternative but to buy his food—imported from the US—at plantation wages, in the landlord's grocery store.)

Britain—then the richest nation on earth, with an empire stretching around the globe—could seemingly do nothing to help its starving citizens. A toxic combination of laissez-faire economic policies, racial bigotry, and religious self-righteousness conspired to blind the English to the plight of the Irish. While the English tend to blame the famine on overpopulation (Ireland's population doubled in the 40 years leading up to the famine), many Irish say there actually was no famine—just a calculated attempt to starve down the local population. For this reason, devout Irish Nationalists do not refer to this period as "the famine" (implying a lack of food) but rather as "An Gort Mór" (The Great Hunger... imposed by British colonial policies). Over the course of five long years, Ireland was ruined. To this day, Irish weather reports include mention of potential potato-blight conditions.

The population was cut by nearly a third (from 8.4 million to 6 million), many of their best and brightest had fled, and the island's economy—and spirit—took generations to recover. The Irish language, spoken by the majority of the population before the famine, became a badge of ignorance, and was considered useless to those hoping to emigrate. Ireland, which remained one of Europe's poorest countries for over a century, was slow to forget Britain's indifference. Ireland's population has only recently begun to grow again. Irish Nationalists point out that Britain's population, on the other hand, has grown from 12 million in 1845 to around 60 million today.

Before the famine, land was subdivided—each boy got a piece of the family estate (which grew smaller with each generation). After the famine, the oldest son got the estate and the younger siblings, with fewer ways to stay in Ireland (primarily joining the priesthood), emigrated to Britain, Australia, Canada, or the US. Because of the huge emigration to the US (today there are 45 million Irish Americans), Ireland began to face west, and US influence increased. (As negotiations between Northern Ireland and the Irish Republic continue, US involvement in the talks is welcomed and considered essential by nearly all parties.)

Occasional violence demonstrated the fury of Irish nationalism, with the tragedy of the famine inflaming the movement. In 1848, the **Young Irelander** armed uprising was easily squelched. In 1858, the **Irish Republican Brotherhood** was formed (the forerunner of the IRA). Also called the **Fenians,** they launched a campaign for independence by planting terrorist bombs. Irish Americans sent money to help finance these revolutionaries. Uprising after uprising made it clear that Ireland was ready to close this thousand-year chapter of invasions and colonialism.

On the political front, Home Rule Party leader **Charles Stuart Parnell** (1846–1891), an Irishman educated in England, made "the Irish problem" the focus of London's Parliament. Parnell lobbied for independence and for the rights of poor tenant farmers living under absentee landlords, pioneering the first boycott tactics. Then, in 1890, at the peak of his power and about to achieve Home Rule for Ireland, he was drummed out of politics by a scandal involving his mistress, scuttling the Home Rule issue for another 20 years.

Culturally, the old Gaelic, rural Ireland was being swamped by the Industrial Revolution and was dominated by Protestant England. The **Gaelic Athletic Association** was founded in 1884 to resurrect pride in ancient Irish sports such as hurling (see page 67). Soon after, in 1893, writers and educators formed the **Gaelic League** to preserve the traditional language, music, and poetry. Building on the tradition of old Celtic bards, Ireland produced some of the great early-modern writers: **W. B. Yeats, Oscar Wilde, G. B. Shaw,** and **James Joyce,** whose rambling, stream-of-consciousness *Ulysses* chronicles a day in the life of 1904 Dublin, and set new standards for the modern novel (see "Irish Literature" on page 374).

Easter Rising, War of Independence, Partition, and Civil War (1900–1950)

As the century turned, Ireland prepared for the inevitable showdown with Britain.

The **Sinn Fein** party (meaning "We, Ourselves") lobbied politically for independence. The **Irish Volunteers** were more Catholic and more militant. Also on the scene was the **Irish Citizens Army,** with a socialist agenda to clean up Dublin's hideous tenements, where 15 percent of the children died before the age of one.

Of course, many Irish were Protestant and pro-British. The **Ulster Volunteers** (Unionists, and mostly Orangemen) feared that Home Rule would result in a Catholic-dominated state that would oppress the Protestant minority.

Meanwhile, Britain was preoccupied with World War I, where it was "fighting to protect the rights of small nations" (except Ireland's), and so delayed granting Irish independence. The increasingly militant Irish rebels, believing that England's misfortune was Ireland's opportunity, decided to rise up and take independence on their own.

On Easter Monday, April 24, 1916, 1,500 Irish Volunteers, along with members of the Irish Citizens Army, marched on Dublin, occupied the General Post Office, and raised a green, white, and orange flag. The teacher and poet **Patrick Pearse** stood in front of the Post Office and proclaimed Ireland an independent republic.

British troops struck back—in a week of street fighting and intense shelling, some 300 died. By Saturday, the greatly outnumbered rebels had been killed or arrested. The small-scale uprising—which failed to go national and was never even popular in Dublin—was apparently over.

However, the British government overreacted by swiftly executing the 16 ringleaders, including Pearse. Ireland was outraged, no longer seeing the rebels as troublemakers but as martyrs. From this point on, Ireland was resolved to win its independence at all costs. A poem by W. B. Yeats, "Easter 1916," captured the struggle with his words: "All changed, changed utterly: A terrible beauty is born."

In the 1918 elections, the Sinn Fein party won big, but the new Members of Parliament refused to go to London, instead forming their own independent Irish Parliament in Dublin. The following year, Irish rebels ambushed and shot two policemen, sparking two years of confrontations called the **War of Independence.** The fledgling Irish Republican Army faced 40,000 British troops, including the notorious "Black and Tans" (named for the color of their clothes: black for police and tan for army-surplus uniforms). A thousand people died in this war of street fighting, sniper fire, jailhouse beatings, terrorist bombs, and reprisals (for a more detailed timeline of the war and events leading up to it, see the sidebar on page 60).

Finally, Britain, tired of war after more than four years in the meat grinder of World War I, agreed to Irish independence. But Ireland itself was a divided nation—the southern three-quarters of the island was mostly Catholic, Gaelic, rural, and for Home Rule; the northern quarter was Protestant, English, industrial, and Unionist. The solution? In 1920, in the **Government of Ireland Act,** the British Parliament partitioned the island into two independent, self-governing countries within the British Commonwealth: **Northern Ireland** and the **Irish Free State.** While the northern six counties (the only ones without a Catholic majority) chose to stay with Britain as Northern Ireland, the remaining 26 counties became the Irish Free State. (For a review of the ongoing Troubles between the North and the Republic, see the Northern Ireland chapter.)

Ireland's various political factions wrestled with this compromise solution, and the island plunged into a yearlong **Civil War** (1922–1923). The hard-line IRA opposed the partition, unwilling to accept a divided island, an oath of loyalty to the queen, or the remaining British Navy bases on Irish soil. They waged a street war on the armies of the Irish Free State, who supported the political settlement. Dublin and the southeast were ravaged in a year of bitter fighting before the Irish Free State led by **Michael Collins** emerged victorious. The IRA went underground, moving its fight north and trying for the rest of the century to topple the government of Northern Ireland.

In 1937, the Irish Free State severed more ties with the British Commonwealth, writing up a new national constitution and taking an old name—**Éire** (pronounced AIR-uh—a Gaelic word possibly derived from the early Greeks' name for the island, Ierne). Ireland called World War II "The Emergency" and remained neutral. In 1949, the separation was completed, as the Irish Free State officially became the **Republic of Ireland.**

Celtic Tiger in the South, Troubles in the North (1950–2000)

Beginning in 1960, the Republic of Ireland—formerly a poor, rural region—was transformed into a modern, economic power, thanks to foreign investors and, in 1973, membership in the European Union. Through the mid-1990s, Ireland's booming, globalized economy grew a whopping 40 percent, and Dublin's property values tripled (between 1995 and 2005), earning the Republic the nickname "The Celtic Tiger."

Big social changes were also reflected in the 1990 election of Mary Robinson (a lawyer who was outspoken on issues of divorce, contraceptives, and abortion) as the first female president of a once ultraconservative Ireland.

Meanwhile, Northern Ireland—with a 55 percent Protestant majority and a large, 45 percent disaffected Catholic minority —was plagued by the Troubles. In 1967, the Northern Ireland Civil Rights Movement, inspired by the African-American civil rights movement in the US, organized marches and demonstrations demanding equal treatment for Catholics (better housing, job opportunities, and voting rights). Protestant **Unionist Orangemen** countered by marching through Catholic neighborhoods, flaunting their politically dominant position in the name of tradition, and thus provoking riots. In 1969, Britain sent troops to help Northern Ireland keep the peace, and met resistance from the IRA, which saw them as an occupying army supporting the Protestant pro-British majority.

From the 1970s to the 1990s, the North was a low-level battlefield, with the IRA using terrorist tactics to achieve their political ends. The **Troubles,** which claimed some 3,000 lives, continued with bombings, marches, hunger strikes, rock-throwing, and riots (notably Derry's **Bloody Sunday** in 1972), interrupted by cease-fires, broken cease-fires, and a string of peace agreements.

Then came the 1998 watershed settlement known as the **Good Friday Peace Accord** (to pro-Irish Nationalists) or the **Belfast Agreement** (to pro-British Unionists). After years of negotiation, in 2005 the IRA formally announced an end to its armed campaign, promising to pursue peaceful, democratic means to achieve its goals. In 2006, I was stunned to discover that the British Army surveillance towers in Derry—disturbing fixtures since my very first visit—had been torn down. And in spring 2007, the unthinkable happened when **Gerry Adams,** leader of the ultra-Nationalist Sein Fein party, sat down across a table from **Reverend Ian Paisley,** head of the ultra-Unionist DUP party. It was their first face-to-face meeting. Also in 2007, London returned control of Northern Ireland to the popularly elected Northern Ireland Assembly. Perhaps most important of all, after almost 40 years, the British Army withdrew from Northern Ireland that summer.

Global Nations (2000 and Beyond)

Today, both Northern Ireland and the Republic of Ireland have every reason to be optimistic about the future, as their economies boom and the political and cultural Troubles lessen. The formerly isolated island is welcoming tourists with open arms, and reaching out to the rest of the globe. In 1999, the number of tourists visiting Ireland topped the 6 million mark, exceeding for the first time the actual native population on the island (5.7 million).

Visitors returning to Ireland are amazed at the country's transformation. Although there are still some tense areas in the North—as there are in all big cities—the peace process is grinding forward.

Now, for the first time in history, the Irish are importing labor, and they've surpassed the English in per-capita income. Since 1980, when Apple Computer set up its European headquarters here, a stream of multinational and US corporations have opened offices in Ireland. Ireland has one of the youngest populations in Europe. And those young Irish, beneficiaries of one of Europe's best educational systems, provide these corporations with a highly skilled, youthful, and educated workforce. Ireland's pharmaceutical, chemical, and software industries are booming—this little country is second only to the US in the exportation of software.

Of course, with rapid growth come problems. Urban sprawl, big-city traffic snarls, rising housing prices, water and air pollution, and the homogenizing effects of globalization have left their mark. By 2003, the rising economic tide had lifted Ireland to float beside Finland as one of the two most expensive countries in the European Union. Per-capita consumption of alcohol has also tripled since 1970 (the dark side of recent prosperity). Still, the Celtic Tiger, although slightly muffled by the tech bubble bursting, continues to roar.

The challenges of immigration (new arrivals into Ireland) have replaced problems associated with the generations of emigration (young people leaving Ireland). Until recently, Ireland had the most liberal citizenship laws in the European Union, granting Irish citizenship to anyone born on Irish soil (even if neither parent had an Irish passport). This led to a flood of pregnant immigrant women arriving from Eastern Europe and Africa to give birth in Ireland for their children to gain EU citizenship. Families with a child

Irish Brogue with a Polish Accent

As you walk down the street in an Irish city these days, you might be perplexed overhearing an unfamiliar language being spoken by groups of enthusiastic young adults. It's Polish and it may soon be to Ireland what Spanish is to the US: a good language to know if you want to better communicate with a huge immigrant population. Polish food sections are popping up in grocery stores. Bilingual English-Polish menus have made an appearance in some restaurants. And ask that chambermaid or waiter with the unusual accent where they're from. Chances are good they'll say Warsaw or Kraków.

When 10 mostly Eastern European nations joined the EU in 2004, Sweden, Britain and Ireland immediately removed major barriers for employment of these new EU nationals. Ireland's booming economy was yearning for a cheap labor force to fill the growing number of minimum-wage jobs. Hardworking, ambitious young Poles headed west to the land of opportunity. Ireland was their first choice because of its Catholicism, stronger economy, and opportunity to learn English (the international language of business).

Granted, the Poles are not the only Eastern Europeans learning about capitalism, Irish-style. But the numbers of arriving Poles dwarf the number of Slovakians, Latvians, Estonians, and other Eastern Europeans headed to the Emerald Isle. Many Irish have taken to calling them all "Poles," just as many Americans might mistake a Guatemalan or Venezuelan for a "Mexican."

The healthy influx of new blood has added ethnic diversity to Ireland not seen since Spanish Armada sailors washed ashore 400 years ago. The Catholic Church has been reenergized with Poles attending Mass. And intermarriage is creating fun new combinations of names like Bridgit Jaruzelski or Colleen Kraszewski.

born in an EU country face fewer border restrictions, increasing their chances of moving into one of the 27 EU nations. In 2004, the Irish people closed that legal loophole in a referendum vote.

While the Irish are embracing the new economies and industries of the 21st century, when it comes to sex and marriage, many still see their island as an oasis of morality and traditional values (homosexuality was decriminalized only a dozen years ago). The Catholic Church continues to exert a major influence on Irish society. But since the Church no longer controls the legislature, the Irish government—driven by the popular demands of the youngest population in Europe—will undoubtedly push for some changes on the following issues.

Birth Control: People in the US take for granted that birth control is readily available. But Ireland only began allowing the widespread sale of condoms in 1993.

Abortion: In Ireland, women who choose to terminate their pregnancies must go to England for help. Abortion is still illegal in Ireland. And it's only been legal since 1993 to counsel Irish women to go to England for abortions. This was a big issue in 2001, when the Dutch anchored their "abortion ship" in Dublin's harbor, and again in 2002, when a referendum legalizing abortion was narrowly defeated. Watch for more referendums proposing the legalization of abortion. Many Irish refer to this as their next Civil War.

Divorce: Ireland voted to legalize divorce in 1995—but only on very strict conditions. After the divorce papers are signed, it takes a four-year waiting period before the divorce is considered official, and little compensation is offered to Irish women who work as homemakers.

IRISH ART

Megalithic tombs, ancient gold- and metalwork, illuminated manuscripts, high crosses carved in stone, paintings of rural Ireland, and provocative political murals—Ireland comes with some fascinating art. To best appreciate this art in your travels, kick off your tour in Ireland's two top museums (both in Dublin): the **National Museum: Archaeology and History** (see page 53) and **National Gallery** (see page 54). Each provides a good context to help you enjoy Irish art and architecture—from ancient to modern and both rural and urban. Here's a quick survey.

Megalithic Period: During the Stone Age 5,000 years ago, farmers living in the **Valley of the Boyne,** north of Dublin, built a "cemetery" of approximately 40 **burial mounds.** The most famous of these mound tombs is the passage tomb at Newgrange (part of Brú na Bóinne). More than 300 feet in diameter and composed of 200,000 tons of loose stone, Newgrange was constructed so that the light from the winter solstice sunrise (Dec 21) would pass through the eastern entrance to the tomb, travel down a 60-foot passage, and illuminate the inner burial chamber. (Not bad engineering for Stone Age architects.) The effect is now re-created daily, so visitors can experience this ancient ritual of renewal and rebirth any time of year (see the Near Dublin chapter).

Some of Europe's best examples of megalithic (big rock) art are also at Newgrange. Carved on the tomb's stones are zigzags, chevrons, parallel arcs, and concentric spirals. Scholars think these designs symbolize a belief in the eternal cycle of life and the continuation of the life force, or that they pay homage to the elements in nature on which these ancient peoples depended for their existence.

Exploring these burial mounds (only Newgrange and Knowth are open to the public), you begin to understand the reverence that these people had for nature, and the need they felt to bury their dead in these great mound tombs, returning their kin to the womb of Mother Earth.

Bronze Age: As ancient Irish cultures developed from 2000 B.C., so did their metalworking skills. Gold and bronze were used to create **tools, jewelry,** and **religious objects.** (The National Museum: Archaeology and History in Dublin houses the most dazzling of these works—see page 53.) Gold neck rings worn by both men and women, cufflink-like dress fasteners, bracelets, and lock rings (to hold hair in place) are just a few of the personal adornments fashioned by the ancient Irish.

Most of these objects were deliberately buried, often in bogs, as votive offerings to their gods or to prevent warring tribes from stealing them. Like the earlier megaliths, they're decorated with geometric and organic motifs.

Iron Age: The Celts, a warrior society from Central Europe, arrived in Ireland perhaps as early as the seventh century B.C. With their metalworking skills and superior iron weaponry, they soon overwhelmed the native population. And, though the Celts may have been fierce warriors, they wreaked havoc with a flair for the aesthetic. **Shields, swords,** and **scabbards** were embellished with delicate patterns, often enhanced with vivid colors. The dynamic energy of these decorations must have reflected the ferocious power of the Celts.

The Age of Saints and Scholars: Christianity grew in Ireland from St. Patrick's first efforts in the fifth century A.D. In the sixth and seventh centuries, its many great saints (such as St. Columba) established monastic settlements throughout Ireland, Britain, and the Continent, where learning, literature, and the arts flourished. During this "Golden Age" of Irish civilization, monks, along with metalworkers and stonemasons, created imaginative designs and distinctive stylistic motifs for **manuscripts, metal objects,** and **crosses.**

Monks wrote out and richly decorated manuscripts of the Gospels. These manuscripts—which preserved the written word in Latin, Greek, and Irish—eventually had more power than the oral tales of the ancient pagan heroes.

The most beautiful and imaginative of these illuminated manuscripts is the **Book of Kells** (c. A.D. 800), on display in the Old Library at Trinity College in Dublin (see page 46). Crafted by Irish monks at a monastery on the Scottish island of Iona, the book was brought to Ireland for safekeeping from rampaging Vikings. The skins of 150 calves were used to make the vellum, which is painted with rich pigments from plants and minerals. The entire manuscript is colorfully decorated with flat, stylized human or angelic forms and intricate, interlacing animal and knot patterns. Full-page illustrations depict the life of Christ and many pages are given over to highly complex yet symmetrical designs that resemble an Eastern carpet. Many consider this book the finest piece of art from Europe's Dark Ages.

The most renowned metalwork of this period is the **Ardagh Chalice,** dating from the eighth century. Now on display at the National Museum in Dublin, the silver and bronze gilt chalice is as impressive as the Book of Kells. Ribbons of gold wrap around the chalice stem, while intricate knot patterns ring the cup. A magnificent gold ring and a large glass stone on the chalice bottom reflect the desire to please God. (He would see this side of the chalice when the priest drank during the Mass.)

The monks used Irish high crosses to celebrate the triumph

of Christianity and to provide a means of educating the illiterate masses through simple stone carvings. The **Cross of Murdock** (Muiredach's Cross, A.D. 923) is 18 feet tall, towering over the remains of the monastic settlement at Monasterboice (north of Dublin, see page 97). It is but one of many monumental crosses that visitors will discover throughout Ireland. Typically, stone carvers depicted Bible stories and surrounded these with the same intricate patterns seen in the Book of Kells and the Ardagh Chalice.

Early Irish art focused on organic, geometric, and linear designs. Unlike Mediterranean art, Irish art of this early period was not preoccupied with a naturalistic representation of people, animals, or the landscape. Instead, it reflects Irish society's rituals and the elements and rhythms of nature.

The Suppression of Native Irish Art: The English, after invading Ireland in 1169, suppressed Celtic Irish culture. English traditions in architecture, painting, and literature replaced native styles until the late 19th century, when revivals in Irish language, folklore, music, and art began to surface.

Painters in the late 19th and early 20th centuries went to the west of Ireland, which was untouched by English dominance and influence, in search of traditional Irish subject matter.

Jack B. Yeats (1871–1957, brother of the poet W. B. Yeats), Belfast-born painter **Paul Henry** (1876–1958), and **Sean Keating**

(1889–1977) all looked to the west for inspiration. The National Gallery in Dublin holds many of these artists' greatest works, with an entire gallery dedicated to Jack Yeats. Many of his early paintings illustrate scenes of his beloved Sligo. His later paintings are more expressionistic in style and patriotic in subject matter.

Henry's paintings depict the rugged beauty of the Connemara region and its people, with scenes of rustic cottages, mountains, and boglands. Keating, the most political of the three painters, featured patriotic scenes from Ireland's struggle against the English for independence.

Contemporary Irish art is often linked to the social, political, and environmental issues facing Ireland today. Themes include the position of the Church in the daily lives of the modern Irish, the effects of development on the countryside, the changing roles of women in Ireland, and the Troubles. Look for this provocative art at the Irish Museum of Modern Art in Dublin (on Military Road, www.imma.ie) and at city galleries.

Today's Irish respect the artistic process so much so that a provision in the tax system in the Republic of Ireland allows income from art sales to go untaxed. This is one reason many artists immigrate to Ireland.

In Northern Ireland, murals in sectarian neighborhoods (e.g., the Shankill and Falls Roads in Belfast and the Bogside in Derry) are stirring public testaments to the martyrs and to the heroes, to resistance and to confrontation, and to the full reconciliation that continues to elude the people of Northern Ireland. (For more on these murals, see the Derry and County Donegal chapter).

IRISH LITERATURE

Since the Book of Kells, Ireland's greatest contributions to the world of art have been through words. As there was no Irish Gaelic written language, the inhabitants of Ireland were illiterate until Christianity came in the fourth century. Far from ignorant, Celtic society maintained a complex set of laws and historical records and legends...verbally. The druidic priests and bards who passed this rich oral tradition down from generation to generation were the most respected members of the clan, next to the king. After Christianity transformed Ireland into a refuge of literacy (while the rest of Europe crumbled into the Dark Ages), Charlemagne's imported Irish monks invented "minuscule," which became the basis of the lowercase letters we use in our alphabet today. The cultural importance placed on the word (spoken, and for the past 1,500 years, written) is today reflected in the rich output of modern Irish writers.

Three hundred years ago, **Jonathan Swift** created his masterpiece, *Gulliver's Travels,* as an acidic satire of British colonialism, which, ironically, has survived as a children's classic. **William Butler Yeats** dedicated his early writings in the 1880s to the "Celtic Twilight" rebirth of pride in mythic Irish heroes and heroines. His early poems and plays were filled with fairies and idyllic rural innocence. His later poems reflected Ireland's painful transition to independence as "a terrible beauty" was born. His Nobel Prize for

literature (1923) was eventually followed by three more prizewinning Irish authors: **George Bernard Shaw** (1925), **Samuel Beckett** (1969), and **Seamus Heaney** (1995).

Oscar Wilde wrote the darkly fascinating novel *The Picture of Dorian Gray* and the witty play *The Importance of Being Earnest,* making him the toast of London in the 1890s—before the scandal of his homosexuality turned Victorian society against him. Meanwhile, **Bram Stoker** was conjuring up a Gothic thriller called *Dracula.* Most inventive of all, perhaps, was **James Joyce,** who broke new ground and captured literary lightning in a bottle when he developed his complex stream-of-consciousness style in his masterpiece novel, *Ulysses.*

The **Abbey Theatre** (championed by Yeats) was the world's first national theater, built to house plays intended to give a voice to Ireland's flowering playwrights. When **J. M. Synge** staged *The Playboy of the Western World* there in 1907, his unflattering comic portrayal of Irish peasant life (and mention of women's underwear) caused riots. Twenty years later, **Sean O'Casey** provoked more riots at the Abbey when his *Plough and the Stars* production depicted the 1916 Uprising in a way that was at odds with the audience's cherished views of their heroes.

In recent decades, the bittersweet Irish literary parade has been inhabited by tragically volcanic characters like **Brendan Behan,** who exclaimed, "I'm not a writer with a drinking problem...I'm a drinker with a writing problem." Bleak poverty experienced in childhood was the catalyst for **Frank McCourt**'s memorable

Angela's Ashes. Among the most celebrated of today's Irish writers is **Roddy Doyle,** whose feel for working-class Dublin resonates in his novels of contemporary life, like *The Commitments,* as well as in historical slices of life, like *A Star Called Henry.*

IRISH LANGUAGE

The Irish have a rich oral tradition that goes back to their ancient fireside storytelling days. Part of the fun of traveling here is getting an ear for the way locals express themselves. Ask an Irish person for directions and you'll more often than not have an interesting, memorable experience. Being excessively verbal seems to be a fundamental part of being Irish: "How do I know what I think until I hear what I say?"

Irish Gaelic is one of five surviving Celtic languages, along with Scottish Gaelic, Welsh, Breton (spoken in parts of French Brittany), and Cornish (spoken in Cornwall). A couple of centuries ago, there were seven surviving Celtic languages. But two have died out: Manx (the Isle of Man), and Galician (spoken in Northern Spain). Some proud Irish choose to call their native tongue "Irish" instead of "Gaelic" to ensure that there is no confusion with what is spoken in parts of Scotland.

Only 150 years ago, the majority of the Irish population spoke Irish Gaelic. But most of the speakers were of the poor laborer class that, during the famine, either died or emigrated. After the famine, Irish Gaelic was seen as a badge of backwardness. Parents and teachers understood that English was the language that would serve children best when they emigrated to better lives in the US, Canada, Australia, or England. Children in schools wore a tally stick around their necks, and a notch was cut by teachers each time a child was caught speaking Irish. At the end of the day, the child received a whack for each notch in the stick. It wasn't until the resurgence of cultural pride, brought on by the Gaelic League in 1884, that an attempt was made to promote use of the language.

Gaeltacht Regions

AREAS SHOWN IN BLACK
ARE GAELTACHTS

These days, less than 5 percent of the Irish population is fluent in their native tongue. However, it's taken seriously enough that all national laws passed must first be written in Irish, then translated into English. Irish Gaelic can be heard most often in the western counties of Kerry, Galway, and Donegal. Each of these three counties has a slightly different dialect. You'll know you're entering an Irish Gaelic-speaking area when you see a sign saying *Gaeltacht* (GAIL-tekt).

Irish Gaelic doesn't use the letters "j," "k," "x," "q," or "z." And there's no "th" sound—which you can hear today when an Irish person says something like "turdy-tree" (33). There is also no equivalent of the simple words "yes" or "no." Instead, answers are given in the affirmative or negative rephrasing of the question. For example, a question like "Did you mail the letter today?" would be answered with "I did (mail the letter)," rather than a simple "yes." Or "It's a nice day today, isn't it?" would be answered with "It is," or "'Tis."

Irish Place Names

Here are a few words that appear in Irish place names. You'll see these on road signs or at tourist sights.

Irish	Phonetics	English
Alt	ahlt	cliff
An Lár	ahn lar	city center
Ard	ard	high, height, hillock
Baile	BALL-yah	town, town land
Beag	beg	little
Bearna	bar-na	gap
Boireann	burr-en	large rock, rocky area
Bóthar	boh-er	road
Bun	bun	end, bottom
Caiseal	CASH-el	circular stone fort
Caislean	cash-LOIN	castle
Cathair	caht-HAR	circular stone fort, city
Cill	kill	church
Cloch	clockh	stone
Doire	dih-ruh	oak
Droichead	DROCKH-ed	bridge
Drumlin	DRUM-lin	small hill
Dun	doon	fort
Fionn	fin	white, fair-haired person
Gaeltacht	GAIL-tekt	Irish language district
Gall	gaul	foreigner
Garda	gar-dah	police
Gort	gort	field

Irish	Phonetics	English
Inis	in-ish	island
Mileac	mee-luch	low marshy ground
Mór	mor	large
Muck	muck	pig
Oifig an Phoist	UFF-ig un fwisht	post office
Poll	poll	hole, cave
Rath	rath	ancient earthen fort
Ross	ross	peninsula
Sí	shee	fairy mound, bewitching
Slí	slee	route, way
Sliabh	sleeve	mountain
Sraid	shrawd	street
Teach	chockh	house
Trá	traw	beach, strand
Tur	toor	tower

Irish Pleasantries

When you reach the more remote western fringe of Ireland, you're likely to hear folks speaking Irish. Although locals in these areas can readily converse with you in English, it's fascinating to hear their ancient Celtic language spoken. Here are some basic Irish phrases:

Irish	Phonetics	English
Fáilte	FAHLT-shuh	Welcome
Conas ta tu?	CONN-us A-thaw too	How are you?
Go raibh maith agat	guh riv mah AG-ut	Thank you
Slán	slawn	Bye

Irish Pub and Music Words

The Irish love to socialize. Pubs are like public living rooms, where friends gather in a corner to play tunes and anyone is a welcome guest. Here are some useful pub and music words:

Irish	Phonetics	English
Poitín	po-CHEEN	moonshine, homemade liquor
Craic	crack	fun atmosphere, good conversation
Bodhrán	BO-run or BOW-run	traditional drum
Uilleann	ILL-in	elbow (uilleann pipes are elbow bagpipes)
Trad	trad	traditional Irish music
Ceilidh	KAY-lee	Irish dance gathering

Fleadh	flah	music festival
Slainte	SLAWN-chuh or SLAWN-tuh	cheers, to your health
Táim súgach!	thaw im SOO-gakh	I'm tipsy!
Lei thras	LEH-hrass	toilets
Mná	min-AW	women's room
Fír	fear	men's room

Irish Politics

Politics is a popular topic of conversation in Ireland. Whether you pick up a local newspaper or turn on your car radio, you'll often encounter these Irish political terms in the media:

Irish	Phonetics	English
Taoiseach	TEE-shock	Prime Minister of Irish Republic
Seanad	SHAN-ud	Irish Senate
Dáil	DOY-ill	Irish House of Representatives
TD, *Teachta Dála*	TALK-ta DOLL-a	Member of Irish Parliament

IRISH–YANKEE VOCABULARY

If some of these words seem more British than Irish, those are ones you're likely to hear more often in Northern Ireland (part of the UK).

advert—advertisement
anticlockwise—counterclockwise
aubergine—eggplant
banger—sausage
bang on—correct
banjaxed—messed up
bank holiday—legal holiday
beer mat—coaster
bespoke—custom
billion—a thousand of our billions (a trillion)
biro—ballpoint pen
biscuit—cookie
black pudding—sausage made from dried blood
Black Mariah—police van

blather—rambling, empty talk
bloody—damn (from medieval blasphemy: "Christ's blood")
blow off—fart
boffin—nerd
bog—slang for toilet
bolshy—argumentative
bonnet—car hood
boot—car trunk
braces—suspenders
bridle way—path for walkers, bikers, and horse riders
brilliant—cool
bum—bottom or "backside"
busker—street musician
cacks—trousers, underpants

candy floss—cotton candy

caravan—trailer

car boot sale—temporary flea market, often for charity

car park—parking lot

casualty—emergency room

cat's eyes—road reflectors

ceilidh—dance, party

champ—mashed potatoes and onions

chemist—pharmacist

chicory—endive

chippy—fish-and-chips shop

chips—french fries

chock-a-block—jam-packed

chuffed—pleased

cider—alcoholic apple cider

clearway—road where you can't stop

coach—long-distance bus

concession—discounted admission

cos—romaine lettuce

cotton buds—cotton swabs

courgette—zucchini

craic (pronounced "crack")—fun, good conversation

crisps—potato chips

crusties—New Age hippies

culchie—hick, country yokel

cuppa—cup of tea

Da—father

deadly—really good

dear—expensive

digestives—round graham crackers

dinner—lunch or dinner

diversion—detour

dodgy—iffy, risky

done and dusted—completed

donkey's years—until the cows come home, forever

draughts—checkers

draw—marijuana

dual carriageway—divided highway (four lanes)

Dubs—people from Dublin

eejit—moron

en suite—bathroom attached to room

face flannel—washcloth

fair play (to you)—well done, good job

fanny—vagina

fell—hill or high plain

fiddler's fart—worthless thing

first floor—second floor

fluthered—drunk

flutter—a bet

football—Gaelic football

fortnight—two weeks

full monty—the whole shebang, everything

GAA—Gaelic Athletic Association

gallery—balcony

gammon—ham

gangway—aisle

gaol—jail (same pronunciation)

Garda—police

gargle—to have an alcoholic drink

give way—yield

giving out—chewing out, yelling at

glen—valley

gob—mouth

gobsmacked—astounded

goods wagon—freight truck

grand—good, well ("How are you?" "I'm grand, thanks")

gurrier—hooligan

half eight—8:30 (not 7:30)

heath—open treeless land

hen night—bachelorette party

holiday—vacation

homely—likable or cozy

hoover—vacuum cleaner

hurling—Irish field hockey

iced lolly—popsicle

interval—intermission

ironmonger—hardware store

jacket potato—baked potato
jacks—toilet
jars—drinks (alcohol)
jelly—Jell-O
jumble—sale, rummage sale
jumper—sweater
just a tick—just a second
kipper—smoked herring
knackered—exhausted
knickers—ladies' panties
knocking shop—brothel
knock up—wake up or visit
ladybird—ladybug
left luggage—baggage check
let—rent
lift—elevator
listed—protected historic building
lorry—truck
Ma, Mam, Mammy—mother
mac—mackintosh (trench) coat
mangetout—snow peas
mate—buddy (boy or girl)
mean—stingy
minced meat—hamburger
mobile (MOH-bile)—cell phone
mod cons—modern conveniences
naff—dorky, tacky
nappy—diaper
natter—talk and talk
norn iron—Northern Ireland
nought—zero
noughts & crosses—tic-tac-toe
off-license— liquor store
Oirish—exaggerated Irish accent
on offer—for sale
paddywhackery—exaggerated Irish accent
paralytic—passed out drunk
pasty—(PASS-tee) crusted savory (usually meat) pie
pavement—sidewalk

pear-shaped—messed up, gone wrong
petrol—gas
pissed (rude), paralytic, bevvied, wellied, popped up, ratted, -pissed as a newt—drunk
pitch—playing field
plaster—Band-Aid
publican—pub manager
pull—to attract romantic attention
punter—partygoer, customer
put a sock in it—shut up
quay—waterside street, ship offloading area
queue—line
queue up—line up
quick smart—immediately
quid—pound (money in Northern Ireland, worth about $2)
ramps—speed bumps
randy—horny
redundant, made—laid off
return ticket—round-trip
ride—intercourse
ring up—call (telephone)
roundabout—traffic circle
RTE—Irish Republic's broadcast network
rubber—eraser
sanitary towel—sanitary pad
sausage roll—sausage wrapped in a flaky pastry (like a pig in a blanket)
scarlet—embarrassed
Scotch egg—hard-boiled egg wrapped in sausage meat
self-catering—apartment with kitchen
sellotape—Scotch tape
serviette—napkin
session—musical evening
shag—intercourse
shag all—hardly any

single ticket—one-way ticket
skint—broke, poor
skip—Dumpster
slag—to ridicule, tease
smalls—underwear
snogging—kissing, making out
solicitor—lawyer
spanner—wrench
spend a penny—urinate
stag night—bachelor party
starkers—buck naked
starters—appetizers
stick—criticism
stone—14 pounds (weight)
strand—beach
stroppy—bad-tempered
subway—underground pedestrian passageway
sultanas—golden raisins
surgical spirit—rubbing alcohol
sort out—figure out
swede—rutabaga
take the mickey—tease
tatty—worn out or tacky
taxi rank—taxi stand
theatre—live stage
tick—a check mark
tight as a Scotsman (derogatory)—cheapskate
tights—panty hose

tip—public dump
tipper lorry—dump truck
tin—can
to let—for rent
top up—refill a drink or your mobile phone credit
torch—flashlight
towpath—path along a river
trad—traditional music
Travellers—itinerants, once known as Tinkers
turf accountant—bookie
twee—corny, too cute
twitcher—bird watcher
underground—subway
verge—grassy edge of road
victualler—butcher
way out—exit
wean—small child
wee (v.)—urinate
wee (n.)—tiny (in the North)
Wellingtons, wellies—rubber boots
whacked—exhausted
whinge (rhymes with hinge)—whine
witter on—gab and gab
woolies—warm clothes
your man—that guy, this guy
zebra crossing—crosswalk
zed—the letter z

APPENDIX

CONTENTS

RESOURCES

Tourist Information Offices

In the US

Ireland's national tourist office in the US—called **Tourism Ireland**—offers a wealth of information on both the Republic of Ireland and Northern Ireland. Before your trip, get the free general-information packet and request any specific information you want, such as regional and city maps, walking routes, and festival schedules.

Ireland Tourist Office: www.tourismireland.com, info.us @tourismireland.com, tel. 800-223-6470 or 212/418-0800.

In Ireland

Virtually every town in Ireland—both the Republic and Northern Ireland—has a TI. Take full advantage of this service. Arrive (or telephone before it closes) with a list of questions and a proposed sightseeing plan. Pick up maps, brochures, and walking-tour information. For all the help TIs offer, steer clear of their room-finding services (bloated prices, booking fee up to €5, no opinions, and they take a 10 percent cut from your B&B host).

Republic of Ireland: In Dublin, try to get everything you'll need for Ireland in one stop at the TI in the old church on Suffolk Street (see page 38). The general nationwide tourist-information phone number for travelers calling from within Ireland is 1-850-230-330 (and their nationwide room-booking phone number is 1-800-363-626; office open Mon–Sat 9:00–20:00, closed Sun).

Resources from Rick Steves

Guidebooks and Online Updates

This book is updated every year in person. The telephone numbers and hours of sights listed in this book are accurate as of mid-2007—but even with annual updates, things change. For the

very latest, visit www.ricksteves.com /update. Also at my website, you'll find a valuable list of reports and experiences—good and bad—from fellow travelers (www.ricksteves.com /feedback).

This book is one of more than 30 titles in my series on European travel, which includes country guidebooks (such as my Great Britain guide, which covers nearby Wales, Scotland, and England), city and regional guidebooks, and my budget-

travel skills handbook, *Rick Steves' Europe Through the Back Door*. My phrase books—for French, Italian, German, Spanish, and Portuguese—are practical and budget-oriented. My other books are *Europe 101* (a crash course on art and history, newly expanded and in full color), *European Christmas* (on traditional and modern-day celebrations), and *Postcards from Europe* (a fun memoir of my travels over 25 years). For a complete list of my books, see the inside of the last page of this book.

Public Television and Radio Shows

My TV series, *Rick Steves' Europe*, covers European destinations in 70 shows, with four episodes on Ireland. My weekly public radio show, *Travel with Rick Steves*, features interviews with travel experts from around the world, including several hours on Ireland and Irish culture. All the TV scripts and radio shows (which are easy and free to download to an MP3 player) are at www.ricksteves.com.

Appendix

Begin Your Trip at www.ricksteves.com

At our travel website, you'll find a wealth of free information on European destinations, including fresh monthly news and

helpful tips from thousands of fellow travelers.

Our **online Travel Store** offers travel bags and accessories specially designed by Rick Steves to help you travel smarter and lighter. These include Rick's popular carry-on bags (wheeled and rucksack versions), money belts, totes, toiletries kits, adapters, other accessories, and a wide selection of guidebooks, planning maps, and DVDs.

Choosing the right **railpass** for your trip—amidst hundreds of options—can drive you nutty. We'll help you choose the best pass for your needs, plus give you a bunch of free extras.

Rick Steves' Europe Through the Back Door travel company offers **tours** with more than two dozen itineraries and 450 departures reaching the best destinations in this book... and beyond. We offer a 14-day Ireland tour, as well as multiple tours in nearby England, Wales, and Scotland. You'll enjoy great guides, a fun bunch of travel partners (with small groups of generally around 25), and plenty of room to spread out in a big, comfy bus. You'll find European adventures to fit every vacation length. For all the details, and to get our Tour Catalog and a free Rick Steves Tour Experience DVD (filmed on location during an actual tour), visit www.ricksteves.com or call the Tour Department at 425-608-4217.

Free Audiotours

If your travels take you beyond Ireland to France or Italy, take advantage of the free, self-guided audiotours we offer of the major

sights in Paris, Florence, Rome, and Venice. The audiotours, produced by Rick Steves and Gene Openshaw (the co-author of seven books in the Rick Steves series) are available through iTunes and at www.ricksteves.com (Italy tours available after January 2008). Simply download them onto your computer and transfer them to your iPod or MP3 player. (Remember to bring a Y-jack and extra set of ear buds for your travel partner.)

Maps

The black-and-white maps in this book, drawn by Dave Hoerlein, are concise and simple. Dave, who is well traveled in Ireland, has designed the maps to help you locate recommended places and get to the TIs, where you'll find more in-depth, cheap (or free) maps. Better maps are sold at newsstands—take a look before you buy to be sure the map has the level of detail you want.

Train travelers can do fine with a simple rail map (available as part of the free Intercity Timetable found at Irish train stations) and city maps from TIs. (You can get free maps of Dublin and Ireland from Tourism Ireland before you go; see "Tourist Information Offices" at the beginning of this chapter.) If you're driving, get a road atlas covering all of Ireland. Ordnance Survey maps are best, available for about €12.50 in TIs, gas stations, and bookstores. Drivers, hikers, and cyclists may want more detailed maps for Dingle, Connemara, Donegal, Wexford, the Antrim Coast, the Ring of Kerry, and the Valley of the Boyne (easy to buy locally at TIs).

Other Guidebooks

If you're like most travelers, this book is all you need. But racks of fine guidebooks are sold at bookstores throughout Ireland and in the US, and each place you will visit has plenty of great little guidebooks to fill you in on local history. You may want some supplemental travel guidebooks, especially if you're traveling beyond my recommended destinations. When you consider the improvements they'll make in your $3,000 vacation, $30 for extra maps and books is money well spent. Especially for several people traveling by car, the extra weight and expense are negligible.

For cultural and sightseeing background in bigger chunks, Michelin and Cadogan guides to Ireland are good. The Lonely Planet and Let's Go books on Ireland are fine budget-travel guides, although neither is updated annually; check the publication date before you buy. Lonely Planet's guidebook is more thorough and informative; *Let's Go Ireland* is youth-oriented, with good coverage of nightlife, hostels, and cheap transportation deals. Also consider *Culture Shock: Ireland* and *Living Abroad in Ireland*, especially if you'll be in the Emerald Isle for an extended stay.

Recommended Books and Movies

To get the feel of Ireland past and present, consider reading some of these books:

Non-Fiction

For a quick overview, Richard Killeen's *A Short History of*

Ireland is a well-illustrated walk through key events. *Ireland: A Concise History* (O'Brien) is just that, while *How the Irish Saved Civilization* (Cahill) shows how this "island of saints and scholars" changed the course of world history. In *Traveller's History of Ireland*, Peter Neville leads readers on a tour through Ireland's complicated history.

Frank McCourt's autobiography, *Angela's Ashes,* recounts his impoverished childhood in 1930s Limerick. *Are You Somebody? The Accidental Memoir of a Dublin Woman* (Faolain) and *To School Through the Fields* (Taylor) are well-written memoirs. Two New Yorkers move to a tiny Irish village in *O Come Ye Back to Ireland* (first in a series of four books by Williams and Breen). For a humorous jaunt through the Irish countryside read *Round Ireland with a Fridge* (Hawks) or *The Back of Beyond: A Search for the Soul of Ireland* (Roy).

Fiction

Ireland is the home to its share of great writers, among them masters such as James Joyce (try his *Dubliners* for a look at Irish life in the 1900s), Oscar Wilde, Jonathan Swift, W. B. Yeats, George Bernard Shaw, and Samuel Beckett. Other classic Irish authors include Brendan Behan, Oliver Goldsmith, Thomas Kinsella, and Seamus Heaney.

Edward Rutherfurd's thick, two-part *Dublin Saga* traces key events in Irish history from A.D. 430 to the fight for independence. Other historical epics include *Trinity* (Uris), *The Last Prince of Ireland* (Llewelyn), and *Ireland* (Delaney).

The Bódhran Makers (Keane) is a heartwarming look at poor families in 1950s Ireland. Roddy Doyle's gritty novels, such as *The Barrytown Trilogy* and *A Star Called Henry,* capture the day-to-day life of working-class Dubliners. Also set in Dublin, *Finbar's Hotel* and *Ladies' Night at the Finbar's Hotel* (Bolger) were written collaboratively, with each chapter penned by a different modern Irish author. Consider also any of Maeve Binchy's soapy novels such as *Circle of Friends.*

Films

The Quiet Man (1952), starring John Wayne as a disgraced boxer, remains a sentimental favorite. David Lean's epic WWI love story *Ryan's Daughter* (1970) was filmed near Dingle. For hard-hitting drama, see *The Field* (1991, an Irish farmer fights to keep his land) or *Angela's Ashes* (1999, based on the Frank McCourt memoir). In *Evelyn* (2002), single-dad Pierce Brosnan goes to court to keep his kids, and unwed mothers struggle to survive the harsh life of a 1960s nunnery in *The Magdalene Sisters* (2003).

For insight into the struggle for independence from Britain, see

Michael Collins (1996, Liam Neeson), a biopic about the Irish Free State revolutionary, and *The Wind that Shakes the Barley* (2006), told through the story of two brothers. *Odd Man Out* (1947) is a film noir about the early IRA, with a great scene filmed in Belfast's Crown Bar. The Troubles haunt a widow and her lover in *Cal* (1984). *In the Name of the Father* (1993, Daniel Day-Lewis) is a biopic of accused bomber Gerry Conlon. The families of IRA hunger strikers are the focus of *Some Mother's Son* (1996), while the documentary-like *Omagh* (2004) recounts a deadly 1998 IRA bombing.

Equally bleak but worthwhile films include *My Left Foot* (1989), which garnered an Academy Award for Daniel Day-Lewis, and *Veronica Guerin* (2003), in which Cate Blanchett fights corruption as a journalist.

For a fun, throw-away romantic film, try *Far and Away* (1992), with Tom Cruise and Nicole Kidman as penniless Irish immigrants. For a comedic break, watch at least one of the films adapted from books by Roddy Doyle: *The Commitments* (1991), *The Snapper* (1993), or *The Van* (1996). In *Waking Ned Devine* (1998), a deceased villager wins the lottery (it's funnier than it sounds). Children bring Irish folk tales to life in *Into the West* (1993) and *The Secret of Roan Inish* (1995).

MONEY MATTERS

Damage Control for Lost Cards

If you lose your credit, debit, or ATM card, you can stop people from using it by reporting the loss immediately to the respective global customer-assistance centers. Call these 24-hour US numbers collect: Visa (410/581-9994), MasterCard (636/722-7111), and American Express (623/492-8427).

At a minimum, you'll need to know the name of the financial institution that issued you the card, along with the type of card (classic, platinum, or whatever). Providing the following information will allow for a quicker cancellation of your missing card: full card number, whether you are the primary or secondary cardholder, the cardholder's name exactly as printed on the card, billing address, home phone number, circumstances of the loss or theft, and identification verification (your birth date, your mother's maiden name, or your Social Security number—memorize this, don't carry a copy). If you are the secondary cardholder, you'll also need to provide the primary cardholder's identification-verification details. You can generally receive a temporary card within two or three business days in Europe.

If you promptly report your card lost or stolen, you typically won't be responsible for any unauthorized transactions on your account, although many banks charge a liability fee of $50.

Tipping

Tipping in Ireland isn't as automatic and generous as it is in the US, but for special service, tips are appreciated, if not expected. As in the US, the proper amount depends on your resources, tipping philosophy, and the circumstance, but some general guidelines apply.

Restaurants: At pubs where you order at the counter, you don't have to tip. At a pub or restaurant with wait staff, check the menu or your bill to see if the service is included; if not, tip about 10 percent.

Taxis: To tip the cabbie, round up. For a typical ride, round up to a maximum of 10 percent (to pay a €4.50 fare, give €5; or for a €28 fare, give €30). If the cabbie hauls your bags and zips you to the airport to help you catch your flight, you might want to toss in a little more. But if you feel like you're being driven in circles or otherwise ripped off, skip the tip.

Special Services: It's thoughtful to tip a euro to someone who shows you a special sight and who is paid in no other way. Tour guides at public sites often hold out their hands for tips after they give their spiel; if I've already paid for the tour, I don't tip extra, though some tourists do give a euro, particularly for a job well done. I don't tip at hotels, but if you do, give the porter about a euro for carrying bags and leave a couple of euros in your room at the end of your stay for the maid if the room was kept clean. In general, if someone in the service industry does a super job for you, a tip of a euro or two is appropriate...but not required.

When in doubt, ask. If you're not sure whether (or how much) to tip for a service, ask your hotelier or the TI; they'll fill you in on how it's done on their turf.

Getting a VAT Refund

As is the case throughout the European Union, wrapped into the purchase price of your Irish souvenirs is a Value Added Tax (VAT) of about 21 percent. If you purchase goods at a store that participates in the VAT-refund scheme, you're entitled to get most of that tax back. Getting your refund is usually straightforward and, if you buy a substantial amount of souvenirs, well worth the hassle. If you're lucky, the merchant will subtract the tax when you make your purchase. (This is more likely to occur if the store ships the goods to your home.) Otherwise, you'll need to:

Get the paperwork. Have the merchant completely fill out the necessary refund document, called a "Tax-Free Shopping Cheque." You'll have to present your passport at the store.

Get your stamp at the border or airport. Process your cheque(s) at your last stop in the EU (e.g., at the airport) with the customs agent who deals with VAT refunds. It's best to keep your purchases in your carry-on for viewing, but if they're too large or dangerous (such as knives) to carry on, track down the proper customs agent to inspect them before you check your bag. You're not supposed to use your purchased goods before you leave. If you show up at customs wearing your new Irish sweater, officials might look the other way—or deny you a refund.

Collect your refund. You'll need to return your stamped document to the retailer or its representative. Many merchants work with services, such as Global Refund (www.globalrefund.com) or Premier Tax Free (www.premiertaxfree.com), which have offices at major airports, ports, or border crossings. These services, which extract a 4 percent fee, can refund your money immediately in your currency of choice or credit your card (within two billing cycles). If the retailer handles VAT refunds directly, it's up to you to contact the merchant for your refund. You can mail the documents from home, or quicker, from your point of departure (using a stamped, addressed envelope you've prepared or one that's been provided by the merchant)—and then wait. It could take months.

Customs for American Shoppers

You are allowed to take home $800 worth of items per person duty-free, once every 30 days. The next $1,000 is taxed at a flat 3 percent. After that, you pay the individual item's duty rate. You can also bring in duty-free a liter of alcohol (slightly more than a standard-size bottle of wine; you must be at least 21), 200 cigarettes, and up to 100 non-Cuban cigars. Food in cans or sealed jars is permissible as long as no meat is included. Some, but not all, types of cheese are allowed. Fresh fruits and vegetables are prohibited. Note that you'll need to carefully pack any bottles of wine and other liquid-containing items in your checked luggage, due to the three-ounce limit on liquids in carry-on baggage. To check customs rules and duty rates before you go, visit www.cbp.gov, and click on "Travel," then "Know Before You Go."

TELEPHONES, EMAIL, AND MAIL

Telephones

Smart travelers learn the phone system and use it daily to reserve or reconfirm rooms, get tourist information, reserve restaurants, confirm tour times, or phone home.

Types of Phones

You'll encounter various kinds of phones in Ireland:

Irish public pay phones are easy to find and easy to use, but relatively expensive. Phones are either coin- or card-operated. They clearly list which coins they'll take, and a display shows how your money supply's doing. Only completely unused coins will be returned, so put in biggies with caution. (If money's left over, rather than hanging up, push the "make another call" button.)

As more people switch to cell phones, the maintenance of public phones has been neglected. Be prepared to encounter the occasional dead phone (without a dial tone) in both urban and rural phone booths.

Hotel room phones, rare in B&Bs, can be fairly cheap for local calls, but expensive for international calls—unless you use an international phone card (see below).

American mobile phones work in Europe if they're GSM-enabled, tri-band (or quad-band), and on a calling plan that includes international calls. They're convenient but pricey. For example, with a T-Mobile phone, you'll pay $1 per minute for calls. If your phone works in Europe, ask about getting it "unlocked" so you can buy an Irish SIM card (a fingernail-sized chip that holds the phone's information, available at mobile-phone stores) to make calls cheaply abroad.

Irish mobile phones are sold with prepaid calling time, which you can add money to as you use up your credit. The cheapest new phones cost around $60 plus about $20 for the necessary SIM card to make it work (includes some prepaid calling time). Incoming

calls are free within the Republic with an Irish mobile phone, and outgoing domestic calls generally run about €0.30 per minute, including to Northern Ireland. If you're traveling to multiple countries within Europe, make sure the phone is electronically "unlocked," so that you can swap out its SIM card for a new one when you cross the border.

For more information on mobile phones, see www.ricksteves .com/plan/tips/mobilephones.htm.

Using Phone Cards

For calls within Ireland, consider buying a **Telecom Éireann phone card** (€4, €7, or €15 at newsstands, TIs, and post offices). Insert the card into the phone and dial away.

Prepaid **international calling cards** are the cheapest way to make international calls from Ireland (they also work for domestic calls). The cards are sold at many post offices, newsstands, mini-marts, and exchange bureaus. Some are rechargeable (you can call up the number on the card, give your credit-card number, and buy more time). There are many different brands, so ask the clerk which one has the best rates to the States. Because cards are occasionally duds, avoid the high denominations.

You can use these cards from anywhere, including most hotel rooms (if your phone is set on "pulse," switch it to "tone"), avoiding pricey hotel rates. Make sure, however, that your hotel isn't overcharging you to dial the access number.

To use a card, scratch off the back to reveal your code. After you dial the access phone number, the message tells you to enter your code and then dial the phone number you want to call. To call the US, see "Dialing Internationally," below. To make calls within Ireland, dial the area code plus the local number; when using an international calling card, the area code must be dialed even if you're calling across the street. International calling cards work only within the country of purchase, with the exception of some brands of cards, which are usable in both the Republic of Ireland and the UK. But confirm before buying a card by checking for both a 1800 access number (used in the Republic of Ireland) and an 0800 access number (for the UK).

To make numerous, successive calls with an international calling card without having to redial the long access number each time, press the keys (see instructions on card) that allow you to launch directly into your next call. Remember that you don't need the actual card to use a card account, so it's sharable. You can write down the access number and PIN (Personal Identification Number) in your notebook and share it with friends. Give the number of a still lively card to another traveler if you're leaving the country.

Using Hotel-Room Phones, VoIP, or US Calling Cards

The phone in your **hotel room** is convenient...but expensive. While incoming calls (made by folks back home) can be the cheapest way to keep in touch, charges for *outgoing* calls can be a very unpleasant surprise. Make sure you understand all the charges and fees associated with outgoing calls before you pick up that receiver.

Dialing direct from your hotel room—without using an international phone card (described above)—is usually quite pricey for international calls. Before you dial, get a clear explanation from the hotel staff of the charges, even for local and (supposedly) toll-free calls.

If your family has an inexpensive way to call Europe, either through a long-distance plan or prepaid calling card, have them call you in your hotel room. Give them a list of your hotels' phone numbers before you go. Then, as you travel, send them an email or make a quick pay-phone call to set up a time for them to give you a ring.

If you're traveling with a laptop, consider trying **VoIP (Voice over Internet Protocol)**. With VoIP, two computers act as the phones, allowing for a free Internet-based call. The major providers are Skype (www.skype.com) and Google Talk (www.google.com /talk).

US Calling Cards (such as the ones offered by AT&T, MCI, or Sprint) are the worst option. You'll nearly always save a lot of money by paying with a phone card (see above).

How to Dial

Calling from the US to Ireland, or vice versa, is simple—once you break the code. The European calling chart on page 394 will walk you through it.

Dialing Long Distance Within Ireland

Ireland, like much of the US, uses an area-code dialing system. If you're dialing within an area code, you just dial the local number to be connected; but if you're calling outside your area code, you have to dial both the area code (which starts with a 0) and the local number.

You'll find area codes listed throughout this book, or you can get them from directory assistance (dial 11811 in the Republic, 192 in Northern Ireland).

The Republic of Ireland has a special way to call Northern Ireland: dial 048, then the local number without the area code. For instructions on how to call the Republic of Ireland from Northern Ireland, see "Dialing Internationally" below.

Dialing Internationally

I've listed below the sequence of numbers you'll need to make your calls. For a handy online dialing tool for international calls, check out www.countrycallingcodes.com.

Calling from the US or Canada to the Republic of Ireland: Dial 011-353, then the area code without its initial 0, then the local number. For example, Dublin's area code is 01. To call one of my recommended Dublin hotels from the US, dial 011 (US international access code), 353 (the Republic of Ireland's country code), 1 (Dublin's area code without its initial 0), then 679-6500 (the hotel's number).

From European countries—including Northern Ireland— to the Republic of Ireland: Dial 00-353, then the area code without its initial 0, then the local number.

From the US or Canada to Northern Ireland: Dial 011-44-28 (28 is Northern Ireland's area code without its initial 0), then the local number.

From the Republic of Ireland to Northern Ireland: Dial 048, then the local number. (In this case, Northern Ireland's area code, 028, is omitted entirely.)

From any European Country (except the Republic of

European Calling Chart

Just smile and dial, using this key:
AC = Area Code, LN = Local Number.

European Country	Calling long distance within ...	Calling from the US or Canada to ...	Calling from a European country to ...
Austria	AC + LN	011 + 43 + AC (without the initial zero) + LN	00 + 43 + AC (without the initial zero) + LN
Belgium	LN	011 + 32 + LN (without initial zero)	00 + 32 + LN (without initial zero)
Bosnia-Herzegovina	AC + LN	011 + 387 + AC (without initial zero) + LN	00 + 387 + AC (without initial zero) + LN
Britain	AC + LN	011 + 44 + AC (without initial zero) + LN	00 + 44 + AC (without initial zero) + LN
Croatia	AC + LN	011 + 385 + AC (without initial zero) + LN	00 + 385 + AC (without initial zero) + LN
Czech Republic	LN	011 + 420 + LN	00 + 420 + LN
Denmark	LN	011 + 45 + LN	00 + 45 + LN
Estonia	LN	011 + 372 + LN	00 + 372 + LN
Finland	AC + LN	011 + 358 + AC (without initial zero) + LN	999 + 358 + AC (without initial zero) + LN
France	LN	011 + 33 + LN (without initial zero)	00 + 33 + LN (without initial zero)
Germany	AC + LN	011 + 49 + AC (without initial zero) + LN	00 + 49 + AC (without initial zero) + LN
Greece	LN	011 + 30 + LN	00 + 30 + LN
Hungary	06 + AC + LN	011 + 36 + AC + LN	00 + 36 + AC + LN
Ireland	AC + LN	011 + 353 + AC (without initial zero) + LN	00 + 353 + AC (without initial zero) + LN

European Country	Calling long distance within ...	Calling from the US or Canada to ...	Calling from a European country to ...
Italy	LN	011 + 39 + LN	00 + 39 + LN
Montenegro	AC + LN	011 + 382 + AC (without initial zero) + LN	00 + 382 + AC (without initial zero) + LN
Netherlands	AC + LN	011 + 31 + AC (without initial zero) + LN	00 + 31 + AC (without initial zero) + LN
Norway	LN	011 + 47 + LN	00 + 47 + LN
Poland	LN	011 + 48 + LN (without initial zero)	00 + 48 + LN (without initial zero)
Portugal	LN	011 + 351 + LN	00 + 351 + LN
Slovakia	AC + LN	011 + 421 + AC (without initial zero) + LN	00 + 421 + AC (without initial zero) + LN
Slovenia	AC + LN	011 + 386 + AC (without initial zero) + LN	00 + 386 + AC (without initial zero) + LN
Spain	LN	011 + 34 + LN	00 + 34 + LN
Sweden	AC + LN	011 + 46 + AC (without initial zero) + LN	00 + 46 + AC (without initial zero) + LN
Switzerland	LN	011 + 41 + LN (without initial zero)	00 + 41 + LN (without initial zero)
Turkey	AC (if no initial zero is included, add one) + LN	011 + 90 + AC (without initial zero) + LN	00 + 90 + AC (without initial zero) + LN

- The instructions above apply whether you're calling a land line or mobile phone.
- The international access codes (the first numbers you dial when making an international call) are 011 if you're calling from the US or Canada, or 00 if you're calling from virtually anywhere in Europe (except Finland, where it's 999).
- To call the US or Canada from Europe, dial 00, then 1 (the country code for the US and Canada), then the area code and number. In short, 00 + 1 + AC + LN = Hi, Mom!

Ireland) to Northern Ireland: Dial 00-44-28 (Northern Ireland's area code without its initial 0), then the local number.

   From anywhere in Ireland (Republic and Northern Ireland) to the US or Canada: 00-1, then the area code and local number. To call my office in the US from Ireland, I dial 00 (Ireland's international access code), 1 (US country code), 425 (Edmonds' area code), then 771-8303.

Useful Numbers in the Republic of Ireland

Note that calls beginning with 1-800 are free throughout Ireland, but 1-850 calls cost the same as local calls.
Emergency: tel. 999
Operator Assistance: tel. 10 for Ireland, tel. 114 to call outside Ireland
Directory Assistance Within Ireland: tel. 11811 (free from phone booth)
International Info: tel. 11818 (free from phone booth)

Useful Numbers in Northern Ireland

Emergency (police and ambulance): tel. 999
Operator Assistance: tel. 100 for Britain, tel. 155 to call outside Britain
Directory Assistance Within Britain: tel. 192 (20p from phone booth, otherwise £1.50)
International Info: tel. 153 (20p from phone booth, otherwise £1.50)

US Embassies

In the Republic of Ireland: 42 Elgin Road, Dublin, Mon–Tue and Thu–Fri 8:30–11:30, closed Wed and Sat–Sun, tel. 01/668-7122 or 01/668-8777, http://dublin.usembassy.gov
In Northern Ireland: Danesfort House, 223 Stranmillis Road, Belfast, tel. 028/9038-6100, http://london.usembassy.gov/nireland

Airlines

These are phone numbers for the Republic of Ireland. (To call the special 1-800 numbers from the US, dial 011-353, then the 800 number without the initial 1).
Aer Arann: tel. 081-821-0210 (www.aerarann.com)
Aer Lingus: tel. 081-836-5000 (www.aerlingus.com)
American: tel. 01/602-0550 (www.aa.com)
bmi british midland: tel. 01/407-3036 (www.flybmi.com)
British Airways: tel. 1-890-626-747 (www.ba.com)
Continental Airlines: tel. 1-890-925-252 (www.continental.com)

Delta: tel. 01/407-3165 (www.delta.com)
Lufthansa: tel. 01/844-5544 (www.lufthansa.ie)
Ryanair (cheap fares): tel. 081-830-3030 (www.ryanair.com)
Scandinavian Airlines System (SAS): tel. 01/844-5440
(www.scandinavian.net)
United Airlines: tel. 01/819-1760 (www.united.com)
Virgin Atlantic: tel. 01/500-5500 (www.virginatlantic.com)

Dublin Car-Rental Agencies

Avis: 35–39 Old Kilmainham Road, tel. 021/428-1111, airport tel.
01/605-7500, www.avis.ie
Hertz: 151 South Circular Road, tel. 01/676-7476, airport tel.
01/844-5466, www.hertz.ie
Budget: 151 Lower Drumcondra Road, tel. 01/837-9611,
central reservations tel. 09066/27711, airport tel. 01/844-5150,
www.budget.ie
Europcar: 2 Haddington Road, tel. 01/614-2888, airport tel.
01/812-0410, www.europcar.ie

Email and Mail

Email: Many travelers set up a free email account with Yahoo, Microsoft (Hotmail), or Google (Gmail). Internet cafés are easy to find in big cities. Most of the towns where I've listed accommodations in this book also have Internet cafés. Many libraries offer free access, but they also tend to have limited opening hours, restrict your online time to 30 minutes, and may require reservations. Look for the places listed in this book, or ask the local TI, computer store, or your B&B host. Some hotels have a dedicated computer for guests' email needs. Small places are accustomed to letting clients (who've asked politely) sit at their desk for a few minutes just to check their email.

If you're traveling with a laptop, you'll find that Wi-Fi, or wireless Internet access, is gradually being installed in many hotels and progressive B&Bs. Most are free, while others charge by the minute.

Mail: Get stamps at the neighborhood post office, newsstands within fancy hotels, and some mini-marts and card shops. To arrange for mail delivery, reserve a few hotels along your route in advance and give their addresses to friends. Allow 10 days for a letter to arrive. Phoning and emailing are so easy that I've dispensed with mail stops altogether.

TRANSPORTATION

By Car or Train?

To see all of Ireland, especially the sights with far-flung rural charm, I prefer the freedom of a rental car. Connemara, the Ring of Kerry, the Antrim Coast, Donegal, Wexford, and the Valley of the Boyne are really only worth it if you have wheels. Cars are best for three or more traveling together (especially families with small kids), those packing heavy, serious photographers (who want to get off the beaten track), and those scouring the countryside. Trains and buses are best for solo travelers, blitz tourists, and city-to-city travelers.

Travelers who don't want (or can't afford) to drive a rental car find they still enjoy their travels using public transportation. Most rail lines spoke outward from Dublin, so you'll need to mix in bus transportation to bridge the gaps. Ireland has a good train-and-bus system, though departures are not as frequent as the European norm. Buses pick you up when the trains let you down.

Rails, Wheels, and Wings in Ireland

Schedules: The best overall source of schedules for public transportation in the Republic as well as Northern Ireland—including rail, cross-country and city buses, and Dublin's DART and LUAS transit—is the Discover Ireland website: www.iol.ie/~discover/rail.htm.

Trains: Ireland's various passes offer a better value than BritRail's pricey "BritRail plus Ireland" pass (see chart on page 400). Irish railpasses can be purchased easily and cheaply in Ireland at major stations (Dublin info tel. 01/836-6222).

Most tourists do not travel enough in Ireland to make a rail or bus pass pay off. Chances are you'll save money by buying point-to-point tickets as you go. Fares are often higher for peak travel on Fridays and Sundays. To avoid long station lines in Dublin, you can book train tickets in advance by phone with your credit card or in person at the Iarnrod Éireann Travel Centre (Mon–Fri 9:00–17:00, closed Sat–Sun, 35 Lower Abbey Street, tel. 01/703-4070).

Research options in advance by studying Irish train schedules at www.irishrail.ie or listening to a recorded timetable at 01/805-4222.

Students are eligible for an **Irish Rail Student Travelcard** (which offers varying discounts per ride), but you have to plan a couple months ahead: Go to www.studenttravelcard.ie, print the application form, get it stamped at your university student-travel office, and mail it to Ireland (include two passport photos and €12, payable by credit card; they'll mail you the card in 4–6 weeks).

Buses: Buses are about a third slower than trains, but they're

Public Transportation in Ireland

also a lot cheaper. Round-trip bus tickets usually cost less than two one-way fares (i.e., Tralee to Dingle costs €9 one-way and €15 round-trip). The Irish distinguish between "buses" (for local runs with lots of stops) and "coaches" (long-distance express runs). On some Irish buses, sports games are piped throughout the bus; have earplugs handy if you prefer silence.

If you're going from Dublin to Dingle without a car, you'll need to take a train to Tralee and then catch a bus from there. From Dublin to Kinsale without a car, you'll need to take a train to Cork and then a bus from there.

If you're traveling up and down Ireland's west coast, buses are best (or a combination of buses and trains); relying on rail-only here is too time-consuming. Note that some rural coach stops are by "request only." This means the coach will drive right on by unless you flag it down by extending your arm straight out, with

Railpasses

Prices listed are for 2008 and are subject to change. For the latest prices, details, and train schedules (and easy online ordering), see my comprehensive *Guide to Eurail Passes* at www.ricksteves.com/rail.

BRITRAIL PLUS IRELAND PASS

	1st Class	2nd Class
5 days in 1 month	$601	$407
10 days in 1 month	1,059	711

This pass covers the entire British Isles (England, Wales, Scotland, Northern Ireland, and the Republic of Ireland). No longer covers ferries. Consider the BritRail passes (online) over the 10-day version. The fare for kiddies 5–15 is half the fare. Kids under age 5 travel free.

IRELAND PASS— REPUBLIC ONLY

	1st Class	2nd Class Senior	2nd Class
5 days in 1 month	$220	$166	$187

Map key:
Approximate point-to-point one-way second-class fares in US dollars by rail (solid line), bus (dashed line), and ferry (dotted line). First class costs 50 percent more. Add up fares for your itinerary to see whether a rail and/or bus pass will save you money.

DEALS ONCE YOU GET TO IRELAND:

These local specials are sold at major train stations in Ireland. €1 = about $1.50 US.

Pass Name	Version	Area	Duration	Price
Emerald Card	Rail & Bus	Republic & North	8 out of 15 days	€236
			15 out of 30 days	€406
Irish Explorer	Rail & Bus	Republic only	8 out of 15 days	€210
Irish Rover	Bus only	Republic & North	3 out of 8 days	€73
			8 out of 15 days	€165
			15 out of 30 days	€245

Open Road Pass
This pass covers buses in the Republic of Ireland.

Duration	Price	Duration	Price
3 out of 6 days	€47	10 out of 20 days	€142
4 out of 8 days	€61	11 out of 22 days	€155
5 out of 10 days	€74	12 out of 24 days	€169
6 out of 12 days	€88	13 out of 26 days	€182
7 out of 14 days	€101	14 out of 28 days	€196
8 out of 16 days	€115	15 out of 30 days	€209
9 out of 18 days	€128		

INTERNATIONAL FERRY CONNECTIONS

Ireland has good ferry connections with Britain and France, thanks to various ferry companies. Check the websites listed per route below for specifics on price, frequency, and length of journey.

Republic of Ireland

Irish Port	To...	Web Site
Dublin	Liverpool (England)	www.poirishsea.com and www.steam-packet.com
Dublin	Birkenhead (near Liverpool)	www.norfolkline-ferries.co.uk
Dublin	Holyhead (Wales)	www.irishferries.com
Dun Laoghaire (near Dublin)	Holyhead (Wales)	www.stenaline.com
Rosslare	Fishguard (Wales)	www.stenaline.com
Rosslare	Pembroke (Wales)	www.irishferries.com
Rosslare	Cherbourg (France)	www.irishferries.com and www.aferry.to/celtic-link-ferries.htm
Rosslare	Roscoff (France)	www.irishferries.com
Ringaskiddy (near Cork)	Roscoff (France)	www.brittanyferries.ie

Northern Ireland

Belfast	Stranraer (Scotland)	www.stenaline.com
Belfast	Liverpool (England)	www.steam-packet.com
Belfast	Birkenhead (near Liverpool)	www.norfolkline-ferries.co.uk
Larne (near Belfast)	Troon (Scotland)	www.poirishsea.com
Larne	Cairnryan (Scotland)	www.poirishsea.com
Larne	Fleetwood (near Blackpool, England)	www.stenaline.com

your palm open.

Bus stations are normally at or near train stations. The Bus Éireann Expressway Bus Timetable comes in handy (free, available at some bus stations or online at www.buseireann.ie, bus info tel. 01/836-6111).

Some companies offer **backpacker's bus circuits.** These hop-on, hop-off bus circuits take mostly youth hostelers around the country super-cheaply and easily with the assumption that they'll be sleeping in hostels along the way. For instance, Paddy Wagon cuts Ireland in half and offers three- to six-day "tours" of each half (north and south) that can be combined into one whole tour connecting Dublin, Cork, Killarney, Dingle, Galway, Westport, Donegal, Derry, and Belfast (May–Oct, 3 days/£119, 6 days/£209, 5 Beresford Palace, Dublin, tel. 01/823-0822, toll-free from UK tel. 0800-783-4191, www.paddywagontours.com). They also run one-day tours of Belfast from Dublin (£29).

Students can use their ISIC (student card, www.isic.org) to get discounts on cross-country coaches (up to 50 percent). Children 5–15 pay half-price on trains, and wee ones under age five go free.

Renting a Car

Car rental is cheapest if arranged in advance from home. Call various companies, look online, or arrange a rental through your hometown travel agent, who can help you out if anything goes wrong during your trip. Rent by the week with unlimited mileage. Expect to pay about $400 per week ($600 for an automatic), including gas and insurance, for a basic rental.

Big companies have offices in most cities (ask to be picked up at your hotel). Small local rental companies can be cheaper but aren't as flexible. Some companies such as Auto Europe (www.autoeurope.com) or Dan Dooley (www.dan-dooley.ie) will do longer-term rentals at a slight discount. You can no longer lease a car in Ireland; you can only rent.

Car-rental companies have age restrictions. Most companies will not rent to someone under 21, and some won't rent to people under age 25 (confirm age requirements when you make your reservation). Restrictions and "under-age fees" can apply if you're 21–26. If that describes you, try STA Travel, which seeks young renters (www.statravel.com, tel. 800-781-4040). In the Republic of Ireland, you can't rent a car if you're 75 or over, and you'll pay extra if you're 70–74. Some companies in Northern Ireland won't rent to anyone over 69.

If your trip covers both the islands of Ireland and

AND LEARN THESE ROAD SIGNS

STOP

(50) Speed Limit (km/hr)

Yield

No Passing

End of No Passing Zone

One Way

No Stopping

Roundabout Ahead

Freeway

Road Narrows

No Entry

No Entry for cars

All Vehicles Prohibited

P Parking

No Parking

Customs

Peace

Great Britain (Scotland, England, and Wales), you're better off with two separate car rentals, rather than paying for your car to ride the ferry between. On an all-Ireland trip, you can drive your rental car from the Republic of Ireland into Northern Ireland, but be aware of drop-off charges ($75–150) if you drop it off in the North. You'll pay a smaller drop-off charge ($25–50) for picking up the car at one place and dropping it off at another within the same country (even picking up in downtown Dublin and dropping off

Driving in Ireland: Distance and Time

at Dublin Airport). If you pick up the car in a smaller city, you'll more likely survive your first day on the Irish roads. If you drop the car off early or keep it longer, you'll be credited or charged at a fair, pro-rated price.

The Ford 1.3-liter Escort-category car costs about $50 more per week than the smallest cars, but feels better on the motorways and safer on the small roads. Remember, minibuses are a great budget way to go for five to nine people.

Since automatics are less common in Europe, they are expensive to buy and therefore expensive to rent. An automatic transmission is going to add about 50 percent to the car-rental cost over a manual transmission. Weigh this against the fact that in Ireland you'll be sitting on the right side of the car, and shifting with your left hand...while driving on the left side of the road. The floor pedals are the same locations as in the US, and the gears are still found in the same basic "H" pattern as at home (i.e., first gear, second, etc).

Tips on Driving

Driving gives you access to the most rural sights and is my favorite mode of transportation in Ireland. Here's what I've learned in the school of hard brakes and adrenaline rushes:

- The *Complete Road Atlas of Ireland* by Ordnance Survey (€12.50, handy ring-binder style, 1:210,000 scale) is the best Irish road map, and includes translations of Irish place names on the last pages. It covers every road your car can wedge onto. Flipping to the next page of an atlas is easier to manage in a cramped front seat than wrestling with a large, ungainly folding map. Buy the atlas at the first TI or gas station you come to.

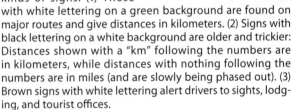

- Study your map before taking off. Know the areas you'll be lacing together, as road numbers are inconsistent.

- Road signs can be confusing, too little, and too late. There are three main kinds of signs: (1) Those with white lettering on a green background are found on major routes and give distances in kilometers. (2) Signs with black lettering on a white background are older and trickier: Distances shown with a "km" following the numbers are in kilometers, while distances with nothing following the numbers are in miles (and are slowly being phased out). (3) Brown signs with white lettering alert drivers to sights, lodging, and tourist offices.

- Figure out your lights, wipers, and radio before you're on the road.

- Adjust your side-view mirrors and get in the habit of using them. Many are spring-loaded to snap back into place (a pragmatic solution on narrow roads). Get comfortable with the sound of vegetation whisking the side of your car (it rarely scratches).

- Drive with your lights on to make your vehicle more visible.

- You'll get used to shifting with your left hand. Find reverse... before you need it. (I love the smell of burnt clutch in the morning.)

- The most common mistake is getting a late start, which causes you to rush, which makes you miss turns, which causes you stress, which decreases your enjoyment, which makes it feel less like a vacation.

- Car travel in Ireland isn't fast. Plan your itinerary estimating your average speed at 40 miles per hour (roughly 1 km per minute). Give your itinerary a reality check by finding distances and driving times between destinations on the driving map (page 403) or online (www.viamichelin.com).

- The shortest distance between any two points is usually the motorway (highway). Miss a motorway exit and you can lose 30 minutes.
- Avoid driving in big cities if possible; use ring roads to skirt the congestion. Dublin traffic has gotten clogged over the years, and you'll find sightseeing easier on foot, by bus (particularly the hop-on, hop-off tours), or by taxi. Spare yourself the traffic stress and parking expense (€3/hr) of trying to drive in Dublin.
- When it comes to narrow rural roads, adjust your perceptions of personal space. It's not "my side of the road" or "your side of the road." It's just "the road"—and it's shared as a cooperative adventure. Locals are usually courteous, pulling over against a hedgerow and blinking their headlights for you to pass while they wait. Return the favor when you are closer to a wide spot in the road than they are. Pull over frequently—to let faster locals pass and to check the map.
- Watch the road ahead and always expect that a slow tractor, a flock of sheep, a one-lane bridge, and a baby stroller are lurking around the next turn. Honk when approaching blind corners to alert approaching drivers.
- Tune in RTE One, the national radio station (89 FM), for long drives. Its interviews/music are an education in Irish culture and good company.
- Make your road trip fun. Establish a cardboard-box pantry of munchies. Keep a rack of liter boxes of juice in the trunk. Buy some Windex and a roll of paper towels for cleaner sightseeing.
- Don't drink and drive. The Gardí (police) set up random checkpoints, and if you've had more than one pint, you're legally drunk in Ireland.
- If you're driving between the Republic and Northern Ireland, keep these basic differences in mind: In the Republic, the speed limit is in kilometers per hour, unleaded costs €1.15 per liter ($5.60 per gallon), and the roads can be bumpy, narrow, and winding. In Northern Ireland, the speed limit is in miles per hour, unleaded costs £0.95 per liter (about $7 per gallon), and roads are better maintained.
- Travelers who want to use designated disabled parking spaces in Ireland can bring their Disabled Persons Parking Card from the US (even though the Irish have a different card that they set on their dashboard). For more information, call the Irish Wheelchair Association at tel. 045/893-094 (from the US, dial 011-353-45-893-094).

Car Insurance Options

In recent years, Ireland has run neck-and-neck with Portugal for the most traffic accidents in Western Europe. When you rent a car, you are liable for a very high deductible, sometimes equal to the entire value of the car. You can limit your financial risk in case of an accident by choosing one of these two options: buy Collision Damage Waiver (CDW) coverage from the car-rental company or get coverage through your credit card (free, if your card automatically includes zero-deductible coverage).

CDW includes a very high deductible (typically $1,000–1,500). When you pick up the car, you'll be offered the chance to "buy down" the deductible to zero (for $10–30/day; this is often called "super CDW").

If you opt instead for credit-card coverage, there's a catch. You'll technically have to decline all coverage offered by the car-rental company, which means they can place a hold on your card for the full deductible amount. In case of damage, it can be time-consuming to resolve the charges with your credit-card company. Before you decide on this option, quiz your credit-card company about how it works and ask them to explain the worst-case scenario.

Buying CDW insurance (plus "super CDW") is the easier but pricier option. Using the coverage that comes with your credit card saves money, but can involve more hassle.

For more fine print about car-rental insurance, see www.ricksteves.com/cdw.

Driving

Your US driver's license is all you need to drive in Ireland, but if you'll be driving throughout Europe, you can get an International Driver's Permit at your local AAA office before you go ($15 plus two passport photos, www.aaa.com).

Driving in Ireland is basically wonderful—once you remember to stay on the left and after you've mastered the roundabouts. Don't let a roundabout spook you. After all, you routinely merge into much faster traffic on American highways back home. The traffic in a roundabout has the right-of-way; entering traffic yields (look to your right as you merge). It helps to remember that the driver is always in the center of the road.

But be warned: Every year I get a few cards from traveling readers advising me that, for them, trying to drive Ireland was a nerve-racking and regrettable mistake. If you want to get a little slack on the roads, drop

How to Navigate a Roundabout

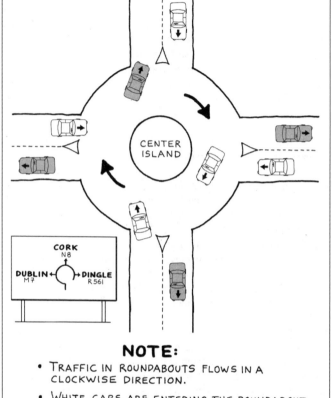

NOTE:

- TRAFFIC IN ROUNDABOUTS FLOWS IN A CLOCKWISE DIRECTION.

- WHITE CARS ARE ENTERING THE ROUNDABOUT, GRAY CARS ARE EXITING

- VEHICLES ENTERING A ROUNDABOUT MUST YIELD TO VEHICLES IN THE ROUNDABOUT.

- LOOK TO YOUR RIGHT AS YOU MERGE! ☺

by a gas station or auto shop and buy a red "L" (new driver with license) sign to put in your back window.

An Irish Automobile Association membership comes with most rentals (www.aaireland.ie). Understand its towing and emergency-road-service benefits.

Seat belts are required by law. Speed limits are 50 kilometers per hour (roughly 30 miles per hour) in towns, 80 kph (approximately 50 mph) on rural roads (such as R-257, R-600, etc.), 100 kph (about 60 mph) on national roads (N-8, N-30, and so on), and 120 kph (roughly 75 mph) on motorways (M-1, M-50, etc.). Some sections of the motorways near Dublin may charge tolls of as much as €2.50.

Note that road-surveillance cameras strictly enforce speed limits. Any driver (including foreigners renting cars) photographed speeding will get a nasty bill in the mail. (Cameras—you'll see the foreboding gray boxes—flash on your rear license plate in order not to invade the privacy of anyone sharing the front seat with someone they shouldn't be with.)

Parking is confusing. One yellow line marked on the pavement means no parking Monday through Saturday during business hours. Double yellow lines mean no parking at any time. Broken yellow lines mean short stops are OK, but you should always look for explicit signs or ask a passerby.

Even in small towns, rather than fight it, I just pull into the most central "disk" or "pay-and-display" parking lot I can find. Disks can be bought at nearby shops. You buy one disk for each hour you want to stay. Scratch off the time you arrived on the disk and put it on your dashboard. I keep a bag of coins in the ashtray for meter/voucher machines (no change given for large coins). These modern pay-and-display machines are solar-powered and placed regularly along the street (about six feet tall, look for blue circle with white letter P). Signs along the street will state whether parking disk or pay-and-display laws are in effect for that area.

Cheap Flights

If you're visiting one or more cities on a longer European trip, look into cheap flights offered by Ryanair (Irish tel. 081-830-3030, www.ryanair.com), Aer Lingus (Irish tel. 081-836-5000, www.aerlingus.com), bmi (British Midland, Irish tel. 01/407-3036, US tel. 800-788-0555, www.flybmi.com), and easyJet (flies in and out of Belfast only, Irish tel. 1-890-923-922, British tel. 0871-244-2366, www.easyjet.com). To comparison-shop inexpensive flights, check www.cheapflights.co.uk and www.skyscanner.net.

Be aware of the potential drawbacks of flying on the cheap: nonrefundable and nonchangeable tickets, rigid baggage restrictions (and fees if you have more than what's officially allowed), use of airports far outside town, tight schedules that can mean more delays, little in the way of customer assistance if problems arise, and, of course, no frills. To avoid unpleasant surprises, read the small print—especially baggage policies—before you book.

Round-trip can be cheaper than one-way—ask. To get the best prices, book in advance as soon as you have a date set (the best fares are generally available online, not by phone). Each flight has an allotment of cheap seats; these sell fast, leaving the higher-priced seats for latecomers. Ryanair is the exception, offering promotional deals throughout the year.

Airports and Intra-Ireland Airlines

All direct flights from the US land in either Dublin or Shannon. Dublin's booming population has outgrown the Dublin Airport and plans are being developed to expand it. If you're offered a choice and have no interest in sightseeing in Dublin, you'll find Shannon Airport to be a far less stressful entry or exit point into or out of Ireland. Drivers will especially appreciate getting used to the "other side of the road" around rural Shannon, as compared to urban Dublin. Be aware that smaller regional airports may not have car-rental offices.

If you're flying within Ireland, try Aer Arann (Irish tel. 081-821-0210, British tel. 0800-587-2324, if calling from the US dial 011-353-61-704-428, www.aerarann.com). They fly from Dublin to Cork, Kerry, Galway, Knock, Sligo, and Donegal.

HOLIDAYS AND FESTIVALS

This is a partial list of holidays and festivals. Some dates have yet to be set. For more information, contact **Tourism Ireland** (tel. 800-223-6470 or 212/418-0800, www.tourismireland.com, info .us@tourismireland.com).

Jan 1	New Year's Day (banks closed)
Jan 23–27	Temple Bar Trad—Irish Music and Culture Festival, Dublin (www.templebartrad.com)
March 15–19	St. Patrick's Day celebration throughout Ireland (parades, drunkenness, 5-day festival in Dublin, www.stpatricksday.ie)
March 21	Good Friday (banks closed)
March 23–24	Easter Sunday and Monday
March 25–30	Pan Celtic International Festival, Donegal Town (festival rotates locations every year, www.panceltic.ie)
May 5	Early May Bank Holiday, Ireland and UK (banks closed)
May 26	Spring Bank Holiday, UK only (banks closed)
June 2	June Holiday, Ireland (banks closed)
June 16	Bloomsday, Dublin (James Joyce festival, www.jamesjoyce.ie)
July 12	Battle of the Boyne anniversary, Northern Ireland (Protestant marches, protests)
July 14–27	Galway Arts Festival, Galway (www .galwayartsfestival.com)
July 28–Aug 3	Galway Races, Galway (www.galwayraces .com)
Aug 4	August Bank Holiday, Ireland (banks closed)

2008

JANUARY

S	M	T	W	T	F	S
		1	2	3	4	5
6	7	8	9	10	11	12
13	14	15	16	17	18	19
20	21	22	23	24	25	26
27	28	29	30	31		

FEBRUARY

S	M	T	W	T	F	S
					1	2
3	4	5	6	7	8	9
10	11	12	13	14	15	16
17	18	19	20	21	22	23
24	25	26	27	28	29	

MARCH

S	M	T	W	T	F	S
						1
2	3	4	5	6	7	8
9	10	11	12	13	14	15
16	17	18	19	20	21	22
23/30	24/31	25	26	27	28	29

APRIL

S	M	T	W	T	F	S
		1	2	3	4	5
6	7	8	9	10	11	12
13	14	15	16	17	18	19
20	21	22	23	24	25	26
27	28	29	30			

MAY

S	M	T	W	T	F	S
				1	2	3
4	5	6	7	8	9	10
11	12	13	14	15	16	17
18	19	20	21	22	23	24
25	26	27	28	29	30	31

JUNE

S	M	T	W	T	F	S
1	2	3	4	5	6	7
8	9	10	11	12	13	14
15	16	17	18	19	20	21
22	23	24	25	26	27	28
29	30					

JULY

S	M	T	W	T	F	S
		1	2	3	4	5
6	7	8	9	10	11	12
13	14	15	16	17	18	19
20	21	22	23	24	25	26
27	28	29	30	31		

AUGUST

S	M	T	W	T	F	S
					1	2
3	4	5	6	7	8	9
10	11	12	13	14	15	16
17	18	19	20	21	22	23
24/31	25	26	27	28	29	30

SEPTEMBER

S	M	T	W	T	F	S
	1	2	3	4	5	6
7	8	9	10	11	12	13
14	15	16	17	18	19	20
21	22	23	24	25	26	27
28	29	30				

OCTOBER

S	M	T	W	T	F	S
			1	2	3	4
5	6	7	8	9	10	11
12	13	14	15	16	17	18
19	20	21	22	23	24	25
26	27	28	29	30	31	

NOVEMBER

S	M	T	W	T	F	S
						1
2	3	4	5	6	7	8
9	10	11	12	13	14	15
16	17	18	19	20	21	22
23/30	24	25	26	27	28	29

DECEMBER

S	M	T	W	T	F	S
	1	2	3	4	5	6
7	8	9	10	11	12	13
14	15	16	17	18	19	20
21	22	23	24	25	26	27
28	29	30	31			

Appendix

Early to mid-Aug	Féile an Phobail, West Belfast Irish cultural festival, Northern Ireland (www.feilebelfast.com)
Aug 15	Kenmare Fair, Kenmare (www.kenmare.com)
Aug 25	Late Summer Bank Holiday, UK only (banks closed)
Second weekend in Aug	Dingle Races, Dingle (boat races) Puck Fair, Killorglin, Kerry ("Ireland's Oldest Fair" and drink-fest, www.puckfair.ie)
Third weekend in Aug	Dingle Regatta, Dingle
Mid-Aug	Rose of Tralee International Festival, Tralee
Late Aug–early Sept	Blessing of the Boats, Dingle (maritime festival)
Sept 8–10	Galway Races, Galway (www.galwayraces.com)

Near end of Sept	Galway Oyster Festival, Galway (4 days, www.galwayoysterfest.com)
Oct 26–27	Galway Races, Galway (www.galwayraces.com)
Oct 27	October Holiday, Ireland (banks closed)
Late Oct	Belfast Queens Festival, Belfast (music, 12 days, www.belfastfestival.com)
Dec 25	Christmas holiday, Ireland and UK
Dec 26	St. Stephen's Day, Ireland (religious festival); Boxing Day, UK

CONVERSIONS AND CLIMATE

Numbers and Stumblers

- Europeans write a few of their numbers differently than we do. 1 = 1, 4 = 4, 7 = 7.
- In Europe, dates appear as day/month/year, so Christmas is 25/12/08.
- Commas are decimal points and decimals commas. A dollar and a half is 1,50, and there are 5.280 feet in a mile.
- When pointing, use your whole hand, palm down.
- When counting with fingers, start with your thumb. If you hold up your first finger to request one item, you'll probably get two.
- What Americans call the second floor of a building is the first floor in Europe.
- On escalators and moving sidewalks, Europeans keep the left "lane" open for passing. Keep to the right.

Metric Conversions (approximate)

1 foot = 0.3 meter	1 square yard = 0.8 square meter
1 yard = 0.9 meter	1 square mile = 2.6 square kilometers
1 mile = 1.6 kilometers	1 ounce = 28 grams
1 centimeter = 0.4 inch	1 quart = 0.95 liter
1 meter = 39.4 inches	1 kilogram = 2.2 pounds
1 kilometer = 0.62 mile	32°F = 0°C

Dublin's Climate

First line, average daily high; second line, average daily low; third line, days of no rain. Note that temperatures are moderate throughout the country, so use the Ireland temperatures listed below as a model. For more detailed weather statistics for destinations throughout Ireland (as well as the rest of the world), check www.worldclimate.com.

J	F	M	A	M	J	J	A	S	O	N	D
46°	47°	51°	55°	60°	65°	67°	67°	63°	57°	51°	47°
34°	35°	37°	39°	43°	48°	52°	51°	48°	43°	39°	37°
18	18	21	19	21	19	18	19	18	20	18	17

Temperature Conversion: Fahrenheit and Celsius

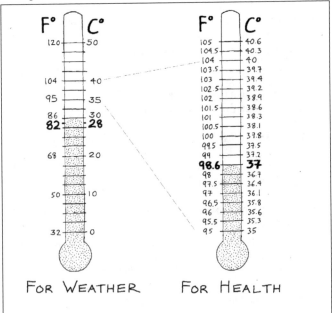

FOR WEATHER   FOR HEALTH

Ireland uses both Celsius and Fahrenheit to take its temperature. For a rough conversion from Celsius to Fahrenheit, double the number and add 30. For weather, remember that 28°C is 82°F—perfect. For health, 37°C is just right.

Essential Packing Checklist

Whether you're traveling for five days or five weeks, here's what you'll need to bring. Remember to pack light to enjoy the sweet freedom of true mobility. Happy travels!

- ❏ 5 shirts
- ❏ 1 sweater or lightweight fleece jacket
- ❏ 2 pairs pants
- ❏ 1 pair shorts
- ❏ 1 swimsuit (women only—men can use shorts)
- ❏ 5 pairs underwear and socks
- ❏ 1 pair shoes
- ❏ 1 rainproof jacket
- ❏ Tie or scarf
- ❏ Money belt
- ❏ Money—your mix of:
  - ❏ Debit card for ATM withdrawals
  - ❏ Credit card
  - ❏ Hard cash in US dollars
- ❏ Documents (and backup photocopies)
- ❏ Passport
- ❏ Airplane ticket
- ❏ Driver's license
- ❏ Student ID and hostel card
- ❏ Railpass/car-rental voucher
- ❏ Insurance details
- ❏ Daypack
- ❏ Sealable plastic baggies
- ❏ Camera and related gear
- ❏ Empty water bottle
- ❏ Wristwatch and alarm clock
- ❏ Earplugs
- ❏ First-aid kit
- ❏ Medicine (labeled)
- ❏ Extra glasses/contacts and prescriptions
- ❏ Sunscreen and sunglasses
- ❏ Toiletries kit
- ❏ Soap
- ❏ Laundry soap (if liquid and carry-on, limit to 3 oz.)
- ❏ Clothesline
- ❏ Small towel
- ❏ Sewing kit
- ❏ Travel information
- ❏ Necessary map(s)
- ❏ Address list (email and mailing addresses)
- ❏ Postcards and photos from home
- ❏ Notepad and pen
- ❏ Journal

Appendix

Hotel Reservation

To: _____   _____
           hotel   *email or fax*

From: _____   _____
             name   *email or fax*

Today's date: _____ /_____ /_____
                      day   *month*   *year*

Dear Hotel _____ ,
Please make this reservation for me:

Name: _____

Total # of people: _____   # of rooms: _____   # of nights: _____

Arriving: _____ /_____ /_____   My time of arrival (24-hr clock): _____
               day *month* *year*   (I will telephone if I will be late)

Departing: _____ /_____ /_____
                 day *month* *year*

Room(s): Single___   Double ___   Twin ___   Triple ___   Quad___

With: Toilet ____   Shower ____   Bath ____   Sink only ___

Special needs: View___   Quiet___   Cheapest ___   Ground Floor___

Please email or fax confirmation of my reservation, along with the type of room reserved and the price. Please also inform me of your cancellation policy. After I hear from you, I will quickly send my credit-card information as a deposit to hold the room. Thank you.

_____
Name

_____
Address

_____
City   *State*   *Zip Code*   *Country*

Before hoteliers can make your reservation, they want to know the information listed above. You can use this form as the basis for your email, or you can photocopy this page, fill in the information, and send it as a fax (also available online at www.ricksteves.com/reservation).

INDEX

Rick Steves' Guidebook Series

Country Guides

Rick Steves' Best of Europe
Rick Steves' Croatia & Slovenia
Rick Steves' Eastern Europe
Rick Steves' England
Rick Steves' France
Rick Steves' Germany & Austria
Rick Steves' Great Britain
Rick Steves' Ireland
Rick Steves' Italy
Rick Steves' Portugal
Rick Steves' Scandinavia
Rick Steves' Spain
Rick Steves' Switzerland

City and Regional Guides

Rick Steves' Amsterdam, Bruges & Brussels
Rick Steves' Florence & Tuscany
Rick Steves' Istanbul
Rick Steves' London
Rick Steves' Paris
Rick Steves' Prague & the Czech Republic
Rick Steves' Provence & the French Riviera
Rick Steves' Rome
Rick Steves' Venice

Rick Steves' Phrase Books

French
German
Italian
Spanish
Portuguese
French/Italian/German

Other Books

Rick Steves' Europe Through the Back Door
Rick Steves' Europe 101: History and Art for the Traveler
Rick Steves' Postcards from Europe
Rick Steves' European Christmas

(Avalon Travel Publishing)

Travel smart...carry on!

The latest generation of Rick Steves' carry-on travel bags is easily the best—benefiting from two decades of on-the-road attention to what really matters: maximum quality and strength; practical, flexible features; and no unnecessary frills. You won't find a better value anywhere!

Rick Steves' Convertible Carry-On $99.⁹⁵

Our roomy, versatile 9" x 21" x 14" carry-on has a large 2600 cubic-inch main compartment, plus four outside pockets (small, medium and huge) that are perfect for often-used items. Wish you had even more room to bring home souvenirs? Pull open the full-perimeter expando-zipper and its capacity jumps from 2600 to 3000 cubic inches. When you want to use it as a suitcase or check it as luggage (required when "expanded"), the straps and belt hide away in a zippered compartment in the back. It weighs just 3 lbs.

Rick Steves' Classic Back Door Bag $79.⁹⁵

This ultra-light (1½ lbs.) version of our Convertible Carry-On features the same 9" x 21" x 14" dimensions and hideaway straps, but does not include a waistbelt or expandability. This is the bag that Rick lives out of for three months a year!

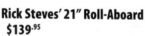

Rick Steves' 21" Roll-Aboard $139.⁹⁵

Our sturdy 21" Roll-Aboard is rucksack-soft in front, but the rest is lined with a hard ABS-lexan shell to give maximum protection to your belongings. We've spared no expense on moving parts, splurging on an extra-long button-release handle and big, tough inline skate wheels for easy rolling on rough surfaces. It features the same 9" x 21" x 14" carry-on dimensions, pocket configuration and expandability as our Convertible Carry-On—and at 7 lbs. it's the lightest roll-aboard in its class.

Prices and features are subject to change.

For great deals on a wide selection of travel goodies, begin your next trip at the Rick Steves Travel Store!

Visit the Rick Steves Travel Store at
www.ricksteves.com

Start your trip at
www.ricksteves.com

Rick Steves' website is packed with over 3,000 pages of timely travel information. It's also your gateway to getting FREE monthly travel news from Rick—and more!

Free Monthly Travel News

Fresh articles on Europe's most interesting destinations and happenings. Rick will even send you an email every month (often direct from Europe) with his latest discoveries!

Timely Travel Tips

Rick Steves' best money-and-stress-saving tips on trip planning, packing, transportation, hotels, health, safety, finances, hurdling the language barrier...and more.

Travelers' Graffiti Wall

Candid advice and opinions from thousands of travelers on everything listed above, plus whatever topics are hot at the moment (discount flights, politics, nude beaches, scams...you name it).

Rick's Guide to Eurail Passes

The clearest, most comprehensive guide to the confusing array of railpass options out there, and how to choo-choose the railpass that best fits your itinerary and budget.

Great Gear at Our Travel Store

In the past year alone, more than 50,000 travelers have enjoyed great online deals on Rick's guidebooks, maps, DVDs—and his custom-designed carry-on bags, day packs, and light-packing accessories.

Rick Steves Tours

This year, 12,000 lucky travelers will explore Europe on a Rick Steves tour. Learn about our 28 different one- to three-week itineraries, read uncensored feedback from our tour alums, and get our free Tour Experience DVD.

Rick on TV, Radio and Podcasts

Read the scripts from the popular Rick Steves' Europe TV series, and listen to or download your choice of over 100 hours of our Travel with Rick Steves radio show.

Respect for Your Privacy

Whether you buy something from us or subscribe to Rick's monthly Travel News emails, we'll never share your name or email address with anyone else. You won't be spammed!

Have fun raising your Travel I.Q. at
www.ricksteves.com

Rick Steves®

More *Savvy.* More *Surprising.* More *Fun.*

COUNTRY GUIDES

Croatia & Slovenia
England
France
Germany & Austria
Great Britain
Ireland
Italy
Portugal
Scandinavia
Spain
Switzerland

CITY GUIDES

Amsterdam, Bruges & Brussels
Florence & Tuscany
Istanbul
London
Paris
Prague & The Czech Republic
Provence & The French Riviera
Rome
Venice

BEST OF GUIDES

Best of Eastern Europe
Best of Europe

As the #1 authority on European travel, Rick gives you inside information on what to visit, where to stay, and how to get there—economically and hassle-free.

www.ricksteves.com

PHRASE BOOKS & DICTIONARIES

French
French, Italian & German
German
Italian
Portuguese
Spanish

MORE EUROPE FROM RICK STEVES

Europe 101
Europe Through the Back Door
Postcards from Europe

RICK STEVES' EUROPE DVDs

All 70 Shows 2000–2007
Britain
Eastern Europe
France & Benelux
Germany, The Swiss Alps & Travel Skills
Ireland
Italy
Spain & Portugal

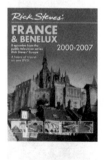

PLANNING MAPS

Britain & Ireland
Europe
France
Germany, Austria & Switzerland
Italy
Spain & Portugal

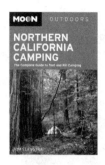

CREDITS

Researcher

To help update this book, Rick and Pat relied on…

Darbi Macy

Darbi, who's worked for Rick for eight years, spends summers in Scotland and Ireland researching guidebooks, guiding tours, and searching for the perfect piece of banoffee pie.

Contributor

Gene Openshaw

Gene is the co-author of seven Rick Steves books. For this book, he wrote material on Europe's art, history, and contemporary culture. When not traveling, Gene enjoys composing music, recovering from his 1973 trip to Europe with Rick, and living everyday life with his wife and daughter.

IMAGES

Location	Photographer
Republic of Ireland (full page): Cliffs of Moher, near Galway	Pat O'Connor
Dublin: Ha' Penny Bridge	Pat O'Connor
Near Dublin: Newgrange, in Valley of the Boyne	Pat O'Connor
Kilkenny and Cashel: Rock of Cashel	Pat O'Connor
Waterford and County Wexford: Waterford's Waterfront	Pat O'Connor
Kinsale and Cobh: Kinsale's Summer Cove Area	Pat O'Connor
Kenmare and Ring of Kerry: Ring of Kerry	Pat O'Connor
Dingle Peninsula: Great Blasket Island	Pat O'Connor
Galway: High Street	Pat O'Connor
County Clare and the Burren: Poulnabrone Dolmen, The Burren	Pat O'Connor
The Aran Islands: The Aran Islands	Pat O'Connor
Connemara and County Mayo: Lough Corrib, Connemara	Pat O'Connor
Northern Ireland (full page): Giant's Causeway, Antrim Coast	Pat O'Connor
Belfast: Donegall Square and City Hall	Pat O'Connor
Portrush and Antrim Coast: Portrush Harbor	Pat O'Connor
Derry and County Donegal: Derry's Walls	David C. Hoerlein

Avalon Travel Publishing
A member of the Perseus Books Group
1700 Fourth Street
Berkeley, CA 94710

Text © 2008 by Rick Steves.
Maps © 2008 by Europe Through the Back Door.
Printed in the United States of America by Worzalla.
Second printing April 2008.

ISBN(10) 1-56691-859-6
ISBN(13) 978-1-56691-859-6
ISSN 1538-1587

Thanks to Rozanne Stringer for her writing on the Celts, Celtic Tiger, St. Brendan, and Irish art. Thanks also to Gene Openshaw and Mike Kelly for their help.

For the latest on Rick's lectures, guidebooks, tours, public radio show, and public television series, contact Europe Through the Back Door, Box 2009, Edmonds, WA 98020, tel. 425/771-8303, fax 425/771-0833, www.ricksteves.com, rick@ricksteves.com.

Europe Through the Back Door Managing Editor: Risa Laib
ETBD Editors: Cathy McDonald, Jennifer Hauseman (Senior Editor), Gretchen Strauch
Avalon Travel Publishing Senior Editor and Series Manager: Madhu Prasher
Avalon Travel Publishing Project Editor: Kelly Lydick
Research Assistance: Darbi Macy
Copy Editor: Amy Scott
Indexer: Carl Wikander
Proofreader: Patrick Collins
Production & Typesetting: McGuire Barber Design
Cover Design: Kari Gim, Laura Mazer
Cover Art Manager: Laura VanDeventer
Maps & Graphics: David C. Hoerlein, Laura VanDeventer, Lauren Mills, Barb Geisler, Mike Morgenfeld
Front Matter Color Photos: p. i and p. viii, © Pat O'Connor
Cover Photos: front image, Celtic High Crosses © Rick Steves; back image: Dingle Peninsula Countryside © Mike Neelley